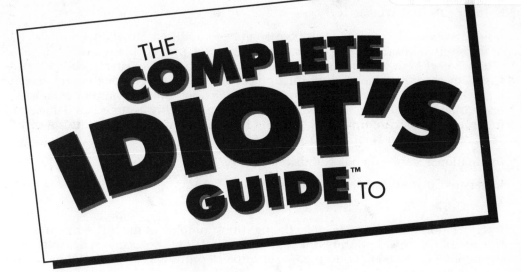

THE COMPLETE IDIOT'S GUIDE™ TO

Beer

by Stuart Kallen

alpha books

A Division of Macmillan Reference USA
A Simon & Schuster Macmillan Company
1633 Broadway, New York, NY 10019

International Standard Book Number: 0-02-861717-7

Library of Congress Catalog Card Number: 97-071182

99 98 97   8 7 6 5 4 3 2 1

Interpretation of the printing code: the rightmost number of the first series of numbers is the year of the book's printing; the rightmost number of the second series of numbers is the number of the book's printing. For example, a printing code of 97-1 shows that the first printing occurred in 1997.

Printed in the United States of America

Executive Editor
Gary M. Krebs

Production Editor
Whitney K. Ward

Copy Editors
Mike McFeely
Whitney K. Ward

Cover Designer
Michael Freeland

Designer
Glenn Larsen

Illustrator
Judd Winick

Indexer
Craig Alan Small

Production Team
Angela Calvert, Tricia Flodder, Christopher Morris, Pamela Woolf

Contents at a Glance

Contents

Foreword

I was flying by the seat of my pants in 1982 when I started out to build one of the first post-Prohibition brewpubs in California (and the United States). The art and lore of brewing beer seemed to be locked up in a mysterious enigma known only to a few. The books I could find that delved into the brewer's art were dusty old tomes written around the turn of the century. Sure there were some technical manuals, but they were for mega-brewers who produced millions of gallons of product.

My how things have changed since then.

Today the exciting world of beer and beer-making is consumer-friendly and burgeoning. Folks are learning to brew their own, hundreds of microbrews line grocers' shelves, and it seems there's a new brewpub popping up on every corner. But with all this choice comes the confusion of too much conflicting beer information. That's why I'm so proud to write the foreword to Stuart A. Kallen's latest beer book, *The Complete Idiot's Guide to Beer.*

Written in a light and easy style, Stu's witty and informative text leads you through the fascinating world of brew. He drops in little-known facts of beer history, discusses the many ingredients of beer, and even helps you figure out which beer to drink with dinner tonight. In addition, Stu's perfect party beer list, consumer warnings, and fabulous "Foamy Facts" make this book a matchless read for beer professionals and amateurs alike. Stu explains the ins and outs of beer with "brews you can use."

For the brew traveler, Stu's reach covers the globe with a thorough list of beer sites from Cucamonga to China. There are addresses of Europe's oldest and most respected brewer-ies, locations of micro-beer in the Bahamas, and a large listing of brewpubs in the United States and Canada. If you cook with beer, Stu's got some recipes. If you want to brew beer, there's a chapter that covers it. If you want to open your own brewpub or buy stock in a fledgling brewery, Stu gives you the lowdown. In fact, there's hardly anything I can think of that's not covered in this book.

As the publisher of *American Brewer* magazine, I work with dozens of writers who attempt to unravel the riddle of beer. I can safely say that, among the writers I've worked with, Stuart Kallen is one of the leading authors on the subject. He's concise, he's funny, and he knows of what he speaks. The book that you're holding in your hands is an entertain-ing romp through the malty world of brewing. I wouldn't hesitate to read it while I was drinking one of the world's greatest beers. And I can't think of a higher compliment than that.

BILL OWENS
Founder of Buffalo Bill's Brewery and
Publisher of *American Brewer* magazine

Introduction

There once was a fellow named Marty,
Who drank swill 'cause he wasn't a smarty
His pals thought him drear
Bought him Idiot's Guide to Beer
Now Marty's the hit of the party.

Back about 15 years ago, in the early 1980s, if you wanted a beer, life was simple. You had your Miller, your Bud, your Coors, and a few other brands. There was no confusion about the beer's style, pedigree, or ingredients. It was simply a yellow, bubbly, sweet libation—usually served up in a can. For real connoisseurs there was imported beer from Canada or Holland. It was a little more full-bodied, a little more potent, and a few bucks more a case. The beer aisle in the liquor store was cluttered with 24-can "suitcases" brewed by a handful of giant American breweries. Life was simple; beer was so-so.

How the world has changed in a few short years. A full-scale revolution in brewing has taken place, and the genie is out of bottle—or should I say *into* the bottle? Beer stores carry hundreds of brands. Restaurants have multi-page beer lists. And a new generation of mini-breweries, microbreweries, and brewpubs have shot up faster than the space shuttle. To further add to the confusion, modern transportation systems allow instant import of beers made on foreign soils from Argentina to New Zealand. Faced with such a dizzying array of choices, how can a consumer ensure that he or she is getting great beer at a good price? That's why I wrote this book.

In *The Complete Idiot's Guide to Beer* I'll separate the ambrosial from the abominable. I'll explain what goes into a beer and how you can discover what you like. Most important, I'll help you separate fact from fiction on beer labels and advertising. That way you won't end up paying a premium price for a mediocre beer in a fancy bottle.

How to Use This Book

This book could have been called *Everything You Always Wanted To Know About Beer,* because I'll be covering all the bases, from basic ingredients to reading a beer list to brewing your own. For those of you completely beer-crazed, I'll even discuss the ins and outs of starting your own small brewery.

Part 1: New to Brew? Here's Beer for Beginners explores the basic ingredients in beer, from malt and hops to exotic ingredients like herbs and spices. This part explains the difference between a brewpub, microbrewery, regional brewery, and other breweries. After a thorough discussion of ingredients, the brewing process is explained in detail. Part 1 wraps up with mouth-watering explanations of the 50 or so basic beer styles from pale ale to porter to Pilsner. There's a short history of every style, its region of origin, and some of the best brand names brewed in that style.

Part 2: 99 Bottles of Beer on the Wall: Cruisin' for a Brewsin' is the consumer's section of the book that explores beer stores, brewpubs, microbreweries, and beer festivals. We'll walk through a bottle shop and learn how to interpret the often confusing information on beer labels. I'll share helpful hints on where, when, and how to find the best and freshest beers for your money. Then we'll discuss the best deals at brewpubs, microbreweries, and anywhere else beer is sold, including beer-in-the-mail clubs, ballparks, and airplanes.

Part 3: Let Me Entertain You—with Beer will fill you in on the perfect beer list for a party, how to match beer with cigars, beer games, and the care and feeding of beer kegs. There's a chapter on beer tasting with everything you've ever wanted to know about beer flavor, color, and bouquet. Part 3 also tells about a marriage—of beer and food. There's a helpful listing of the best beer styles to match with almost any food. The part ends with dozens of recipes you can prepare with beer, from soups and appetizers to main courses and desserts.

Part 4: Around the World in 80 Beers: A Beer Lover's Travel Guide takes you on a visit to the global beer village. This section will tell you where to find a great beer anywhere in the world from Nebraska to Nepal. This part of the book covers brewpubs, microbreweries, and other beery sights in every state in the union and all the provinces of Canada. Then it's across the Atlantic to the notable brewing countries of Great Britain and Europe, where 90% of today's beer style originated. If you've still got wanderlust, Part 4 continues from South and Central America, to the Caribbean, Japan, China, India, and Africa. It's a thirsty world.

Part 5: Will Work for Ale—The Business of Beer, if you've had enough of drinking beer, will clue you in on ways beer can make (or break) your financial world. From enjoyable hobbies such as collecting beer cans, we move to Wall Street to discuss the ups and downs of beer stocks on the Big Board. For those of you completely beer nuts, Part 5 continues with basic information you need to build your own brewery. And last but not least, there's a detailed lesson on homebrewing, including all the equipment and procedures you need to know to make your own beer.

Extras

Beer has an ancient history that is rife with fascinating facts and amusing quotes. There are also pitfalls you should know about when buying, brewing, or drinking beer. To help guide you through this world of brew, I've included sidebars with important facts, tips, warnings, sayings, and definitions. Look for these signposts as you read through the text:

Foamy Fact

Did you know the Pilgrims disembarked at Plymouth Rock because they ran out of beer? This anecdote is one of the many Foamy Facts scattered throughout the book.

Terms of Enbeerment

Definitions of beer, brewing terms, and other jargon that you might not be familiar with. Learn these, and you can talk beer among and with the best of them.

Bar Talk

Almost every famous person has made a wise crack about beer at one time or another. Bar Talk tells it like is from ancient Sumeria to Shakespeare to Jerry Lee Lewis.

Tasty Tip

These are little tidbits of advice that will help you in your beer education. Tasty Tips include insider hints about purchasing beer, as well as books, addresses, Web sites, and other sources related to beer.

Stale Ale Alert

Consumer warnings, untruths exposed, myths uncovered, and other alerts. These facts will help you separate the ale from the stale.

Acknowledgments

This book is dedicated to Patti Marlene Boekhoff for her emotional, physical, intellectual, and spiritual support.

Special thanks to the folks at Macmillan Publishing: Gary M. Krebs, Theresa Murtha, Francisco Rios, and Whitney Ward.

I'd also like to thank my friends in the beer business: Mary and Crayne Horton, Buffalo Bill Owens, George Saxon, Jim Dorsch, Bill Metzger, Joe Barfield, Cathy Noah, Lynn Kastner, Charles Finkel, Wendy Littlefield, Don Feinberg, and Sherri Casey. And a great bow of appreciation to all those too numerous to name. Hats off to the folks who work day in and day out to bring us the best brew in the world.

Special Thanks from the Publisher

The Complete Idiot's Guide to Beer was reviewed by an expert in the field who not only checked the technical accuracy of what you'll learn here, but also provided insight to help us ensure that this book gives you everything you need to know about beer. Our special thanks are extended to Jim Dorsch, who is a recognized authority on beer and beer writing. He has contributed to publications such as *The Washington Post, Chicago Tribune, The Washingtonian, American Brewer, BrewPub, The New Brewer,* and *Beer: the magazine.* Jim has also contributed to "Michael Jackson's Beer Hunter Online" Web site, as well as other electronic projects affiliated with eminent beer expert, Michael Jackson, and The Discovery Channel.

Part 1
New to Brew? Here's Beer for Beginners

It's hard to believe, but almost all beer, from ballpark swill to black-as-night imperial stout, is made up of four or five simple ingredients. Like a painter with a few primary colors, a beer maker (known as a brewmaster, or if a woman, a brewster) can combine the basic elements of beer into dozens of styles. But a complete list of brewing regions, beer flavors, and beer styles can make your head spin—even before you lift your glass. That's why I'm here.

If you don't know a German bock beer from an English old ale, don't worry. Beer has been brewed for thousands of years for one main reason: human enjoyment. Relaxation is as important to a long, happy life as eating well and exercise. And medical research has shown that two beers a day can lower your blood pressure and reduce your risk of heart disease. Five beers a day is another story…

So pour yourself a tall one. Put on some relaxing music. And learn all about beer basics from ale to zymurgy. There's a lot to learn, and it's a lot of fun. Some consider it a hobby. So before we embark on a sea of beer, let me paraphrase Bobby McFaren and say, "Don't worry. Be hoppy."

Chapter 1

Why Beer?

In This Chapter

➤ Why cool beer is such a hot fad

➤ Where was beer invented?

➤ What is beer?

➤ The origins of today's beer styles

➤ How to pour your first glass

Younger readers may find this hard to believe, but even as recently as a dozen years ago, there were only a handful of giant breweries operating in the United States and Canada. A few small breweries, called craft breweries, brewpubs, or microbreweries, were starting to pop up on the West Coast. Today, America's 95 million beer drinkers are served by over 1,200 breweries, and that number is literally growing every day. One might go as far as saying that a beer revolution is taking place.

It all started with homebrewers, whose numbers have grown to an estimated 1.6 million as of this writing. While merely a speck among the millions of beer drinkers in the United States, homebrewers represent a segment of beer aficionados that brewing companies can no longer afford to ignore. Research has shown that homebrewers cover a wide spectrum of society professionals, from lawyers and doctors, to computer programmers, to scientists, and so on.

Brewpubs, microbreweries, and imported beer are all part of an unstoppable movement that experts believe has the potential for amazing growth. It's fun, it's exciting, and it gets better every day. And isn't that what a revolution is supposed to be all about?

Beer by Numbers

It's easy to keep track of how much brew is commercially sold in the United States. The government taxes its production and keeps very accurate records on the matter. Beer production is measured by the U.S. government in barrels, and each barrel has 31 gallons of beer.

Foamy Fact

Tut the Taxman: Taxes on beer are nothing new. Records from Egypt's Middle Kingdom—about 1,800 B.C.—show that the royal court received 130 jars of beer *every day* for tax payments. The queen herself rejoiced with five jars a day.

In 1995, total beer production in the U.S. added up to 199.1 million barrels. It's estimated that there are about 95 million beer drinkers in the U.S. Those numbers tell us that the average beer drinker consumed roughly two 31-gallon barrels of beer that year—or 110 six-packs. At $4 to $8 or more for a six-pack (retail), it's not hard to figure out why so many are jumping on the homebrewing bandwagon.

Beer sales have recently dropped or remained flat for America's brewing giants, while sales of craft-brewed beer rose an amazing 50% average in 1994 and 1995. The market share of craft-brewed beer was 1.3% in 1995, and rose to 2% in 1995. Forty-eight states and Washington, D.C. have legalized brewpubs since 1983. In the United States, 287 new breweries opened in 1995. That breaks down to 96 brewpubs and 91 microbreweries. One more foamy fact: Of that 196.5 million total barrels, Anheuser-Busch (makers of Budweiser, Michelob, and Busch) made about 89 million barrels—or almost half.

Located in Hopland, California, Mendocino Brewing Co. opened in 1983. It was the first brewpub to open in the United States since Prohibition began in 1920.

So There Are New Breweries: What's the Big Deal?

So who cares if breweries are sprouting up faster than barley on a sunny spring day? Well, if they were brewing the same kind of beer brewed by the mega-breweries, it would elicit a huge yawn. For those of you conditioned to think of beer as the main product made by Budweiser, Miller, or Coors, it's not even a blip on the radar screen. But for those of us whose mouths have watered over a Taddy Porter or whose kitchens have been turned upside-down in pursuit of perfect homebrewed Pilsner, it's another story. Once you've gone *bock*, you can never go back.

With all the new brands and beer styles currently on the market, it's like a small version of the World Wide Web. You can effortlessly surf from a bitter to a brown ale, or from a barley wine to a doppelbock. Like becoming liberated from boring, corporate swill—akin to a 13-inch black-and-white TV—we can now buy beer with all the bells and whistles. If it were only pretty labels we were buying, the whole thing would simply be a fad, and it wouldn't last

Terms of Enbeerment
Bock is a rich, malty beer usually brewed in the spring. The name derives from a town in Prussia famous for its beer.

Terms of Enbeerment
When small breweries, called **brewpubs** or **microbreweries**, first opened their doors they were called "boutique breweries" or **"craft breweries."** Technically, brewpubs are restaurants or bars that make their own beer for sale on the premises. Microbreweries are small breweries that make beer to sell in liquor stores, grocery stores, and other retail outlets. While the boutique term has fallen by the wayside, craft brewery is sometimes used interchangeably with brewpub or microbrewery.

long. But it's more than labels. It's flavor. It's integrity. It's refined taste from antique traditions. Whoever can put that in a bottle is selling a sort of magic. And whoever drinks that product is participating in that sorcery.

The problem is, like any other hot trend, there will be a few people willing to take advantage of folks who are simply looking for better brew. With all the new *microbrewery* products on the market, the big, bad, mega-brewers are releasing plenty of product that *looks* like *craft-brewed* beer, but is simply re-tooled brew in a fancy new bottle.

That's why the modern beer lover has to become an educated consumer. It's not too hard, and once you start, you'll want to keep going. What could be more fun than a six-pack on a Saturday night? How about six beers with wild heather from the Scottish coast? Or a meal of French onion soup with a bottle of Pilsner poured in it? Or a tour of a beautiful brewery, after which, plenty of free beer is handed out to the tourists?

Foamy Fact

Monster of a Beer: Heather has been used in Scottish beer for centuries. The Picts, a tribe who brewed heather ale over 1,800 years ago, painted their faces blue, drank the magic potion, and ran the Roman legions out of Scotland. The beautiful flower has a delicate, honey-like taste. Research has shown that heather leaves sometimes contained the ergot fungus, the psychoactive substance in LSD. Maybe that's the explanation for all those Loch Ness Monster sightings. Of course, modern heather ale is brewed with only pure heather flowers, so you don't have to worry about flashbacks after drinking a bottle.

I could go on and on, and in fact, I have. It's so easy to wax poetic about good beer. The following pages will take you on a tour from Sumeria to Egypt to the United States today. In later chapters, there are beer spots listed for almost every country on the planet, and all the details of every beer style known to humankind. So if there has ever been anything that you've always wanted to know about beer, here it is. Sit back, relax, and pour yourself a tall one.

Heather ale has been brewed in Scotland since 2,000 B.C. Fraoch Heather Ale is brewed there today from a recipe that's over 500 years old.

Where Was Beer Invented?

Beer is an ancient drink—it's been brewed since the time of the ancient Sumerians. The first record of a beer recipe is on a clay tablet written in 6,000 B.C. The same tablet details religious rituals that had to be performed before the beer was consumed. And lest you think that Uncle Sam is unique in collecting taxes on beer, the Sumerians gathered tariffs on brew about 77 centuries before George Washington was born.

The Sumerians brewed their beer with barley and wheat. In fact, they quit their nomadic wanderings and settled down so they could grow barley specifically to make beer. Many centuries later, methods for barley brewing evolved, and dozens of different beer "flavors," or styles, were the result. (For more on the Sumerians, see Chapter 3.)

As time went on, ancient peoples such as the Greeks and the Romans also brewed beer. During the times of the great pharaohs, workers of the great Egyptian pyramids were actually paid for their services in beer.

The Egyptians brewed beer using half-baked loaves of barley bread which they soaked in water for several days. Then they threw the bread into six-foot-tall vats and stomped on it. The brewers filtered the mash through tightly woven reed baskets into clay jars, which were sealed with mud from the Nile. The final product was flavored with nutmeg, lavender, cedar, honey, and other flowers.

Foamy Fact

Drink to Me Only with Thine Beers: The Greeks and the Romans called beer *cerevisia.* The word comes from the Roman goddess of agriculture, *Ceres,* and the word *vis,* which means strength. The word "beer" comes from the Latin *bibere,* which means "to drink."

Beer Today, Gone Tomorrow

Skipping way ahead to the 20th century, in 1920, Prohibition—the law banning the manufacture and sale of all alcoholic beverages—became the 18th Amendment to the United States Constitution. Prohibition all but destroyed America's booming brewery business, and over 1,400 breweries closed their doors. When beer was banned, organized crime took up the slack, supplying moonshine and smuggling hard liquor to the thirsty populace. Al Capone became the country's biggest brewer, making a million dollars a day on five-cent beers at the height of the mob era. When Prohibition was repealed, America was left with less than 10% of its original breweries. Many of those closed within a few years. And besides a dearth of good beer, the last years of Prohibition were in the Great Depression. Unemployment, homelessness, and no brew. Those were the days. Prohibition lasted 14 years, until December 5, 1933, when the 21st Amendment to the Constitution repealed it.

About 20 years ago, the United States Congress passed a law allowing folks to make their own beer at home. Home winemaking had already been legalized in 1933 when Prohibition was repealed. After President Jimmy Carter signed the law legalizing homebrewing in 1978, dozens of folks began making their own beer. When the novice homebrewers realized the rich, dark, sweet beer they made in their kitchens was better than the weak, watery, yellow brewskis they could buy at their local bottle shop, the homebrewing business boomed: What a difference being born on the right side of the century can make!

What Is Beer?

Simply put, beer is an alcoholic beverage made from grains of ground-up barley (and sometimes wheat and other grains) that have been *fermented*—converted chemically with the addition of yeast. The barley is usually brewed with *hops*—flowers from a plant also called hops. Barley used in beer is cured in a heating process called *malting,* and the final product is called *malt* or *malted barley*. Depending on the type of yeast used during fermentation, beer may be an ale or a lager. Generally speaking, beer is less than 5% alcohol by volume, although some is stronger.

Malt, hops, yeast, water, and occasionally wheat and other grains have been combined over the years into many different beer styles. Some ale styles include pale ale, brown ale, porter, and stout. Some lager styles include Pilsner, bock, and American lager.

Each style of beer contains:

➤ Either ale yeast or lager yeast—or occasionally wild yeast

➤ A unique color, ranging from pale straw to gold, amber, copper, brown, or black

➤ A specific degree of malt flavor and sweetness

➤ A specific degree of hop bitterness and hop aroma or bouquet

Terms of Enbeerment
Fermentation is the process whereby yeast manufactures enzymes to break down sugar molecules. The result is that sugar is turned into alcohol and carbon dioxide (CO_2), which is also known as the bubbles in your beer. **Hops** are flowers from the hop plant. When barley is heated through a **malting** process, the final product becomes known as **malt** or **malted barley**.

In addition, each style probably originated in a specific region of Ireland, Great Britain, Europe, or in rare cases, the United States.

If compared to food, beer styles may be as different as broccoli is from lobster. For a complete rundown on beer styles, see Chapters 5, 6, and 7.

Most of today's ale styles came into their own in the 17th and 18th centuries, though some are even older. Lager arrived on the scene in the mid-19th century. Great beer styles evolved in regions of Belgium, Germany, the Czech Republic, Ireland, and Great Britain. The unique flavors and aromas of each style had to do with a particular region's brewing water, climate for farming, barley types, hop varieties, and other factors. Before modern transportation systems, a region's beer tasted a certain way and stayed that way for decades.

In these changing times, classic hop types from Kent, England might be grown in eastern Washington. German barley is exported all over the globe. And yeast that once lived only in Bavarian caves can be cultured in a homebrewer's kitchen. That means you can drink a classic English porter brewed in Pittsburgh, an ancient Egyptian wheat beer brewed in California, or a Belgian pale ale brewed at your house.

What all this modern mixing of ancient beer ingredients means to the average consumer is *choice*. But how much choice is too much? Even a beer professional such as myself can occasionally have his mind blown by all the hundreds of beers screaming "Drink me!" on the bottle-shop shelves. But all revolutions are about choosing a new way over the old, entrenched way, and the new brewing revolution is no different.

Pouring Lore and Tasting Grace

Brewers spend oodles of time, talent, and money to make sure the beer that you're drinking is good. What good means is another story. Everyone has different tastes, and one person's "Great!" might be another person's "Blah."

But whatever beer you're drinking—especially if it's a microbrewed or imported beer—it can add to your personal enjoyment to try a few tasting tips from the experts. For instance, beer drunk out of a glass—as opposed to a bottle—allows you to get your nose near the brew. That way you can breathe in the hoppy bouquet and sweet malt aroma. And that's just one tip.

Bar Talk
A quart of ale is a dish for a king.

—William Shakespeare

Beer experts and people in the world of beer take long, involved courses on beer tasting. But don't let that scare you. Pouring a good beer and really tasting it is simple, easy, and fun. And hey, if you want to swill out of the bottle, no one's going to stop you. It's a free country, right? But if you want to taste the best a beer has to offer, try these tips. The payoff is, you get to drink beer while you're doing it. I've delved into the deepest secrets of beer taste, aroma, color, glassware, and more in Chapter 12.

This section is to give you an excuse to drink a beer right now. Then you can have another when you get to Chapter 12.

First, take your beer out of the refrigerator. Beer that's too cold loses its flavor subtleties. Let the beer sit on the counter for about 30 minutes. It should be between 45 and 55 degrees Fahrenheit. (For each beer style's proper serving temperature, turn to Chapter 5 for ales or Chapter 7 for lagers.)

Next find yourself a nice, clean, wide-mouthed beer glass. Rinse it well with lukewarm water, but don't use soap, as any residue will kill the foamy head of the beer. After you've rinsed your glass with water, rinse your mouth. Leftover food tastes can distort or destroy a beer's true flavor. If you've been smoking or eating onions, a piece of neutral cracker or French bread clears the palate nicely. Get a bottle opener and pry the cap from the bottle of beer. If you have a lively brew, you might get a little foam out of the bottle's top. That's all right.

There are two schools of thought as to how to pour beer. School one says, dump the beer straight down the middle of your glass. That way you end up with a lot of foam in your mug. School two says tilt the glass at a 60-degree angle and pour the beer gently down the glass's side. This is my preferred method. That way I can regulate the amount of head I end up with. If I see the beer is looking a little flat, I can straighten the glass out and pour harder to get about two fingers of foam. If the beer is excessively foamy, I can pour very slowly down the side of the glass so I don't end up with a nose full of beer head when I taste.

After your beer is poured, give it a small swirl in the glass. Take two or three sniffs. Some folks like long, slow pulls; some like quick, deep sniffs. (I prefer the former.) What do you smell? The floral or piney smell is hops—the beer's bouquet. The sweet smell is the malt. A fruity smell would be from ale yeast. Lagers don't usually smell fruity but are malty, dry, and crisp.

Bar Talk
They who drink beer will think beer.

—Washington Irving

After about three sniffs, your nose gets used to the smell, and you can't really glean much more aroma information from the brew. Next, take a few small sips of the beer into your mouth and roll it around on your tongue. Swallow it slowly while making chewing motions with your mouth.

After swallowing, exhale through your nose. It may look a little strange, but that chewing motion sends the beer's flavor up to sensors in your nasal cavity to help you taste the

beer better. Take another small sip. Stop for a moment and do a little analysis. Does the beer have a balance between the hops and the malt or is one more outstanding than the other? Are there any flavors you find disagreeable? Are there any flavors you find ambrosial?

Tasty Tip
Once you've finished the beer, ask yourself if you would have another just like it. Was it worth it? Would you buy that beer again? If you're so inclined, write your impressions down in a beer diary or notebook. This comes in handy when you're tasting several beers and want to remember the one you liked best later when you're at the store.

Notice the beer's aftertaste. Is it pleasant? Is it lacking in flavor? Does it taste yucky?

Now you're ready to go for it. Drink the beer. Notice how the head in the beer collapses. A cheap beer's head might simply vanish. A great beer might leave a rocky, craggy, rich head. Great beers also leave a pattern of semi-dried bubbles on the side of the glass that is called Belgian Lace because it looks like the famous hand-crocheted lace of (where else?) Belgium.

As you happily consume your beer, keep noticing the flavors and aromas. I've had beers with certain flavors that were not noticeable until the beer was halfway gone.

That's the long and the short of it. Well, actually the short of it. For more on beer tasting, see Chapter 12.

The Least You Need to Know

➤ Beer is an extremely popular beverage; there are over 95 million beer drinkers in America alone.

➤ Beer is an ancient drink that has been around for at least 8,000 years.

➤ Beer comes in many "flavors," called styles, that can trace their lineage back to Europe, England, and Ireland.

➤ For your first tasting, pour the beer into a glass so you can breathe in the bouquet.

Chapter 2

Breaking Down Beer—What's in Your Glass?

In This Chapter

➤ Eat, drink, and be merry—but be careful, too

➤ Facts and myths about alcohol and beer strength

➤ What are the main ingredients of beer?

➤ Some exotic beer ingredients, such as fruit, vegetables, and spices

---

It may sound simple, but beer can be as complex and unique as a fine wine. To say beer is made up of four basic ingredients is true, but it's cheating a little. Over the centuries those basic elements have been modified, picked at, mulled over, baked, and manipulated—possibly more than any other crop or foodstuff known to humankind.

The results of this beer evolution have been astounding. Even as recently as the early 1800s, beer tended to be a cloudy, dark, chewy affair: warm, flat, and drunk instead of water for breakfast, lunch, and dinner. Today, some fine beers parallel wine or champagne in flavor complexity and *joie de vie* (or joy of life, if you will). And the list of great beers grows every day.

Still and all, when you're talking about beer, you're actually referring to barley soup that's been allowed to ferment with a few natural flavorings and preserving agents thrown in for good measure. But there are over 20,000 commercially produced beers in the world. And it could be said that each one is as different as the individual brewmaster's fingerprints. But each brew must start with four basic elements. Not earth, wind, water, and fire, but malted barley, hops, yeast, and water. Maybe not the name of a great rock band, but the initial makings of a fine beer.

While it's my intent to help you savor and enjoy the myriad pleasures of beer, it's also my hope that you remain safe, happy, and healthy. In order to help you do that, I've provided some information on the negative effects of alcohol consumption on you and the people around you.

How Much Is Enough? A Blood-Alcohol Chart

Drinking beer is a right. Driving an automobile is a privilege. As we are all well aware, the two do not mix. Drinking even one beer can prohibit you from performing certain tasks properly. The following chart details your blood-alcohol content (BAC). The numbers tell how much alcohol is in your blood. A reading of .05 means you have five parts alcohol to 10,000 parts blood. If your BAC is between .05 and .09, in many states you are presumed to be impaired and you may be subject to tickets, fines, and arrest. In California and 13 other states, a BAC reading over .08 will get you arrested for driving while intoxicated (DWI). Most state laws allow a BAC of .10 before a DWI arrest. (The move is on right now by Mothers Against Drunk Driving [MADD] to lower *all* states to .08.)

After you get arrested for DWI, your auto insurance rates may go as high as $1,000 a month because you are considered a menace to yourself and others. A DWI arrest may mean time in jail, expensive fines, forced public service, mandatory attendance at Alcoholics Anonymous, immediate revocation of your driver's license, and even surrender of your automobile. In fact, your first DWI arrest will cost you approximately $18,000. No one needs that kind of grief, and it's not worth it when all you end up with is a hangover anyway.

Your blood-alcohol content (BAC) depends on a few different factors:

➤ How much you weigh.

➤ How much you've eaten. Food slows alcohol absorption but does not keep your BAC from rising. Proteins and fats delay alcohol absorption more than carbohydrates.

➤ The strength of your drink. Beer dilutes alcohol more than a straight shot of whisky.

➤ The time since your last drink. It takes one hour for your body to metabolize the alcohol in 12 ounces of an average beer.

Note: The chart below is only a guide and may not be used as legal evidence in a court of law. Individuals absorb alcohol at different rates and may vary somewhat. Health problems, medication, or other physical or mental conditions should also to be taken into consideration.

To get an idea of your limits, find your weight in the left-hand column. Under the number of drinks, you'll see a row with the numbers 4, 3, 2, 1; these indicate the number of hours that have passed since you've had the first drink. The numbers below that indicate your BAC (your *blood-alcohol content* after the specified number of drinks and hours).

1 Drink = 12 oz. of beer, 4 oz. of wine, or 1.25 oz. of 80-proof liquor

Blood-Alcohol Content by Weight After Hours Elapsed

	1 Drink After x Hours				2 Drinks After x Hours				3 Drinks After x Hours			
Weight	*4 hrs.*	*3 hrs.*	*2 hrs.*	*1 hr.*	*4 hrs.*	*3 hrs.*	*2 hrs.*	*1 hr.*	*4 hrs.*	*3 hrs.*	*2 hrs.*	*1 hr.*
100 lbs.	-	-	-	.03	-	.02	.04	.06	.05	.07	.08	.10
120 lbs.	-	-	-	.03	-	-	.03	.05	.03	.04	.06	.08
140 lbs.	-	-	-	.02	-	-	.02	.05	.02	.03	.05	.07
160 lbs.	-	-	-	.02	-	-	.02	.04	.01	.02	.04	.07
180 lbs.	-	-	-	.01	-	-	.01	.04	-	.02	.03	.05
200 lbs.	-	-	-	-	-	-	.01	.03	-	.01	.03	.05
220 lbs.	-	-	-	-	-	-	-	.03	-	-	.01	.04

	4 Drinks After x Hours				5 Drinks After x Hours				6 Drinks After x Hours			
Weight	*4 hrs.*	*3 hrs.*	*2 hrs.*	*1 hr.*	*4 hrs.*	*3 hrs.*	*2 hrs.*	*1 hr.*	*4 hrs.*	*3 hrs.*	*2 hrs.*	*1 hr.*
100 lbs.	09	.10	.12	.13	.13	.14	.16	.17	.16	.18	.19	.21
120 lbs.	.06	.08	.09	.11	.09	.11	.13	.14	.13	.14	.16	.17
140 lbs.	.02	.03	.05	.07	.07	.09	.10	.12	.10	.12	.13	.15
160 lbs.	.03	.04	.06	.08	.06	.07	.09	.10	.08	.09	.11	.13
180 lbs.	.02	.04	.05	.07	.04	.06	.07	.09	.06	.08	.09	.11
200 lbs.	.01	.03	.04	.06	.03	.04	.06	.08	.05	.07	.08	.10
220 lbs.	-	.01	.03	.06	.01	.03	.05	.07	.04	.06	.07	.09

What you need to know from the previous chart:

➤ With a BAC up to .05, drive carefully.

➤ With a BAC from .05 to .08, you are driving impaired and may be arrested.

➤ With a BAC over .08, DO NOT DRIVE!

The Good News

The good news is that a few beers a day can actually help you live longer. Unless you have an addictive problem with alcohol, beer (and wine) have been shown to have positive health effects. In fact, the Dietary Guidelines for Americans, published jointly by the Agricultural Department and the Health and Human Services Department, were rewritten in 1995 to include this statement: "There is evidence to suggest that moderate drinking may lower the risk of heart attacks." This statement is based on a 12-year study conducted by Danish researchers that monitored the health of 7,234 women and 6,015 men. Dr. Morten Gronbaek, with the Institute of Preventative Medicine in Copenhagen, concluded that the lowest risk for coronary heart disease was for those who consumed up to six drinks per week.

Bar Talk
He was a wise man who invented beer.

—Plato

Two beers a day have also been shown to have other health benefits. For one thing, beer is fat-free! (It's the carbohydrates in brew that give people "beer bellies.") Second, a Harvard University study found that people taking one to three drinks per day have lower blood pressure than non-drinkers. Finally, epidemiologists Sir Richard Doll and Professor Richard Peto of Oxford University put a very positive spin on the relationship of alcohol to mortality after studying 12,000 male moderate drinkers over a 13-year period. They found that death rates for moderate drinkers were not only significantly lower for heart disease, but for other types of vascular and respiratory diseases and cancers as well. The reason that alcohol has these benefits has not yet been proven. My theory is that the more relaxed a person is, the longer he or she will live.

The key phrase in these studies is *two drinks a day*. Any more than that and you're opening yourself up to a whole host of other possible problems. Those include cirrhosis of the liver, stomach cancer, brain damage, and a wide range of social problems like lost jobs, destroyed lives, and dysfunctional families. So, like everything else, moderation is the key.

Beer has been considered medicine since ancient times. Before modern science, it was used as the base for many medicines and thought to cure everything from boils to cancer to snake bites. Today we know that fermentation increases the vitamin and mineral content of barley fourfold. The yeasts that turned the barley mush into beer contain protein, C and B complex vitamins, as well as trace elements of minerals.

For more on how alcohol affects your body, see "Squeezing the Cat: Hangovers" in Chapter 11.

The Beautiful Basics of Brew

Considering that beer is made from four simple ingredients, it's hard to fathom all the fretting and verbosity that's been expended on the subject. That is until you realize that in the distant past, beer could contain anything from parsnips to tree bark to chicken entrails. Beer has come a long way, and the worst thing you're likely to find in your beer these days is corn syrup and a few unpronounceable chemical preservatives.

Be that as it may, *real* beer should be made from malted barley, water, hops, and yeast. Period. That's it. Wheat beer may contain from 20% to 60% wheat. Preservatives, chemical additives, and artificial colorings are rampant in cheap swill, but are generally verboten in breweries making quality product.

Mass-market beer brewers use a chemical panoply to make their beer stand up to time, heat, light, shipping, and other beer killers. These include over 50 different *antioxidants*, dozens of *foam enhancers*, and several *enzymes,* which are not listed on their labels. Small craft brewers eschew such preservatives in favor of a more pure, wholesome product.

Bar Talk
If barley be wanted to make into malt

we must be content and think it no fault.

For we can make liquor to sweeten our lips

of pumpkins and parsnips and walnut tree chips

—Popular song from the 17th century

Terms of Enbeerment
Brewers of huge quantities of beer need to protect their product from long periods of storage, exposure to heat and light, and the hazards of cross-country shipping. To combat these problems, large breweries use **antioxidants** to keep oxygen from giving the beer a "wet cardboard" flavor. They use **foam enhancers** and **head stabilizers** to make sure the beer's head foams up properly. Brewing **enzymes** are naturally occurring proteins that aid in brewing.

John Barleycorn and Other Great Grains

The Latin name for barley is *Hordeum vulgare.* Along with wheat, it has been used in beer making since time immemorial for two purposes:

Stale Ale Alert
Grains other than barley that are added to beer are called "adjuncts," or as I call them, "add junk." Adjuncts like corn and rice are cheaper than barley and give beer a lighter color and flavor. While common as rain, corn gives beer a "chicken-feed" flavor. Look for beer that says "all-malt" on the label (unless it's wheat beer). Beer brewed with corn and rice should cost less than all-malt brews.

➤ Barley provides fermentable sugars in beer that allow yeast to produce alcohol and carbon dioxide (a.k.a. beer bubbles).

➤ Barley gives beer its conditioning (carbonation), alcohol, and sweetish flavor.

Almost any grain has starches and sugars that may be converted into alcohol and CO_2. Wheat, rye, oats, corn, and millet have all found their way into beer over the centuries. While quality microbrewers shun corn and rice as cheap additives, industry giants like Miller, Budweiser, and Coors use up to 40% of the stuff in some of their recipes.

Wheat beers are all the rage these days, and they are valued for their unique flavor. Most people either love 'em or hate 'em. Wheat beers tend to be lighter, summertime beers.

Rye literally gives beer a rye bread sort of flavor. A few modern brewers are experimenting with rye beers, some of which are quite tasty.

Oats are added to oatmeal stout with great effect, giving the beer a sweeter, smoother character.

What's the Buzz About Malt?

Terms of Enbeerment
A barley **kiln** is a large furnace with perforations in the floor. To dry the barley, the kiln is set at a temperature of about 200°F. To produce dark-colored barley for dark-colored beer, the barley is kilned at higher temperatures.

For yeast to best utilize the sugars in barley, the grain must be converted to barley *malt.* Fortunately, barley is the grain that best lends itself to malting.

To malt barley, people who do the malting, called *maltsters,* soak the raw grain in water until it starts to germinate. Then it's dried, or *kilned,* at high temperatures for 35 to 40 hours. The length and temperature of the kilning process determine the color and flavor of the malt.

Malting barley converts the grain's starch into a type of sugar called maltose. Beer yeast thrives on maltose and eagerly converts it into alcohol.

How Do Hops Happen?

Hops are the cone-shaped flower of the hop vine, *Humulus lupulus.* The flowers are savored for brewing because of their bitterness and bouquet. They also help counter the sweetness of malt. Hops have been used down through the ages in sedatives and tonics. The plant is from the botanical family *Cannabinaceae*, which has two family lines— Humulus and Cannabis. This makes hops the first cousin to *Cannabis sativa*—a.k.a. marijuana—and flowers of the two plants have a similar, calming effect upon the body. Hop pillows were once believed to cure insomnia.

Luscious hop flowers hang on the summer vine. Credit: Hop Growers of America, Yakima, Washington.

Hops have been used in beer since at least A.D. 800. A sticky substance in hops called lupulin helps preserve beer, and hops were used mainly for that purpose in the days before airtight bottles and refrigeration.

Like grapes, hops grown in different regions are valued for their varying qualities of bittering, bouquet, or flavor.

Yeast Makes It All Happen

Yeast is a single-celled, living organism that eats sugar and multiplies rapidly. The by-product of this action is carbon dioxide and alcohol. In biological terms, yeast is a fungus.

In beer and brewing terms, it's the organism that makes beer a living product. Yeast is everywhere in the air. Some of it turns barley water to beer. Other strains turn bread to mold. The yeast used in brewing naturally evolved over the centuries.

Many people become confused trying to figure out the difference between ale and lager. It's simpler than you think. When you hear of a beer referred to as an ale or a lager, it's the type of yeast that differentiates the two. Ale yeast produces a complex, fruity, sweet flavor in beer. Since ale yeast works its magic on the top of the beer, ales are sometimes called "top-fermented."

Foamy Fact

What's Reinheitsgebot?: In 1516, Bavarian Prince William IV enacted a beer purity law called the Reinheitsgebot (rine-HITES-ga-bote). The law stated that beer should only be made with barley malt, hops, and water. Yeast was unknown at the time. The law made exceptions for wheat beers, which were usually brewed with 20% to 60% malted wheat.

Lager yeast was first used in brewing in the 1400s, but it wasn't isolated and named until the mid-1800s. Lagers are less complex in flavor, soft, crisp, dry, and refreshing. Lager yeast works at the bottom of the fermenting brew. For that reason, beers brewed with lager yeast are sometimes called "bottom-fermented."

Whetting Your Whistle with Water

Like the human body, beer is up to 98% water. In the old days, before modern sanitation, sources of pure water were rare. As a matter of fact, polluted water in places like London killed tens of thousands of people. When a good source was discovered, a brewery usually sprang up next to the spring. Great brewing centers like Burton-on-Trent in England and Pilsen in the Czech Republic were known far and wide for their pure water. The natural mineral content of the water also affected the taste and character of beers brewed with it.

Bar Talk
He that drinks strong beer

and goes to bed mellow

Lives as he ought to live

and dies a hearty fellow

—17th-century English drinking song

Today, most breweries simply use tap water whose mineral content has been adjusted to fit individual beer styles. But some breweries still use spring water, mountain water, or, in one case I know of, water from Alaskan glaciers. Whatever the quality of the water, it is reflected in the taste of the beer. Hence the popularity of beers from Colorado, Oregon, and other clean-water locales.

Ingredients Beyond the Big Four

In the 1990s, some American breweries are following in the footsteps of their European kin by brewing beer with fruit, fruit extracts, and/or brewing sugars. The quality of beers with these additives varies from brand to brand. But in today's anything-goes world of beer, you're liable to find an interesting array of strange and unusual ingredients in your beer.

Sergeant's Pepper Wort's Glub Beer: Fruits and Vegetables in Brewing

Adventurous homebrewers throw everything in beer from kiwis to garlic. Commercial breweries, however, can't get away with anything that strange. But it's been a recent trend (that dates back many centuries) to flavor some beers with fruit. I've seen ale with cranberry, raspberry, cherry, currants, peaches, and blackberries. I've even seen banana ale! Several Belgian imports ferment their beer with macerated cherries or raspberries. Those beers are ambrosial, more like wine than beer, and well worth drinking.

Basically any fruit that people eat—and can be added to beer—probably will be incorporated sooner or later. Most commercially available beers use fruit extracts as opposed to the real thing.

To most people, the idea of vegetables in beer is a stomach churner. Broccoli beer? Ugh. But let's not forget chili peppers. If you want a fire in your belly and gleam in your eye, there is a chili-pepper beer on the market. This offering actually has a pepper floating right in the bottle for visual as well as gastronomic enjoyment. Watching your friends foam at the mouth after partaking of a chili beer is always good for a quick laugh.

In the old days, when barley was scarce, vegetables such as parsnips, zucchini, potatoes, and peas were thrown into beer. Several years ago, California brewer Bill Owens revived a recipe for pumpkin ale that was a favorite of George Washington, who was an avid homebrewer. The recipe called for a large, baked pumpkin to be added to the brew. Pumpkin Ale, complete with nutmeg, cinnamon, and clove, is unusual, delicious, and widely available.

> **Tasty Tip**
> *Tutti Frutti:* Words cannot describe the wondrous taste of Belgian fruit beers. If you want a real taste treat, try fruit beers like Liefmans Frambozenbier, Boon Kriek Lambic, Lindemans Kriek Lambic, and Chapeau's outrageous Banana.

Herbs and Spice and Everything Nice

At one time, beer was one of the world's first medicines. And, like many home remedies, it was often combined with healing herbs and spices to cure any number of ailments. In this fashion, ancient homebrewers pitched all manner of leaves, flowers, twigs, and roots into their brew kettle.

While brewing with herbs fell out of fashion during the last century, modern micro-brewers are reviving the tradition. The easiest time of year to find spiced beers is between Thanksgiving and Christmas. "Winter Warmers" pop up on retailers' shelves faster than snowmen on a playground. The brewers usually hold the (recipe) cards close to their chests, but I've detected ginger, coriander, cardamom, and cloves among other "secret" ingredients in holiday beers.

In small amounts, spices add a delicious dimension to a brew. They can quickly become overpowering, however, as many intrepid homebrewers have discovered.

> **MMM**
>
> **Tasty Tip**
> *Warms You on the Inside:* In the past few years, the coming of the Christmas season has been marked by the appearance of "Winter Warmers" on retailers' shelves. These beers tend to be stronger, darker, and spicier than your average brew. Winter Warmers may contain spices ranging from anise to cloves to yarrow.

Brewers may also add ginger, licorice, spruce, chocolate, or smoke flavor to their beers. The recent espresso fad has prompted several breweries to toss some coffee beans right into the brew kettle. Talk about cross-marketing! They're great beers and are conducive to long conversations deep into the night.

Some other surprising herbs and spices added to beer are basil, bay, cassia, angelica, nutmeg, orange peel, vanilla, woodruff, and chamomile.

Sweetening the Pot: Brewing Sugars

As mentioned earlier, barley sugar, or maltose, is the main (but not only) sugar that yeast converts to alcohol and carbon dioxide. But brewers can add other sugars to beer to take the place of maltose or add to the flavor. Many British brewers add what's known as brewing sugars to their beers to give them a "rummy" taste. Lactose, or milk sugar, may be added to so-called milk stouts from Britain. Brown sugar, molasses, maple syrup, and honey have all found their way into the brewer's kettle. Maple syrup and honey in partic-ular are experiencing a comeback among microbrewers.

Alcohol Facts and Beer Strength

There's plenty of fact, fable, and fantasy circulating on the subject of beer strength. No matter what you've heard, beer is usually less than 5% alcohol by volume. Some strong

English and German beers do contain higher amounts of alcohol. The strong English beer styles are old ale, barley wine, and imperial stout. The strong German styles are bock and doppelbock.

The confusion is due to the different systems used to measure beer strength. The United States, the Netherlands, and a few other countries measure beer alcohol content by weight, not volume. Alcohol is lighter than water—by 79.6% to be exact. So measuring alcohol content by weight gives a lower percentage number, making the beer sound lighter. For instance, 3.2% beer is 3.2% alcohol by weight, about 4% by volume. The volume of the alcohol is what affects you when you're drinking, and it's used in blood-alcohol charts, so that number seems easier for people to use. The United States' wine industry and brewers in the rest of the world express alcoholic content by volume. That is the method used in this book.

The Bureau of Alcohol, Tobacco and Firearms (BATF)—besides having an interesting moniker—is very nitpicky about every little thing that goes—or does not go—into beer. Until recently, the BATF would not allow beer producers to list alcoholic strength on the label. Ever the paternal agency, they were afraid that we irresponsible types might go out searching for the strongest beers. Gasp! How could they think such a thing?

There are some myths about beer strength I'd like to dispel while I'm at it:

➤ Myth Number One: Homebrew (beer made at home by amateur brewers) is stronger than commercial beer (beer made by professional brewers).

That's definitely not true. Actually, homebrewers have a harder time efficiently utilizing the sugars available in their beer. A bucket in the basement can't compete with today's high-tech brewing systems. Some homebrew might be stronger than your average store-bought beer. But unless your homebrewer is quite skilled, the strength of his or her beer will be about the same or below commercially available beer.

➤ Myth Number Two: Dark beer is stronger than lighter beer.

Again, it's not necessarily true. *Some* dark beers are stronger, some aren't. A few notoriously strong Belgian beers, like Duvel, are light and straw-colored. And they weigh in at 8%. A few dark stouts are about average in strength. It's more the style, rather than the color, of the beer that determines strength.

➤ Myth Number Three: Import beers are stronger than American beers.

That might have been more accurate before the microbrewery revolution. Some imports are stronger than your average commercially brewed beer, but again, not always.

The Least You Need to Know

➤ Beer can be good for you if you don't drink too much, and if you don't drink and drive.

➤ Traditionally, beer is made from malted barley, hops, yeast, and water.

➤ Other ingredients such as fruit, vegetables, and spices may be added to beer without sacrificing quality.

Chapter 3

The Four Elements— Beer Ingredients

In This Chapter

➤ Everything you need to know about barley

➤ Hop facts and hop puns

➤ Ale and lager yeast characteristics

➤ The differences between hard water and soft water brewing

Okay, so beer is made of barley, hops, water, yeast, and occasionally wheat. So how do we get stout? Pale ale? Bock? Pilsner? Fortunately, the four elements of beer are so versatile that they can be combined into dozens of flavors and styles. To fully understand beer, this chapter looks deep into the glass to learn the fascinating facts that lurk behind beer's basic components.

Barley Naked

Barley is beer's basic ingredient. After it's been malted, barley gives beer its flavor, sweetness, and *mouthfeel* (a term used to describe the body of the beer). When malted barley mixes with yeast, the sugars in the malt give beer its alcohol and carbon dioxide.

The Grain of the Ancients

Beer is made from barley. But did you know that it was the first grain to ever be domesticated? Back when our ancestors were wandering the hills of ancient Sumeria, they accidentally discovered that wild barley could make a bodacious, consciousness-altering concoction. Once that cat was out of the bag, the nomads quit their wandering ways and learned how to farm. Some anthropologists believe that growing barley for beer was the sole reason that the first agricultural civilization was formed. Besides, who can wander too far after they've had a few Sumerian ales?

Terms of Enbeerment
The way the beer feels in your mouth is called (you guessed it) **mouthfeel**. Mouthfeel describes the thickness of the beer's body. Beer is described as light-bodied, medium-bodied, or full-bodied. Usually, the darker the beer, the fuller the body. To wit: Light beer is light-bodied; pale ale is medium-bodied; stout is full-bodied. Other mouthfeel terms might be creamy, chewy, humongous, gargantuan, and poo poo.

Over 7,000 years ago, the first known recipe for the "wine of grain" was etched on stone tablets in Mesopotamia. Even before that time, barley grew wild in the ancient hills of Sumeria for more than a million years.

The ancients worshipped the goddess Ninkasi and believed that she gave barley to *women* (not men). Women were in charge of brewing, and dozens of goddesses were associated with beer, brewing, drinking, and even hangovers. Men, of course, also enjoyed beer.

In addition to brewing, women also acted as tavern keepers, servers, staff, and even bouncers. No man, no matter how drunk, would question a woman who had Ninkasi on her side. The taverns lured male patrons by displaying stone signs with pictures of bare-breasted vixens carved in high-relief.

Foamy Fact

The Lady Who Fills the Mouth: By 1,800 B.C., the Sumerians worshipped Ninkasi, the goddess of brewing. Ninkasi was also called "the lady who fills the mouth." She lived on the legendary Mount Sabu, whose name roughly translates as "mountain of the saloon keeper."

How Does Your Barley Grow?

The barley used in brewing is called either two-row barley or six-row barley. The terms two-row and six-row define how may rows of grains grow on each ear of the plant.

Two-row barley *(Hordeum distichon)* grows with (you guessed it!) two long rows of grain on each ear. Two-row is considered to be a finer grain for brewing. It has a thinner husk, making beers brewed from it less astringent.

German beers use high-quality two-row barley, as do most English beers. Most American microbrewed beers also use two-row barley. Some finer beers boast on their labels of using two-row barley. This is the good stuff.

Six-row barley *(Hordeum vulgare)* has six rows of grain on each ear. Eighty percent of the barley cultivated in North America is six-row. It's cheaper to grow, as it yields more barley per acre. Six-row has a high *protein* and *tannin* content, which imparts a coarser flavor and causes cloudiness in beer.

Most giant American breweries use six-row malt, but cut the haziness it causes with adjuncts such as corn and rice. They also use chemical haze deterrents. Six-row is not favored among micro- and craft-brewers.

Terms of Enbeerment
Protein is a class of organic compounds that contain amino acids. Excessive protein in beer can cause cloudiness known as chill haze when the beer is cooled. **Tannins** are naturally occurring acids found in tea and tree bark. Tannins in barley result in harsh flavors and haze in beer. During the brewing process, tannins (which have a negative charge) attract proteins (which have a positive charge) and they both settle out of the beer. Poorly made beer may have excessive tannins.

Making Malt

It's not surprising that the ancients attributed the miracle of beer to goddesses. The process that renders barley useful is long, strange, and exacting.

➤ Malt is barley that has been soaked in water, sprouted, then exposed to high temperatures in a kiln (as mentioned earlier, a large furnace with perforations in the floor) for up to 35–40 hours.

➤ In the kiln, hot air—about 200°F—is passed over the barley. To produce dark-colored barley for dark-colored beer, the barley is kilned at higher temperatures.

➤ Beer is made mostly of lightly kilned barley. Darker styles such as porter, bock, and stout use varying percentages of barley that has been kilned to darker colors.

To turn barley into malt, the following procedures are performed:

1. Barley is soaked, or steeped, in a vat for 40 hours. The water is changed several times to prevent bacterial contamination and spontaneous fermentation. As the barley steeps, its moisture content within the grain rises from 12% to 40%.

2. After the barley has steeped, the water is drained, and it sits in the vat for six to 12 hours.

3. The barley is then laid out in a germination room. Here, the grains are held at 60°F while they begin to germinate and sprout. Sprouting requires plenty of oxygen and generates a lot of heat. The sprouting barley is periodically turned while tiny rootlets poke their tails out from the grain husk. This barley is called green malt.

4. Finally, the green malt is loaded into a kiln. At first the temperature of the kiln is kept very low. Later, it is raised to cure the malt. This process develops the flavor and color of the malt. Some malts are kilned for up to 35–40 hours. Maximum kiln temperatures reach 400°F.

The entire process takes about six to ten days. Of course, modern maltsters (folks who make malt) speed up the process by using modern methods. Still and all, malting barley is a traditional science performed by a few giant malting houses throughout the world.

In the past, homebrewers and small breweries would malt their own barley. They might soak it in a net sack in the river for a few days, dry it on the attic floor with the windows wide open, and kiln it on a screen over a fire. Large breweries, too, malted their own barley well into the twentieth century. The economics of small-scale brewing does not allow today's craft brewers to malt their own grain, except in very special circumstances.

Barley is converted to malt by passing through the steeping tanks (top), *germination tanks* (center), *and circular kiln* (bottom).

Malt Varieties

A brewer uses malted barley like a painter uses various colors to create a masterpiece. Some beers utilize only one type of malt; others may have seven types of malt, giving the brew an overwhelmingly complex flavor and unique color. Here's a basic list of malt types, listed from lightest to darkest.

➤ *Lager malt* is sown in spring. It's a two-row used in microbrewed and imported lagers. It is light in color and has a cereal-like flavor.

➤ *Pale ale malt* is sown in winter. Pale ale malt gives British and Irish beer styles their distinctive flavor. The malt imparts a biscuity, toasted flavor and hints of toffee.

➤ *Crystal* or *caramel malt* is prepared in a different process from most malts—it is wet-kilned to give it a delicious burnt-sugar flavor and reddish hue. Caramel malt is used in amber lagers, Oktoberfest, and bock beers.

➤ *Chocolate malt* gives beer a coffee-like flavor along with hints of burnt caramel. It's named for its color, not its flavor. Chocolate malt gives beer a rich, brown color and provides brown ales, porters, and sometimes stouts with their roasty "bite."

Foamy Fact

Testament to Beer: Beer is mentioned frequently in the *Talmud* and in the Bible. Three of the rabbis who wrote the *Talmud* were brewers. David, the King of the Jews, was a brewer. When a brewery went into business, the sign hung outside the door was the six-pointed Star of David. The Star also represented alchemy—the turning of water into…beer.

➤ *Black malt* was originally roasted in England in a drum like a coffee roaster in a patented process. Black malt or black patent malt gives sweet stouts and dark ales a sharp, acrid flavor and black-as-night color.

➤ *Roasted barley* is used primarily in Irish stouts like Murphy's. It is strong, dry, and more bitter than black malt. It's characterized by the flavor of burnt coffee. Roast barley also gives Irish stout its famous, rich, creamy head.

Drink Your Wheat

Before Prohibition was enacted in 1919, one of the most popular beer styles in the United States was German wheat beer called *weizen* (VYT-sen). Although wheat makes up less than 10% of brewing grains, its popularity is growing exponentially. These days, many craft breweries brew some style of wheat beer.

Wheat *(Triticum aestivum)* is used in beers in malted and unmalted, or raw, form. German and American wheat beers tend to use malted wheat, while Belgian wheat beers tend to use unmalted wheat.

Malted wheat is light in color and gives beer a thick mouthfeel, a strong head, and an unmistakable flavor. Some wheat beers taste like clove chewing gum. A light cloudiness is usually associated with wheat beers and is to be expected. There are many styles of beer brewed with wheat. For more information, see "American Wheat Beer," toward the end of Chapter 6.

Rye and Other Strange Grains

Today we forget that for thousands of years, people experienced shortages of many important daily necessities, from sandals to huts. In centuries past, there always seemed to be a scarcity of good malted barley for brewing. Not to worry. Yeast's mission in life is to convert sugar into alcohol, and it doesn't care if the sugar is from pumpkins or pale ale malt. Human taste buds do care, however, but many grains make passable beer, and some are quite unique and enjoyable. Seventeenth-century Dutch brewers used wheat, unmalted spelt, barley malt, malted rye, and oats in a single recipe.

➤ A few microbreweries have recently introduced rye beers. Rye gives beer a spicy, uh, *rye bread* sort of flavor.

➤ In Africa, a traditional beer called *chakalow* is made from the cereal grass, millet.

➤ Spelt, a type of wheat, creates a lighter, more flavorful beer than wheat.

➤ Oats give beer a silky, smooth, sweet flavor and are used in small amounts in oatmeal stout.

Don't Worry, Be Hoppy

After malt, hops are probably the most noticeable ingredient in beer. They provide beer with a *bitterness* that balances the sweetness of malt. They give beer its floral bouquet. And hops act as a natural *preservative*, which was no small concern in the days before refrigeration and modern bottling.

Hops grow in different varieties and regions. Just as malt varieties determine beer styles, so too do hop varieties. Some varieties of hops are grown for their

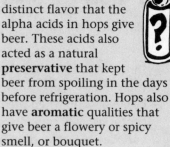

Terms of Enbeerment
Bitterness describes the distinct flavor that the alpha acids in hops give beer. These acids also acted as a natural **preservative** that kept beer from spoiling in the days before refrigeration. Hops also have **aromatic** qualities that give beer a flowery or spicy smell, or bouquet.

aromatic qualities; some are grown for their *bittering* qualities. As a result, most beers have several varieties of hops.

Czech Pilsner is unique in flavor and bouquet because of the Saaz hops it is brewed with. Many American microbrewed beers are notable for their abundant use of Cascade hops.

Hoppiness Is a Warm Pun

Although hops have been used in brewing for more than a millennium, they have only been used with some consistency for about 200 years. Their popularity grew with brewers as breweries grew larger and beer was more prone to spoil when it was shipped longer distances.

Bar Talk
Hops are the grapes of beer.

—Gold-medal-winning brewer Shaun Franklin of the Rooster Brewery, UK

Hops give beer bouquet. Oils and resins in the hop flower manifest themselves in a sticky, yellow powder called lupulin. Hop oils give beer its unique perfume. Hop resins contribute to its bitterness. Hop oils boil away quickly during the brewing process, so hops used for bouquet and flavor are added during the last few minutes of the brewing process. Some brewers "dry hop," which means hops are added to the finished beer a few days before bottling or kegging. This is the preferred method for the finest bouquet.

Hops make beer bitter, which balances the natural sweetness provided by the malt sugar. When beer lovers discuss bitterness, it isn't bitter "ugh," but bitter "yum." If the term "bitter" bothers you, think of bitter beer as "dry" and less-bitter beer as "sweet."

Hops inhibit the growth of beer-spoiling bacteria. In the early days, herbs such as ginger, spruce, tansy, sage, and even wormwood were used to preserve beer. But as anyone who has grown hops quickly learns, hops are prolific, tenacious, and grow in many kinds of soil. A single hop vine can grow 20 feet during one season and produce a pound of flowers—enough to make 40 gallons of beer.

Let's Grow Do the Hop

Hops are a perennial crop, meaning that they grow to maturity every year without being replanted.

In the old days, hops grew wild in the forests, netting out across trees and bushes in all their sinewy glory. Trouble was, male hops didn't do a thing for beer. And female hops became seedy when bred with males, making them difficult to use in brewing. Over the centuries, wild hop vines were destroyed so that only female hops would grow. Several varieties of British hop, however, are still allowed to breed and are considered higher quality, if fertilized.

Modern hop cultivation takes place in hopyards lined with 20-foot-long poles, 20 feet apart. The poles are connected with strong wire. From that wire, single wires run down to each hop plant. The hops poke their shoots out in spring, and by summer they have snaked 20 feet or more up the wires. In the heat of August, a hop vine can grow more than two feet a day.

When hops are ripe, they are heavy with flowers. The hops are harvested by machinery and dried at 130°F to 150°F for six to 20 hours. They are cured for one to 12 days, compressed into bales, and shipped to cool-storage warehouses. Light and oxygen destroy the oils in the hops, so they must be handled with care.

Who Grows the Hops?

The first written mention of hop cultivation for beer was in the ninth century by a Bavarian nun called Hildegarde. (She also prescribed cannabis for headaches, but that's another story.) During Hildegarde's era, hops were grown in the Hallertau region of Germany and the Bohemian region of the modern Czech Republic.

Foamy Fact

Hops in History: Hops were first noted in records of the Jewish captivity in Babylon. Folks there were given "a strong drink made from hops."

By the early 1400s, hops were well established as a brewing ingredient. Flemish brewers were responsible for taking hop-brewed beers to England. The English were appalled that anyone would put such a decadent plant into their beer and for a time, it was illegal to brew with hops in Britain. Hops were introduced to North America in the early 1600s by the Pilgrims, who truly loved their beer. The skunky flowers were cultivated in Manhattan, Virginia, and other colonies.

Today, Germany grows more hops than any other country—30% of the world's total. The United States runs a close second at 25%. Other major hop-growing countries include Russia, Japan, and—strangely enough—Tasmania.

The rich, black, volcanic soil of the Pacific Northwest makes it ideal for hop cultivation. Almost all of the commercially grown hops in North America are grown in the Yakima Valley in central Washington state, the Willamette Valley in Oregon, the Snake River Valley in Idaho, and in British Columbia, Canada.

Hop Varieties and Where They Grow

Like a vintner artistically blending grape varieties into a fine wine, a brewer carefully measures hops to achieve greatness in beer. Chosen for their bouquet, flavor, preservative, and bittering qualities, the hops in the beer you're drinking may have traveled 10,000 miles to spice your drink. While there are dozens of hop varieties, and new ones being bred and hybridized every year, there are a few basic kinds of hops that every beer lover should recognize.

➤ Cascade hops are grown in the Pacific Northwest and give American and Canadian microbrewed beer its unique floral nose. European brewers consider them "skunky" and shun them, but American microbrewers are die-hard hopheads and use the Cascade to great effect. Cascade hops impart a pine-like, fruity, and citric bouquet to beer.

➤ Fuggles and Goldings are two delightfully named hops, bearing the monikers of the farmers who propagated them in the 17th and 18th centuries, respectively. Fuggles and Goldings give British ales their world-renowned bouquet and bitterness.

➤ Hallertau hops are grown in Bavaria and give German beers their delicate hop aroma. Hallertau is a spicy hop traditionally used in lagers.

➤ Northern Brewer is a strong bittering hop traditionally grown in Germany and used for lager.

➤ Saaz hops are grown in Zatec, Bohemia, and are notable for giving Pilsner Urquell and other Czech Pilsners their divine nose.

Yeast Is Yeast: What's It Doing in My Beer?

Beer is alive. And yeast is what makes it alive. Beer would only be barley soup without yeast, despite the illustriousness of malt and hops. Virtually unknown, unnamed, and unseen by the human eye until the mid-19th century, yeast is the living fungus that makes beer happen.

Foamy Fact

First Things First: Yeast was first observed by Anton van Leeuwenhoek in 1680. In fact, beer was the very first thing the Dutch scientist observed up close and personal when he invented the microscope.

Yeast, like every other living organism, lives to eat and reproduce. It is to our benefit that beer yeast loves to eat maltose (malt sugar). It is to our further benefit that the by-products of the yeast's voraciousness are alcohol and CO_2.

Yeast occurs everywhere. It's responsible for bread, tofu, cheese, yogurt, and other foods. But yeast is more than just food. The process that makes all living things rot when they die is caused by wild yeast. So is the mold on your bread. And those wild fungi are not welcome in the brewhouse. Bad yeast can cause beer to taste like soap, form chunks, or gush in your face when you open the bottle. Trust me, it's not too tasty.

In recent years, dried beer has been discovered in ancient Egyptian pots over 4,000 years old. Scientists managed to awaken the yeast contained therein and actually brew beer with it. This has also been done with centuries-old beer bottles found in ancient ship-wrecks on the bottom of the sea. This clearly illustrates the tenacity and life cycle of yeast.

All Hail Ale Yeast

For the past century or so, most commercially brewed beers in America and Continental Europe have been lagers, or beer brewed from lager yeast. Ale styles, brewed from ale yeast, have been revived in the past 15 to 20 years by the microbrewery revolution. Most microbreweries and brewpubs brew ale because it takes less time and it works in warmer temperatures, saving money on refrigeration costs. Ales are also more complex in flavor, and versatile, making them "fun" to brew.

Foamy Fact

God is Good: Although yeast had not yet been named, Bavarian brewers under-stood that the gunk at the bottom of their beer barrels could be added to the next batch of beer with great results. Without name, this sludge was some-times referred to as "God is Good."

Ale yeast produces a complex, fruity, sweet flavor in beer, which is partially due to the fact that ale yeast does not convert sugars to alcohol as efficiently as lager yeast. This leaves unfermented sugars behind that give ales their sweetness and complexity.

Ale yeast works at the top of the liquid, so ales are sometimes called "top-fermented." During the brewing process, ale yeast prefers temperatures of about 60°F to work.

> ### Foamy Fact
>
> *A Real Head Trip:* The ninth-century Vikings were crazed berserkers from Scandinavia who would get their enemies drunk, burn down the bar, and drink ale from their roasted skulls. Some believe the toast *Skoal!* comes from the word "skull." These Viking warriors brewed their ale with wormwood, a madness-inducing hallucinogen. Entomologists believe that the world "ale" comes from the Viking word for beer, *aul.*

Lager Yeast

Lager yeast was isolated in the mid-1800s by one of the great Munich brewers, Gabriel Sedlmayr of the Spaten Brewery, and his student, Jacob Christian Jacobsen. In 1845, Jacobsen persuaded Sedlmayr to give him two pots of living yeast, which he then used to found Carlsberg Breweries and produce Denmark's first commercially brewed beer. By 1883, Jacobsen was having trouble with his beers. He hired scientist Emil Hansen to flush out his yeast beasts. Carlsberg beer had four yeasts, three bad and one good. Hansen isolated the good yeast, which became known as *Saccharomyces carlsbergensis.* The *carlsberg* part of the yeast's name was to honor the brewery that first isolated lager yeast, even though it was a Bavarian product. This name was later changed to *uvarum.*

> **Terms of Enbeerment**
> Some beers, notably Budweiser, advertise that they are **krausened.** This is a German word describing a process in which a small portion of fermented brew is added to the lager before bottling or kegging. This causes a secondary fermentation and gives the beer a natural effervescence.

Lager yeast works more slowly and efficiently than ale yeast. It produces a cleaner, drier beer with less fruity overtones. Some drinkers sense a bouquet of "new-mown hay" in lager.

Lager yeast works at the bottom of the beer, so it's often referred to as "bottom-fermented." It is fermented at 41°F to 48°F for ten days to two weeks; then the temperature is lowered to 33°F for four to six weeks. Some great beers are lagered for up to six months. Mass-produced lagers are only aged for two or three weeks, the latter being the norm.

Wild Yeasts of Lambic

In Belgium, certain beers are fermented with wild, airborne yeasts. They are called lambics, after Lembeek, the town southwest of Brussels where they have been brewed the same way for centuries. Lambics are something most people either love or hate. Some say they are sour and winy; advocates profess that they're absolutely unique and delicious.

When lambics are fermented, the beer is left in large, open containers in the brewery's attic. The roof vents are left open, and the brew is visited by wild yeasts that float in on the wind.

Most breweries must be kept spotlessly clean to avoid contamination by wild yeasts that may spoil the beer. But some brewers in Belgium depend on wild yeasts to visit their beers and make them unique and flavorful. The flowery-fecund yeast does find the beer, but in (relatively) low doses, so that the resulting brew must be aged in wooden barrels for up to three years. Scientists have identified over 70 different yeasts at work in lambic beer, some of which have taken up residence in the wooden barrels.

There are several styles of lambics, including fruit beers. For more on lambics and Belgian beers, see Chapter 6.

Killing Yeasts with Pasteurization

Modern breweries pasteurize their beer by applying heat of up to 150°F to the brew. This kills ambient bacteria, halts fermentation, and extends the shelf life of bottled or canned beer. Kegged beer is usually unpasteurized.

Some microbrewers, traditional breweries, and knowledgeable consumers still shun pasteurization and prefer the flavor and quality of a "living" beer.

When most people think of Louis Pasteur, they remember their eighth-grade science classes where they discussed pasteurized milk. What they didn't tell you in eighth grade (along with many other things) is that much of Pasteur's work was with *beer.* He originally developed the process named after him so that the French brewing industry could become competitive with German brewers. Pasteur was the first to prove that the production of alcohol during fermentation was the vital function of a living cell. He fought the resistance of other scientists on this issue, and he called the process *la vie sans air,* or life without air. Pasteur went on to pinpoint and classify bacteria that infect beer.

From 1857 to 1868, when Louis was making his early discoveries, many breweries were growing into national and even international marketers. But shipping beer across great distances can be harmful—or even fatal—to the beer. And the same thing that gives beer its life—yeast—can also kill it if it becomes contaminated with bacteria. So the trick was figuring out how to control yeast, making it jump through hoops and produce consistent-quality beer, then go away and leave the finished product alone.

Foamy Fact

Trained Yeast Circus: Yeast can be trained to behave in certain advantageous ways. The Marston's Brewery in Burton, England employs a brewing system called "Burton Unions" in which the yeast does as many tricks as a circus pony. The Burton Unions brewing system uses rows of wooden barrels to ferment the beer. The barrels are connected with swan-necked tubes into long, open troughs. The yeast bubbles and froths, forcing the ale, by natural pressure, up into the series of troughs. For three or four days the foamy beer circulates through the shiny metal troughs like the tides, ebbing and flowing. When the yeast is done, the ale settles down back into its original barrels. This trained yeast gives Marston's Pedigree Bitter a matchless, fruity character.

The Joys of Bottle-Conditioned Beers

Most beers have CO_2 from tanks injected into them to give them bubbles. Beers that are bottle-conditioned have newly fermented beer, sugar, or yeast added to them right before bottling. The beer is then stored for about a month and allowed to condition (carbonate). This carbonates the beer naturally.

Bottle-conditioning allows the beer to travel better and remain fresh longer. When you see the words "bottle-conditioned" on a beer label, you are getting a living product. Unlike most beers that are pasteurized and injected with CO_2, bottle-conditioned brews have natural conditioning, which means a fresher, better-tasting beer.

Bottle-conditioned beers usually have a small cake of yeast on the bottom of the bottle. If the idea of drinking yeasty beer doesn't appeal to you, pour the beer carefully into a glass and leave the last half-inch in the bottle. If you appreciate the B_6 and B_{12} vitamins found in yeast—which help stave off hangovers, by the way—pour the whole thing right in your glass.

Water You Drinking?

Like the human body, beer is about 98% water. Lager beer is usually made with "soft" water, while ale is usually brewed with "hard" water. The terms "hard" and "soft" to describe water hearken back to a time when people first started using soap. Water with a lot of minerals made soap hard to lather. Water with low mineral content was the opposite, hence "soft."

Here are the defining characteristics of hard water:

➤ Hard water contains large amounts of mineral salts such as calcium sulfate, also known as gypsum.

➤ Pale ale, porter, stout, and other English ale styles rely on hard water to give them their unique character and color.

➤ Calcium reduces haze, increases extracts from malt and hops, and stimulates yeast growth and fermentation.

➤ Sulfates contribute to dryness and add to hop bitterness.

➤ The hardest water comes from breweries in Yorkshire and Burton-on-Trent, England; Dortmund, Germany; and Dublin, Ireland.

And here are the defining characteristics of soft water:

➤ Soft water contains lower amounts of minerals such as calcium, magnesium, and sulfates.

➤ Soft water lends a soft, full, sweet flavor to beer.

➤ Lagers tend to be brewed with soft water.

➤ A few brewing centers with soft water are Pilsen, Czech Republic (home of the original Pilsner); Munich, Germany; and Milwaukee, Wisconsin.

Billions of tons of barley and hops are grown each year. They are baked, boiled, heated, and chilled. Thousands of workers bend their backs in the fields and breweries to harvest, pack, isolate, and distill these products of nature. All this work would be for naught, however, if it weren't for the water. Great water—which is sometimes even treated by modern breweries—makes great beer, and the mineral makeup of the water adds subtle characteristics to the final product.

Bar Talk
It takes beer to make thirst worthwhile.

—German saying

The Role of Water

In the past, beer advertising and braggadocio centered on the water: *From the icy cold springs of the sky blue waters of the flowing source of the Rocky Mountain streams…*You know the pitch. Until recently, no ad exec would bother to spend precious ad dollars bragging about a beer's incredible caramel malt or bodacious Fuggles hops. While that may be changing, the concept of beer being as pure as water has a long history.

The reason great brewing centers sprang up around pure water sources is that up until about 75 years ago, the water in many cities of the world was so polluted that it would sicken or kill whomever drank it. The water's still polluted, of course, but chemicals are added to purify it of disease-causing bacteria. In the old days, almost everybody drank beer whether they liked it or not because beer was boiled when it was brewed, thus killing the microscopic nasties. Lest you think people were stumbling around drunk all the time, remember that beer was brewed in several strengths, the weakest being for children, the strongest being for sailors and other hardy folk.

Bar Talk
Americans can fix nothing without a drink. If you meet you drink, if you part you drink…if you close a bargain you drink…they drink because it's hot; they drink because it's cold; they begin to drink early in the morning, they leave off late at night; they commence it early in life and continue until they soon drop off dead. As for water, it's very good for navigation.

—British naval officer Captain Frederick Marryat writing in 1837

Water is used in every aspect of the brewing process, from germinating malt to cleaning the kettles. Breweries employ detailed chemical analysis of their water and treat it accordingly for each style of beer. Some breweries tap into springs, glacial runoff, or deep wells. With groundwaters becoming more polluted from fertilizer and pesticide runoff, many breweries simply use tap water. They filter the water, or boil it to neutrality, then add back salts and minerals as required by style.

No matter how good the water, great beer can only be made with great ingredients overall, along with the talented hands of a skilled brewer. But when you're talking about an ingredient that makes up 98% of your brew, the advertiser's words take on a new meaning: it really *is* the water.

The Least You Need to Know

➤ Many types, colors, and flavors of malt are made from drying sprouted barley in a kiln.

➤ Hops are the flowers of a fast-growing plant. There are many different kinds of hops, classified by where they grow as well as their bittering, bouquet, and flavor qualities.

➤ Beer may contain ale, lager, or wild yeasts. Ale is complex, fruity, and sometimes sweet in flavor. Lager is less complex, dry, soft, and refreshing. Wild yeasts are used primarily in the brewing of Belgian lambic beer.

➤ Beer is 98% water. Hard water and soft water are used for different beer styles.

Chapter 4

Malted Magic: The Art and Science of Brewing

In This Chapter

➤ Who brews beer?

➤ A step-by-step guide to how beer is made

Brewing beer is one of the oldest industrial processes known to the human race. It might be *the* oldest. As you can imagine, malting barley, boiling it with herb and hop, and cooling, fermenting, and preserving it afterwards are not accidental processes. Down through the ages, almost every up-to-date modern invention, from the microscope to refrigeration, has been utilized in the name of brewing. Some archeologists believe that pottery itself was first invented solely for beer storage. And a few years ago, German scientists conducted brewing experiments aboard the space shuttle.

So next time you crack the cap on a simple bottle of beer, be aware that you're getting in touch with many millennia worth of industry and providence. To you it may simply be a beer, but to hundreds of thousands of people for thousands of years, its been a life's work. As long as there's been civilization and industry, there's been brewing.

Today's beer consumers are bombarded with a slew of slogans boasting beer that is craft-brewed, brewed in small batches, microbrewed, made in a brewpub, and on and on. Some of these terms are meaningless advertising froth. Some have true industry definitions. To separate the foam from the fluff, this chapter takes a close look at brewery definitions as set forth by the people in the brewing business.

Brewpubs—Beer Brewed and Food

Brewpubs are taverns or restaurants that make their own beer to sell on the premises. In many states, brewpubs are only allowed to sell their beer over the counter to customers—not to distributors or liquor stores. Many states allow brewpubs to sell take-away containers to customers. Brewpubs first became legal in the United States when California changed its liquor distribution laws in 1982. Before that time, it was illegal in many states for a brewery to self-distribute beer or sell direct to the public. Since then, most states have changed their laws to allow for brewpubs. Self-distribution by microbreweries is still not allowed in many parts of the country.

In the old days, every town of consequence had several restaurants that made their own beer as they baked their own bread. In 1920, Prohibition wiped those establishments off the map. In Europe, the tradition has been carried on for thousands of years. And why not? The idea dates back to ancient Sumeria. While not specifically called brewpubs, there are breweries all over the world that brew beer for sale on the premises. Some have been doing it for centuries.

Goose Island Brewing Co. in Chicago offers an old-fashioned speakeasy atmosphere that would do Al Capone proud.

Since 1983, almost 500 brewpubs have opened in the United States. About 100 have opened in Canada. About 100 are expected to open every year from now on. Now *that's* good news.

Foamy Fact

The Brewing Godfather: One of the first brewpubs to open in America since Prohibition was Buffalo Bill's Brewery in Hayward, California. The pub was founded by the Godfather of the brewpub business, Buffalo Bill Owens.

Owens, an award-winning photographer and a homebrewer, badgered the California legislature to change the liquor laws so beer manufacturers could sell directly to the public. When the revised brewpub law went into effect in September 1983, Owens opened the taps. Since that time, almost 500 brewpubs have opened in the United States and another 100 or so in Canada.

Microbreweries—Big Beer on a Small Scale

Brewpubs sell the beer they make on the premises. Microbreweries put beer in bottles or kegs for distribution to and sale in taverns, liquor stores, bottle shops, or grocery stores. Some microbreweries—in places where it's legal—sell beer fresh, right at the brewery.

Rockies Brewing Co. in Colorado is a microbrewery with a cozy tasting room where beers flow after brewhouse tours. Credit: George Jayne.

Two quick facts you should know about beer barrels:

➤ All breweries, large and small, measure their output in barrels per year.

➤ A barrel of beer contains 31 gallons.

The term microbrewery (a.k.a. micro) was coined in the late 1970s when the average national brewery produced upwards of 500,000 barrels of beer a year. Anheuser-Busch produced that much Budweiser in *two weeks*. The first microbreweries were lucky if they sold 2,500 barrels a year. As a matter of fact, some micros sold only 500 barrels of beer per year.

You can imagine that somebody making 2,500 barrels of beer every year is going to put more effort and better ingredients into the brew than someone brewing half a million barrels. On that small a scale, it's a labor of love. Also, large breweries are entirely automated and computerized. This is great for quality control, but in general, many folks believe that "smaller is better" when it comes to brewing.

Once the idea of beer brewed in small batches caught on, some microbreweries couldn't keep up with the demand for their quality product. As the breweries knocked down walls and expanded, so did the term microbrewery, which crept up to meaning 15,000 barrels per year. Then it went to 25,000 barrels per year. Today there are microbreweries that produce 100,000 barrels of beer per year. Some successful micros are building new breweries from the ground up and are expecting to grow indefinitely.

While the numbers may change, it's more of the commitment to craft that separates the micros from established old-line breweries. Micros usually brew all-malt beer without adjuncts. They tend to give their beer the time it needs to age properly. And they almost all put their beer in bottles as opposed to cans, which many of us find more esthetically pleasing. Think of a microbrewery as a small café that makes everything fresh from scratch, as opposed to a large chain restaurant with factory-packed, frozen food.

Many microbreweries give tours on Saturday afternoons, and they're a lot of fun. You get to see how the beer is made, and there are usually plenty of free samples. For more about that, see Chapter 10.

Regional Breweries—Local Lager Landmarks

Regional breweries are older, mid-sized breweries that have been making beer for a long time in a limited region. Consumer loyalty to a locally produced product kept many of these regionals in business during hard times. During the mid-1980's merger-mania, dozens of regionals such as Leinenkugel got gobbled up by giant breweries. The big breweries would assume the regional's well-known brands and, at the same time, gain a new location for brewing their flagship brands. A lot of regionals that were not bought closed their doors forever. They just couldn't compete price-wise with the big, bad giants.

Olympia Brewing Co. in Washington is a former regional now owned by a national brewing company.

Regionals are more flexible than giant breweries, so they can tailor their product to please local tastes. The craft-brew revolution has been good to the regionals that survived, because the smaller breweries have been able to introduce higher-quality products made in small batches. Regionals also do quite a bit of contract brewing.

Foamy Fact

Golden Age of Golden Beer: The late 18th century was a golden age of brewing in America. In 1890, there were 94 breweries in Philadelphia, 77 in New York, 41 in Chicago, 38 in Brooklyn, 33 in Detroit, 29 in St. Louis, 26 in San Francisco, 24 in Cincinnati, and 20 in Buffalo. As the 20th century progressed, however, hundreds of breweries closed as giant breweries gobbled up smaller ones. Prohibition drove the final nail in the brewery coffin, and the number of American breweries would not increase again until the mid-1980s.

Contract Brewing—Brewery in an Office

Contract brewing is when a few people establish a beer name, set up a sales office, and have their beer made by an established brewery. This is very cost-effective because a contract brewery can put a product on retailers' shelves in months without incurring the multi-million-dollar cost of building a brewery. Some of the biggest names in microbrewed beer, like Pete's Wicked Ale, and Samuel Adams, have been contract-brewed at large breweries. Contract brewing is the bread-and-butter gig for many regional breweries.

Tasty Tip

You can some-times tell a contract-brewed beer from a microbrewed beer by reading the label. If the address of the brewing company is different than that of the brewery, it's usually a contract beer. Some contract beer labels say "Brewed under special license by XYZ Brewing Co." While there are some great-tasting contract-brewed beers, if you want real craft-brewed beers, look for a label that says "Brewed and bottled by XYZ Brewing Co."

National Breweries— The Big Boys

National breweries are old, established breweries that make and sell huge amounts of beer. Anheuser-Busch leads the pack, selling 86 million barrels of beer a year. Many of the nationals have breweries in several geo-graphic locations so they don't have to ship their beer all over the place. They also contract their beers in foreign countries. Budweiser sold in Europe, for instance, is brewed at the Guinness brewery in Dublin, Ireland.

National breweries are all-pervasive. Their logos are in nearly every movie and sporting event. Their beer is everywhere. The nationals are committed to delivering a product that is always exactly the same, whether in Bangkok or Bangor. Lately some of the nationals have been brewing products that look just like microbrewed beers, leaving their familiar logos and names off the labels. Most of them can't compare to the lager of love produced by small breweries.

Alchemy—Turning Water to Beer

Anyone who has toured the gigantic breweries of Anheuser-Busch in St. Louis or Coors in Golden, Colorado, may not realize that brewing is a simple process that millions accom-plish with great success in their kitchens. And it is essentially two separate processes: the brewing and fermenting of beer; and the bottling, kegging, and canning of the finished product. The basics of the first process haven't changed in centuries. The basics of the second get more sophisticated every year.

Bar Talk

Once during Prohibition, I was forced to live for days on nothing but food and water.

—W.C. Fields

The most efficient brewhouse relies on gravity to facilitate production. The grain starts at the top, and the finished product is cooled in the lowest levels. This is not always the case, however. Many space-constricted microbreweries use pumps and hydraulics to move the tons of barley, hops, and water from place to place.

As technology changes, so do breweries. The oldest breweries have centuries-old buildings standing next to buildings that are 50 years old, which stand next to buildings that are brand new. As breweries grow and new processes come on line, whole buildings are erected and swept away to improve efficiency. The more historic buildings are sometimes remodeled and rebuilt as office space for the growing business. And yet, as no two breweries are the same, they are all carrying out, in one manner or another, processes that haven't really changed that much in a thousand years.

Below I've provided a quick list of the steps involved in brewing beer. The subheadings that follow describe them in much greater detail.

1. Malted, and some unmalted, grain is carried to the highest levels of the brewhouse via a screw conveyor, or it is carried in 50-pound sacks by brewery workers.

2. The grain is ground into crunchy grist in a mill.

3. The grain travels by gravity down a pipe to a large cookpot called a mash tun.

4. The grist is mixed with very warm water in the mash tun and held at various temperatures until enzymes in the malt convert starch to malt sugar, called maltose. This is called mashing the grain.

5. After most of the starches in the malt have been converted to sugar, the mash is fed into a giant strainer called a lauter tun. Rotating arms in the lauter tun gently spray water on the mash in order to further rinse the sugars from the grain. This step is called sparging.

6. The liquid, called wort (pronounced *wert*) is transferred to the brew kettle. The grain left behind in the lauter tun is shoveled out and used as animal feed. The wort is brought to a rolling boil, and hops are added at various stages.

7. After an hour or more in the boil, the wort is sent through a whirlpool that removes unwanted protein and spent hops by centrifugal force.

8. The wort moves through a heat-exchanger, which cools it down to temperatures suitable to fermentation.

9. The wort moves to large vessels called fermentation tanks or unitanks. Yeast is added, or pitched.

10. After the yeast has done its job, the wort is now beer and is moved to conditioning tanks where it ages and clarifies.

Terms of Enbeerment
As the Grist Tuns: **Grist** is coarsely ground grain used to brew beer. A **mash tun** is the large cookpot where the grain's starches are converted to malt sugar, which is fermented into beer. The **lauter tun** is a vessel where the grain is rinsed with water to remove the final malt sugars. This process is called **sparging**.

Terms of Enbeerment
The thick froth of yeast foam floating on top of fermenting wort is called **barm**. Barm is more often called "krausen."

11. The finished beer is filtered into holding tanks where it is prepared for bottling, kegging, or canning. Many beers are filtered or pasteurized at this point to kill any living yeasts still in the beer.

12. The beer is shipped to your bottle shop and eventually makes it to your waiting hands.

Milling the Malt

After that quick tour through the brewing process, some of you might be interested to learn the operation in greater detail. What follows is an up-close-and-personal trip through the brewing procedure. It all starts with the grain.

Crispy malted barley is cracked and crushed during the milling process in such a way that the husk is left as large as possible.

Rollers in the mill are adjusted to properly grind different types of malt. Proper milling gives brewers the maximum yield from their barley.

Milling causes a lot of dust that bacteria love. That's why milling must be done separately from the other brewing process, usually in a room atop the brewery.

This diagram shows the simplified brewing process. After the malt goes into the mill, the finished product is beer.

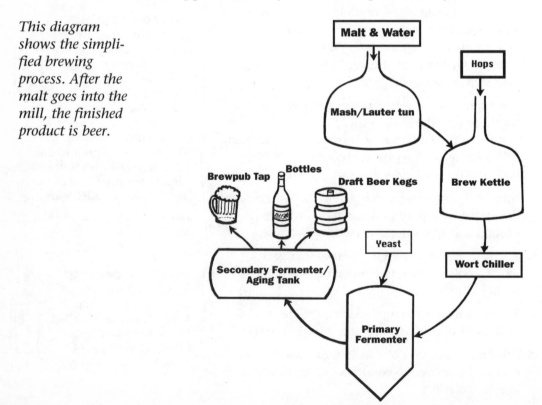

Mashing and Lautering

Once the grain is crushed, it is dropped into hot water in the mash tun. The mash is held at temperatures around 140°F for a period of time, then the temperature is raised several times. While in the mash tun, the grain resembles hot porridge, which in fact is what it is.

Different temperatures activate different enzymes in the malt, which in turn break down the grain's stored starches into fermentable sugars.

Although this process can be done in one vessel, many breweries employ two vessels, the second called the lauter tun.

The sugar-rich liquid, now called wort, is strained through the bottom of the lauter tun. As this liquid drains, warm water is sprayed on top of the spent grain to recover the maximum amount of sugars. This process is called sparging.

Millions of pigs and cattle the world over are fed the non-alcoholic grain that is left after sparging. Anheuser-Busch uses so much grain that their leftovers feed four percent of all dairy cows in the United States.

Boiling with Hops

The wort is brought to a boil in the brew kettle. Many complex chemical reactions take place during the 60- to 120-minute boil that affect the outcome of the beer.

Boiling sterilizes the wort and extracts bitterness from the hops. It also causes undesirable tannins and proteins to clump together and fall to the bottom of the kettle. Commercial breweries install agitators in their brew kettles to aid this process.

Hops—either whole flower hops, compressed hop pellets, and/or concentrated hop oil—are added to the kettle: Those added early in the boil impart bitterness to the beer; those added in the middle of the boil impart flavor; those added at the finish give great beer its hop bouquet. Sometimes hops are added after the beer is fermented. This process, called *dry hopping*, gives beer an extra punch of hop bouquet.

When the boil is finished, the hops are filtered out in a device called a *hopback*. The wort is sent to a whirlpool where centrifugal force removes the bits of grain, hops, and long molecules of protein that cloud beer.

> **Terms of Enbeerment**
> A **hopback** is a stainless-steel vessel that filters the hops out of the wort. When brewers add hops to beer after the first fermentation, it is called **dry hopping**. Dry-hopped beer will have a lovely hop bouquet bursting out of the glass.

This gleaming copper brewkettle is where gallons of wort are brewed with hops.

Pitching the Yeast

The wort is transferred from the whirlpool to a heat exchanger, which cools the liquid to 70°F, a temperature at which yeast can thrive. The heat exchanger is made of coils of tubing that run cold water over hot wort. As the wort becomes cool, the cold water becomes very hot. This water is used to mash the next batch of beer or to wash the equipment after the brewing is over.

Terms of Enbeerment
A brewer uses a **hydrometer** to tell the specific gravity (SG) of unfermented beer. The hydrometer looks like a thermometer and floats out of the beer, depending on the density of the dissolved sugars within.

After the wort has cooled, the brewer must measure the amount of fermentable sugars. For this he or she uses a *hydrometer,* a glass instrument that measures the density of liquid by floating in it. The more sugar there is in a liquid, the higher out of it the hydrometer will float.

When the wort is cooled, it is transferred to a fermenting tank that is lined with refrigeration coils. Sometimes non-refrigerated tanks are set in a large, cold room in order to cool the liquid.

The yeast is pitched, or added to the beer. If the beer is an ale, the temperature of the wort is lowered to 55° to 65°F. If it's a lager, it's lowered to 40° to 55°F.

Yeast sets to work slowly. But it's in the fermenter where the alchemical action of water into beer takes place. As the hours, days, and weeks pass, the hungry yeast absorbs oxygen, gobbles up the sugars in the brew, and excretes alcohol and carbon dioxide. The yeast also breeds like mad in this fecund environment.

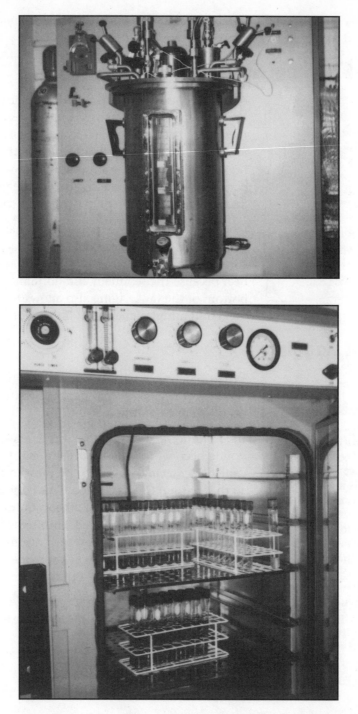

Living yeast cells are propagated in a bio-reactor (top) *and incubated in test tubes* (bottom) *under strict sterile conditions.* Credit: Wyeast Laboratories, Mt. Hood, Oregon.

The yeast only ferments certain sugars such as glucose, maltose, and sucrose. Other sugars are left behind to give the beer body and mouthfeel.

Racking and Rolling: Storing the Beer

Terms of Enbeerment
When finished beer has sweet, young beer added to it, the process is called **kraeusening**. This process wakes up the dormant yeast in the finished beer so that natural carbon dioxide is created. Budweiser is the world's most famous kraeusened beer.

After the yeast does its thing, it settles into dormancy on the bottom of the fermenter and creates a layer of sediment. The beer, by now, looks like regular, drinkable beer, and millions of yeast cells are still quietly existing in the brew. The brewer takes another hydrometer reading, compares it with the reading before the yeast was added, and determines the alcohol content of the brew.

Once the brewer is sure fermentation has completely stopped, he or she moves the beer, or racks it, into the conditioning tank. Here the beer ages. Aging improves beer because the sediment and dormant yeast sink to the bottom of the tank. Aging also allows the beer's flavors to meld and mingle—marinate, if you will.

Bottling and Kegging

Terms of Enbeerment
In England, and in some North American micro-breweries, kegged beer is sometimes **cask conditioned**. This means sugar syrup, hops, and a natural clarifying agent are added to the keg before it leaves the brewery. This causes a second ferment in the cask, giving the beer a fine dose of CO_2. The beer is then dispensed through a "beer engine" like those commonly used in pubs in Britain. Cask conditioning gives beer a soft, smooth, velvety mouthfeel.

When the beer has aged to perfection, it is time for bottling or kegging. What happens to the beer at this point depends on the brewery.

In a traditional brewery, the finished beer is primed with young beer, which still has its sugars intact. This process, called *kraeusening,* wakes up the yeast in the finished beer, so that natural CO_2 is created. This conditioned beer is held in a conditioning tank, then put into bottles or kegs. It may or may not be filtered. Unfiltered beer comes with a thin pad of yummy yeast on the bottom of the bottle. When you see that yeast, you know the beer is still alive, and usually fresh.

In Europe and a very few microbreweries, sugar syrup, hops, and a natural clarifying agent are added to the keg before it leaves the brewery. This process is called *cask conditioning,* and it gives the beer natural carbon dioxide and a smooth mouthfeel.

Modern breweries filter their beer and pasteurize it before bottling. Pasteurizing exposes beer to high heat for a few seconds. This kills any yeast left alive in the beer. In many people's opinion, it also kills some great flavors left in the beer and hastens the development of off flavors. Pasteurized beer will travel better, store longer, and not give too many unpleasant surprises—like massive foaming—if mishandled.

Since kegged beer is used up faster, it is usually not pasteurized. This is why kegged beer tastes better to some people.

The Least You Need to Know

➤ Malt is first crushed in a mill so that it can be used for brewing.

➤ Malt is soaked, or mashed, in very hot water for about an hour so that its sugars can be utilized for beer.

➤ After it's mashed, the malt is rinsed, and the final liquid is called wort.

➤ Wort is boiled with hops for up to two hours.

➤ Wort is cooled and yeast is added to begin the fermentation process.

➤ After the yeast works its magic, the wort is beer, which is stored, then bottled, kegged, or canned.

Chapter 5

A Grail of Ale: Basic Ale Styles

In This Chapter

➤ How beer color is measured

➤ How beer bitterness is measured

➤ English ale styles fully explained

If there are only a few basic ingredients in beer, you might ask, then why are there hundreds of different beers in the bottle shop? Like many other aspects of life, it's all a matter of style. With a beer tradition that goes back thousands of years, every nook and cranny of Great Britain and continental Europe has developed its own brewing style. So too did many countries not usually associated with beer. In fact, with all the breweries in the world making five or six different styles of beer, there might be 20,000 different beers in the world. Like fingerprints, each one is slightly different. But almost all of them fit into about 40 styles and several sub-styles.

Ale Flavors and Lager Essence

Most people in North America were weaned on American and Canadian lagers, with an occasional European lager thrown in. But in terms of beer history, lagers are relatively new—they've only been on the scene about four centuries, and they've only been popular worldwide for 155 years or so. Millions of people enjoy lagers, but their breadth and depth of *style* does not cast as wide a net as ale. There are fewer lager styles than ale styles.

Terms of Enbeerment
The word **style** is used to describe a broad category that defines a beer by color, bitterness, bouquet, yeast type, ingredients, overall flavor profile, and region where it originated. These qualifications make a bock different from a porter, which is different from a Pilsner. To fit into a particular style, a beer is brewed within that style's parameters. These parameters are broad enough to make each brand of beer unique within a style.

Ales have been around since before the time of Tut. They were the beers of our founding fathers, but practically disappeared after the turn of the last century, except in Great Britain, Ireland, and Belgium. When the micro-brewing revolution planted its malty footprint on American shores, dozens of ale styles that were dead and buried were resurrected. Today, as we happily swill pale ales, barley wines, and other great ale styles, remember that they were almost driven to extinction by lagers in the last 100 years.

Because ales are more fruity and complex, they are more versatile when it comes to style. Ales tend to absorb and reflect much more flavor than lagers and can be brewed with oatmeal, cherries, wheat, and/or at heavy hopping rates.

If a comparison were made to wine, lagers might be thought of as champagne—limited in color and depth, but bubbly, sparkling, light and delicious. Ales might be thought of as all other wines with their broad range of colors, flavors, sweet notes, and tart tastes.

Brew Speak—Defining the Terms

Before we get into the ins and outs of each beer style, it's necessary to define the terms that beer folks use to describe lagers and ales in such loving detail. The numbers assigned to color and bitterness may seem confusing at first, but they're only meant to be a guide for comparing, say, a nut-brown ale to a black-as-night stout.

A Lighter Shade of Ale: The Rainbow of Beer Color

Beer color is measured by using a system called the Standard Reference Method or SRM.

The colors of beer may be as varied as the colors of tree leaves in autumn. From pale gold to deep red and orange through umber and burnt black, beer can be as lovely to gaze upon as nature's palette. And while all those beautiful colors may be hard to describe, that hasn't stopped anyone from trying. The problem is that beer colors are as changeable as the vessel that holds them. What looks amber in a skinny test tube looks deep brown in a standard pint glass because less light can pass through the larger quantity of liquid.

Chemists and brewing scientists have had to develop a standardized language to describe beer color. To this end, they came up with the not-so-excitingly named Standard Reference Method (SRM), which uses light-analysis meters to measure light intensity as reflected off the beer in question. While few of us need gauges, dials, and meters to judge beer color, the SRM is useful when describing each style. For comparison's sake, just remember that the lighter the beer, the lower its SRM number. The chart below will give you an idea of SRM compared to color.

Terms of Enbeerment
The **Standard Reference Method (SRM)** uses light analysis to measure the exact color of beer and then assigns a number to each color. Light beers have a low SRM number; dark beers have a higher SRM number.

Standard Reference Method Numbers

Color	Style	Example	SRM
Pale yellow	American Pilsner	Budweiser	3
Gold	European Pilsner	Pilsner Urquell	4
Copper	English Pale Ale	Bass	6–12
Amber	California Micro	Anchor Steam	12–20
Dark amber	German Bock	Salvator	20–30
Brown	English Brown	Newcastle	25
Deep red/brown	Porter	Samuel Smith	25–35
Opaque	Stout	Guinness	40+

Bite Your Tongue—Beer Bitterness

Beer bitterness is measured in International Bitterness Units (IBU). The more bitter the beer, the higher the IBU rating.

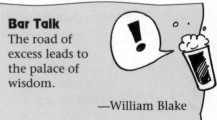

Bar Talk
The road of excess leads to the palace of wisdom.

—William Blake

Like color, the bitterness of a beer has been defined by science. And like beauty and beer color, taste is still in the eye—or should I say tongue—of the beholder. Even the most scientific readings won't change the fact that a lot of hops in a sweet, malty porter will not taste as bitter as a lot of hops in a light lager. Be that as it may, brewing scientists have developed a unit of measure called the International Bitterness Unit (IBU) to measure beer bitterness. It is based on a mathematical formula of interest to homebrewers and brewmeisters, who use

Terms of Enbeerment
The amount of hop bitterness in a beer is measured in **International Bitterness Units (IBU)**. The IBU of a beer is based on a mathematical formula that's based on the amount of alpha acid (bittering agent) in the hops.

it to figure out how much hops to add to a brew in order to achieve the desired bitterness and not pucker one's tongue.

For our purposes, let's just say that bland, mass-produced American Pilsners have about 5–15 IBUs. Bohemian lagers like Pilsner Urquell have about 25–30 IBUs. Noticeably bitter beers like Anchor Liberty Ale have about 30–50 IBUs. And over-the-top strong beers like Samuel Smith's Imperial Stout or Young's Barley Wine might have 50–90 IBUs. The bitterness of the latter ales is tempered by the sweetness of the malt used in such dark offerings.

Ale-Phenalia—Basic Styles of Ale

Ales fall into a few broad categories determined by the brewing region. There are English and Irish ales, Belgian and northern French ales, and German and Eastern European ales which also include some—but not all—wheat beers. And of course, there are American-brewed ales, which are mostly based on European styles, with many interesting hybrids.

If this all seems a little complicated, don't worry. If you think of malt and hops as different hues of paint, you can think of beer styles as different paintings: Some are sparse and simple; some are dark, complex, and brooding. It's all a matter of blending and synthesis at the hands of the brewer.

Since English ale styles are the most prominent and well known, we start out here with them, moving from the lightest and mildest to the darkest and most bitter.

All Hail English Ales

Contrary to popular myth, English ales are not served warm and flat. It's just that the beers North Americans are used to are served too cold and over-carbonated. English ales are served at cellar temperature (about 55°F) so that their full flavors can be appreciated. Ideally, the ales are cask-conditioned, meaning that they are naturally carbonated and less bubbly than Milwaukee barley pop.

Bar Talk
Always remember that I have taken more out of alcohol than alcohol has taken out of me.

—Winston Churchill

Eighty-five percent of all beer in Great Britain is served in a pub, club, or restaurant. In the United States, only 15% of the beer is consumed outside the home.

The British call their lager-swilling soccer hooligans "lager louts." That says a lot about the nation's dedication to its ale. While golden lagers made a clean sweep across the globe in the late 19th century, the Brits clung to their ales with all the tenacity of a great empire. Thank goodness that you can still walk into almost any pub in Great Britain and drink antique ale styles, served properly, in all their authentic glory.

Pale Ale

Pale ale, the classic beer style of Great Britain, is a medium-bodied ale with a complex, medium-dry palate. It's honey-gold to copper red with a nutty malt character and a tart finish. There's a noticeable hop bitterness, a subtle hop bouquet, and a long hop finish. Pale ale should be served at cellar temperature—about 55°F—and is about 5% alcohol by volume, 8–12 SRM, and has 20–50 IBUs.

The first pale ales were brewed in London around 1750, but they quickly became associated with the brewing town of Burton-on-Trent. Monks had been brewing in the Trent Valley since the 1200s, and even in those ancient days, Burton's gypsum-rich water was considered unique for brewing.

The Allsopp Brewery in Burton has been owned by one family since the time of the Crusades. Allsopp's head brewer mixed up the first batch of pale ale in the mid-18th century. Legend has it that he brewed it up in a teapot.

Long ago, most ales were muddy brown brews. When pale ale came along, it was considered lucidity pale by comparison. Though the style is much darker copper than today's commercial Pilsners, this ale was as pale as things got in those days. As a matter of record, pale ale was the first luminously crystal sparkling beer, not Bohemian Pilsner, as is commonly believed. This beer style also came into being around the time that bottled beer was growing in popularity and perceived sophistication.

Today pale ale is the flagship style of the North American craft brewing boom. Although brewed since the days of George Washington, the style fell out of favor when German lagers began to dominate the market at the end of the 1800s. After Prohibition, only one American company, Ballantine, brewed pale ale.

Foamy Fact

Pale Ale Has Sailed: Although pale ale is usually associated with Great Britain, the style is also brewed in Belgium, the Netherlands, Australia, New Zealand, and even Malta and the Falkland Islands. Today at least 25% of new brands introduced by craft brewers are pale ale.

India Pale Ale (IPA)

India pale ale is a more bitter and higher-alcohol version of pale ale. IPA should be served at 50–55°F, and is 6.4–8.2% alcohol by volume, 6–15 SRM, and has 40–60 IBUs.

When British soldiers, merchants, bankers, and bureaucrats were busy colonizing India in the late 18th century, they didn't do it without their beloved ale. And beer was more than a luxury—the water in India killed more than one mad dog and Englishman. Problem was, shipping kegs of ale down the African coast, around the Cape of Good Hope, and up to India wreaked havoc on porter, the most popular beer style of the time. The beer was all shook up and went through hundreds of temperature changes on the journey that took up to five weeks.

The problem was solved by a London brewer named George Hodgson, who is credited with inventing India pale ale. He brewed IPA to be high in alcohol and added a tongue-twisting quota of hops. The rocking and rolling of the ship ensured maximum fermentation, and as the beer criss-crossed the equator, it also got two warm ferments. The result was a sturdy, restorative brew for the colonialists. As paler malts were developed, more brewers got into the market, and Allsopp and Burton soon dominated the IPA trade, which also caught on at home.

Bitter

Bitter, brewed from very hard water, is the most popular beer style in England. Bitter and pale ale are very similar, except pale ale is bottled and slightly higher in alcohol content. Bitter is dispensed on draft and is often cask-conditioned. Bitter is served at cellar temperature (about 50–60°F), is 3–4.4% alcohol by volume, 7–23 SRM, and has 28–40 IBUs.

It's been mentioned that bitter is not exactly an appealing name for a commercial product. True, but hops are *good* bitter. And for those folks who lived around the hop fields of southeast England, around Kent and Canterbury, it made perfect sense to pitch plenty of the local agricultural product into the brewing vats. Besides, the stuff was considered medicine.

Extra Special Bitter (ESB)

Extra Special Bitter (ESB) is a stronger version of bitter. It has an alcohol content of 4.5–5.5%, 12–14 SRM, and 28–48 IBUs.

Amber or Red Ale

Red isn't a beer style; it's a color. Most beers called red or amber are more a product of the brewery's marketing department, though some micros brew a tasty, reddish ale. Most reds are pale ales with some crystal malts thrown in for color's sake. Some ambers or reds are lagers, and they are basically German Pilsners with a slightly reddish cast.

Brown Ale

Brown ale is an English style, the most famous of which is Newcastle Brown, a medium-bodied ale, reddish to nut-brown, dry, and bitter. Brown ale should be served at cellar temperature (about 50–55°F), is about 4–5.5% alcohol by volume, 16 SRM, and has 20 IBUs.

The muddy, or "foddy," beer of yesteryear was dark enough for people to consider pale ale pale. But it was also chewy enough that it made brown ale also seem lucent. Brown ale was first developed in Newcastle in 1890. The term "brown" was a boast by Newcastle Brewing Co. that theirs was an unclouded, reddish-brown ale, considerably lighter than the average muddy beer of the time.

American microbrewers have adopted the style and made it their own, making it—of course—stronger and more bitter than the traditional brown. To be true to style, a brown must be only slightly darker than an IPA.

Foamy Fact

Twenty People Drown in Beer: On October 16, 1814, a 22-foot-high beer vat ruptured at the Meux Brewery in London, releasing a tidal wave of beer. With a boom heard five miles away, the vat popped its cast-iron bands, releasing 124,000 gallons of beer that broke another vat containing 75,000 gallons of brew. The sticky wave of porter knocked down dozens of buildings in a five-mile radius and killed eight people. Twelve more were killed later—trampled under the crush of people who were trying to drink the free beer.

Mild

Mild is a traditional English brew that is sweet, malty, dark brown, and has a full-flavored hop bitterness and bouquet. Mild is also known as southern brown ale because it originated and is mainly consumed in southern England. There are very few mild browns available in the United States, as Americans prefer less sweet, higher-alcohol browns. Milds are low-alcohol affairs, around 3–4% by volume, with an SRM of 17–34, and have an IBU of 12–25.

Old Ale

Old ale is also called English strong ale and is brewed strong and sweet, meant for cellar aging by consumers for up to five years. Old ale is reddish-brown, full-bodied, rich, creamy ale with a complex, malt-sweet palate. It has a raisin or currant finish which is achieved with the addition of brewing sugars. Old ales should be served at 55–60°F, are 6.5–8.5% alcohol by volume, 12–25 SRM, and have 30–85 IBUs.

Old ales are often stronger or special versions of a brewery's regular beer. Not all old ales are powerful, though some are virtually indistinguishable from potent barley wines. While old ales hearken back to the "good old days," some of them are actually old—they've been stored in a cellar for several years. Old ales are not always fermented completely in order to leave a sweetness and body that give them a delicious creamy consistency.

Bar Talk
That Beer's a Mother: The British used to call a mixture of bitter and old ale a "Mother-in-Law." Bitter and old? What about stout and pale?

British brewers love to give droll names to their old ales. Some of my favorites are Wobbly Bob, Old Peculier (with an "e" not an "a"), Old Buzzard, Owd Roger, Old Jock, and the infamous Old Fart.

Some old ales, most notably Thomas Hardy, can be aged up to 20 years. This increases the alcohol content from 7% to about 12%.

Scottish Ale

Scottish ale is the classic beer style of Scotland, where a bracing ale is necessary to shield one from the damp chilly weather. Scottish ale is a full-bodied ale, strong, dark, and creamy. It's deep copper to light brown with a sweetish malt character and a low hop bitterness.

Scotch ale should be served at a temperature of 50–55°F, is 6.2–8% alcohol by volume, 15–40 SRM, and has 25–35 IBUs.

Monks first contributed to Scotland's long brewing heritage in 12th-century Edinburgh. Ancient Scots used to brew with heather flowers, which sometimes had hallucinogenic properties resulting from the ergot fungus found on the plant. Today, Scotland's whisky industry is world famous for its malt products.

Scotch ales come in different strengths and are noted by a "shilling" designation, which is an extinct British currency. Light Scotch ale, comparable to an English mild, is called 60 shilling. Seventy shilling is compared to pale ale and is also called a "heavy." Eighty shilling is like a bitter and also called an "export." Ninety shilling is the strongest beer and has the quaint name "wee heavy." The shilling numbers are said to have represented the price of a barrel of beer, or the tax on a barrel, and were stamped into the wood.

Maclay Oat Malt Stout is the world's only Scotch ale brewed with malted oats.

Porter

Porter is a classic English beer style and is a robust, full-bodied ale with a complex, chocolate or coffee-like palate. Porters are brewed with roasted, unmalted barley, chocolate, and black patent malts. They are ruby brown to almost black in color with a toasted malt character and a dry, smooth finish. There's a high hop bitterness, and a medium hop bouquet and finish. Porter should be served at a temperature of 55–60°F, is 5–6.5% alcohol by volume, 25–45 SRM, and has 20–40 IBUs.

Porter, once the most popular beer style in the British Isles, started out as a combination of beer styles. A barman would pour some pale ale, some brown ale, and some old ale into one glass. Carters and haulers of London's Victoria Station would order such a beer by asking for "an entire." In 1722, Ralph Harwood decided to brew a ready-made entire and name it after his best customer—the porter. Soon England's brewing giants picked up the style, and porter caught on from India to China to America.

Foamy Fact

Pilgrim's Progress: The Pilgrims were not planning to land at Plymouth Rock. They meant to go to Virginia but overshot their mark. They finally disembarked at Plymouth when they ran out of beer. A scribe on the *Mayflower* wrote:

So in the morning…we came to this resolution—to go presently ashore and make better view of the two places we thought most fitting for us; we could not take time for further search or consideration, our victuals being much spent, especially our beer, *and it being now the 19th of December.*

In 1817, a new drum-roasting method was patented for malt. Working like a coffee roaster, this malt machine allowed for high heat to produce a black roasted malt. This added a whole new dimension to porter and, later on, stout. Porter's eminence began to diminish, however, when advanced malting and brewing techniques in the mid-1800s allowed for pale, sparkling beers like Pilsner and pale ale. Porter faded into history between the two world wars. The last porter brewery in Ireland closed in 1973.

During the great beer counter-revolution of the 1980s, porter rose from the ashes of its former glory to recapture its place in the hearts and stomachs of beer lovers everywhere. Today there are scores of porters on the market to choose from. If you love your beer dark, toasty, and bitter, porter provides a lot to cheer about.

Foamy Fact

Beer for Kids and Sailors: In the early 18th century, there were four main styles of beer: Small beer was the weakest, enjoyed at meals, even by small children. Ship's beer was next in strength, followed by table beer. Strong beer was at the top of the list, and in the later years, dark, roasty porter became very popular.

Stout

Stout is a rich, dark, full-bodied ale with a creamy tan head. It has an incredibly complex palate with burnt-malt notes and hints of molasses in the finish. Stout is black to opaque in color, with a high hop bitterness, a medium hop bouquet, and a long hop finish.

Stout should be served at a temperature of 55–60°F, is 4–8% alcohol by volume, 40+ SRM, and has 30–60 (that's bitter!) IBUs.

There are several styles of stout, all with their own characteristics. They are dry or Irish stout, milk stout, sweet stout, oatmeal stout, and imperial or Russian stout.

Stout is porter times two. It's pale ale times ten; it's…well, you get the idea. As the name implies, stout's flavor is thick, deep, big, and broad. It represents the apex of the brewer's art, with up to eight types of malt and six kinds of hops. Stouts are generally high in alcohol, though not always. The drum-style malt roaster that allowed for dark malts for porter also gave stout its defining characteristics. Stout was the logical extension of porter and was originally called stout porter.

Foamy Fact

Guinness—First in Stout: When Arthur Guinness opened his brewery in Dublin in 1759, porter was the best-selling beer. Guinness & Co.'s porter was so good that it dominated the Irish and the English markets. Guinness tinkered with the recipe, added the newly available black malt, and began to sell Guinness Extra Stout in 1820. The rest, as they say, is "beerstory." By the early 20th century, Guinness was the largest brewery in the world, and stout was the national drink of Ireland. Guinness is still the world's largest stout brewery.

Stout, like porter, made quite a comeback when microbreweries and brewpubs began their ascent. Today any micro worth its malt brews one or more styles of stout. The styles are as follows.

Dry Stout

Dry stout, like the name says, is dry, though it is also known as Irish stout. Dry stout has scads of hop bitterness and is black as night. It has an alcohol content of about 5%, an SRM of 35–70, and an IBU of 25.

Guinness is the world's best-selling dry stout. Most North American microbrewed stouts are of the dry Irish variety. Guinness and Murphy's Irish Stout serve their ale with a nitrogen charge mixed with the carbon dioxide. This removes the acidic CO_2 bite and gives their beers an incredibly smooth, creamy, rich mouthfeel. These beers come in pint cans with a nitrogen charge and are well worth seeking out for their whipped-cream consistency.

Foamy Fact

10,000 Years of Beer-itude: Arthur Guinness leased a brewery in 1759 at St. James's Gate, where his brewery still stands today. Guinness leased the brewery for *10,000 years* at an annual rent of £45. What a deal!

Sweet Stout

In simpler times, folks who wanted a sweet stout simply stirred a spoonful of sugar into their dry stout. Brewers began marketing sweet stout during the late 1800s.

Sweet stouts are usually low in alcohol, around 3.5%, and were considered a healthy tonic. Sweet stouts are less bitter, with around 15–25 IBUs and an SRM of 40+. The best known sweet stout is Mackeson.

Milk Stout

Milk stout was invented by a doctor and two chemists who envisioned a beer made from whey, milk, lactose (milk sugar), and hops. Sounds gross, but these folks were thinking of a medicinal beer with food value. In 1907, Mackeson brewery in Hyth, Kent, made its first batch of milk stout by adding lactose—which does not ferment—to the beer.

By the 1930s, Mackeson Milk Stout was boasting that "each pint contained the energizing carbohydrates of ten ounces of milk." The low-alcohol beer was considered a restorative for nursing mothers, the sick, and the invalid.

Modern beers with the word "cream" in their label do not have the lactose sugar of real milk stout.

Oatmeal Stout

Oats give stout a nutty flavor and a unique silkiness in body and mouthfeel. Oatmeal stout is 3–6% alcohol by volume.

Long ago and far away, brewers used whatever grains they could find to make beer. Thus, many a batch of ale had oats pitched into the tun. During the health craze of the late 1800s, oatmeal beer came back into fashion. The last oatmeal stout was made in England by Eldridge Pope in 1975. In 1980, beer importer Charles Finkel of Merchant du Vin in Seattle persuaded Samuel Smith Brewery in Tadcaster, England, to revive the style. Since then, dozens of breweries have begun to brew oatmeal stout.

Foamy Fact

Brew for Breakfast: In the 1800s, English dock workers and sailors could not get a decent cup of coffee. So they started each day with a hot, spicy ale called Purl. The men who sold it from small boats were called Purlmen.

Imperial or Russian Stout

What stout is to porter, imperial stout is to dry stout. It's deeply complex, opaque, and as hoppy as they come. Imperial stout is robust, intricate, and high in alcohol, 9.5–10.5% in volume. It is opaque, with an SRM of 40+, and has IBUs of up to 65.

There is a fruitiness and a burnt, almost tar-like flavor that leaves an aftertaste resembling coffee, sherry, and a Cuban cigar. Now that's complex!

Imperial stout was originally brewed as strong porter in London circa 1780. In barrels marked with XXXXX, the porter was exported to Germany, Scandinavia, Kaliningrad, and other Baltic ports. Catherine the Great, Empress of Russia, was said to drink gallons of the stuff daily to ward off the incredibly frigid Russian winters. Imperial stout was exported from England to Russia until the dawn of World War I.

Real imperial stout is aged in wooden casks for two months and in bottles for one year. The beer will keep for up to ten years, or even longer.

Samuel Smith makes an excellent, widely available imperial stout. Grant's Imperial Stout is a fine, Washington-brewed stout. Other breweries brew stouts of this magnitude under the name barley wine.

Foamy Fact

There's a Bivalve in My Beer!: Oysters in beer? Yuck! Yet it was done earlier this century. The first commercially produced mollusk ale was made in 1929 by Young & Son of New Zealand. They used actual oysters in the beer recipe of Victory Oyster Stout. Castletown Brewery on the Isle of Man brewed oyster-laden Manx Oyster Stout from 1938 to the 1960s with the granulated extract of oysters. The beer was not overly fishy and was even exported to Asia, Africa, and the United States. Today, wild and crazy homebrewers whip up batches of oyster stout using oyster juice. Yum!

Barley Wine

Barley wine is as strong as ale gets. It's full-bodied, with a complex, dry palate. It's brick red to mahogany in color, resembling fine sherry in flavor character and finish. There's plenty of bittering hops in barley wine and not a little hop bouquet. Since high alcohol kills ale yeast, some American barley wines are made with champagne yeast. Other ingredients may include molasses and maple syrup.

Barley wine should be served at a temperature of 60°F, is 7–15% alcohol by volume, 14–22 SRM, and has 50–100 IBUs. BATF rules forbid the mixing of wine and beer in a commercial product, so to quell consumer confusion, American barley wine is labeled "barley wine–style ale."

Barley wine is the zenith of the brewer's art. It requires a long aging period, from six months to several years, and a profound understanding of yeast that has to be prodded to achieve the high alcohol content.

The first commercial product to use the term barley wine was Bass No. 1 Barley Wine. Before that, the term was used by homebrewers to designate their best brew—and usually the strongest. To keep cranking out the alcohol, the barrels were periodically rolled around the yard to wake up the exhausted yeast.

Barley wine was revived in the United States in 1975 by Anchor Brewing Co. of San Francisco when they began brewing Old Foghorn. Sierra Nevada brews a seasonal Bigfoot Barley Wine.

The Least You Need to Know

➤ Most ale styles come from Great Britain, Ireland, and Belgium.

➤ Pale ale, bitter, brown, porter, Scottish ale, and stout are from Great Britain.

➤ American microbreweries usually brew ales, most of them based on English styles, except for the popular German-style wheat ales.

Chapter 6

Wheat Brew and Belgian, Too: Belgian Ales, Lambics, and Wheat Beers

> **In This Chapter**
>
> ➤ A primer on ale and lambic styles from Belgium
>
> ➤ Wheat beers fully explained

For years beer critics have agreed that Belgium brews some of the greatest beers on the planet. Fortunately, today's consumers are also learning this salient fact.

Unfortunately, the number of breweries in Belgium has steadily decreased since 1900, when there were 3,000 breweries. Today, only 150 remain. The demise of thousands of Belgian breweries was caused by business consolidation, changing tastes, and the effects of two horrific world wars. One thing Belgium does have is cafés (taverns)—some 60,000, or one for every 170 people in the country.

Brewing in Belgium was once the work of farm families. But in the 11th century, monks began brewing beer in abbeys and selling it to the masses. Five Belgian abbeys still brew to this day, and their beers are a hot commodity the world over. (A sixth abbey brewery is in the Netherlands.) By the 16th century, beer was such an entrenched part of Belgian society that well-to-do brewers built the fabulously adorned *Maison de Brasseurs* (Guild Hall of the Brewers) on the Grand-Place in Brussels.

Unique Belgian Styles

Belgians believe that brewing is an art, and trying to classify their beers by style is somewhat difficult. A Belgian ale might be anything from a cidery-tart Rodenbach to a leathery Trappist ale like Orval or an ambrosial cherry beer like Lindemans.

Belgian brewers have taken the wine tradition of France, the beer tradition of Germany, and the ale tradition of Great Britain and combined them into dozens of unique and wonderful beers found nowhere else.

Part of the uniqueness of Belgian beer may be the varying ingredients. A Belgian beer might contain unmalted wheat, fruit, invert sugar, aged hops, or three different kinds of yeast.

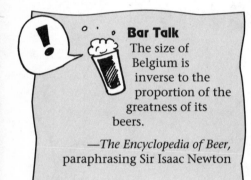

Bar Talk
The size of Belgium is inverse to the proportion of the greatness of its beers.

—*The Encyclopedia of Beer,* paraphrasing Sir Isaac Newton

Many Belgian beers are treated like fine champagne—corked, wired shut, and wrapped in tissue paper. Many Belgian styles have their own special glass, to be used only with that specific beer. The glasses allow a drinker to enjoy the beer's aroma, or conversely, to let the beer breathe. Occasionally drinkers in Belgian pubs are refused a certain beer because all the glasses for serving that style are in use.

Belgian ales cost a little more than most beer but, as the saying goes, you get what you pay for. These beers are brewed with the finest ingredients, aged to perfection, and handled by experts who can trace their brewing heritage back centuries.

Foamy Fact

Old Brewer Wanted for New World: The first professional brewer in America was Belgian. He was recruited by the British to ensure a vital supply of good beer in the 17th century.

Flanders Brown Ale

Flanders brown is a mildly acidic beer sometimes called *zuur,* or sour beer. Some may contain *lactobacilli,* a yeast used in yogurt, or occasionally *brettanomyces,* a wild yeast. These are beers whose full flavor can take you back to medieval times. Flanders brown is (not surprisingly) brown in color with a medium hop bitterness, a low hop bouquet, and a fruity, spicy-sour palate.

Flanders brown should be served at a temperature of 50°F, is 4.5–5.5% alcohol by volume, 12–18 SRM, and has 15–25 IBUs.

Liefmans Frambozen is a Flanders brown ale with raspberries added to it. The most widely available Flanders brown is Goudenband from Liefmans Brewery. The wort is boiled *six hours,* as opposed to 60–90 minutes for most beers. Goudenband has six malts, four hop varieties, and is 5% alcohol by volume. It's blended from young and old beer and is stored for up to two years.

The dancing cherubs of Liefmans Frambozenbier represent one of the world's finest raspberry beers.

Belgian Red Ale

Belgian red is called the Burgundy of Belgium. It's *extremely* tart and fruity and may contain up to 20 strains of yeast. The light-red color comes from the beer's aging in old oak tuns.

Belgian red ale should be served at a temperature of 55°F, is 6.3% alcohol by volume, 12–18 SRM, and has 15–25 IBUs.

Terms of Enbeerment
Back before the advent of steel barrels, all beer was stored in wooden casks. The skilled artisans who built these casks were called **coopers**. The barrels had to withstand over 40 pounds of pressure per square inch. Empty, the 36-gallon (or so) barrels weighed 140 to 160 pounds. The casks absorbed flavors, yeast, and bacteria that added to the beer's character. The watertight barrels lasted for up to 60 years. Today only a handful of coopers still work to make beer barrels.

The most famous Belgian red is Rodenbach from the family Brauereij Bios van Steenberge in Flanders. It was first brewed in 1890. The beer is sweet on the first taste, and sour and tart on the aftertaste. It's aged in wooden tuns for up to two years, where it picks up caramels, tannins, and acidity usually associated with wine. The brewery employs *coopers* who maintain these giant tuns, which range from 4,000 to 16,000 gallons and contain strains of yeast that have been living there for more than 100 years.

Belgian Golden Ale

Belgian golden ales are honey-golden, deceptively strong ales, usually named after the devil (more on that later). Belgian goldens are light-bodied because they are brewed with Pilsner malt and have dextrose added to lighten the body. They're bottle-conditioned and have a rich, rocky head, strong alcohol punch, a perfumy hop bouquet, and bitterness.

Belgian golden ale should be served cold, at a temperature of 45–50°F, is 6.3–8.5% alcohol by volume, 3–5 SRM, and has 30 IBUs.

Foamy Fact

Beer Saves the Human Race: The Egyptians believed beer was started by the sun god, Re, who was mad at the human race when he saw his temples fall to squalor. To teach them a lesson, Re sent Hathor down to Earth in the form of a leopard. Hathor went to work murdering the miscreants. After one day, the streets flowed red with blood. Re thought Hathor had gone too far, so he came down to Earth in the form of a baboon and planted (you guessed it!) barley and dates in the blood in the streets. The barley turned to beer in the morning's sun and Hathor the leopard began to drink the stuff. The vengeful cat fell asleep under a tree and snoozed for two days. Humans were saved, and—by the way—they got beer. Hathor thus became the Goddess of Beer.

A Belgian golden is a devil of a beer. That's because the beer—invented by the Moortgat Brewery (near Breendonk, north of Brussels)—was named Duvel, a Flemish corruption of the word devil. When the brew was first concocted after World War II, a brewery worker said it was "a Devil of a beer!" Duvel's unsurpassed character is the result of a painstaking, labor-intensive, triple-fermentation process that is unique to the brewery. A sign on the brewery in massive red letters says "Shhhh…Duvel is ripening here." The beer is stabilized in bottles for six weeks in cold storage before its release. Duvel aficionados like to store it in their basements for up to three months for further blending.

Belgian Wit Is No Joke

Belgian white is generally a bottle-conditioned, medium-bodied ale made with 50% unmalted wheat and a Lactobacillus fermentation that gives the beer a very cloudy, white (wit) appearance and a cumulous-cloud white head. It's tangy and refreshing, containing hints of plum, orange, honey, and Muscat-wine flavor. There's a noticeable hop palate and bouquet. Wits made with all barley malt, Curaçao orange peel, coriander, and other spices are called Grand Cru.

Belgian wit should be served at a temperature of 50°F, is 4.8–5.2% alcohol by volume, 3 SRM, and has 10–15 IBUs.

Foamy Fact

Does that Beer Come with Pepperoni?: Belgians brew an eccentric variety of brews found nowhere else. Take, for instance, Shii-Take, brewed at Piessens Brewery. The strong, black beer is 9% alcohol. The mash water is 15% juice from—you guessed it—boiled Japanese shiitake mushrooms.

Belgian wits have been brewed in Hoegaarden (pronounced "who-garten"), east of Brussels, since the 1700s. At one time there were 50 wit breweries in Hoegaarden, but the last one closed in the 1950s. In 1966, Pierre Celis, who lived next door to an abandoned wit brewery and once worked there, decided to revive the style. By the 1980s, the style's popularity was booming. Celis was bought out by a large brewing concern, Interbrew S.A., in 1989, and he moved to Austin, Texas, where he introduced wit to the truckers, kickers, and cowboys of east Texas. Celis's wit, and his other beers, grew popular nationally, and Miller Brewing bought a partial interest in the company in 1994. Meanwhile, wit is again brewed and happily drunk in Belgium, the Netherlands, France, and the United States.

Saison

Saison, which is bottle-conditioned with yeast added at bottling time, is a farmhouse ale from the French-speaking Walloon region of southern Belgium. It is snappy, bright, refreshing, citrusy, well-hopped, mild, and occasionally flavored with orange peels and star anise. The dense white head is like a meringue.

Saison should be served at a temperature of 50–55°F, is 5–7% alcohol by volume, 3.5–9 SRM, and has 20–30 IBUs.

Saison was originally brewed in *la saison de mars* (the season of March) for consumption by farm families and their workers during fall harvest time. Saison breweries resemble museums more than modern breweries because the beer is made according to strictly old-fashioned standards. Because of this, the beer is sometimes only 50% fermented.

Foamy Fact

Belgian Beer Folks: The specialty beers of Belgium and Northern France are the passion of Wendy Littlefield and Donald Feinberg. In 1982, they founded Vanberg & DuWulf Co. in New York, NY, to import Belgian "gastronomic beers" from the richest repository in the world. Their collection numbers 34 beers from 10 breweries representing 18 different styles. Wendy and Don have recently opened a farmhouse-style brewery in Cooperstown to bestow peerless Belgian quality ales on America.

Saison Dupont defines the style. The brewery was built in 1850 and has been operated by the third generation of Duponts since 1920. It is a working farm, and eggs are sold from the "executive" offices. If you want to buy their beer for retail sale, you have to come pick it up at the brewery. The Duponts are brewers, not truck drivers, and they don't deliver.

Trappist or Abbaye Ale

Trappist or abbaye ales are the bottle-conditioned beers available from only six breweries in the world, all run by Cistercian Trappist monks. Together, the six Benedictine monasteries produce about 20 beers, and like many other Belgian beers, each is singular and unique. Trappist ales are generally strong, fruity/sour, spicy, "leathery," and full-bodied with a medium hop bouquet. Trappist ales are made from mostly organic ingredients and are considered by critics to be among the finest ales in the world.

Foamy Fact

The First King of Beers: The real King of Beers was Jan Primus, fourth duke of Brabant, Antwerp, Belgium. Also known as Gambrinus, Primus introduced the toast as a prelude to imbibing.

Trappist ales should be served at a temperature of 55–60°F, are 5–11% alcohol by volume, 4–20 SRM, and have 20–45 IBUs.

The six Trappist beers, their monasteries, and locations are:

➤ Chimay, brewed at Abbaye de Notre-Dame de Scourmont, founded in 1850 in the province of Hainaut near the French border. This abbey was the first to sell its beer to the general public and label it Trappist. Their three beers are Chimay Red (red cap), Grand Rèserve (blue cap), and Cinq Cents (white cap).

Founded in 1850, Chimay was the first Trappiste ale sold to the public.

➤ Orval is brewed at Abbaye de Notre-Dame d'Orval, founded in 1070 in the province of Luxembourg near the French border. Orval is the oldest Trappist brewery. Three separate strains of yeast, three kinds of organic barley, three kinds of organic hops, brewing sugar, and a triple fermentation process make Orval one of the highest-quality beers in the world.

➤ Rochefort is brewed at Abbaye de Notre-Dame de St. Rémy, founded in 1230 in the province of Namur, which began brewing in 1595.

➤ La Trappe is brewed at the Koningshoeven Monastery at Schaapskooi in the Dutch province of Brabant, on the Belgian border. The brewery was founded in 1884 to finance the monastery.

➤ Westmalle is brewed at Abdij der Trappisten, founded in 1821, in the province of Antwerp, which began brewing in 1836.

➤ Westvleteren is brewed at Abdij Sint Sixtus, founded in 1899, in West Flanders.

Abbey Beer

Abbey beers are brewed in the Trappist tradition by commercial breweries. These beers cannot use the word *Trappiste* unless they are brewed under the strict supervision of a Trappist monastery. While some of these beers are quite good, abbey beers are not the same as genuine Trappist beers.

Lambic Beer

Lambic beers are brewed mainly in Payottenland, southwest of Brussels in the River Zenne valley. Lambics are not ales or lagers, but fermented with wild yeasts, as all ancient beers once were. Sometimes lambics are called wild beers.

Lambics are bottle-conditioned, medium-bodied, oaky, smoky, winy, and more complex than simple words can describe. Fruit lambics are sweet, fruity, and absolutely delicious.

Foamy Fact

Gaze upon Belgian Lace: Visitors to Brugge, Belgium, are treated to the sight of dozens of women—working outdoors in the summer—spinning intricate and exquisite Belgian lace, which is for sale in shops around town. The lovingly hand-crafted beers of Belgium are also expected to have some Belgian lace. That's the pattern of bubbles left clinging to the side of the glass as the beer is drunk. A great beer will usually leave behind a beautiful Belgian lace.

Lambics are aged up to three years and are brewed with up to 35% raw, unmalted wheat. Lambics that are a blend of young and aged beer are called *gueuze* (pronounced "gurrs"). Lambics are sometimes brewed with fruit. These ambrosial, heavenly beers are called Kriek (cherry), Framboise (raspberry), Cassis (black currant), Pèche (peach), and Druiven (Muscat grape). Lambic sweetened with candy sugar or other sweeteners is called *faro*.

Lambics are probably the world's most difficult beers to bring to market. All other commercial breweries function under strict standards of sanitation to make sure that not one strain of wild yeast contaminates the brew. Lambic brewers, however, leave their wort in large, flat open containers in the attics of their breweries. Louvered vents are left wide open and the brew is visited by up to 70 strains of wild yeast. Lambics are aged up to three years in oak barrels.

> **Terms of Enbeerment**
> **Gueuze** (pronounced *gurrs*) is a Belgian beer that is a blend of old and young aged lambics. When lambics are sweetened with candy sugar they are called **faro**.

In another eccentric process, lambics are made with hops that have been aged for *three* years. They smell like stinky cheese at that point and have lost all their bittering properties. They have, however, retained strong antibacterial resins and powders which protect the lambic from contamination as it ages for up to three years. The amount of hops used in lambic is four times that of other beers, but the bitterness is very low—about the same as an American lager.

Lambics ferment in dark cellars filled with cobwebs that brewers are afraid to sweep away lest they lose some of the natural yeasts that reside there. Spiders are desirable because they kill bacteria-bearing fruit flies.

If all this sounds strange, just think of it as museum beer, as it's made using authentic processes from the 17th century. Because of the complicated and time-consuming brewing process, lambics are expensive. But they come highly recommended, and they aren't any more pricey than a cheap bottle of wine. They're great for special occasions or for everyday indulgence.

What's Up Wit Wheat Beer?

Wheat has been used in beer since before the time of the Pharaohs. The Babylonians grew wheat and barley mixed together in the fields and harvested them together for beer. The Egyptians brewed dozens of wheat beers. The Iberian Celts concocted a beer of honey and wheat called Corma. Wheat shortages led to laws in medieval England prohibiting brewers from using wheat in beer. It seems that the powers that be thought bread was more important than beer. Can you imagine? By 1517, German brewers had two separate guilds, the Weissbrauers (white or wheat brewers) and Rothbrauers (red or barley brewers). Wheat beers were popular in the United States until Prohibition. Today they're making a comeback at the hands of craftbrewers who are reintroducing us to a style that is—in theory—more than 6,000 years old.

Weizenbier or Weissbier

Bavarian white beer is technically called Suddeutche *weizenbier* (south German wheat beer) or *weissbier*. This is the most popular of the German wheats. Brewed with 40–60% malted wheat, this top-fermented ale is aged like a lager, which makes the beer much cleaner and clearer than beers of old.

Terms of Enbeerment
What's Up with Wheat, Wit, Weizenbier, and Weisse?: Beers brewed with wheat seem to have a dizzying array of names applied to them. Because wheat makes beer cloudy and gives it a foamy white head, these beers are sometimes called "white" beers. **Wit** and **weisse** mean white. **Weizen** (VITE-sen) means wheat, and **weizenbier** means wheat beer. So don't call them "wheezin' beers" unless you want your friends to laugh so hard they get foam up their noses.

Weizenbier is bubbly, light to medium in body, and golden in color with a white cloudiness. It has a rocky white head, light hops, and a clove-like bouquet with slight banana overtones. Weizenbier should be served at a temperature of 45–50°F, is about 4.9–5.5% alcohol by volume, 3–9 SRM, and has 10–15 IBUs.

Weizenbier is brewed with a special type of yeast that gives the golden brew a clove-like bouquet that will remind you of clove chewing gum. It's sometimes served with a slice of lemon, though purists shun the lemon juice. Weizen is a crisp, fruity, tart drink with a thick meringue head. Weizenbiers make up 25% of all beers sold in Bavaria— and they drink lots of beer.

Weizen bottled with yeast is called *hefe-trub* (yeast sediment) or hefe-weizen. Filtered weizen is called *kristalklar*, or crystal-clear. This is a sparkling beer that might be considered the equivalent to wheat champagne.

Dunkel Weissbier and Weizenbock

Dark wheat beer is called dunkel (dark) weissbier, or dark white beer, if you prefer. This beer is medium- to full-bodied, and dark copper in color.

Weizenbock is copper to dark brown in color, and very malty, with a low hop bite. This is bock made from wheat and may be up to 9.3% alcohol by volume. For my money, the best weizenbock, and maybe one of the best beers anywhere, is Aventinus, brewed by G. Schneider & Sohn, in Kelheim, Bavaria, Germany.

Berliner Weisse

Berliner weisse–style beer was once the most popular style of German beer in the United States before Prohibition. It is a light, low-alcohol, top-fermented beer. Today, the beer must be brewed in Berlin, Germany to legally carry the name Berliner Weisse, as it's an appellation like Burgundy. Sometimes the beer is called the *Kuhle Blonde* or cool blond of Berlin. It has a citrus palate, and lactobacillus is added during the secondary fermentation. This yogurt yeast gives the beer a milky appearance, a sour, acidic bite, and a thick, white head. Sometimes woodruff (green) or raspberry (red) syrup is added to Berliner weisse to offset the sourness.

Berliner weisse should be served at a temperature of 45–50°F and is 3.4% alcohol by volume, 2–4 SRM, and has 3–8 IBUs.

> **Tasty Tip**
> *German Mix-Ups:* Beer-loving Germans sometimes mix beer into interesting and unique concoctions. Imbibers in Germany can taste a Heller Moritz, which is equal parts wheat beer and champagne. Or how about a drink of wheat beer and lemon soda called a Russ?
>
> MMM

American Wheat Beer

American wheats are usually fermented with regular ale yeast so they lack the clove-like flavor of their German parents. American wheat beer may be considered a new style unto itself with little resemblance to traditional European wheat styles.

Generally, American wheats should be served at a temperature of 45–50°F, are 3.8–5.5% alcohol by volume, 2–16 SRM, and have 12–20 IBUs.

Oh, those crazy American microbrewers. They make wheat beer with honey and maple syrup. They brew it with fruit. There's even a wheat *wine*, the staggeringly delicious cousin of barley wine. The folks over at Hart Brewing Company in Kalama, Washington (now Pyramid Ales in Seattle) rolled out Pyramid Weizen in the mid-1980s. It was the first wheat beer to be brewed in the U.S. since Prohibition. The beer got Hart lots of notice and contributed to its success in the microbrew-laden Pacific Northwest. Today brewers large and small are wheatin' our appetites for wheat beer.

The Least You Need to Know

➤ Belgians brew a wide variety of beer styles not found anywhere else.

➤ Belgian beer can include fruity lambics, strong ales, and beer brewed by Trappist monks.

➤ Wheat beers are ales, most originating in Germany and Belgium, with today's micro-wheats coming from the United States.

Chapter 7

For the Love of Lager: Basic Lager Styles

In This Chapter

➤ Lager styles from Europe

➤ American beer styles

➤ Unusual beer styles such as alt, organic, rye ale, steam, and smoked beer

Lagers were developed in Bavaria, spread through Northern Europe, and were brought to America by German immigrants after the Civil War. Once lagers arrived in America, they slowly became lighter, more carbonated, less hoppy, and loaded with adjuncts like corn. In recent years, the rise in imports has reintroduced North Americans to real German bocks and Czech Pilsners. Microbrewers have also revived long-ignored lager styles.

While the craft-beer revolution recently brought ales back into prominence, the *first* beer revolution was the lager revolution. By the mid-20th century, only Great Britain, Ireland, and Belgium continued drinking old-fashioned ales in quantity. And while there are some strong, dark lagers, a greater percent of lagers drunk in the world resemble Bohemian Pilsner or Munich Helles.

Terms of Enbeerment

A Sudsy Reminder: **SRM** stands for Standard Reference Method, which measures the color of beer. The higher the number, the darker the beer. **IBU** stands for International Bitterness Units. The higher the number the more bitter the beer. For more information on SRM and IBU see Chapter 5.

MMM **Tasty Tip**

Pilsner, named after the town where it was originally brewed in 1842, has been imitated by just about every brewery in the world—in name and in style. Around the world you might find it called plzen, pilsener, pils, German pils, or Bohemian-style Pilsner. Frustrated with the pilferage of their name, the original brewers in Plzen, Czech Republic, changed it in 1893 to Pilsner Urquell, which means "original Pilsner." Even today, the Pilsner label appears on the rankest of beers. If you want to know what all the fuss was about, drink Pilsner Urquell. Then you'll know why it's the most imitated beer on the planet.

Continental Lagers: Bohemian Bliss

Lagers generally can be divided into two broad categories: continental lagers, from Europe; and American lagers, for better or worse, the best-known lagers in the world. But American lagers are only take-offs of their better-brewed European cousins. The real stars of lager come from Eastern Europe and Germany.

Czech Out Some Bohemian Pilsner

Bohemian Pilsner, from the Czech Republic, is the classic lager style that has been much imitated, but rarely duplicated, all over the globe. It is medium-bodied, straw-colored, with a light, crisp taste. It has a fragrant, perfumy, hop aroma, and it's malty and well-balanced with a complex palate. Bohemian Pilsner is rich yet thirst-quenching. Brewed with soft water and Saaz hops using traditional methods, Pilsner Urquell invented and defines the style.

Bohemian Pilsner should be served at a temperature of 45–50°F, is about 4.5–5.5% alcohol by volume, 2.5–4.5 SRM, and has 25–45 IBUs.

Whenever you crack the top of a mass-produced American barley pop, you are drinking a pale imitation of Bohemian Pilsner. When Pilsner Urquell was first brewed in Plzen, Czech Republic, in 1842, the lager became an overnight sensation in the sidewalk cafes of Prague, Vienna, Berlin, and beyond. Not far behind were commercial brewers who recognized a winner when they tasted one. Before you could say "Czechoslovakia," the style—and even the name—was filched by dozens of breweries from Stuttgart to St. Louis.

It's said that the further one travels from Plzen, the poorer quality the Pilsner beer becomes. The Germans make some pretty good Pilsners; Scandinavia—passable. By the time one travels to China, Argentina, or Milwaukee, the Pilsners are barely in the same league. (Unless you're talking about a microbrewed Pilsner.) That's not to say that these mild, straw-colored lagers are bad, it's just that they lack the perfume, balance, and overall quality of Pilsner Urquell—the Pilsner original.

Brilliant Beer—Münchener Helles

Münchener Helles means Munich pale and was first brewed in the 1920s to compete with Bohemian Pilsner. Its darker progenitor is called Munich dunkel, or dark. Münchener Helles is deeply golden, very malty and caramelly, with very little hop bite and low alcohol content.

Münchener Helles should be served at a temperature of 45–50°F. It is 4.5–5.5% alcohol by volume, 3–5 SRM, and has 20–30 IBUs.

Münchener Helles is the most popular beer style in Germany. Helles means "light" or "brilliant." The malty flavor of the beer comes from the complex brewing process and the Munich-style malt, which is cured at low temperatures.

Export a Quart of Dort: Dortmunder Beer

Dortmunder is also called Export style. It's very pale, medium-bodied, and brewed with hard water in the city of Dortmund, Westphalen, the largest brewing city in Germany. A special malting process gives Dortmunder a unique malty flavor.

Dortmunder should be served at a temperature of 45–50°F. It is 4.8–6% alcohol by volume, 4–6 SRM, and has 23–30 IBUs.

At the turn of the century, Dortmunder had 121 breweries. Today, only nine are left, but it's still the largest brewing city in Germany, accounting for 25% of German beer production—and that's a lot of suds. Dortmunder beer was of such high quality, even in the 1300s, that other brewing towns tried to keep the Dortmunder brew out of their territory by force. The Pilsner revolution of 1842 quickly spread to Dortmunder and by 1873, the Dortmunder Union Brewery was brewing the original Dortmunder style.

A special malting process with a long steep gives Dort its pale color. The beer has more taste and strength than Bohemian but less hops. It is lighter and drier than Munich. Dortmunder's water is very hard, only

> **Tasty Tip**
> *More German Mix-Ups:* In a country with the highest per capita beer consumption, the drink of choice is sometimes beer mixed with whatever else is on hand. An Alsterwasser is equal parts Münchener Helles and lemonade. A Honigbier (Honey Beer) is made from 12 ounces light-colored lager, a few tablespoons of honey, and half a cup of oatmeal. It's to be consumed with a shot of whisky. (Good luck with this one.)

slightly less than the famous gypsum-laden water of Burton, England. Meticulous care is used in the preparation and filtering of Dortmunder because it is brewed to be exported all over Europe. The style was popular in the U.S. before Prohibition and was brewed here and there until the 1960s.

Marching with Märzen, Vienna Beer, and Oktoberfest

Vienna beer is made with Vienna malt, which gives it a unique toasty flavor and aroma, and a reddish-amber color. Vienna has a sweet malt bouquet, a medium-bodied light malt flavor, and toasty grain aftertaste. More malty than hoppy, Vienna is the grandaddy of the recent "red" or "amber" lager fad taken up by America's brewing giants.

Vienna beer should be served at a temperature of 45–50°F, is 4.8–5.4% alcohol by volume, 8–12 SRM, and has 22–28 IBUs.

Although the Vienna style vanished for nearly a century, similar beers were, and still are, brewed in Germany for Oktoberfest. These Vienna taste-alikes may be called Märzenbier (March beer) or Oktoberfest. Today a few breweries have revived the true Vienna style.

Foamy Fact

Oktoberfacts: Oktoberfest is an annual celebration in Munich, Germany, that commemorates the marriage of Crown Prince Ludwig I and Princess Therese in 1810. Germans do not generally need an excuse to drink beer, but this one serves admirably. Oktoberfest begins in mid-September and ends the first Sunday in October. Ten million pints of beer are consumed during the festivities, most of it resembling Vienna style. In the old days, Oktoberfest beer was Vienna-style beer also called Märzenbier or "March beer," a term developed when brewers had to quit brewing in March because warm weather might contaminate the brew. The March beer was stored in caves until mid-September and opened for Oktoberfest. Today almost all Oktoberfest beer is a pale "fest beer."

Vienna was the cultural capital of the 19th-century Austro-Hungarian Empire, which stretched from today's Czech Republic, through Yugoslavia, Slovakia, and central Europe, to northeastern Italy. While the great lager styles were popping up in Bohemia and Dortmund, master brewer Anton Dreher introduced Vienna beer. The malt for Vienna was dried at higher temperatures that gave the lager its amber color. Dreher brewed his beer in Vienna, Budapest, Michelob, Bohemia, and Trieste, Italy.

The Austro-Hungarian Empire collapsed after World War I, and Vienna lager became extinct on the continent. Oddly, it is still brewed by Dos Equis and others in Mexico, where quite a few Eastern European immigrants settled. Today the beer is making a comeback as microbrewers resurrect the great old styles of yore. When America's brewing giants tried to hitch their wagons to the micro-revolution, they started brewing quasi-Vienna-style lagers with adjuncts and called them red or amber.

Third Bock from the Sun

Bock beer is German in origin and is rich in flavor, powerful in potency, and sweet and malty with a low hop bite. According to tradition, bocks should be either richly golden or amber brown. There are several types of bock. Maibocks are lighter, hoppier, and bronze in color. Doppelbocks, or double bocks, may be up to 13.5% alcohol by volume.

Bocks should be served at a temperature of 50–55°F. By German law, bocks must have an alcohol content of 6.7% by volume (bock brewed elsewhere may be between 4.5 and 7% alcohol). Doppelbocks must be 7% alcohol by volume or higher. Bocks are 20–30 SRM and have 20–30 IBUs.

Bocks are bracing beers that are traditionally brewed at the beginning of winter for release in early spring when the chill winds are still blowing. Maibock, or May bock, is a lighter, hoppier affair brewed for the warmer days of late spring.

When you take a sip of rich, creamy bock, the alcohol warmth protects you from spring's chill like a warm coat. And there's history in that sip. Bock can trace its roots back to the springs of Crooked Waters creek, a tributary of the Ilm River near Einbeck, Lower Saxony, Germany. Those crystal-clear waters put Einbeck on the map as an international brewing center as early as the 11th century.

Tasty Tip
The Secret Beer Fest: All beer drinkers probably know of Munich's Oktoberfest. But the Starkbierfest (Strong Beer Fest) is Munich's March beer festival celebrating the annual release of the doppelbocks. The Starkbierfest is as wild and rowdy as Oktoberfest, but without the blind-drunk tourists. By the way, the locals call doppelbock the "spring beer cure." Think about it.

The beer of Einbeck was a popular libation in Munich by the mid-16th century. Thirsty Munichers asked for *einbeckischbier,* or beer imported from Einbeck. After a few mugfuls, the name got shorter—to *ein beck,* or *ein bock,* in the Bavarian accent. The name stuck and the spring beer from Einbeck became bock beer. Now it just so happens that "bock" is the German word for "goat." Before long, the rutting, strutting billy goat was linked to bock beer as a symbol of spring and a drink with a kick. The billy goat has long been a symbol of fertility and even lechery. Early ads, labels, and posters for bock beer showed a lascivious, leering goat—sometimes in *lederhosen*, those leather shorts traditionally worn with suspenders by the Bavarians.

Eventually the bock style became so important that its qualities were written into law. Today's German bock beers must have an alcohol content of at least 6.7% by volume. The color has been deemed to be either amber-brown or golden, but not in between.

Bock was brought to America by German immigrants after the Civil War. Bock, like many other great styles, was corrupted after it hit the shores of the U.S. Large breweries produced weak, corn-laden beer with caramel coloring and passed it off as bock.

Stale Ale Alert

For years rumors have circulated in North America that bock was "made from the dregs of the tanks," in breweries "when they were cleaned every spring." Brewers keep their kettles and kegs spotless: they clean them after every batch of beer lest they become contaminated with bacteria. There are no such things as dregs of tanks. Real bock is a high-quality beer that is the apex of a brewer's art.

Most North American craft breweries are ale-based and generally aren't equipped to make a lager like bock. But a few make some great bock beers.

Doppelbock

Doppelbock is not really double the strength of bock, but may seem that way if consumed too heartily. It's powerful, thick, and delicious. Paulaner Brewery brewed the first doppelbock in 1780. To honor its roots as a former monastery brewery, Paulaner dubbed this strong beer *Salvator* or "savior." After that, most breweries producing doppelbock tacked the suffix "-ator" on the end. This has given us such amusing doppelbock names as Celebrator, Optimator, Navigator, Animator, and Kulminator. It has also given us the Terminator.

Celebrator Doppelbock kicks like a billy goat.

Red, White, and Brew: American Lager

American lager is the generic name given to the very pale, lightly hopped, light-bodied lager commercially brewed in most parts of the world, except Europe. It is the main style brewed in Canada, Mexico, Central and South America, Australia, Japan, and the Far East, and it makes up 85% of the beer sold in the United States.

American lager has a minimal taste profile. It is usually brewed with 6-row barley malt, processed corn or rice, and very little hops. American lager, which should be served at a temperature of 45–50°F., comes in several styles: 3.2 beer, light beer, premium beer, dry beer, ice beer, and malt liquor. Standard American lager is 4.7% alcohol by volume, 2.7 SRM, and has 10–15 IBUs.

Even with the microbrewery revolution in full gear, 85% of the beer sold in North America is so-called American lager. Loosely based on Bohemian Pilsner, American Pilsner is brewed and aged for shorter times, has adjuncts like rice and corn added to the

Bar Talk
What's made Milwaukee famous, has made a loser out of me.

—Jerry Lee Lewis

recipe, and has a bare minimum of hops. This is the beer whose very blandness spawned the microbrewery revolution.

We all know what American beer tastes like. We've seen the logos in every movie and sporting event in the past 25 years. We've seen the cans next to the highway. And since so many billions of gallons of the stuff are consumed every year, here's a primer of American lager styles from lightest to heaviest.

Beer by Numbers—3.2 Beer

Your familiarity with 3.2% most likely has to do with your age and where you live. This beer was legalized in the United States right before the repeal of Prohibition in 1933. When Prohibition was finally repealed, states were given the right to regulate alcohol however they chose, or of remaining "dry"—no alcohol sales at all. Some opted to sell only 3.2 beer. In the old days, before the drinking age was raised federally to 21, some states sold only 3.2 beer to people who were 18 to 21 years old. Some states sold it only on Sunday.

Foamy Fact

Fresh, Creamery Ale: There's no milk in cream ale. It's actually a very pale Pilsner-style beer fermented at warm temperatures like an ale, then aged at cold temperatures like a lager. Cream ale is a top-fermenting beer handled like a bottom-fermenting beer. The yeast rises like cream to the top of the brew, hence the name. It was invented by German immigrant brewers who could not find proper bottom-fermenting yeast in America.

Generally, 3.2 beer is standard American lager that's been watered down. It has no more than 4% alcohol by volume, so it is 3.2% by weight. In states like Utah, it's the only beer available that's not sold in specially licensed liquor stores. It seems overall that Big Brother has given up on the concept of beer that's 4% instead of 4.7% alcohol by volume, and 3.2 may soon become a thing of the past.

Light Up Your Beer

Light beer is a low-calorie beer with a lower gravity than regular beer—some have a lower gravity than *water*. There is no law in the United States that regulates exactly what constitutes "light." In Canada, beer labeled "light" must be 3.2. In my opinion, light beer was the straw that broke the camel's back, causing millions of beer lovers to go out and build their own microbreweries.

Light beers are extremely pale and have even less taste than standard American lager. Regular beers have 155 calories per 12-ounce serving, while light beers have one-third to one-half fewer calories. Light beer is brewed with special enzymes that convert unfermentable dextrins to fermentable sugars, which convert to alcohol. Alcohol contributes 7.1 calories per gram no matter what, so water is added.

In these days of "no-fat" and "low-fat" foods, consumers forget that these "light" foods still have calories. The same may be said for light beer. And the tasteless, bland product known as light beer is a pox on 5,000 years of beer tradition. Since good beer is all about enjoyment, my advice is to drink *real* beer, but drink less of it.

Bar Talk
Whoever called it near beer was a poor judge of distance.

—Prohibition saying

Gas Up with Super-Premium Beer

Premium or super-premium American lager is usually the top-of-the-line beer mega-brewers make. Many times its simply a fancier label than standard beer. Premium might also mean fewer or higher-quality adjuncts (rice instead of corn). Some might have real 2-row barley and higher-quality hops. American beer sold in Europe tends to be brewed with higher bitterness and fewer adjuncts, and would fit into the premium style.

Freeze Your Ice Off: Ice Beer

If you want a *real* ice beer, try the astounding Reichelbräu Eisbock from Kulmbach, Bavaria, Germany. That beer weighs in at 10% alcohol by volume and is a thick, rich, malty nectar. Eisbock is made by freezing beer and removing the ice (water), which concentrates the alcohol.

Ice beer was first introduced in the United States by Canadian brewer Labatt in 1992. Molson quickly came out with their own ice beer. The idea of ice beer is that it is stronger than regular beer—something the brewers couldn't state directly because of labeling laws. Ice beer is brought down to 25°F for two days, after which the ice crystals are filtered out, leaving a beer with a concentrated flavor and alcohol content—Molson's is about 6% by volume. American ice beer is similar, if somewhat lighter.

Wet Your Whistle with Dry Beer

One of my favorite Groucho Marx jokes is when a bejeweled society matron tries to pour a glass of champagne and the bottle is empty. Nothing comes out, so Groucho says, "That must be dry champagne."

Groucho aside, dry means "less sweet" in reference to alcoholic libations. Dry beer was first brewed in 1987 by Asahi Brewing Co. in Tokyo, Japan. Asahi Super Dry is slightly higher in alcoholic content, has reduced malt sweetness, and little or no aftertaste—a flavor profile achieved by adding enzymes like those used in light beer. The dry flavor complements broiled fish, seafood, and Eastern cuisine, and has 8% fewer calories than regular beer.

> **Foamy Fact**
>
> *Marketing Programs Are Hard to Swallow:* A writer in the *Financial Times* wrote about dry beer in 1989: "These people are drinking a marketing program. They're not drinking beer."

The beer became so popular in Japan that the brewery's sales increased by a third. With numbers like those, you can bet that the style spread quickly across Japan and to North America.

Stale Ale Alert
While malt liquor has a higher "liquor" content than regular beer, it has very little malt. The words "malt liquor" must be on labels in states that require beer above 5% alcohol to be called something other than "beer." Those two words corrupt more than the constitutions of those who drink it. Many great European beers are higher than 5% alcohol, so they must have the words "malt liquor" on their labels. Consumers shun these great beers thinking they are like cheap American malt liquor. If you see a German or British beer labeled malt liquor, give it a try. You'll like it.

Malt Liquor

American malt liquor is made for a quick cheap buzz, often followed by nausea and a headache. It's very pale and strong with a minimum taste profile. There are almost no hops. It's brewed with 50–60% malt, 30–40% corn grits, and 10–20% dextrose sugar. Its production values are further cheapened by warm fermenting temperatures and extremely short lagering periods—as little as one week.

Strange and Wonderful Beer Styles

There are a few beers that don't fit into any obvious categories. Some are regional styles that have been brewed quietly for centuries. Some are styles that were once thought extinct but have been revived by modern brewers looking for new products to dazzle micro-jaded customers. Every beer lover should try these strange and wonderful styles. Some are readily available; some need to be hunted down. But once you crack the cap on a wood-smoked or organic beer, you'll be glad you took the extra effort.

In with the Altbier and Kölsch

Alt, meaning "old" in German, describes several styles that differ depending on region. German alts come from Düsseldorf, Münster, Dortmund, Cologne, and Bavaria.

Altbiers date back to the time before lager's ascendancy as Germany's most popular beer. Like lager, each region's altbier is different. Not all altbiers are top-fermented, but most are. Some are fermented at warm temperatures like most ale, while some are fermented at cold temperatures, like lager. Cold-fermentation subdues the fruitiness usually associated with ale.

Altbiers are top-fermented, pale bronze to copper brown, with a smooth, dry, balanced character. They have a subtle to medium hop bouquet and a low bitter finish. They may be 10–15% malted wheat. Altbiers should be served at a temperature of 50–55°F, are 4.5–4.7% alcohol by volume, 25–35 SRM, and have 30–50 IBUs.

The most famous altbier is from Düsseldorf, and it's top/warm-fermented and cold-aged like lager. It is dark and hoppy. Munich's old Bavarian dark (alt-Bayrisches dunkeles) is a dark, cold-fermented lager. In Dortmund, altbier is a top/warm-fermented ale, dark in color. The altbier of Münster is pale and tart, brewed with 40-wheat malt.

Tasty Tip
Tutti Frutti: Folks in the Düsseldorf region pour their altbier over goblets of fresh fruit. The resulting delicacy is called an Altbier Bowl.

Kölsch is an appellation, like Bordeaux, meaning it can only be brewed in Cologne (Kölsch, in German) or adjoining towns. It's a pale, fruity, top/warm-fermented ale that is cold-aged like a lager. Kölsch is a little darker than Pilsner and has an alcohol content of 4.9%. It may contain 20% wheat malt. Kölsch was originally brewed to compete with Pilsner. It is served at 55°F in a tall narrow glass. Kölsch is rarely imported to the United States because few of Cologne's 26 regional brewers bottle their product. A few craft breweries are producing Kölsch-style beers.

Bière de Garde

Bière de garde is French country ale from northwest France. It's similar in flavor to Belgian ales. Bière de garde is strong, malty, fruity, and rich golden to reddish brown. Most bières de garde are bottle-conditioned in cork-finished champagne bottles, while a few modern products are bottom-fermented and filtered. Bière de garde should be served at a temperature of 50–65°F, is 6.5–8.5% alcohol by volume, 12–14 SRM, and has 25–28 IBUs.

Northwestern France, in the Calais-Dunkerque area, is a hop-growing region whose hops have been used in brewing since the ninth century. Barley is grown in the Flanders, Champagne, and Burgundy regions. Before the destruction of World War I, every town in the region had a few breweries. The bière de garde style was developed because average-strength beers would not make it through the region's warm summers. A strong beer had to be brewed that could be drunk in the late summer. Thus bière de garde, or "beer to be guarded" (cared for, or laid away), was developed. To survive, the beer needed to be strong and bottle-conditioned.

Don't Panic, It's Organic Beer

As in food production, all sorts of questionable chemicals are used in beer production. Chemicals are used in the farming of barley and hops. They are also used during sprouting and germination of green malt. Brewers who want to brew organic have a hard time finding enough malt and hops to do it. But the trend in food today is towards organics, so why not beer?

Tasty Tip

Drink Your Pinkus: Pinkus Müller makes the longest-standing organic beers sold in the U.S. The brewery in Münster, Germany, dates to 1816. Not too long ago, Pinkus began to brew the organic Ur-Pils for a Dutch health-food store. The brewery went all-organic when Barbara, the youngest daughter of the current generation of Müllers, completed her studies at Munich's Weihenstephan brewing school. The Pinkus Home Brew Haus, the brewery's brewpub, is famous for its "Altbier Bowl," a refreshing drink made by pouring Pinkus Altbier over seasonal fruit.

Organic ingredients are just fine, but the beer still has to be good. The organic beers I've sampled have an appealing cleanliness to them that makes them worth paying a little extra for. Most organic beers in regular production are from Europe.

Golden Promise Ale (Organic) brewed by the Caledonian Brewing Company in Edinburgh, Scotland, is not only organic, it's one of the best pale ales I've ever tasted. The smell of Kent hop perfume wafts right out along with the sweet smell of Scottish malt. The beer is light, well-balanced, and rich. The organic ingredients have a certain cleanliness and wholesomeness that is both reassuring and refreshing. The neck label informs that the organic barley and Kentish hops have been guaranteed by the British Soil Association. The back label explains that natural methods of sustainable (organic) agriculture are used in the growing of the ingredients.

Golden Promise is a mouth-watering organic ale brewed in Scotland.

The folks who brew the Belgian farmhouse ale, Saison Dupont at the Brasserie Dupont in Tourpes, Wallonia, Belgium, offer a highly recommended beer called Foret, which is the only certified organic saison beer in Belgium.

Wry Smiles over Rye Ale

Rye ale is brewed with 10–60% malted rye. It's tangy, fruity, spicy, and slightly bitter. Rye ale should be served at a temperature of 45–50°F, is 4.5–5% alcohol by volume, 2.5–5 SRM, and has 15–20 IBUs.

Rye grows well in cold climates and has been used in traditional alcoholic drinks from Russian vodka to Pennsylvania rye whisky. Less beloved than barley or wheat, and associated with poor rural peasants, rye is cultivated less in Europe's beer-drinking countries. Very difficult to work with in a brewery, rye beers have not yet made a comeback like other strange and unusual beer styles.

Until recently, the most famous (and available) rye beer was Germany's Schierlinger Roggen (roggen meaning "rye" in German). Brewed in Schierling, Bavaria, the ale has a whopping 60% rye malt, is about 5% alcohol, and is low in hop bitterness, but high in rye bitterness. It resembles a wheat beer in flavor.

Today, Redhook Brewery and Pyramid Brewery, both in Seattle, brew rye ales that are popping up everywhere. Try them with a pastrami and rye sandwich. Skoal!

Light Up Your Life with Smoked Beers

Smoked beer is called rauchbier (ROWK-beer) in German. Brewed by various methods, smoked beers are characterized by their noticeably smoky flavor and dark-copper, smoky color. If you love smoked meat and cheese, you'll love these beers. If you don't, you'll probably hate them.

Smoked beer should be served at a temperature of 50–55°F, is 3.8–6.5% alcohol by volume, 10–40 SRM, and has 20–50 IBUs.

Tree These Beers Out: Wood and Peat-Smoked Beers

In the old days, before gas heat, all beers were smoked beers. That's because the malt was dried over wood or peat-fueled fires. Peat was used in Scotland as it was the main source of fuel at the time. The wood used in modern rauchbier is beech wood. Direct wood-fired kilns leave malt partially roasted and smoky, giving beer brewed with it a unique taste. The most widely available rauchbier is Schlenkerla Rauchbier, brewed at Brauerei Heller-Trum, Schlenkerla, in Bamberg, Germany.

To get the unique flavor of Schlenkerla Rauchbier, the malt is smoked over an open wood fire. The barley sits on a mesh screen in a smokehouse, while beech wood smoke swirls around it. The malt is made twice a week. The beer is made entirely from smoked malt. It's unpasteurized, bottom-fermented, and matured for seven weeks. The beer has a light head, cloudy dunkel color, very slight smoke nose, and *deep* smoke flavor. The beer has a dryness and a smoky palate that lingers long in the finish.

The peat-smoked Adelscott Bièr au Malt à Whisky from the Fischer Brewing Co. in France is as unique as Schlenkerla because of its musky peat-smoked flavor. Rogue Ales in Oregon also makes a great rauchbier called Rogue Smoke with Rauchbier malt and home-smoked alder malt.

Foamy Fact

Spruce Juice: Beech wood isn't the only tree product used in beer. The young shoots of red or black spruce trees were used in place of hops in North America in the 17th and 18th centuries. Today, a few homebrewers are reviving the spruce juice tradition.

Everybody Must Get Stone Beer (Rauchenfels Steinbier)

The most dramatic brewing process in the world is found at the Ewald Werner Brewery in the Bavarian town of Neustadt near Coburg, Germany. That is home of stone beer—Rauchenfels Steinbier. Once upon a time, it was impossible to construct giant brewing kettles from metal. To raise the temperature of wort, brewers plunged white-hot rocks into their wooden tubs. Agrarian homebrewers in northern Europe used this method of "boiling stones" until the mid-1800s.

In the 1980s, Gerd Borges, owner of a small brewery near Coburg, Bavaria, read an article from 1906 about beer made in this traditional way. Later, Borges located a tape-recorded message—made in 1965—from an old brewer who brewed with stones and wanted to preserve his knowledge. Borges found a quarry in southern Austria that had mined rocks for this exact purpose until World War I. The stone from the quarry is called *graywacke*. It's a type of sandstone that can stand very intense heating and cooling without shattering.

In 1982, Borg began brewing stone beer. He heats boulders over a beech wood fire for four hours until they are white hot. When the stones reach 2,200°F, they are transported in a basket to the brewhouse by an overhead monorail. Then they are lowered into the kettle. The wort, which is half wheat malt, is close to boiling when the stones are put in and comes to a boil immediately afterward. The angrily crackling brew fills the room with steam and instantly caramelizes the malt.

The stones become coated with the caramelized malt. When they cool, they are placed in the lagering tanks so the caramelized sugar on the stones primes the brew. The beer, which is a true labor of love that takes a Herculean effort to produce, is well worth the effort.

Terms of Enbeerment
The stones used to boil the wort in Rauchenfels Steinbier are called **graywacke**. This type of sandstone can take the intense heating and cooling process without shattering, which would ruin the beer.

Bar Talk
Everybody must get stoned.

—Bob Dylan

Dream a Little Steam Beer

Steam beer is the style brewed only by Anchor Brewing, in San Francisco, California. It is medium-bodied, caramel in color, with a high hop bitterness and bouquet. Steam beer should be served at a temperature of 45–50°F, is just under 5% alcohol by volume, 8–20 SRM, and has 30–45 IBUs.

Steam beer is thought to be the only beer style indigenous to the United States (although some say cream ale is also an American invention). Also known as California common beer, the style can trace its heritage to the Gold Rush of 1849. German immigrant brewers made steam beer with cold-brewing lager yeast, but in California's temperate weather, were forced to ferment the beer at warm temperatures. The finished beer was kraeusened with new beer in the German style, rather than primed with sugar as is the English style. (Kraeusening gives beer a rich, creamy head.) This hybrid of bottom/warm-fermenting beer had a rich, creamy head and—served at warm temps—a powerful CO_2 charge. The name "steam beer" supposedly derived from the loud hissing sound the gas made when the kegs were tapped.

Even with the advent of ice machines in 1871, steam beer remained popular on the West Coast. By the end of the 19th century, there were more than a hundred steam breweries. After Prohibition ended in 1933, only Anchor Brewing Co. remained. Founded in 1896, the already small brewery was brewing only 700 barrels a year by 1965.

If you want a steam beer, you have to buy it from Anchor Brewing in San Francisco. It's the only steam brewery in the world.

On the day the brewery was going to close its doors forever, Fritz Maytag, heir to the Maytag washing machine fortune, stopped by the brewery to pay his condolences. Maytag ended up buying the brewery "for the price of a good used car," and changed the brewing world forever. Maytag rebuilt the business, trademarked the term "steam beer," and single-handedly (if inadvertently) started the microbrewing revolution.

By 1976, the brewery was turning a profit. By 1988, Anchor had gone from producing 600 barrels of beer a year to 82,000 barrels. And it's still growing. Maytag made history by brewing porter and barley wine again in America for the first time in almost half a century. The beer is brewed in wide, shallow open-fermenting vessels in a unique process that creates a singular beer, well worth drinking.

Foamy Fact

Not So Common Beer: "Common beer" was a name given to any American beer that did not utilize standard brewing methods. Although it should be called "uncommon" beer, steam beer fit into that category. But there were others. Kentucky common beer was a dark, sour-mash beer popular in Louisville in the 1800s. The deliciously named Pennsylvania Swankey was flavored with anise seed.

The Least You Need to Know

➤ Lager styles of beer originated in Bavaria, Austria, and in Bohemia—today's Czech Republic.

➤ Authentic lager styles are still primarily brewed only in the regions mentioned above.

➤ Most mass-market American beer is loosely based on the Pilsner style that originated in today's Czech Republic.

➤ There are many strange and unusual beer styles to try, such as smoked beer, rye ale, and steam beer.

Part 2
99 Bottles of Beer on the Wall: Cruisin' for a Brewsin'

There are almost 50 different identifiable beer styles, and maybe 5,000 breweries making them. It's enough to give one the vapors just thinking about it. On the other hand, it's a beer-lover's delight. If you were so inclined, you could drink a different beer every day of the week for the rest of your life. Starting…NOW!

But seriously, not all beer is created equal. And even the greatest beers have been mercilessly murdered by too much rockin' and rollin' during shipping and too much time spent languishing in warehouses. What's a hop head to do? Well, there are almost as many ways of finding good beer as there are beers themselves. These days, practically every major city has at least one brewpub and microbrewery. Quality beer is being sold in grocery stores, through the mail, in ballparks, and even on airplanes. Part 2 of this book will examine the ins and out of beer hunting and give you some insight into stalking the wily wort.

Chapter 8

Hop into the Bottle Shops

> ## In This Chapter
>
> ➤ Interpreting the information on beer labels
>
> ➤ Everything you need to know about beer kegs
>
> ➤ Helpful hints for buying the best beer

The best place to find the greatest number of beers at the lowest prices is your friendly neighborhood bottle shop—that is, a store that specializes in beer, wine, and liquor sales. And like beer, all bottle shops are not created equal. As an aficionado, I often find myself driving across town to find a special beer or get a good deal on a few of my favorites. I also prefer shops that let me mix and match, buying single bottles from six-packs. As my job requires that I taste as many beers as possible (someone's got to do it) I usually don't buy more than one or two of the same beers. Variety is the spice of life, and there have never been so many great beers to choose from. The trouble is, in my opinion, at least half the beers available are not worth paying for. (For more on judging a beer's quality, see Chapter 12.)

I have spent literally hundreds of hours in bottle shops, reading labels, sniffing out new and interesting products, talking to proprietors, and becoming an informed consumer. What follows are some carbonated clues to help you separate the ambrosial from the awful. Happy hunting!

Labels and Fables

Almost nothing inspires more exaggeration, palaver, and prevarication than the labeling and marketing of beer. The mega-brewers are losing scads of market share to uppity, upstart, backroom brewing companies. The Big Boys didn't get to the top of the malt-money mountain by rolling over to their competition. They want you to think that their chemical-laden, adjunct-added, factory-brewed beer is equivalent to the all-malt beer brewed in small batches in your hometown.

But it's not just giant brewers who enrich and adorn their product with superlatives worthy of Shakespeare. The marketing of beer is a tough, competitive business, and if a few well-turned sentences can get you to buy beer ABC instead of beer LMNOP, well then, who's to argue?

Throw in the archaic laws of the BATF and government bodies of other countries, and buying beer is probably the *least* informed decision a consumer can make these days. There's more information on the label of canned soda pop than on the label of your beer. Go figure. But you're laying down your hard-earned bucks for some pleasure and relaxation. You don't want to be disappointed or—worse—made queasy. Here's a list of label jargon that may help you find what's fine and leave the rest behind. I listed them in order of importance so you can zero in on what your hoppy heart desires.

> **Stale Ale Alert**
>
> *Don't Let the Sun Shine In:* Three things ruin beer—time, heat, and light. Old beer that's been stored in hot warehouses may be stale. Refrigerated stock is the best. Light brings out an unpleasant skunky odor in hops. Beer can get light-struck in a store window and by florescent lights in display cases. The darker the bottle, the more it protects the beer. Gushing, flat, or stinky beer should be returned.

The Yeast Beast: Ale or Lager?

The BATF requires that every beer state on its label whether it's an ale or a lager. Not too much confusion there. Pick one.

What's Your Style?

There is no legal requirement that says a label must say if the beer is a porter, bock, or whatever. With the "amber" or "red" craze, you really don't know what style it actually is. But most brewers, especially microbrewers, are more than happy to tell you you're buying a bock or a stout. It's a no-brainer. If you can't figure out from the label what kind of beer is in the bottle, my advice is to skip it.

Where's It From?

Every beer sold in the U.S. must list the name and address of the bottler, but not the actual brewer of the beer. It's crazy. Brewing-giant Miller brews Red Dog, which simply says "Brewed at the Plank Road Brewery," the original name for Miller Brewing Co. back in the 19th century. Many biggies try to skirt the issue by implying that their beer is brewed at some homey little brewery. My advice is, if you want craft-brewed beer, look for labels that clearly state the name and address of the brewer. If the brewing company is in one town, and the brewery in another, you're probably not buying beer brewed in small batches.

A Mighty Moniker: Reinheitsgebot

Although not a guarantee of quality, if the label says "Brewed in strict accordance with the Reinheitsgebot," or "German purity law of 1516," at least you know you're getting an all-malt beer. That's got to be better than some chicken-feed-flavored, corn-laden product. There's no law in the U.S. that says Reinheitsgebot-labeled beer has to conform to any standards, but I've never heard of a brewery lying about it. It's a worthy moniker.

Ironically, some imported German beers sold in North America are "dumbed down" to American tastes and may be brewed with adjuncts and preservatives. Generally speaking though, fresh import beer is usually a superior product to mass-produced American lager.

Stale Ale Alert
We may love oxygen for breathing, but beer is killed when it's been sitting around too long and it becomes oxidized. Oxidized beer tastes and smells like wet cardboard. As Elvis recommended: Return to sender.

How About a Date? Freshness Dating

Pasteurized beer—the most common type—generally remains fresh in a bottle for about three months. Strong, dark, and well-hopped beers last longer. Bottle-conditioned beers last the longest and some may be aged like wine. The trend today is toward freshness dating. Some beers proudly display "Drink before (month) and (year)." It's an indication that your beer is fresh. Not enough brewers date for freshness, but it's nice to know how old your beer is. Reduced-price products are generally older beers. They may still be good, but if they aren't, *take them back*.

Corny but True: Ingredients

If a beer clearly states its ingredients, so much the better. You know what you're buying. Some, however, proudly state that they contain corn or rice. Whatever.

Labeling No-Nos

Although it's been proven that beer is nutritious, and a couple of beers a day are good for you, brewers cannot state any health benefits on their labels. The overprotective BATF does not want anyone thinking that drinking (a few brews) can be good for them. Bottle-conditioned beer contains live yeast that is rich in B vitamins, but that information is also verboten.

Better Brown Bottles and the Can Can

I'm a beer writer. I have a License to Swill. If I was seen drinking canned beer, my license would be revoked. Metal cans spoil the ancient beer tradition for me. Maybe it's just a snob thing. Plus, there are not that many canned beers that I'd even bother to drink (maybe two). But as an official beer snob, I don't drink from a bottle either. If I can't smell the beer while I'm drinking it, I can't enjoy it. *Always pour your beer in a glass—it's worth it.* Now that I've gotten that off my chest, I will relate some facts about beer receptacles so you may ignore me and draw your own conclusions.

In 1935, Krueger Cream Ale was the first beer sold in cans. Aluminum cans were first used by Coors in 1952. Canned six-packs offered convenience; they were easy to chill, lightweight, and one could wing 'em out the window of their '39 Desoto. Unfortunately, the beer they contained *tasted* like a '39 Desoto. For a time, cans were lined with a very thin layer of plastic. When aluminum cans were introduced, the liner disappeared, and it's been that way ever since.

Americans today throw away enough aluminum annually to rebuild our entire fleet of airplanes three times over. Aluminum is also the most recycled product. Personally, I think aluminum is less inert than glass, and I don't like drinking the stuff. But if great beer was sold in aluminum, maybe I'd buy it. *Maybe.* Most good beer is sold in good old brown glass bottles. And I'm a dedicated recycler, though I would prefer returnable bottles.

Kollege of Keg Knowledge

Great beer comes in kegs. It's usually fresh and unpasteurized, and some bottle shops carry upwards of 80 different brands of kegged beer. So if you're planning on entertaining 20 to 2,000 people, limber up your drinking elbow and roll out the barrel.

Beer makers measure their production in 31-gallon barrels. Kegs, or half-barrel kegs, hold 15.5 gallons of beer—enough for 165 12-ounce servings. Quarter-barrel kegs hold (uh…) 7.75 gallons, enough for 82 12-ounce servings. Full kegs run from about $50 for mega-brewed beer to $150 for a good import. Imports generally come in 50-liter (13.2 gallon) barrels only, while micro and mega-brews come in quarter-barrel kegs of 7.75 gallons. You pay a deposit for the keg and the tap handle. Don't use them for jack stands for your truck unless you want to lose $50 or so.

Foamy Fact

One for the Ladies: Vassar College for Women was founded in 1861 by Matthew Vassar, the first well-to-do American brewer. Vassar made his money selling 30,000 barrels a year of Poughkeepsie Do and Ale.

Keep kegged beer cold. Giant refrigerators are the best method, or put it in a large garbage can or bathtub and pack it with plenty of ice. Don't forget to put ice on top, too. Let the keg sit for a few hours, if possible, or else the first gallon is gonna be foam. Pumping the air pressure pump too much will also foam your flagon. Use clean pitchers for serving.

After the party's over, leftover beer can be stored in plastic, sealable milk cartons for a couple of days in the refrigerator. For more info about buying 15 gallons of beer at a time, see "Tappa Kegga Brew" in Chapter 11.

A Six-Pack to Go: Buying Take-Home Beer

Here are a few tips on how to root out the righteous at your local bottle shops.

At Your Service

Many bottle shops have a resident beer geek, whose job is to keep up with the dozens of new brewskis introduced each month. That person is paid to help you. Ask a clerk who the beer warden is and *make friends with that person.* He or she will tell you about new products, good deals and sales, and products you might like. You will probably also get straightforward answers about a specific product's age and quality.

Beers R Us: Specialty Shops

In the 1980s, many bottle shops recognized the wine trend and began to specialize in wines. And, like wine, there is a bigger profit margin in high-end beers. In a few cities—following a newer trend—there are retailers who specialize in beer. While beer specialty shops might be slightly higher in price, the selection, knowledgeable staff, attention to handling, and high rate of turnover add to the probability that you'll be a hoppy customer. One note of caution: Take wads of cash or a credit card. Many beer enthusiasts act like 5-year-olds on Christmas morn when they see 1,000 bottles of beer on the wall for the first time.

Stale Ale Alert

Dusty and Crusty: Try to avoid beer sold in places where there is a slow turnover. Examine the bottle. If it's very dusty, or the beer has chunks floating in it (unless it's bottle-conditioned), don't buy it. Also avoid beer that's stored in brightly lit deli cases.

Pickles and Beer: Supermarkets

In states where it's legal, some supermarkets probably offer the freshest beers at a reasonable price. The drawback is that the beers might be mishandled, limited in selection, and exposed to bright lights in display cases. In some places, like California, consumers may find great beers in supermarkets. In other states, food stores may only sell 3.2 beer, or mass-produced suds.

1,000 Bottles of Beer: Massive Beer Stores

There are dozens of stores in the U.S. that carry 1,000 different beers. Others have around 500. The selection changes all the time, and some stores can get more than 100 new additions *every week*! During holiday seasons, like Oktoberfest and Christmas, breweries flood their distributors with seasonal beers. New imports also add to the list. With scores of new microbreweries opening every year, we ain't likely to run out of beer any time soon. Pinch me, I must be dreaming. Less than a decade ago, we were lucky to get one new beer a year.

That said, if you want to find the greatest selection, you've got to go where you'll find lots of people. A dense population (physically, not mentally) makes for fast-moving, high-quantity beer choices. But each state has its own beer retail laws, some of them quite Byzantine. Naturally, we can't go into the beer laws in every state, so my advice is to get out the phone book and go beer hunting on a Saturday afternoon. After you've tracked and captured your prey, you can enjoy the fruits of your labors on Saturday night.

Bottle Shop Tips

Here's some free advice if you're browsing a bottle shop:

➤ **Think Globally, Drink Locally**   If you love a great California-brewed microbrew but you live in New Hampshire, you might not be able to get the beer. You'll probably be better off drinking a locally made product that might be nearly as good.

➤ **Saturday Specials**   Many beer retailers have in-store tastings on Saturday afternoons where you can try before you buy.

➤ **Speak Up**   The customer is always right. If you can't find what you want, just ask. Retailers should be happy to track down your favorite brew for you.

➤ **Micro Media**   Some retailers have toll-free phone numbers, books, videos, newsletters, and World Wide Web pages featuring pertinent info.

➤ **I Gar-ohn-tee**   Some retailers have a cash-back guarantee if you're not satisfied with your purchase.

If you live in an area where great beer is hard to find, you may want to consider joining a beer-by-mail club, covered in Chapter 10.

Tasty Tip
I've Got a Ph.D. In Beer: As any well-seasoned beer drinker may (vaguely) remember, college students and beer go together like…well, college students and beer. Folks in college are the most adventurous beer drinkers. Hence, some of the most well-stocked beer stores in the nation are near college campuses.

Great Bottle Shops

Here is a by-no-means-complete list of well-stocked beer stores. This information was gleaned from an article by Daria Labinsky in *Beer: the magazine*. Thanks to her.

The 1,000 Beer Club

➤ Mesa Liquor & Wine Co., San Diego, CA (619) 279-5292

➤ Shangy's: The Beer Authority, Emmaus, PA (610) 967-1701

➤ Grand Opening Liquors, North Haledon, NJ (201) 427-4477

The 500 Beer Club

➤ Chevy Chase Wine & Spirits, Washington D.C. (202) 363-4000

➤ Ollie's Pub, Ocean City, MD (410) 289-6317

➤ Goldberg Liquors, Baltimore, MD (410) 789-1234

➤ Surdyk's, Minneapolis, MN (612) 379-3232

➤ Liquor Mart, Boulder, CO (303) 449-3374

➤ Big Z Beverages, Huntington, NY (516) 499-3479

The Least You Need to Know

➤ You can learn a lot about a beer from the label, but some things, like the original brewery and alcohol strength, are not always offered. Let the buyer beware.

➤ Better brew is usually sold in bottles. Recycle!

➤ Beer usually tastes better from a keg. A full keg is enough for 165 12-ounce servings. Half-kegs hold enough for 82 12-ounce servings.

➤ You can buy beer anywhere, but specialty shops offer the best selection, quality, and service, while supermarkets offer the best prices.

Chapter 9

You're Drafted: Brewpubs and Beer Bars Want You

In This Chapter

➤ Tips and taps at beer bars, restaurants, and brewpubs

➤ The benefits of brewpubs and beer dinners

➤ Great beer in ballparks and on airplanes

These days there's no reason not to drink good beer. New brewpubs are opening up every week. Taverns are replacing their mega-brewed beer line with dozens of tap handles to deliver fresh micro and imported beer. Restaurants are updating their beer lists to resemble wine lists. Some are even installing brewing equipment in the back room or in the middle of the dance floor. So forget about that dingy pub with the orange plastic tables where you can have any kind of beer you want, as long as it's watery American lager. It's an aficionados' market, and all it takes to drink the best is mere money.

Playing Taps: Variety in Beer Bars

The best way to drink a wide variety of fresh beer is in a bar that features a diverse selection of beer. The distinct advantage here is, if you're unfamiliar with a specific beer, you can usually ask the barkeep about it. If it's a tap beer, you might even get a little taste before you buy. You might pay a little more in a beer bar, but the people who run that type of establishment know their beer, and they know how to store and serve it.

Today, in most major cities, there are a few bars that can boast a beer list of 500 or more beers. Scores more have 50 to 100 brews. While quantity is great, quality might suffer (see Stale Ale Alert). Nonetheless, nothing warms the heart more than walking into a tavern and seeing dozens of tap handles sprouting up behind the bar.

Tapping into the Best

Tap beer is fresher and usually unpasteurized. It's generally lacking in the acidic carbonic bite of bottled beers, and is served the way beer was meant to be served: in a nice, tall glass or mug. Since kegs cost more than bottles, they're usually stored and handled properly. And if you're really lucky, you'll find a tavern with genuine *hand-pulled* English ale or nitrogen-charged Irish stout.

Before tanks were used to charge beer with CO_2, all ale was cask-conditioned. With natural CO_2 in the barrel, the real ale is delivered by a beer engine that works like a siphon and suctions beer into a pint glass with three good pulls. A special restricted hole in the opening of the tap forces the beer out, making tiny bubbles, and giving the brew a rich, creamy head that sits up above the glass. Divine! If you can find hand-pulled beer in North America, move next door to the pub that serves it.

Stale Ale Alert
It's very impressive when a bar stocks hundreds of beers. But be aware that the more beer in stock, the greater the possibility that it's old or mishandled. Use the same criteria in bars as in bottle shops. If the bottle is dusty or there's chunks floating in the beer, give it back immediately. Ditto if it smells like wet newspaper or used kitty litter.

Terms of Enbeerment
If you've ever been lucky enough to enjoy your ale in an English pub, you've seen the barkeep pulling on the long tap handle to fill your glass. The British have long known that **hand-pulled** English ale means freshness from the keg to the glass.

House Brand Beers

A few bars that feature pretty good beer selections also have their own house brand on tap. These are usually beers brewed to the specifications of the bar by a local micro- or regional brewery. House brands may vary from the ridiculous to the sublime. Ask for a taste.

Beer in Restaurants

The focus of most restaurant libations is, understandably, wine, which has a greater profit margin. But I'm still amazed when I go into an upscale eatery and can chose from only among the blandest of beers. I mean, if a restaurant is pushing *Oven-Braised Raddichio with*

Free-Range Oysters à la Brooklyn, they should be able to offer a malty miracle to accompany it. That said, many restaurants are climbing on the beery bandwagon and hipping up their beer lists to match those of their wine. If you're unsure which beer to drink with your above-mentioned and totally fictional Oysters à la Brooklyn, a knowledgeable wait-staff should be able to recommend an appropriate beer. (For more on food and beer pairings, see Chapter 13.)

Malty Mastications: Beer Dinners

Your favorite restaurant may not have scores of great beers everyday. But a few are offering formal beer dinners. (No, a seven-course beer dinner is *not* a six-pack and a pizza.) Beer dinners are gourmet meals that incorporate several courses, each of which has beer as an ingredient in the recipe and is summarily consumed with a matching brew. If you've never had a Chocolate Stout Bourbon Pie with Belgian grand cru wit beer, you haven't lived. (Or maybe you'll outlive us all.) Be that as it may, beer dinners prove that in heaven there *is* beer.

Beer dinners usually feature a speaker from the beer industry who will wax poetic about the victuals and potions you're greedily consuming.

A few tips for attending beer dinners:

➤ They're not cheap.

➤ They fill up quickly. Make reservations right away.

➤ This is no joke: Wear loose-fitting clothes that can absorb stains. I've had a waitress accidentally dump night-black stout on my pastel silk suit coat. The need for loose-fitting clothes is self-evident.

Birth of the Brews: Cruising the Brewpubs

Brewpubs are restaurants that brew their own beer just as they might bake their own bread. Some brewpubs' main focus is beer. Some focus more on the food. Some do a superb job creating both. Brewpubs range from hole-in-the-wall, brats-and-brew places to white-tablecloth, yup-scale eateries. The thing they have in common is (usually) great-tasting, fresh beer made with love, varying amounts of skill, and lots of malt.

The first brewpubs were established in Sumeria around 8,000 years ago. They've flourished throughout history as places where the public could find two of life's basic needs: beer and food. Today, they're opening across America at the rate of one a day, fueled by the profusion of small, easy-to-use brewing systems and economics. (A glass of beer that costs 50¢ to produce sells for up to $4.) But most brewpub owners do it as a labor of love.

Many of them are former homebrewers who simply had to have a great glass of ale. And once you've been bitten by the brewpub bug, there's no going back. Good brewpubs add to the quality of life in almost any town and deserve your support.

Foamy Fact

In with the Inn Crowd: In the 1500s, merchants needed a place to sleep, drink, and do business deals. And so the inn was born. As competition increased, innkeepers began to put shows, music, and balls in their barrooms. Like today's brewpub boom, the number of inns increased exponentially. By the middle of the 16th century, there were almost 20,000 inns throughout Europe. Folks who didn't live the good life of the traveling merchant were usually relegated to establishments called taverns. Those even poorer found themselves in what were called ale houses.

Brewpub Benefits

It's so easy to sing the praises of brewpubs. They've forever changed the way beer is drunk on this planet. Here, in no particular order, are some benefits to beer brewed on premises.

➤ **The Best Beer Around:** You can't get it any fresher than at a brewpub. The beer hasn't been shaken for days during shipping. It's been stored at exact optimum temperatures since it was hatched. And it's been minimally handled by ale aficionados who know what they're doing. A beer that travels 30 feet between kettle and glass has *got to* be better than one that travels 300 miles in a bottle.

➤ **The House of Styles:** Brewers in brewpubs love to experiment with styles, flavors, and malt combinations that you won't find anywhere else. Besides always having a fresh IPA, porter, and stout on hand, you're just as likely to find a maple-raspberry or honey-barley wine on the menu. Besides exotic brews, brewpubs have rotating seasonal styles, such as spiced Christmas brews, wheats, and March beers.

➤ **See Suds Hatch:** If you're of the curious mind, you can watch as beer is brewed. The brewing equipment in most brewpubs is behind large glass windows, or even right out in the open. Many give tours on Saturday afternoons, complete with free samples. Some will let you help them slog in the brewery if you want to apprentice. There's nothing like the sight of steaming, 214-gallon copper brewpots to give you that warm glow inside.

➤ **They Know of What They Speak:** Brewpubs serve their beer at the right temperature in a proper glass. The waitstaff is trained to answer your questions.

➤ **Higher Education:** Some brewpubs offer special beer seminars and tastings for those looking for an erudite beer-ucation. Others open their doors to homebrewing clubs and other masters of malty mirth. Fixed-price beer lunches and dinners are also on some brewpubs' blueprints.

➤ **Eat, Eat, Eat:** Hey, you can even masticate here. Many brewpubs are themed restaurants that cover the spectrum from California healthy to Germanic cuisine to English pub grub. Quite a few of the dishes are prepared with the house beers to great effect, and local specialties pop up often. I've had everything from beer-battered fish and chips to lager-brewed chipotle chicken.

➤ **Attractions, Holidays, and Special Events:** Brewpubs have outdoor beer gardens, live music, dart boards, pool tables, and other accouterments you'd expect from a tavern. Many celebrate Oktoberfest, national holidays, and odd holidays, like the birth of a 13th-century beer saint. A few even sponsor bike races and marathons.

Samplers, Tasters, and Growlers

Another beauty of brewpubs is that you can buy a sampler with five 4-ounce glasses and taste a broad range of offerings. Called *samplers*, *tasters*, or *flights*, these bubbling babies come on a placemat with each beer described in vivid verbosity. Start with the lightest and go to the darkest or hop from side to side. These are great to share with someone, and then go ahead and order a pint (or two) of your fave.

In states where it is legal, brewpubs offer *growlers* to go. A growler is simply a pail—or these days a plastic half-gallon jug—that the barkeep fills directly from the tap. Keep it refrigerated and drink it quickly before it goes flat. Your stomach won't be growling after one of these. The term "growler" originated in the old days when factory workers on lunch break gave children two bits to run to a saloon to fill up their beer bucket. Apparently the growling stomachs of the workers gave the ale pail its quaint name.

Terms of Enbeerment
Flights of Fancy: There are many beauties to imbibing in brewpubs. Among them are **samplers.** You can order four or five 4-ounce glasses containing each beer style the brewpub makes. These little glasses with a wide array of beer flavors are called samplers, **tasters,** or **flights. Growlers** are plastic jugs that the brewpub sells to go.

Brew Trek: Finding Brewpubs While Traveling

For obvious reasons, I can't begin to name all the great brewpubs in the world. I *could* shamelessly plug a book I wrote called *Beer Here: A Traveler's Guide to American Brewpubs*

Bar Talk
Local baseball, local beer. What could be better? What could be more American?

—D. L. Geary, Geary's Brewing Co.

and Microbreweries, with 600 listings. Or I could recommend that you pick up the *brewspapers,* magazines, and books listed in Appendix B. These tomes and bimonthly publications cover the ins and outs of the ever-changing pub crawl and are invaluable when traveling. The "Real Beer Page" on the Internet is also a great place to find beer bars, brewpubs, and reviews. In Chapter 15 you'll find a state-by-state listing of some of my favorite brewpubs in the United States.

Beers, Balls, and Bats at the Old Ball Game

One group of folks benefited from the 1994 baseball strike besides zillionaire owners and players: minor-league baseball teams. Without the Yankees and the Indians to kick around, folks took their families out to watch dedicated players play on natural grass under the open night sky. And while the underdog leagues prospered, the underdogs of the brewing world were not far behind. As fast as you could say "Yer out!" brews like

Terms of Enbeerment
Inexpensive or free regional newspapers that cover the suds scene are known as **brewspapers.** They're usually available at the entrance to brewpubs and liquor stores. Brewspapers contain news of new beer bars, brewpubs, and microbreweries. They cover food and drink, wacky personalities, homebrewing, and just about everything you can imagine about the world of beer.

Blackwell Stout from the New Haven Brewing Co. were selling out at New Haven Ravens games. At minor league parks across the country, craft beer sales were exceeding everyone's expectations.

Not to be outdone, the big boys got into the act. It started when Coors Brewing Co. invested $30 million in a new stadium for the Colorado Rockies for the right to name it Coors Field. But it came out of left field when Coors opened the SandLot Brewery right in the ballpark. Called the first brewery in a ballpark, Coors was selling Squeeze Play Wheat by opening day 1995. They sold 100 kegs in the first two days of play.

Oriole Park at Camden Yards in Baltimore opened several concession stands with seven Maryland microbrews. Other big leaguers are getting into the micro act, hoping that the lure of great beer will keep the fans coming back for more.

Beer of Flying: Airline Brews

You hope your chosen airline's main goal is getting you where you're going safely. Filling the fuel tank and screwing the wings on tight takes precedence over a great beer selection. But still, when you're sitting there white-knuckled nervous and eight miles high, what better way to lower your blood pressure than with a quality beer? Unfortunately, most North American airlines have beer selections as old and tired as their 737s.

If you want something better than Milwaukee's or St. Louis' mediocrity, you better pony up for first class, where you can get a Beck's or a Heineken. But bottles are the main reason airlines don't have great beer. Good beer comes in them, and glass is heavy, adding to fuel costs. And glass is dangerous in an airline cabin.

The Delta Shuttle from Boston to New York to Washington offers Samuel Adams Boston Lager, and Northwest Airlines offers Henry Weinhard's Private Reserve and Augsburger beers. Northwest also offers Asahi, Suntory, and Kirin on its flights to Japan.

If you want the great import beers, you usually have to fly to the great beer-producing countries overseas. Ireland's beautifully named Aer Lingus serves Pub Draught Guinness and the delicious Smithwicks. Scandinavian Airlines offers Carlsberg, Pripps, and Ringnes, along with aquavit. Germany's Lufthansa offers bottled Paulaner, Holsten, and Fürstenberg. Swiss Air probably has the best beer list of all with Dinkelacker, Kronenbourg, Feldschlösschen-Hopfenperle, and Hürlimann.

I guess if you want better beer, you better fly across the ocean to get it.

> **Tasty Tip**
> *Shipyard in the Air Yard:* Waiting for airplanes got a little bit better recently (at least in Orlando, Florida) when Shipyard Brewing Co. of Portland, Maine began operating a 20-barrel microbrewery at Orlando International Airport. Host Marriott will also open two Shipyard Brewpub Restaurants at the airport. For more information, hop on the Internet at http://www.shipyard.com.

The Least You Need to Know

➤ Beer bars offer a wide variety but may serve old beer.

➤ Beer dinners are great events to taste and learn about beer and food, but they are expensive and fill up quickly. Make early reservations.

➤ Brewpubs brew their own beer and often serve small tasters so you can pick your favorites among their offerings.

➤ A few minor-league ballparks serve quality craft brews, and some of their larger brethren are catching on, too.

➤ If you want great beer when flying, fly first class or overseas.

Chapter 10

Microbreweries for the Masses and Ale in the Mail

In This Chapter

➤ The ins and outs of microbreweries

➤ Free beer! Touring the breweries

➤ More beer than you've ever seen before: beer festivals

➤ All about beer-of-the-month clubs

The first American microbrewery was slapped together by Jack McAuliffe in Sonoma, California. With the barest knowledge of brewing, McAuliffe, a former navy submarine mechanic, built his New Albion Brewery out of old pipes, army surplus, and used dairy equipment. He welded, wired, and brewed New Albion Ale with a professional brewing scientist named Don Barkley. In 1976, New Albion brewed about 150 barrels. But with no advertising budget and more demand than cash flow, McAuliffe gave up after six years. Jack's brewing equipment went on to complete many years of dedicated service at Medicino Brewing Co. in the appropriately named town of Hopland, California.

Micro is a relative term and, as demand for all-malt, high-quality beer keeps growing, more than a few microbreweries are busting at the seams trying to keep their products on the shelves. This is of great benefit to you, the consumer, as variety, freshness, and *value* become the new watchwords for the craft-brewing business.

Free Beer! Tour the Breweries

Touring a microbrewery is a fine way to spend a Saturday afternoon. You get to see the kettles, shiny tanks, and miles of pipes humming like a Stradivarius. All to give you your daily ration of suds. It's a lot of beer, and it's impressive.

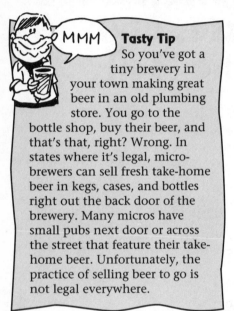

Tasty Tip
So you've got a tiny brewery in your town making great beer in an old plumbing store. You go to the bottle shop, buy their beer, and that's that, right? Wrong. In states where it's legal, micro-brewers can sell fresh take-home beer in kegs, cases, and bottles right out the back door of the brewery. Many micros have small pubs next door or across the street that feature their take-home beer. Unfortunately, the practice of selling beer to go is not legal everywhere.

Most microbreweries offer tours—some on a daily basis, some on a weekly basis. The only way to find out, besides my book *Beer Here,* which lists 350 microbreweries and their tour hours, is to call the brewery. Some, like Anchor Brewing in San Francisco, are booked up weeks in advance. Other smaller breweries will give you a tour whenever you show up. It's fun and informative, and a great way to meet the folks who are brewing your beer.

Most micros are glad to let you sample their products free of charge before, during, and/or after the tour. It always tastes better right there in the brewery, and it's a great way to introduce the public to new products. So if you're wasting away your Saturday afternoons mowing the lawn or studying, get thee to a microbrewery. Take a tour and relax.

Brewery Tours You Don't Want To Miss

Your local microbrewery will give you a fun and friendly tour, but if you really want to have some excitement, there's nothing like touring an old, humongous, commercial brewery. While their beers are shunned by aficionados, brew geeks, and people who know better, one still can't help but be impressed by brew kettles that hold 100,000 gallons of beer and a company that sells 10,000 barrels *an hour* worldwide.

Listed in the following sections, in no particular order, are a few breweries that are worth an afternoon of your time. So drop the family off at the mall and head directly to the brewery. Call ahead to find out when the tours are touring.

Politically Incorrect National Breweries

Author's disclaimer: I strongly recommend that you patronize your local microbrewery. I'm not endorsing any of these mega-breweries or their products, but they are fun to visit. Drink locally, but tour the breweries globally.

➤ Anheuser-Busch, 1127 Pestalozzi, St. Louis, MO 63118; 314-577-2626: The King of Beers is also the king of brewery tours. You'll see the famous Clydesdale horses and the brewpots where America's best-selling beer originates. The original brewhouse was built in 1876, but today these guys spill more in a day than some micros make in a year. You have to drink quickly on the tour. They only give you free samples for 15 minutes. Guess they're afraid of running out.

➤ Coors Brewing Co., Twelfth and Ford, Golden, CO 80401; 303-279-6565: This is the largest single brewery in the world. They pack in more than 300,000 tourists a year while brewing up 22 million barrels of American beer. They give prizes to every millionth visitor, and the number of visitors has surpassed 5 million. The Coors plant in Tennessee (901-375-2100) lets you sample beer in a replica of a 19th-century paddle boat after touring their ultra-modern, high-tech beer factory.

➤ Miller Brewing Co., 4251 West State St., Milwaukee, WI; 414-931-BEER: Miller Brewing offers a spiffy tour starting with a large-screen video and ending in the historic Cave Museum, where beer was once lagered. There's an outdoor beer garden and live music in the summer. The cases and palettes of beer in their warehouse have been described as "beer as far as the eye can see."

➤ Arthur Guinness & Son, St. James's Gate, Dublin 8, Republic of Ireland; 01-453-6700: I know, Dublin is probably not on your local bus line, but if you're ever in Dublin, the control room at the Guinness factory looks like the Starship *Enterprise* from the *Star Trek* TV show. It's a rolling, sprawling brewery taking up a huge portion of downtown Dublin. There's a gift shop where you can buy Guinness-logoed clothing, from socks to underwear to hunting jackets. Tell 'em I sent you.

Bar Talk
The German immigrants didn't give up their beer; they made Milwaukee famous.

—Anonymous

Regional Brewery Tours: Oldies but Goodies

The regionals are a little smaller scale, and many of them do contract brewing, improving the odds that you'll get an all-malt beer to sample.

➤ F.X. Matt Brewing Co., 811 Edward St., Utica, NY 13502; 315-732-0022: Tarry along on a restored trolley at the Matt brewery and enjoy free samples at the 1888 Tavern. Kids get free root beer. The hospitality center is a treasure trove of antique beer advertising and memorabilia.

➤ D. G. Yuengling & Son, Fifth & Manhantongo Streets, Pottsville, PA 17901; 717-622-4141: Established in 1829 in Pottsville PA, Yuengling (rhymes with Ringling) & Son is the oldest brewery in the U.S. Four generations of Yuenglings have brewed beer here, while 400 other Pennsylvania breweries bit the dust. Plenty of free samples, a gift shop, and a museum.

Another load of Pottsville Porter: The Yuengling Brewery was already 44 years old when this photo was taken in 1873. America's oldest brewery, Yuengling continues to offer tours today.
Credit: D.G. Yuengling & Son, Pottsville, Pennsylvania.

➤ August Schell Brewing Co., Schell's Park, New Ulm, MN 56073; 507-354-5528: One of the oldest (but not *the* oldest) continuously operating breweries in America, the Schell family opened this place in 1860. They dug the lagering caves in the hillside by hand. Today, the place sits nestled in a wooded valley. Schell's Victorian mansion has been lovingly restored and the grounds boast a formal garden, peacocks, and deer. They survived Indian wars, droughts, disease, freezing winters, Prohibition, and bad shoes. And they make pretty good all-malt beer, which they generously give away to tour hounds.

➤ Spoetzl Brewery, Shiner, TX 77984; 512-594-3852: If you want to see where the cowboys get their Shiner beer, this is the place. This eccentric little brewery was country before it was cool. It was actually started by a few of the many German immigrants who moved to Texas back in the old days.

Foamy Fact

Hoppy Daze Are Here Again: Prohibition ended on April 7, 1933. A grateful America consumed over a million gallons of beer that night. But the burden was great on the remaining brewers. Of the 1,600 pre-Prohibition brewers, only 700 reopened. With little capital and obsolete equipment, 500 of those folded before long.

Ale Crafters: Microbrewery Tours

It's getting to the point that no matter where you live, you're probably within a few hours (or a few minutes) of a microbrewery. Since most of these places don't have a lot of bucks for ad budgets, the brewers encourage the public to tour their facilities (usually on the weekends) and imbibe in their freshly made products. Of course, some of these folks are too busy brewing to talk to tourists. The only way to find out is to call. Most breweries offer tours and they're fun, friendly, and heavy on the free tasters.

➤ Redhook Ale Brewery (No. 2), 14300 NE 145th Street, Woodinville, WA 98072; 206-483-3232: Redhook's state-of-the-art brewery sits on 22 acres in Woodinville, near Seattle. Ten acres of the land are natural wetlands. These guys started small in the early 1980s, and now they're growing like wild mushrooms in the rain forest. They used to be a microbrewery, but they're making so much beer now, I'm not so sure.

➤ The Santa Fe Brewing Co., Flying M Ranch, Galisteo, NM 87540; 505-988-2340: This might be the only microbrewery on a real ranch, out New Mexico way. They brew the likes of Chicken Killer Barley Wine and Sangre de Frambuesa (whatever that is). They brew from an on-site well, and you have to find mile marker 58 on State Road 41 to attend one of their BBQ cookouts/beer tours.

➤ Bar Harbor Brewing Co., Route 3, Bar Harbor, ME 04609; 207-288-4592: This mini-microbrewery is run by Todd and Suzi Foser, who sell their hand-crafted beers right from the log-cabin farm where they brew and live. Hang out on the front porch or rent an overnight room in the brewery. There's a play area with homemade root beer for the kids. It's a stone's throw from Acadia National Park.

More Beer Than You've Ever Seen Before: Beer Festivals

If you want to find a wide variety of beer under one roof, there's nothing like a beer festival. At these soggy events, brewers large and small set up tables, kegs, and cups to offer small samplers to thirsty hoards who come to quaff their products. Some fests are sponsored by radio stations or entertainment weeklies, some by the craft brewers themselves. From Berkeley to Boston and from Britain to Belgium, beer festivals are popping up wherever loquacious beer lovers love to lap it up.

Most fests offer dozens of different beers from brewers who also give away bumper stickers, buttons, cups, posters, coasters, and other beer-a-phernalia. The variety is there and the quality is there. So put on your rubber waders and jump in.

What Do You Do at a Brew Fest?

Expect to pay a high-gravity fee for entrance to the fest, usually $15 to $20. This should entitle you to taste each and every beer that you desire. If you think about it, it's not more than you'd spend for an evening in a barroom. Sometimes you'll receive a commemorative glass to keep.

You'll first enter a large hall, or parade ground outdoors, with hundreds of different brewers offering their wares. The lines can be long. Most tables only pour a one-ounce serving so that you can *taste* and *savor* each beer. Here are some quick tips for you as you make your way around:

➤ Eat before you go. Drinking a wide variety of beers on an empty stomach may be hazardous to your health, and others around you.

➤ Wear comfortable shoes and clothes that can absorb spills. Expect folks to accidentally spill beer on you. If the festival is outdoors, take sunblock, rainwear, or whatever you'll need for protection against the elements. Be prepared. Fests rarely get canceled because of bad weather, and there's usually a tent or two to crowd into.

➤ I like to carry a backpack with water, extra clothes, and my journal. The last item is invaluable for remembering which beers I liked when I want more later.

➤ Although some fests discourage it, I bring my own carbo-rich food like good bread and pasta salad. Who wants to pay too much at concession stands for food you wouldn't eat if it were free?

➤ Leave the kids at home. Some fests won't let anyone under 21 into the place. Besides, standing around *under* hundreds of beer glasses is no fun for the little ones.

➤ Please take along a designated driver or use public transportation. Don't drink and drive.

➤ Get there early. By the end of the night, lines get ridiculous.

➤ Upon entry, pick up a festival program and study it. It will tell you where to find your favorite beers or new brews you want to try. It's also full of useful information about bathroom locations. A few may even contain articles by yours truly.

➤ Pick up as much brewer paraphenalia as you desire. Some people become walking billboards before the night is out.

➤ Take advantage of other events the fest has to offer. There is usually live music and dancing, homebrew demonstrations, and the like.

➤ Meet and greet the brewers and owners standing behind the tables. These folks usually don't hear enough compliments when they're slogging wort all day.

➤ If there aren't enough bathrooms, there's not much you can do. Find the information booth and let the management know you expect better accommodations next year.

➤ Don't just drink your old stand-by beers. Be adventurous. Experiment. That's what the fests are all about.

Where for Art Thy Fests?

Beer festivals are busting out all over. For up-to-date listings, consult your local brewspaper, homebrew supply store, or the ubiquitous Internet. During the summer, a traveler could go to a different beer fest every weekend. Things slow down after Christmas and resume again for bock season in spring. Here's a list of the most well-known (and well-attended) brew fests.

➤ The Great British Beer Festival (August): This is the great granddaddy of them all, celebrating 20 years of real ale in 1997. Sponsored by CAMRA (the Campaign for Real Ale), the five-day GBBF attracts 50,000 pilgrims to enjoy more than 500 cask-conditioned ales. That's roughly 225,000 pints of ale. It's not just British beer either, with more than 100 imports offered.

Incidentally, CAMRA was founded by four people in 1971. Since then it has become the world's largest consumer organization. It's dedicated to ensuring the continued existence of non-pasteurized, cask-conditioned "real ale." Whenever a small, cask-conditioned brewery closes, CAMRA is there with a funeral march, complete with a band and an open casket filled with the brewery's bottles. Not ones to miss a good story, the British press took notice at the first funeral marches and gave the group tons of free media exposure. Today, CAMRA's membership exceeds 45,000 people in 150 chapters across Great Britain. There are also CAMRA chapters in Canada, Belgium, Scandinavia, and the Netherlands. CAMRA can take credit for helping spur the American micro revolution. For CAMRA's address and publications, see Appendix B.

➤ The Great American Beer Festival (late September/early October): The oldest American beer festival celebrated its 15th event in 1996. This Denver festival features more than 1,700 beers from approximately 400 brewers, and the number of brews and breweries is increasing every year. It's a great love-fest of America's irrepressible microbrewers, homebrewers, beer writers, and 25,000 beer lovers. For more information, see their Web site at http://www.beertown.org/gabf/gabf.html, or call them at 303-447-0816.

➤ Boston Brewers Festival (May): Ten-thousand brew-thirsty patrons attend this event every year. Scores of American and Canadian microbrews are featured under one roof at Boston's World Trade Center. For more information, phone 617-547-2233.

➤ KQED Beer & Food Fest in San Francisco (July): This is the oh-so-cool northern Cal beer-mania that raises money for public radio station KQED, to the tune of $100,000 a year. It features live entertainment and great beer and food, but is very crowded. Advance ticket purchases are recommended. Phone 415-553-2200.

➤ Oregon Brewers Fest in Portland (July): The Pacific Northwest is crawling with microbrewers, and this is their chance to meet and greet. Held at Riverside Park on the scenic Columbia River, this is where old brewers go when they die. Phone 503-778-5917 or get on the Web: http://www.jwh.com/~jhw/brewfest.

➤ Great Eastern Invitational Microbrewers Festival in Adamstown, PA (June, July, September): This sell-out event is held at the Stoudt Brewing Co. in a series of three weekend events that feature the East Coast's finest. Phone 717-484-4386.

➤ New York Beerfest (September): A well-attended event held outdoors, on the waterfront under the Brooklyn Bridge. Phone 718-855-7882, ext. 21.

➤ La Mondial de la Bière in Montreal, Canada (June): The Canadian *pièce de résistance*, with 200 beers from 25 countries held in the Old Port area of Montreal. Phone 514-722-9640.

Your Ale's in the Mail

All this talk of brewpubs and microbreweries is great. But what if you live in a locale far from the nearest brewpub? Or if you're simply too tired to go to the liquor store? Then ale in the mail might be the thing for you. Fresh beer delivered to your doorstep is a monthly joy for people who belong to beer-of-the-month clubs. About a dozen such clubs operate in the United States. The first one was Beer Across America, which started with 400 members in 1992 and now boasts as many as 60,000 monthly customers. (This number is a guesstimate, as the club does not release member numbers.)

The advantages of beer-of-the-month clubs are many. While details vary from club to club, most benefits include:

➤ Members receive two six-packs of fresh beer from two different microbreweries each month.

➤ Most include newsletters with all sorts of fun info about the beer you're drinking. The newsletters have letters, columns, articles, and recipes.

➤ The selection varies with the seasons, guaranteeing you a wide range of Christmas brews, bocks, wheats, Oktoberfest beers, and so on.

➤ You will be exposed to a wide variety of beers you might not be able to find, such as California microbrews on the East Coast.

➤ Some clubs offer hard-to-find brews made by tiny breweries with the highest standards.

➤ The beer is usually fresh. It's received and shipped within a few days.

And now for the downside:

➤ Only 14 states consider beer-of-the-month clubs legal. The National Beer Wholesalers Association has declared war on the clubs for violating the three-tier (brewery/distributor/bottle shop) system in place in many states. Kentucky has made direct shipping of alcohol a felony, punishable by five years in prison. (Negotiations are currently ensuing, however, to change this draconian law.) Check your state laws before signing up.

> **Stale Ale Alert**
> *Watch Out for the Beer Police:* Ale in the mail is a great concept and a valuable resource for the aficionado. But there are a few unfortunate problems, mostly relating to government regulations. For instance, in some states it is illegal to ship alcohol.

➤ There are no safeguards to keep the beer out of the hands of minors; although, most clubs require an adult to sign for the package.

➤ On a less serious note, beer can arrive hot or frozen. Those UPS shipping trucks are not great environments for beer. Make sure your club will immediately replace any bad beer.

➤ You might fall in love with a beer that you can't buy where you live. On the other hand, you might hate one month's selection.

➤ Most clubs require a mandatory two- or three-month sign up.

➤ If you live in a larger city, you could probably find most beers you'd receive cheaper locally.

➤ Some clubs are shipping contract-brewed beers, which are generally not as lovingly made as microbrewed beers.

➤ When you figure in taxes and shipping, you're paying $10–$13 per six-pack of beer that retails for half that much.

Beer Clubs: Who You Gonna Call?

Some of these folks come and go because their profit margins are shaky. Look for ads in brewspapers and magazines for beer clubs in your area. As of press time, here are the names and numbers of a few brew clubs. More can be found using the Yahoo search engine on the Internet and typing "beer+month." If you want to kill your taste buds before drinking the beer, many of these places also offer cigars of the month. (For more on beer and cigars, see Chapter 11.)

➤ 800-MICROBREW: Their phone number is (you guessed it!) 1-800-MICROBREW

➤ Ale in the Mail: 800-573-6325

➤ Barley Malt & Hops: 1-800-705-BREW

➤ Beer Across America: 800-854-BEER: (on the Web: http://www.beeramerica.com)

➤ Beer Basket USA: 800-ITS MICRO; they also offer wine-of-the-month

➤ Beers to You!: 1-800-619-BEER

➤ Hogs Head Beer Cellars: 800-922-CLUB

The Least You Need to Know

➤ If it's legal where you live, you can save money by buying beer directly from a microbrewery.

➤ Touring breweries is a great source of fun, and most offer free beer after the tour.

➤ Beer festivals are a perfect way to sample dozens of beers available in your region (and some from outside your region).

➤ Beer-of-the-month clubs are great places to get exotic beers if you can't find them where you live. Before joining, check to make sure the clubs are legal in your state.

Part 3
Let Me Entertain You— with Beer

It's been said that beer is a social lubricant. Drinking a brew or two relieves one of stress, kindles creative juices, and allows one to enjoy discussions with strangers and near-strangers. Great beer can be central to a successful dinner or party. If you've ever had chicken marinated overnight in rauchbier, or attended a tasting party with a dozen people, you know that outstanding beer can make better conversation than the weather.

In Part 3 of this book, I'm going to discuss the details of beer parties, beer tastings, and cooking with beer. I'll even help out with some tips for hangovers and how to avoid them (besides the obvious abstinence). So crank up the stereo, dim the lights, and pull down the shades. Crack the cap and kick up your heels. There's a party going on right here.

Party Hearty!

When most people think of beer at a party, they think of dozens of cans of mega-brewed swill floating in a tub of ice. Or they might think of a keg of lager lolling around in the bathtub. But it doesn't have to be that way. Serving quality beer at a party can be done with as much *savoir faire* and elegance as serving wine. With a few flourishes and a little inside knowledge, you can make a great impression on your friends and turn your party into a night to remember.

Impress Your Friends

When people begin to drift into your home for a party, it's good to have a light, inexpensive beer to greet them. A microbrewed pale ale or Czech lager goes well with hors d'oeuvres. Present people with a beer and a glass, so they can fully enjoy the offering. When you're greeting people and shaking hands, you don't want a strong, dark beer that is going to detract from socializing.

Once the group has arrived, depending on the size of your party, you can introduce beers one at a time. Start with lighter beers and work your way to the dark offerings. If you want to bring people together and provide a central focus, there's nothing like popping the cork on a one-and-a-half-liter, bottle-conditioned Belgian beer. For the price of a bottle of cheap champagne, you can provide one of the best beers in the world along with the joyous pop. I've even served Belgian fruit beers like framboise (raspberry) and kriek (cherry) in fluted champagne glasses. It's a nice touch. Some Belgians come in giant three-liter bottles. If you can afford them at $50 a pop, they're really impressive.

Of course, a larger group needs more fuel, and many beer stores these days sell kegs of imports and microbrewed beers. As mentioned in Chapter 10, you might be able to buy a keg direct from your local microbrewer. For smaller groups, there are German five-liter mini-kegs that provide beer for about a half-dozen folks.

When I have a dozen or so people over, I like to hold court at the large dining room table. (Maybe that's why I don't have a lot of friends.) Anyway, I bring out beers, one brand at a time, and serve them up with a little chatter about the beer's lineage and history. I pour about three or four ounces into smaller glasses I have for the purpose and pass them around. When everyone's done with their beer, I gather up the glasses and rinse them out before the next pour. (If you're paying extra for that premium beer, you don't want the last beer's dried sludge getting in the way of the flavor.)

Stale Ale Alert

Friends Don't Let Friends…: One more wag of the proverbial finger: In many states, the host or hostess may be held responsible if a drunk person leaving their party gets in a car accident. Serve lots of food to make sure your guests don't get snockered, and keep the phone number of a cab company nearby for friends who've had too much fun (and too much to drink).

Bar Talk

I decided to stop drinking with creeps. I decided to drink only with friends. I've lost 30 pounds.

—Ernest Hemingway

If you're on a budget, BYOB (bring your own bottle) is appropriate. In that case, ask your friends to pick up a specific brand or style of beer. Or just tell them to bring imports or microbrews of their choice. You can always pick up the beer and pass the hat for donations. Not exactly a way to impress your friends, but it beats bankruptcy.

The Perfect Party Beer List

If you're planning to have a party last three or four hours, a six-pack per person is not an unreasonable amount of beer to provide. If you're planning an all-nighter, even more beer is appropriate. This can add up pretty fast, so I've provided a beer list for a party with a dozen people and tried to keep the beer tab around $100. I've listed the beers in the order I'd serve them.

➤ Two six-packs of a Czech Pilsner like Pilsner Urquell

➤ One six-pack of a locally made, microbrewed India pale ale

➤ One six-pack of a micro or German wheat beer

➤ Six single bottles of Belgian ales like Duvel, Orval, and Chimay

➤ One or two bottles of Belgian fruit beer such as framboise

➤ One six-pack of a brown ale like Newcastle

➤ One six-pack of Scottish ale

➤ One six-pack of a German bock or doppelbock

➤ One six-pack of microbrewed porter

➤ One six-pack of an Irish or English stout

Bar Talk
Drink beer, the custom of the land

Beer he drank—seven goblets

His spirit was loosened

He became hilarious

His heart was glad and his face shown

—*The Epic of Gilgamesh* (1200 B.C.)

That should keep your friends busy well into the night. This list could also be a quick reference on which beers to take to a party.

Tappa Kegga Brew

Of course, if you want quantity over variety, you can always pick up a keg, which costs about $70 to $100 per 15.5 gallons of microbrewed beer and $100 to $150 for imported beer. For more on kegs, see Chapter 8. Kegs of import beer can take anywhere from one to five days to deliver, so plan ahead.

Beer, Booze, and You

But life isn't all beer and skittles. Sometimes life is beer, *booze*, and skittles. Matching beer and booze can be tricky, and I don't want to encourage blind inebriation. That said, the reality is that as long as there's been hard liquor, it's been consumed with

Bar Talk
I do not drink more than a sponge.

—Rabelais, 17th-century French satirist

beer. How many headaches have resulted in this combination is unanswered, but if you combine the right booze with your beer, you might be spared that long ride to nowhere on the porcelain bus.

➤ The best booze to drink with beer is single-malt Scotch whisky. It's not a cheap liquor, but it's made from barley malt, so it makes a good combination with beer. They go together like grapes and brandy. Scotch ale is particularly recommended with single-malt Scotch whisky.

➤ Bock beer and Jägermeister make an interesting combination with a German flair, but don't plan on doing much the next day.

➤ Growing up in Cleveland, I saw plenty of guys drinking "boilermakers" prepared thusly: Pour a measure of bourbon or Canadian whiskey into a shot glass. Drop the entire thing into a glass of Pilsner beer. Drink. Don't let the shot glass in the beer glass chip your teeth. Go stoke the boiler. For you non-factory types, this drink is also called a "depth charge."

➤ The excellent, rich, chocolatey, German ice bock, Kulmbacher Reichelbräu Eisbock 24%, can be mixed into coffee with brandy.

➤ The Scandinavians drink a liquor made from rye called aquavit. If you had a mind to, you could drink aquavit with a rye ale.

➤ In centuries past, the Russians were famous for their consumption of imperial stout (at least the ones who could afford it). I imagine that many an imperial stout was consumed with vodka, but I don't recommend it.

➤ Guinness sent me a great list of drinks to mix with Guinness Stout. They're numbered for the sake of convenience, but in no particular order:

1. **Guinness Velvet:** A 50/50 mix of Guinness and champagne.

2. **Tumbril:** Guinness mixed with port wine, brandy, and champagne…in one glass!!! Supposed to *cure* hangovers(?!), it's named after a tumbril, which is a cart used to carry condemned prisoners to the gallows. "You're only supposed to get into one if you feel like death." *Note:* Author takes no responsibility for the effects of this one upon the reader.

3. **Black and Black:** Guinness and blackberry liqueur. (I saw quite a few people drinking this one in Dublin.)

There were others—like Guinness with tomato juice—that I couldn't bring myself to try. With all due respect to the Irish ale magicians, these drinks could be made with any stout.

Foamy Fact

A Flaming George: George Washington's expense account included scores of entries for a drink called *flip* that was made from beer, rum, cream, sugar, and eggs. Really. The *pièce de résistance* in flip preparation was when a red-hot poker, called a loggerhead, was taken from the fireplace and plunged into the gooey drink, expelling foam all over the table and drinker alike.

Smokin'! Beer and Cigars

Beer and cigars go together like…well, beer and cigars. I know that smoking fries the taste buds and I hate cigarettes, so I usually refrain. Cigarettes, it goes without saying, destroy your sense of taste over time. Cigars do it in ten seconds. Fortunately, taste buds can recover.

Lighter beers simply get lost when consumed with cigars. They just can't compete. But a good cigar and a great stout together are a thing of beauty. The rich flavors complement each other, and by the time the cigar is gone and the beer consumed, you don't care about your poor taste buds, or much of anything else. If stout is good with a cigar, imperial stout is even better. With its smoky, sherry-like flavors, and raisiny aftertaste, the beer of the Czar goes great with cigars. Other great cigar beers are porters, old ales, doppelbocks, and German black beer. And since cigars come from the Caribbean, a great dark beer from the region, like Jamaica's Dragon Stout, makes a wonderful tobacco companion.

For those of you who desire to be a little more cigar savvy, here are a few cigar basics:

➤ Cheap cigars sold in drug stores and mini-marts contain such lovely ingredients as paper (for filler), saltpeter (for even burning), and glycerin (to keep them from drying out). "Good" cigars contain only 100% tobacco. Great cigars contain only the finest tobacco leaves. Good cigars are generally only available from tobacconists (so-called smoke shops).

➤ There is no such thing as a "fresh" quality cigar. Expensive cigars are rolled with tobacco that is aged 18 to 24 months. Great cigars might be aged another year before shipping. If stored properly in a humidor, cigars can last decades. Cigars manufactured in the 1860s were recently found deep in the basement of an Irish castle. The humidity and temperature there were perfect for their preservation. The cigars sold for over $1,000 each!

➤ To store a cigar properly, it must be kept in a room that has 70% humidity. Seventy degrees is the optimal storage temperature.

➤ Cigars from different countries have different qualities. Jamaicans are mild. Cigars from the Dominican Republic are medium in strength. Honduran and Nicaraguan cigars are strong and heavy. Cubans are considered the world's best (though illegal in the U.S.). They are rich and creamy.

➤ Thicker cigars generally have a richer flavor. The longer the cigar, the cooler the smoke.

For you folks who are into cyber cigar hunting, check out the Internet Cigar Group at http://www.cigargroup.com. It's got everything you need to know about cigars—and a whole lot more.

Sudsy Songs and Brew Films

Everybody's seen those old black-and-white movies where the beer mugs slide down the bar and onto the floor, or on somebody's lap. The use of beer in theatrical productions is as old as the theater itself. It was Willie Shakespeare who said, "I will give all my fame for a pot of ale and safety," in *Henry V*. Beer and ale have been mentioned in films from *Of Human Bondage* (1930) to *How Green Was My Valley* (1941) to *The Deer Hunter* (1978) to *Glory Daze* (1996).

Some movies are entirely about beer. *Take This Job and Shove It* (1981) details the true story of a small-town brewery threatened by a rich guy. *Strange Brew* (1983) features those wild and crazy guys from *SCTV*, Doug and Bob McKenzie of the "Great White North." They're not exactly Oscar material, but there's a lot of swilling and breweries in the flicks.

The movie *Beer* (1985) is a farce about beer marketing starring Loretta "Hot Lips" Swit of *M*A*S*H* fame. The more recent *Glory Daze* (1996) is about a bunch of folks lying around on the couch drinking beer. Sounds different.

Bar Talk
The stocking cap is to keep your head warm in the winter and your beer cold in the summer.

—Bob McKenzie portrayed by Dave Thomas in the *SCTV* spoof, "The Great White North"

A new phenomenon called cinema drafthouses is cropping up in cities across the nation. These places usually show second-run movies while serving food and beer. It's usually not gourmet on any account, but it's fun to order a pitcher, kick back, and watch a movie on a big screen. It gives "concession stand" a whole new meaning.

A twist on beer and movies can be found on the Internet on the California Beer Guide and Soap Opera, which contains strange soap-opera-like stories featuring famous actors such as James Dean touring around drinking beer and visiting barrooms. The page also has reviews of brewpubs in the west, and want ads for workers in the movie business. Just type "beer+movies" into Yahoo! to find this odd synergy of the brew and film business.

Sing a Song of Swill

Beer has inspired people to song since the days of the Babylonians. The ancient Egyptians had hundreds of songs dedicated to Hathor, the goddess of beer and drunkenness. By the Middle Ages, songs in praise of beer were in the repertoire of every bard and minstrel. In modern times, country and western songs such as Bob Wills' "Bubbles in My Beer," have praised and blamed beer for a whole catalog of consequences.

Foamy Fact

Tears in Your Beer: Beer and country songs go together like, well…heartbreak and country songs. One of the classics by Hank Williams is "There's a Tear in My Beer." Country troubadour Tom T. Hall wrote the anthemic "I Like Beer" with no-nonsense verses such as this: "Whiskey's too rough, champagne costs too much, vodka puts my mouth in gear….I like beer." And for you blues fans, let's not forget "One Bourbon, One Scotch, One Beer" performed so memorably by Amos Milburn.

One of the world's greatest bands for "suckin' on the ale" is an English band named Steeleye Span (no *not* Steely Dan). It does traditional glass-cracking, ale-drinking songs revved up with electric instruments, drums, violins, and incredible harmonies. They've been around for years. Steeleye Span CDs can be ordered at your local record store from Shanachie records. I recommend "Tempted and Tried" (#64020), "All Around My Hat" (#79059), and "Tonight's the Night" (#79080).

For those of you interested in drinking songs of the opera, pick up *Opera's Greatest Drinking Songs* put out by Classics World.

Playing with Your Food: Beer Games

Most beer games are designed to get the players as loopy as possible. I've listed a few here that at least require a modicum of skill and not as much chug-a-lugging. I'll say it again: Be responsible and don't torture yourself and others around you by drinking too much. Most beer games are takeoffs of basic non-beer games.

Beer Ping-Pong

Players place a full glass of beer one paddle-width from the edge of the ping-pong table. If you hit your opponent's cup, you earn a point and your opponent must sip. If you get the ball in your opponent's cup, you earn five points and he or she must drink the whole cup. (Don't swallow the ball!)

Beer Piano

Here's one for the musically inclined. One person blows into a beer bottle that's been all or partially drunk. The player tries to find that note on a piano (or any other instrument). He or she gets three tries. If the person fails, it's time to drink a beer. If the contestant gets the note, the note blower must drink.

Beer Cheers or "Hi Bob!"

This is similar to many television drinking games. Watch *Cheers*. Every time Norm touches his beer, drink a gulp of beer. If he drinks from his beer, drink the entire time he's drinking. Every time the crowd yells "Norm!," drink. Other players can base their consumption on primary character's actions in the show.

A similar game is played with the old *Newhart* show. Every time someone says "Hi Bob!" it's time to chug.

Beer Hunter

This one cracks me up. Take one bottle of beer and shake it for five minutes. Put it in a box with six or more beers just like it. Mix them up while the player is not looking. Have another person mix them up when the first mixer isn't looking and so on. The idea is to have the shaken beer hidden among its unshaken brethren. The first player picks up the beer and opens it. If he or she doesn't get a face full of beer, he or she drinks it. And so on. You may want to try this one outdoors—no sense in damaging any furniture or angering the host.

Three-Legged Pub Crawl

This is for those who like to get out of the house and make public fools of themselves. The game is played, preferably, near a college campus where such behavior is less likely to draw the brain police. It takes a few people, some money, and several bars close together.

People pair off and tie their legs together like a three-legged sack race. Every team starts at the same bar and is equipped with a list of several bars the team needs to visit. Each team consumes two beers (one each) at the bar. The team then quickly moves on to the next pub, still joined at the leg. They finish two more beers and then are on to the next bar. The team that gets to the last bar and finishes their beers first, wins. This game works best when played with about 10 people.

Bar Talk
There are more old drunks than there are old doctors.

—Willie Nelson

Squeezing the Cat: Hangovers

Alcohol is many things to many people. One thing it is to all people is a poison. We all know that it's not a good idea to drink too much of any alcoholic substance. But if you're going to drink, beer is probably the easiest on your body. And, if you drink home-brewed, bottle-conditioned, or cask-conditioned beer, you're getting your B-complex vitamins (B_1, B_2, B_3, B_6, and B_{12}) in living yeast still in the beer. This will help ease you into the next day. B vitamins help your body metabolize fat, carbohydrates, and protein. Without them, we could not live. Drinking alcohol depletes your body of these important vitamins, and without enough of them you get headaches, shakes, low energy, and dehydration.

The Sauerkraut Miracle Cure

You might have heard of the comic strip entitled *The Katzenjammer Kids*, which was very popular in the early days of the 20th century. What you might not know is that "katzenjammer" is a German expression used to describe hangovers. It means, literally, "squeezing the cat."

The Egyptians called the hangover malady "pulling of the hair." Their remedy? Cabbage juice. Don't laugh. Modern science has proven that cabbage juice contains chemicals that neutralize acetaldehydes, the nasty by-product of our livers trying to metabolize alcohol.

Stu's Surefire Hangover Cures

There's nothing foolproof about curing hangovers, but here are some quick tips that should help alleviate some of the symptoms:

1. Only drink high-quality beer and don't drink too much. Strong, dark beer like barley wine should be consumed in smaller amounts.

2. Drink several large glasses of water *before* going to bed even if you feel bloated from the beer. Dehydration is the main cause of hangover pain. I guarantee if you drink lots of water the night before, you'll feel better, if still dazed, in the morning.

3. Take a B-complex vitamin before going to bed. Add an aspirin if you can handle it.

4. Sleep in a bed, or at least lying down, not passed out in a chair.

5. Upon awakening, take a shower (please!). Your pores are clogged from your body trying to eliminate alcohol. Without a shower, the previous night's poisons have a rough time exiting your poor body.

6. The next day, take a multi-vitamin, aspirin, and an antacid if necessary. Drink more water.

7. Eat! Eat! Eat! Food will replace vitamins and settle your stomach. I prefer an Oriental buffet where a good soup is served. Great Vietnamese, Thai, or Chinese soup will definitely make you feel better. So will tea or a good cup of coffee. The soup usually has cabbage in it, the hangover cure known to the ancient Egyptians. If you can stomach it, drink a cup of cabbage juice. Your body will thank you.

8. Exercise. Swimming, weight lifting, or any other aerobic workout will help. Even if you have to drag your body to the gym, a good workout will make you feel 100% better afterwards—especially if your gym has a spa. Steam rooms, saunas, and Jacuzzis are a godsend if you have access to them.

The Least You Need to Know

➤ You can entertain a dozen people with beer for about $100.

➤ Order kegs of imported or microbrewed beer a few days in advance.

➤ If you want to match beer and cigars, pick a strong, dark beer.

➤ Single-malt Scotch, in moderation, goes well with beer.

➤ At a party, you and your friends can have a grand old time playing beer games.

➤ If you drink too much and have a hangover the next day, take vitamins, drink plenty of water, eat well, drink some cabbage juice, and get some exercise.

Speech bubble: CARL, IF YOU WANT TO ENJOY THAT FULL BODIED TASTE, SLOW DOWN A TAD...

Chapter 12

Beer Tasting and Other Tricks of the Tongue

In This Chapter

➤ The mysterious workings of your taste buds

➤ Tips for proper beer serving temperatures

➤ Beer glasses explained

➤ Everything you ever wanted to know about tasting beer like the experts

Some people, à la Bluto Blutarsky of *Animal House* fame, pop the top on a can of beer, swill it down, crush the can on their foreheads, rip off a good belch, and they're done with it. But if you've gotten this far in this book, you're probably not one of those people (unless it's your birthday). With all the different beers on the market competing for your taste buds—and your hard-earned cash—conducting (in)formal tastings and writing down your impressions can save you time and money. Besides, it's fun. And isn't that what this is all about? Your beer can talk to you. So go get one, pour it in a glass, and listen to what it's saying. (Drink me!)

To me, tasting a great beer is like experiencing a five-course meal in a bottle. The first sniff is like the salad course with all its variations of herb, sweet, and fruit. The first small taste is like a bread course, with all the biscuity flavor of malt. The first long draught is the appetizer, with all its mouth-watering implications. The main body of the beer is the main course. And the aftertaste is like dessert, with a sweet taste and a satisfied warmth. To truly appreciate the analogy, you've got to have a great beer.

Tasting beer can be a hobby for some and an all-out obsession for others. A lot of work and effort go into the production of a good beer—from farmers and truck drivers to maltsters and brewers. So it makes sense to enjoy the final product with a certain reverence and regard. Or just swill it down. But don't crush the *bottle* against your forehead.

I Am Joe's Tongue

That pink little muscle flapping around in your maw is as complicated and intricate as any computer ever built. Without the millions of taste buds contained in your tongue and throat, you wouldn't know the difference between a Pilsner and a parsnip.

Your taste buds can recognize four distinct flavors: sweet, sour, bitter, and salt. In primal terms, salty buds tell you that certain foods might replace the vital minerals lost to sweat and other bodily fluids. The sweet buds tell you what food is good. The sour buds warn you away from foods that might make you sick. And the bitter buds set off the mental alarms cautioning you that a substance you're about to eat might be poisonous.

Terms of Enbeerment
If you look at your tongue in the mirror you'll see hundreds of little dots on its surface. These dots are called **papillae**, and each one contains from two to 250 taste buds. Papillae allow you to taste food, beer, and other essential comestibles. Flavors of food also travel up your throat to your nasal cavity, where they stimulate the **olfactory membrane.** The olfactory membrane sends the flavor signals to the part of the brain called the **hypothalamus**, which tells you if the food tastes good or bad.

Each of the little protruding dots on your tongue are called *papillae*. And there are four different kinds of papillae. Each one contains from two to 250 taste buds. There are two kinds of taste buds: receptor or basal. When you taste something, there are chemical reactions with your saliva that send the molecules into the taste buds. They communicate with each other and decide what signal to send to your brain, whether it's "good beer" or "bad meat." Luckily, we don't have to think about our taste buds. It all happens in a split second.

All taste buds are capable of detecting all flavors, although those that are more sensitive to certain flavors are clustered in certain places. The sweet-detecting buds are on the tip of the tongue and the salt-detecting buds on each side. The sour buds are on the back-sides of the tongue. And the last defense against gag-a-licious foods, the bitter buds, are at the back of the tongue. You even have taste buds in your upper palate.

When you eat or drink, the vapors of the food travel up your nose before they ever come in contact with the

140

tongue. When you chew, the vapors go up the back of your throat to your nasal cavities. There, molecules of flavor hit postage-stamp-sized tissue called the *olfactory membrane*. Every nasal cavity has one, and each one contains 100 million receptor cells. Through complicated and miraculous chemical reaction, those billions of cells tell more billions of cells to send *more* signals to different parts of your brain. Some signals go to the part of your brain called the *hypothalamus*, which controls such primitive feelings as appetite, anger, fear, and pleasure. Other signals go to your memory-regulating brain. Some go deeper into your subconscious. That's why odors can provoke such strong memories.

When you taste beer, try to chew, swallow, and exhale through your nose at the same time. This way you can taste the full flavor as provided by your taste buds and your olfactory membrane.

A Matter of Degrees: Serving Temperatures

Ice-cold beer loses its subtlety of flavor. You may prefer that if you're drinking bad beer. But if you just laid down $10 for a six-pack of English porter, you want to serve it properly. This is most important if you're conducting a formal tasting. (Proper serving temperatures per style are detailed in Chapters 5 and 6.)

The average refrigerator keeps food at about 40°F. At this temperature, beer will release less carbonation, and hence, less aroma. Liquid this cold will stun your taste buds, numbing them. So serve lighter beers at 45°, darker beers at 50°, and real dark beers at 55°.

Tasty Tip
Taking Your Temperature: You probably don't have a thermometer to drop into your beer to make sure that it's 50°F. If you live in northern climates, simply store your darker beer in the basement. Except during the hottest part of the summer, your porters, stouts, and doppelbocks should be properly chilled. If you live where it's warm, or if you're drinking lighter beer, take the beer out of the refrigerator 30 to 60 minutes before serving.

The Secret's in the Glass

As with wine, the appreciation of a good beer depends on the look, the smell, and the taste. The best way to record that information in your brain is by first pouring the beer into a proper glass.

I've poured one beer into two separate glasses and have gotten two distinct flavor impressions. I know it sounds weird, but a tulip-shaped Belgian beer glass, the kind recommended by the brewer, worked better than a standard-issue English pub glass. Rather than debate the geometry and physics of each glass, I try to stick with the right glassware for each beer.

For your simple, everyday beers, a simple pint glass or mug with a handle is great. For those pricey imported brews and rich old ales, something a little, shall we say glassier, is called for. Here's a quick class on glass:

➤ English pint glass: For pale ales, IPAs, brown ales, porters, and stouts.

Stale Ale Alert

Freezing Your Glass Off: Unless you like watery frozen beer and frostbitten fingers, storing mugs in the freezer is not recommended. As quaint as the concept might be, frosted mugs are good only for killing the flavor of beer. Of course, if you drink cheap beer, frosted mugs can be a useful tool, as they deaden the off flavors inherent in lower-quality brew.

➤ Tulip-shaped glass with wide mouth: This is the classic Belgian glass. Use with Duvel or other strong Belgian ales. The outward curve of the glass allows the imbiber to consume the beer under the deep layer of foam.

➤ Brandy snifter: For serving imperial stout, old ales, and barley wines.

➤ Long-stemmed flutes: Use with fruited beers such as lambic.

➤ Tall, narrow, footed glasses: The classic Pilsner glass, along with light German lagers.

➤ Wide-bowled goblets: Use with German wheat beers like Berliner weisse and Trappist ales.

➤ Handled mugs: For doppelbocks and darker German lagers.

Cleanliness is Next to Beer-liness

Great beer glasses are usually available at homebrew supply stores, through beer magazines, or in bottle shops. They cost a few bucks extra, but with proper care, can last for years. Here are some tips on the caring and feeding of your glassware:

➤ Beer glasses *must* be clean. This means free of greasy fingerprints, lipstick, and old crusty beer residue. Soap film and dust are also culprits that can ruin your beer. Besides, who wants to pick up a glass with used pink lipstick on it?

➤ Fats in soap and body oils can cause your beer to go flat quickly, and they're disgusting.

➤ If the head of your beer breaks up into large, ugly bubbles, your glassware isn't "beer clean." Get thee to thy kitchen sink.

➤ For ultimate cleanliness, rinse your beer glass with hot water (no soap) immediately after drinking. Shake out excess water, but don't pound it into the faucet. (I've done this more than once, and it's a great way to shatter expensive beer glasses.)

➤ Wash the outside of the glass with a lightly soaped sponge. This gets rid of finger-prints. I avoid soap *inside* my glass unless it gets really filthy. Soap is hard to remove and leaves undesirable flavors and odors.

➤ If you're really obsessive, you can fill the sink with hot water and throw in a few tablespoons of baking soda. Scrub the glasses with a brush and air dry.

➤ Store your clean glasses away from steam, dust, food, and smoke, preferably in a sealed cabinet.

If all this sounds anal-retentive—well, after you've trained your taste buds to properly taste beer, believe me, good, clean glassware makes it all worthwhile. But that shouldn't stop you from drinking from large plastic tumblers or your lover's shoe if the occasion calls for it.

White Line Fever

British pubs serve beer in glasses with a white fill line around the rim. By English law, the barkeep is supposed to pour your ale to that line and the head should rise above it. What most people don't know is the line is called the *plimsoll line*. It's named after Samuel Plimsoll, the guy who standardized a way to mark hull-depth lines on bows of ships.

Those tall glasses presented in pubs with wooden stands to hold them up are called *aleyards* or a yard of ale. They were originally used by Belgian coachmen who, by Napoleonic law, were not allowed to drink with their riders inside the tavern. The coachmen would slip the yard-long glasses into their boots and still enjoy their ale. The bell-shaped glasses with the ball at the bottom hold $2^1/_2$ pints of beer.

Tasting Away in Malt-o-beverage-ville

Now that we know all there is to know about beer glasses, let's taste some beer. (Hooray!) I gave a quick rundown on tasting basics in Chapter 1. What follows are the complete details gleaned from tasting experts and beer connoisseurs.

First, get yourself one of those aforementioned clean, wide-mouthed glasses. Clear your palate with a big glass of water and a piece of French bread or a neutral cracker. Cigarette and cigar smoke seriously interfere with beer tasting, so try to avoid both—at least until later in the evening when your taste buds are tired anyway. Once you're sure your beer is at the right temperature, you're ready to be tasting away again in Malt-o-beverage-ville.

Pop the Top

You can't drink a beer unless you remove the top on the bottle. But like everything else in beerology, it's not as simple as it seems.

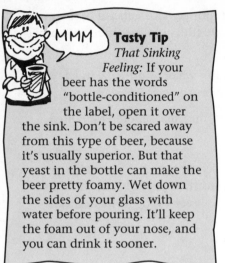

Tasty Tip
That Sinking Feeling: If your beer has the words "bottle-conditioned" on the label, open it over the sink. Don't be scared away from this type of beer, because it's usually superior. But that yeast in the bottle can make the beer pretty foamy. Wet down the sides of your glass with water before pouring. It'll keep the foam out of your nose, and you can drink it sooner.

➤ Before you open your beer, examine the liquid in the bottle, especially the air space in the neck of the bottle. Hold it up to the light.

➤ If there a ring of gunk around the neck, the beer is probably contaminated. If the air space is too large, the beer might be oxidized, another bad sign.

➤ The same goes for chunks floating in the bottle. Unless it's bottle-conditioned beer, chunks are bad news.

➤ Once it's passed the visual test, open the beer and *listen.* Does a great burp of CO_2 escape? Is it just a little *ffftt?* The louder and longer the gas sound, the foamier the beer will be. This is the first sign of what's to come.

Pouring Wars

Now you're ready to pour your beer in a glass and drink it, right? Wrong! Folks with Ph.D.s in subjects like "Colloids and Surfaces" spend their entire lives researching beer foam so that when you pour a beer, you get two point five fingers of foam that lasts for exactly five point three minutes. Those folks spend their lives in laboratories and are highly paid by brewers for finding fantastic foam.

Terms of Enbeerment
Did you know a beer might also have **legs**? That's the visible clear alcoholic coating that streams down the side of the glass after the beer is swirled. This is usually only visible in high-alcohol beers like doppelbocks and barley wines.

For us folks with Ph.D.s in beer-strology, the main argument is this: Do I tilt the glass or pour it straight down the center? I've almost had beers poured on my *head* debating the subject, so let me weigh in with a voice of reason: Do it both ways.

➤ Pouring the beer down the side of a glass held at a 60° angle or so will give you control over how much head you end up with. If it's a deliciously foamy Belgian offering, you will need to regulate the foam, unless you want to wait 10 minutes to enjoy your beer. Most beers foam up nicely if poured down the side of a tilted glass.

Stale Ale Alert
Addendum to the above *Terms of Enbeerment:* If you say "This beer has great legs" at a party, you might end up talking to yourself.

➤ If the beer is a slightly flatter, darker offering, you can pour it directly into the center of your glass, waking up the CO_2 and garnering the desired head space in your glass.

➤ If the beer is bottle-conditioned, it will have a small pad of yeast on the bottom of the bottle. If you love your vitamins, pour out all the beer except the last half-inch. Then roll the bottle around on the table, or shake it slightly. This will liquefy the yeast. Pour the remaining beer into your glass and enjoy. If you don't like chewy beer, leave the last half-inch in the bottle.

Making Scents of Beer Bouquet

Beer bouquet dissipates quickly, so don't dawdle after the brew is poured. Carbon dioxide bubbles release the aromas in the beer. Give your glass a swirl. Put it up to your nose. Clear your mind and inhale. Some folks like to take a few quick sniffs; some like a long, slow pull. Whatever your style, consume it heartily, deeply, and with great relish. Pause. Breathe deeply once again. Enjoy it while you can. After a few sniffs, your nose gets accustomed to the beer, and the subtleties get lost.

You should be thinking of balance when you smell a beer's bouquet. Do you smell malt sweetness or hop bouquet? Does the beer smell good? Does it smell like wet cardboard? You can tell a lot about the beer by its aroma and bouquet.

Hop bouquet in beer can be described as floral, perfumey, herbal, spicy, or piney. I've smelled the Pacific rain forests in some West Coast beers.

Malt aromas might include caramel, licorice, roasty, butterscotch, chocolate, coffee, and sweetness.

Stale Ale Alert
Experts do things like sniff cardboard marinated in beer for a week to be able single out that off-flavor in beer. Just for fun, here's an official list of words experts use to describe the awful smells and flavors found in bad beer: Like Band-aids, astringent, kerosene, tar, sulfur, rotten eggs, garlic, burnt rubber, wet cardboard, shrimp, cooked cabbage, onion, chicken-feed, or corny, cheesy, soapy, fatty, goaty, catty, rancid, moldy, musty, salty, rusty, metallic. Still thirsty?

Beer Appearance: The Eyes Have It

Don't drink your beer yet (sorry). Hold the glass up to the light and take a long (thirsty, mouthwatering) look. Is the beer the right color for the style? Is it cloudy or clear? Is it inviting you to partake? Can you see your future in the bubbles?

Seriously, beer can range from straw yellow to midnight black depending on style. Unless your beer is clear, or purple, there is (almost) no wrong color for beer. To compare your beer's color to the proper style, see Chapters 5 and 6.

The head of the beer should appear as small, tight bubbles. Better beers might have a dense, creamy, rocky head with beautiful peaks and valleys. Superb beer head looks like meringue. If your head isn't up to snuff, the beer is flat or your glass is dirty.

Sip and Swirl

Finally! It's time to taste the beer. Don't gulp. Sip a tablespoon or two slowly into your mouth. Roll it around all over your tongue. Simultaneously swallow and move your jaw in a chewing motion. After you've swallowed, exhale through your nose and keep chewing. I've got a little trick where I inhale the beer into my mouth while exhaling through your nose at the same time.

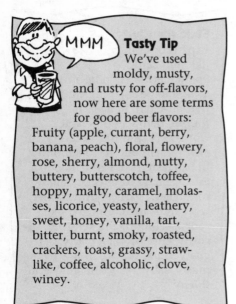

Tasty Tip
We've used moldy, musty, and rusty for off-flavors, now here are some terms for good beer flavors: Fruity (apple, currant, berry, banana, peach), floral, flowery, rose, sherry, almond, nutty, buttery, butterscotch, toffee, hoppy, malty, caramel, molasses, licorice, yeasty, leathery, sweet, honey, vanilla, tart, bitter, burnt, smoky, roasted, crackers, toast, grassy, straw-like, coffee, alcoholic, clove, winey.

Take another small sip. Roll the beer around, coating your entire mouth. Is the beer thick and full-bodied? Thin and light-bodied? What's the mouthfeel? Is the beer complex or a one-note malt? What about negatives? Is it astringent? Puckering?

How is the aftertaste? Is it pleasant, or does it leave a wet paper taste in the back of your throat? A great beer should leave a good finish in the back of your throat and beckon you to drink more. If it's a mega-brewed beer, it may have little or no aftertaste. If it's a microbrewed beer, it may leave an aftertaste of a sinful dessert. The finish is the *pièce de résistance*, the perfection of the brewer's art, or his or her downfall.

Drink Up!

Now is the time to enjoy the rest of the brew and reflect on its deeper and more subtle flavors. Look for balance. Does the bitterness of the hop offset the sweetness of the malt and vice versa? Is this beer worth your time and money? Do you greedily gulp it with wild abandon or are you already thinking of your next beer? Does the alcohol slip by almost unnoticed or does it warm your body and soul? Do the hops bite or are they perfumey? Is the malt cloyingly sweet, or just right? It is a snack or a meal in a glass? Is the beer a stick drawing or the Mona Lisa?

Thank You, Sir! May I Have Another?

The one question every brewer would like to know after you taste his or her brew is "Would you have another?" That should be your final analysis as you drain the last drops of foam from your beer glass. A great beer should leave you wringing the bottle out to get the last delicious drips of ambrosia. A not-so-great beer will leave you shrugging, "So what?" Here are some additional tips as you continue to taste different beer styles:

➤ Use a simple system of assigning points to each beer. Aroma one through five, color one through five, taste one through five, aftertaste one through five, final impressions one through five, and so on.

➤ Try tasting beers of the same style at one time—all porters or all bitters, for instance. It's easier to compare two porters than a porter and an Oktoberfest.

➤ Don't taste more than four or five beers in one sitting.

➤ Only drink three or four ounces of each beer. Once you're snockered, you tend to get real enthusiastic about anything and everything.

➤ If you want to know how the pros have judged a specific beer, go to professional beer tastings or check the Internet. Hundreds of beers are rated on various Web pages. (For beer-related Web addresses, see Appendix B.)

➤ Finally—and I can't emphasize this enough—if you like a beer, it's good. Everyone has different tastes, or we'd all eat the same food, dress the same, and listen to the same music. Beer is fun, relaxing, and for sharing. If you get too hung up on dissecting each and every beer, you might not be having fun. And your friends might call you (gasp!) a beer snob.

Tasty Tip
Beer Diary: I've tasted thousands of beers, but I would be lost without my laptop computer full of beer-tasting notes. (Keep beers and computers on separate tables, unless you like sticky keys and short circuits.) A less high-tech (and infinitely cheaper) method is a beer-tasting journal. In it, you can record your impressions of each beer's look, bouquet, and flavor. Beer journals: Don't drink foam without them.

The Least You Need to Know

➤ Your tongue can detect hundreds of flavors in a beer, if you taste carefully and analyze.

➤ Beer must be served at the proper temperatures for you to fully appreciate the flavor. Beer that's too cold will not reveal its full flavor.

➤ There are different glasses for different beer styles. Keep your glassware clean and soap-free.

➤ Beers are judged by their look, aroma, mouthfeel, flavor, aftertaste, and overall impression. Keep a journal to record your overall reactions to each beer.

Chapter 13

Beer Steining and Dining: Blending Beer and Food

In This Chapter

➤ What beers go well with specific foods

➤ Beers to drink with bread, soups, salads, and cheeses

➤ Beers to serve with seafood, poultry, beef, lamb, pork, and dessert

➤ Beers that go with ethnic cuisines

Many cooks about to entertain at a dinner party have recited the old maxim "Serve white wine with white meat, red wine with red meat, and sweet wines with dessert." But no one ever memorized "Serve stout with oysters and rauchbier with sausage." (Well, *almost* no one.) But in reality there are hundreds of combinations of food and wine. So, too, are there scores of beers that can be paired with victuals.

In this chapter, I discuss the best beers to drink with foods. Many of these same combinations can be served with great recipes featured in the next chapter.

Mixing and Matching

Bar Talk
Every man should eat and drink and enjoy the fruit of all his labor; it is the gift of God.

—Ecclesiastes 3:13

Tasty Tip
Nifty Snifters: Beer can be very filling, and there's no need to serve it in huge mugs along with dinner. If you want to offer several beers with a many-course meal, serve the beer in wine glasses, champagne flutes, or apèritif beer glasses made for this purpose. Barley wines, imperial stouts, and doppelbocks are well presented in brandy snifters.

While wine's acidity is a bonus in cutting through the richness of some foods, most beer does tend to lack in that department. But hops add a spiciness to beer that is reminiscent of thyme, rosemary, and oregano. The malt in beer adds sweetness, bread, cracker, and nutty flavors. Yeast adds tartness, fruitiness, acidity, and savory tastes.

In today's world of choices, there are few hard and fast rules about anything, let alone which beer to drink with what food. Nevertheless, almost all of today's beer styles are hundreds of years old, and they originated in regions where local delicacies naturally blended together in a fusion of food, flavor, and foam. So while no one would stop you from drinking swarthy black stout with filet of sole, you might miss the delicate flavor of the fish and at the same time make your ale taste like low tide.

Yet the beauty of beer is that there is no wrong choice. And it's a good opportunity to mix cultures. For example, I like drinking sweet, malty German lagers to cut the heat of jalapeño peppers, and hoppy California bitters with rich Italian food. A traditional, if decadent, dessert consists of imperial stout poured over vanilla ice cream. Generally, the following guidelines either match a food (say, sweet with sweet) or they balance a food (bitter with sweet). But beer is a versatile drink and, while some matches may be made in heaven, others can bring out the devil in you.

Grateful Bread

Not too long ago, bread was in the same doldrums as beer. You could buy white bread or rye bread. If you were lucky, you could find white bread with caramel coloring, called wheat bread. Like beer, bread began to enjoy a renaissance where it got darker, healthier, and more natural. Today, paralleling the brewpub boom, fresh-baked-bread stores are popping up in corner shops and strip malls. The consumer can now get exotic bread styles fresh from the oven. Once again, the yeast leads the way.

Still and all, bread, like beer, is basically grain, water, and yeast. But these two cousins can work admirably together during the bread course of a meal. In fact, bread can be baked with beer. (More about that later.)

Great bread and beer pairings include the following:

➤ **Saison:** Saison is Belgian farmhouse ale originally brewed for farm workers and their families. The lemony hoppy Saison Dupont has boysenberry overtones that could almost act as a jam with bread.

➤ **German Pilsner:** German Pilsners can be very grainy and sweet. Pinkus Müller Ur-Pils is a light, refreshing lager and a perfect complement to dark, crusty bread.

➤ **Oatmeal Stout:** On the sweet, rich, and dark end of the spectrum, a Samuel Smith's Oatmeal Stout would be a heavenly accompaniment to a bread course.

➤ **Orval or other Belgian Trappist Ale:** Trappist monks at Abbaye D'Orval sell more than 35,000 loaves of whole-grain bread every year. Orval beer is often enjoyed with warm, brown, crusty bread.

Tasty Tip
Dubbel Your Fun: An *enkel* (single) or *dubbel* (double) designation on some Trappist beers indicates that they are lighter in alcohol than *tripel* (triple) or *quadrupel* (quadruple).

Gouda Brews—Beer and Cheese

Cheese is the premier yeasty concoction that makes a heavenly marriage with beer. The sweet/bitter flavors of beer make the perfect escort to the sour/salty flavor of many cheeses. Strong beers go particularly well with strong cheeses.

German beers go with German cheeses, British beers harmonize with British cheeses, and Belgian beers blend well with Belgian cheeses. Some regions of Europe have a local cheese producer *and* a local brewery. If you like a particular regional cheese, ask your bottle-shop proprietor if there is a beer brewed in that region.

With so many types of cheese and beer, the pairings are infinite and endless. Almost any beer can go with almost any cheese, but here are some of the classics.

➤ **German Wheat Beers and Doppelbocks:** Aventinus, from Kelheim, Bavaria, is a top-fermenting, wheat doppelbock that's perfect with German cheese. So is Erdinger Pinkantus Weizenbock, also from Bavaria. Berliner Weisse and other wheat beers are also recommended.

➤ **English Pale Ale, India Pale Ale, Bitter:** English ales make workmanlike alliances when served with cheese-, bread-, and onion-laden ploughman's lunches in the U.K. A grand pale ale like Eldridge Pope Royal Oak makes this traditional combination into a busman's holiday.

Foamy Fact

Eat, Drink, and Be Merry, For Tomorrow We May Diet: Beer gets a bad rap when it comes to calories. But the truth is that 12 ounces of a regular pale American lager have only 151 calories—slightly less than a glass of 2% milk. By comparison, 12 ounces of Chablis contain 264 calories, a Big Mac has 540 calories, and 12 ounces of corn chips have 1,860 calories.

➤ **Barley Wine and Imperial Stout:** Imperial stout and barley wine are sherry-like beers. They come highly recommended with English cheeses, such as Stilton, Cotswold, and cheddar. Samuel Smith from Yorkshire makes one of the world's best imperial stouts. Rogue Old Crustacean is a great Oregon-brewed barley wine.

Imperial stout, like this one from Rogue in Oregon, goes great with English cheeses like Stilton, Cotswold, and Cheddar.

➤ **Strong Belgian Ale:** The malty sweet flavor of the deliciously named Delirium Tremens from the Brouwerij Huyghe in Melle, Belgium, is to die for. The cherry overtones of this strong ale make it almost wine-like and a perfect match with hearty cheese.

➤ **Belgian Fruit Lambics, Gueuze, and Fruit Ales:** Fruit lambics and gueuze are more like wine than beer. Framboise, kriek, and other fruit beers go well with creamier cheeses like brie and camembert. Gueuze is tart and winy, perfect for lighter, nutty cheeses. American-brewed fruit beers are also recommended.

Soupy Ales and Stewy Brews

For many of us, our first experience with beer and soup was some version of beer-cheese soup. (I've had it with popcorn floating in it as a garnish.) But matching a beer with a soup is a little trickier, as soup can contain anything from vegetables to beans to fish to ham hocks. Here are a few general recommendations. For further information, match beers with the ingredients in the soup or stew as detailed on the following pages. (For example, for chicken soup, see "Birdy Brews.")

➤ **Bohemian Pilsner:** A hoppy, fragrant, well-balanced Pilsner Urquell can be a perfect match for many dishes, but it works particularly well with French onion soup and hearty stews. Scrimshaw Pilsner from Fort Bragg, California; Dock Street Bohemian Pilsner from Philadelphia; and Baderbräu Pilsner from Chicago are great American microbrewed Pilsners that are also recommended.

➤ **Belgian Red Ale:** A tart, sour Rodenbach brings out the sweetness of vegetable soup in beef broth. Also recommended with beef stew.

➤ **Pumpkin Ale:** This stuff from Buffalo Bill's Brewery tastes like pumpkin pie in a bottle and goes well with root soups with ingredients such as potatoes, parsnips, and rutabagas.

➤ **Scotch Ale:** A thick, biscuity, malty Scotch ale like MacAndrew's or Maclay makes a nice accompaniment to a hearty black bean soup. Grant's Scottish Ale from Yakima, Washington, blends well with hearty stews. For a fine French-Canadian Scotch ale, check out Le Cheval Blanc Loch Ness Ale.

Lettuce Entertain You: Veggies and Beer

Like soups, salads may contain anything from potatoes to goat cheese to prosciutto ham. Traditional leafy vegetable salads are delicate and need a subtle and mellow beer to wash them down.

Veggies are generally lightly flavored, unless you're talking about jalapeño peppers, garlic, or onions, which need a light, quenching draft. Here's a quick list of suggestions for mixing and matching beer and vegetables:

➤ **Pale Ale:** A good, hoppy North American microbrewed pale ale goes great with any vegetable salad. The spicy, green herbal flavor of the hops complements greens and vegetables in wonderful ways. For those who love organic veggies, try Golden Promise Ale (organic), from Caledonian Brewing Company in Edinburgh, Scotland. Besides using the word "pale" twice in its name, it's organic and one of the best beers around. (Organic usually tastes better anyway.)

➤ **Trappist or Abbey Ales:** Trappist or Abbey ales have an ancient taste that fairly reeks of old leather-bound books, cloistered rooms, and rich earth. Beers such as Chimay Trappist Ale or Corsendonk Monk's Pale Ale make a perfect accompaniment to earthier veggies like asparagus, broccoli, and cabbage.

Tasty Tip
Barley Dressing:
If you want to better blend your lettuce with your beer, try using malt vinegar in the salad dressing.

➤ **Greek Lager:** A medium-bodied lager from Greece goes well with Greek salads and feta cheese. Aegean Hellas or Spartan Lager are two quality beers made for stuffed grape leaves, figs, and all things Grecian.

Drink Like a (Shell)fish

Nothing cuts through a fishy dish like a good beer. The beer you want to drink with your seafood depends on the denizen of the deep you're ingesting. White-fleshed fish like sole, pike, or trout need a lighter offering, while red-fleshed and richly flavored fish can stand up to a stronger beer. Beer and crustaceans are found in many traditional recipes of the British Isles, Ireland, and Northern Europe.

➤ **Belgian Strong Ale, Grand Cru, or Wit:** A Belgian strong ale such as Duvel is an excellent pairing with shellfish, as well as ocean fish such as monkfish and salmon. The coriander and citrus overtones of a Belgian Grand Cru add spice to your dish and cut through fishy overtones of the seafood. The ducky Kwak is a Belgian strong ale that is recommended with salmon and swordfish. Wheat beer and fish go back a long way—since the pyramid builders were pulling finned food from the Nile.

➤ **Porter:** Samuel Smith's Taddy Porter is famous as an accompaniment to oysters on the half-shell. Also good with clams, mussels, crab cocktail, lobster bisque, and other shellfish.

➤ **Dry Stout:** Dry stout and oysters are practically a religion to some. A 50/50 mix of Irish stout and champagne, called a Black Velvet, is the perfect drink to go with oysters Rockefeller, lobster, crab, shrimp, clams, and other crustaceans. Fresh American stouts such as Rogue Shakespeare Stout and Pyramid Espresso Stout also work well for this purpose. Canadian brew fans should check out Brock's Extra Stout by Niagara Falls Brewing.

Birdy Brews

Chicken and turkey are sweet and mild in flavor. A bitter beer contrasts interestingly with the sweet meats. Sweet beers bring out the flavors in various sauces. Game birds like duck and goose are stronger-flavored and more on the oily side and therefore need a stronger potion.

Here are some quick suggestions for mixing fowl and beer:

> **Bar Talk**
> Good beer needs no excuse. One should drink it because it's pleasing to drink and not because it contains any specific number of calories or because it is either good or bad for you.
>
> —Anonymous comment, 1934

➤ **Extra Special Bitter (ESB):** Chicken and turkey benefit from the extra hop kick of an ESB. The buttery flavor found in good ESBs is almost gravy-like in its piquancy. Anderson Valley Belks ESB or Oasis Capstone ESB are a few American varieties worth tasting.

➤ **Fruit Beers and Lambics:** Though not a true lambic, Samuel Adams Cranberry Lambic and turkey are a natural. Liefmans Frambozenbier is so good I hate to ruin it by drinking it with food, but this raspberry ale is ambrosial with chicken, turkey, Cornish hens, and duck. Chapeau makes several exotic lambics that make great refreshers with bird, including their peche (peach) and mirabelle (plum). Lindemans Kriek Lambic is also a fine offering with roast duck made with cherries and turkey made with cranberries.

➤ **Winter Warmers, Spiced Beer:** Goose and turkey tend to be consumed around the holidays, making them perfect for winter-warmer-style beers that pop up in profusion before Thanksgiving. California offerings like Anchor Our Special Ale or Samuel Smith's Winter Welcome Ale work perfectly. Or check your local microbrewery for their winter-warmer and holiday offerings.

➤ **Bock and Doppelbock:** Bocks and doppelbocks are big, malty brews with an alcoholic kick. They are made for feasting and nothing could be finer with a smoked wild turkey leg or smoked duck. Granville Island Bock from Vancouver, Canada, is one fine bock. Celebrator Doppelbock is a profoundly rich doppelbock. German weizenbocks are also excellent with smoked bird.

Oasis Capstone ESB makes any chicken walk like an Egyptian.

Steak Me to Your Liter: Beef Beers

England may have its ale tradition, but they named the yeoman of the queen's guard Beefeaters, not ale-drinkers. Red meat is the richest of meats and needs an assertive brew. While the classic pale ales and bitters are a natural with beefy British cuisine, some of the denser and stronger ales listed below are a nifty fit for your royal table.

➤ **Pale Ale and IPA:** The English classic pairing. Samuel Smith's India Pale Ale makes even hamburger a feast. For a classy Belgian abbey-style pale ale, try Corsendonk Monk's Pale Ale.

➤ **Old Ale:** Old ales have a sherry-like flavor and their princely lineage graces the taste of roast beef, Yorkshire pudding, and steak. Old Peculier and Thomas Hardy are widely available English classics. Third Coast Old Ale from Kalamazoo Brewing in Michigan and Old Foghorn from Anchor Brewing are a few great old American ales.

➤ **Porter:** Porter is a dark, strong brew made for heavier cuts of meat and spicy cold cuts like pastrami, corned beef, and beef salami. Porter and porterhouse steak sound like a winning combo. Pick one up from your local microbrewery.

Lamb Chops and Hops

Lamb is another popular meat in the British Isles and one more food that fits in nicely with British and Scottish beer styles. Here's a quick list of suggestions:

➤ **Brown Ale:** I wouldn't pull the wool over your eyes with this one. A fruity, sweet, and clean brown ale fixes up lamb from chops to spicy gyros. Newcastle Brown Ale is the granddaddy of the style. One of the best browns around is the Canadian Griffon Brown Ale from the Brasserie McAuslan in Montreal.

➤ **Scotch Ale:** There's more sheep than people in Scotland, and this is one beer style that was meant for the local lamby victuals. A lighter offering such as 60 shilling ale is great for the sandwiches, while a more potent 80 or 90 shilling would grace the classic rack of lamb.

➤ **Bière de Garde:** This spicy malty potion from northern France is traditionally drunk with lamb, rabbit, fruit, and strong cheeses. Two wonderful bières de garde are Jade Organic French Country Ale and St. Amand.

Slamming with Ham

The other white meat can be sweet or salty, greasy or lean, depending on whether you're eating ham, bacon, pork chops, or sausage. Whatever the cut, a quenching, malty beer is what's called for. Here's a quick list of beers to mix with various pig products:

➤ **Dortmunder:** Dortmunder is a pale, crisp lager that readily cures the thirst associated with salty meats like ham, sausage, and bacon. Dortmunder Union is the classic in the style, while a great American lager is Stout's Export Gold from Pennsylvania.

➤ **Wheat Ale:** It's a treat to drink your wheat with whatever food you eat. Berliner Weisse is the most refreshing wheat beer around. Other hefe-trub German wheats can grace any table whether you're serving cold cuts or glazed ham. The highly

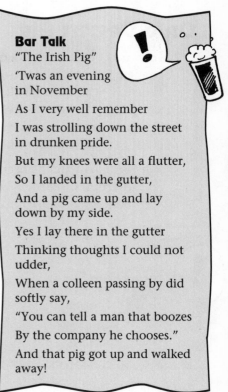

Bar Talk

"The Irish Pig"

'Twas an evening in November
As I very well remember
I was strolling down the street in drunken pride.
But my knees were all a flutter,
So I landed in the gutter,
And a pig came up and lay down by my side.
Yes I lay there in the gutter
Thinking thoughts I could not udder,
When a colleen passing by did softly say,
"You can tell a man that boozes
By the company he chooses."
And that pig got up and walked away!

rated Austrian wheat, Edelweiss Dunkel, and Edelweiss Kristallklar have a clovey, vanilla, and smoke character that brings out the zing in baked ham.

➤ **Amber Ale or Lager:** An ale such as St. Stan's Amber Alt is soft and refreshing; its sweetness draws out the subtle flavors of better cuts of pork. Amber lagers are reminiscent of Vienna-style beer, a natural when it comes to bacon and ham.

➤ **Abbey Ale:** The spicy overtones and dryness of an abbey ale makes this brew an answered prayer to your pork dinner. Affligem Triple is irresistible with sausages.

➤ **Belgian Red:** The talented brewers of Belgium's premier red beer recommend pork chops with Rodenbach and prunes.

On a Dessert Ale

Folks don't generally associate beer and dessert, but as the song goes, the times they are-a-changing. Beer is fermented sugar and it's a neat treat for any sweet. Dessert beers are generally of a higher quality with fruit and spice overtones. Dark-as-night beers side-by-side with chocolate are divine decadence that set the teeth aching at the very thought. The dark beers also work well as after-dinner digestifs poured in a brandy snifter or wine glass. Here are some specific suggestions for matching desserts and beer:

➤ **Wit:** Wits are the beers of choice with dessert because of their orange and spice overtones. Try them with apple pie and ice cream. Blanche de Bruges white beer has been immortalized frozen into a sorbet.

Bar Talk
Now thrice welcome Christmas!

Which brings us good cheer;

Mince pies and plum pudding

Strong ale and strong beer

—17th-century Christmas carol

➤ **Dark Lagers, Doppelbock, Eisbock and Triple Bock:** The strongest lagers in the world are Samichlaus beer at 14.7% and Samuel Adam's Triple Bock, which weighs in at a hefty 17%. These numbers even make a doppelbock blush. But their highly sweet malty overtones and sherry-like aftertaste make them perfect for creamy desserts, cakes, or chocolate. Kulmbacher Reichelbraü Eisbock from Bavaria already tastes like chocolate, whisky, and coffee, and is absolutely fabulous poured over ice cream (if you dare). Try an Optimator, Salvator, or Celebrator Doppelbock frozen into a popsicle.

➤ **Imperial and Oatmeal Stout, Barley Wine:** These are chocolatey beers with coffee, whisky, brandy, and sherry flavor profiles. Big Foot Barley Wine from Sierra Nevada will leave its imprint on puddings, chocolate cake, and ice cream. St. Ambroise Oatmeal stout is smoky, with a deeply roasted flavor. This beer is an apèritif by itself. Grant's Imperial Stout or Samuel Smith's Imperial Stout make dessert fit for a queen.

➤ **Fruit Lambic:** Once again, the fruity brews lend themselves to any fruit, vanilla, or sorbet. Drink Boon Kriek with tropical fruits and deliciously named Mort Subite Framboise with strawberry shortcake.

Foamy Fact

This Beer Is a Killer: One of the most impressive-tasting Belgian lambics is Mort Subite, which means "sudden death" in French. The name actually comes from the Mort Subite Cafe in Brussels, where a dice game was played by bank workers on their lunch hour. When they had to go back to work, they would switch to the "sudden death rule" so the winner would take all. The French word for coffin is *bière*, so Belgians make a pun by saying Mort Subite is *de bière a bière,* or the beer of the coffin.

Barbecue Brew

Now here's a beer tradition! Brews are consumed before, during, and after a barbecue and are occasionally used to put out fires caused by hot grease dripping onto the coals. You won't want to waste these beers on your combustible conflagrations, so keep a bucket of water handy for emergencies. Or just push your grill into the swimming pool.

➤ **Abita Turbo Dog:** I don't know what beer style this is, maybe a dark ale, but I beat a path to the door of anyone serving Abita Turbo Dog. It's made from medicinal spring waters near Lake Pontchartrain.

Abita Turbo Dog is a Louisiana love call that makes any barbecue a Mardi Gras.

➤ **Rauchbier:** Smoked beer with smoked meat might be a little too, well, smoky for some folks, but the flavors complement each other in strange and unusual ways. This is for rauch lovers only. Try Rauchenfels Steinbier, Schlenkerla Rauchbier, or Rogue Smoke. If you want to overdose on smoke, try the French peat-smoked offering Adelscott Bièr au Malt à Whisky from the Fischer Brewing Co.

➤ **American Ale:** Great microbrewed American ales are the long-lost companions to the backyard grill offerings. Find some ale on sale and pick up a case for your pals.

Hasta La Pasta: Beer and Italian Food

Beer is not exactly a specialty in the land of wine and olives. But northern Italy butts up against Austria and Switzerland, two countries rich in beer tradition. Acidic tomatoes call for a soft, smooth lager, while cheeses and cream sauces benefit from more tart and winy offerings. Here are some suggestions for mixing pasta with beer:

➤ **Italian Beer:** There aren't an overwhelming number of breweries in Italy, but the Moretti brewery in Udine, in northeast Italy, makes some of the best the Italians have to offer. Their La Rossa Doppiomalto pairs nicely with Northern Italian cuisine, garlic-laden foods, and hard Italian cheese.

➤ **Vienna Lager:** This red, malty beer is a pasta lover's delight. Try a Spaten Ur-Märzen or an American-brewed red lager.

Spice is Nice: Indian, Oriental, and Spicy Asian Food

Indian and Asian food can be eye-watering, nose-running, and sweat-inducingly hot. Curries, chutneys, and chilies call for a fire-extinguishing beer. I've put white sugar on my tongue to put out a pepper fire, but why mess with sugar when the brewer's done it all for you? Here are a couple of quick suggestions if you're considering mixing fire and brew:

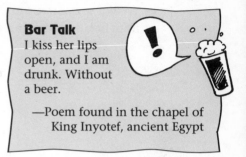

Bar Talk
I kiss her lips open, and I am drunk. Without a beer.

—Poem found in the chapel of King Inyotef, ancient Egypt

➤ **Asian Lagers:** Singha from Thailand, Tiger Pilsner from Singapore, Sun Lik from Hong Kong, and Tsingtao from China can't hold their own against all-malt lagers from the West, but they're the perfect antidote to the beautiful burn of Kung Pao peppers.

➤ **Japanese Beer:** Japanese beers are ricey and light, but some, like Sapporo Black Stout Draft, are full-bodied and high in alcohol and do a good job on the hot stuff. Suntory and Asahi go well with rice, fish, and noodle dishes.

Flying Burrito Brews: Mexican Food

If ever a regional cuisine begged for a brew, it's Mexican munchies. The first brewery in the New World was said to have been in Mexico in the 1500s. Germans immigrated to Mexico in the last century and started brewing lager there. Cheese, chips, beans, salsa, and corn call for light beers. Corn is not a great adjunct in beer, but blends in well with tamales and tortillas.

➤ **Mexican Lagers:** There is a lot of bad Mexican *cerveza* around. It's watery and sour because it's lagered for short periods of time, cut with corn, and barely hopped. The requisite lime adds about the only flavor. There are, however, a few good Latin American beers that are worth serving at your next fiesta. Carta Blanca's not a bad brew, and Superior is a good jalapeño halter. Negra Modelo is a Vienna-style beer that's worth trying. Dos Equis is drinkable as well.

➤ **Chili Beer:** This is more along the lines of a dare than fine dining. See if you can eat five-alarm habeñero salsa and wash it down with some Cave Creek Chili Beer. You better go outdoors for this experiment. And give someone a bucket of water to douse you with.

➤ **Brazilian Black Beer:** Amazonian Indians have been brewing a black beer since before Colombian times. It's black as an Irish stout. According to *The Encyclopedia of Beer*, beer historian Alan Eames "discovered" it and began brewing Xingu (shin-gu) in Brazil from an ancient recipe to go with peppers, corn, potatoes, and other New World delicacies.

161

The Least You Need to Know

➤ Beer can balance the flavors of almost any food.

➤ There are beer styles that have been matched with foods for centuries.

➤ Try the suggestions in this chapter for mixing beer with different kinds of food, from bread to Mexican food.

Chapter 14

A Dash of Pepper, a Splash of Brew: Cooking with Beer

In This Chapter

➤ How to cook with beer

➤ Recipes for marinades, soups, meats, desserts, and more

Cooking with beer is an exhilarating experience. Whether you're using a Pilsner, a stout, or a lambic, beer cookery melds together flavors that are unique in the world of culinary arts. And the beauty of beer is that it will blend with almost any food. The flavors in beer that are bitter, malt-sweet, tart, and tangy can highlight similar flavors in food. Beer can be used in almost any recipe that calls for soup broth or water. You can think of it as a gravy. Homebrewers have even more to work with. The spent malt can be baked into bread and malt syrup can be substituted for honey, sugar, or maple syrup.

The tradition of cooking with beer is as old as the drink itself. Many cultures have favorite recipes that blend in the brew. The national dish of Flemish Belgium is Carbonnade— a beef stew with a beer base. Scots cook gingerbread with 90 shilling ale. The English marinate venison in ale, the Irish poach salmon in porter, and the Danes eat a breakfast soup made from beer.

Saucy Suds: Beer Marinades, Sauces, and Dressings

Throughout its history, beer has been poured over almost every conceivable food (and not a few noggins). Sauces, marinades, and dressings are where beer comes into its own. Here are a few no-muss, no-fuss recipes to get you started.

Rauch-and-Roll Meat Marinade

This smoked beer marinade is to die for. Soak any meat you want to barbecue in this mix—the longer it marinates, the better it tastes. Serves two to four people. Here's what you'll need:

1–2 pounds of chicken, beef, pork, or game
1 bottle Schlenkerla Rauchbier or other smoked beer

1 tablespoon olive oil

2 tablespoons Worcestershire sauce

1 teaspoon chili powder

1 teaspoon curry powder

$1/2$ teaspoon each rosemary, thyme, and marjoram

$1/2$ teaspoon salt or 1 teaspoon soy sauce

1 sliced jalapeño pepper or Tabasco sauce to taste (optional)

1. Combine all ingredients in a plastic food container.

2. Thoroughly wash the meat you are going to use under cold water in the sink, then add it to the liquid marinade in the food container. Make sure the meat is completely covered with liquid.

3. Seal and refrigerate meat and marinade for at least four hours. This marinade will keep for two days in the refrigerator.

4. To prepare, slowly roast meat on charcoal or gas grill. Pour marinade over meat while grilling.

Lovely Lambic Salad Dressing

This is an amazing salad dressing with spicy, fruit flavor. It works great over any salad greens. Try it with endive, raddichio, cucumbers, and butternut lettuce. Here's what you'll need:

2 tablespoons Dijon mustard

$1/4$ cup wine vinegar

$1/2$ cup Lindemans Framboise or other raspberry lambic

$1/2$ cup olive oil

2 tablespoons oregano, chopped parsley, marjoram, and thyme

1 clove finely minced garlic

2 tablespoons freshly squeezed lime juice

salt and pepper to taste

1. Mix all the ingredients in a bowl or food processor.

2. Store leftovers in a cruet or a clean, used salad dressing bottle.

3. This dressing will keep indefinitely in the refrigerator, but the olive oil tends to solidify at cold temperatures. If refrigerated, let warm, and shake well before using.

Tasty Tip
When the recipes call for chicken broth, you can use canned broth that is available in your grocery store. Of course, making your own from chicken or beef is the best. Consult a cookbook for recipes. If you don't have any broth, use water with instant broth powder or bouillon cubes. If you don't have that, just use water or more beer to taste.

Luscious Lager Linguini Sauce

This sauce takes 15 minutes to prepare and works great on angel hair, linguini, tortellini, or other pasta. Serves two to four people. Here's what you'll need:

2 tablespoons butter

3 tablespoons olive oil

1 tablespoon flour

1 or 2 cloves minced garlic

1 cup Moretti Italian beer or other premium Pilsner

$^1/_2$ cup canned chicken broth or water

salt and pepper to taste

1 teaspoon each oregano and thyme

1 can (14 oz.) artichoke hearts, chopped

3 tablespoons fresh, chopped parsley or 1 tablespoon dried parsley

$^1/_4$ cup freshly grated Parmesan or Romano cheese

1 pound linguine, tortellini, or other pasta

1. Put two quarts of water and 1 tablespoon olive oil into a large pot and turn heat on high. Begin to prepare the sauce (see step 2, below). When water comes to a rolling boil, add pasta and cook until tender.

2. Meanwhile, melt butter over medium heat in a saucepan.

3. Add olive oil and stir in the garlic and flour. Continue to stir until flour is brown.

4. Slowly pour in the beer and chicken broth or water and lower heat to simmer.

5. Add salt, pepper, oregano, thyme, artichoke hearts, and parsley. Continue to stir until sauce thickens.

6. Add half the cheese.

7. Pour sauce over drained pasta and toss.

   Serve with the remaining grated cheese for sprinkling on top.

Soupy Suds and Stews

Dinner guests in my kitchen have been shocked when they've seen me open a 22-ounce bottle of premium beer and dump it all into the soup simmering on the stove. Their shock turns to murmurs of satisfaction when they taste the final result. Beer is barley soup, and the soupy possibilities are endless.

Urquell Onion Soup

This is a traditional French onion soup with a twist—a healthy dose of Bohemian Pilsner beer. Serves eight. Here's what you'll need:

4 large white or yellow onions

$1/_4$ cup butter

$1/_4$ cup olive oil

2 tablespoons brown sugar

22 oz. Pilsner Urquell

1 oz. brandy, cognac, sherry, or dry white wine (optional)

6 cups chicken broth or beef broth, or any combination of the two

1 tablespoon fresh thyme

salt and pepper to taste

grated Parmesan or Romano cheese to taste

croutons

1. Peel the onions, cut the top and bottom ends off and discard. Slice the onions as thinly as possible.

2. Melt the butter in a large saucepan. Add olive oil and onions. Sauté the onions until clear, about eight minutes.

3. Add sugar and cook, stirring often, until onions turn brown.

4. Add the chicken and/or beef broth and scrape pan well to loosen food stuck to pan.

5. Pour in Pilsner beer and add the brandy, cognac, sherry, or dry white wine.

6. Add thyme leaves, salt, and pepper and bring to a boil.

7. Reduce heat to simmer; cover and cook for one hour.

8. Skim foam that rises to the top.

   To serve, pour over croutons and top with grated cheese. Serve with a premium porter.

Loch Ness Cock-a-leekie with Scotch Ale

Cock-a-leekie is a traditional Scottish chicken stew with leeks. It's supposed to be made with tough old birds that need hours of cooking. I've substituted tender low-fat chicken breasts, some Scotch ale, and a shot of single malt Scotch whisky to make this dish good enough to lure Nessie from her loch. Serves four to six. Here's what you'll need:

Delicious Cock-a-leekie is made with a great Scotch ale like Loch Ness.

3 whole, skinned, boneless chicken breasts	$1/2$ cup pearl barley
2 tablespoons olive oil	1 bay leaf
4 leeks, white part only	$1/2$ teaspoon salt
3–5 cups chicken broth or water	$1/2$ teaspoon pepper, thyme, and sage
1 pint of Scotch ale	3 tablespoons minced parsley
1 oz. single malt Scotch whisky (optional)	8 whole pitted prunes (optional, but traditional)

1. Preheat oven to 400°F.

2. Cut chicken breasts into long strips. Cut the leeks in half and wash them well.

3. Chop the leeks.

4. In a large frying pan, heat olive oil. Add chicken and cook until brown.

5. Remove the chicken and add the leeks. Sauté leeks until they are slightly brown.

6. Pour the Scotch ale into a measuring cup and add the shot of whisky. (Go ahead, have a taste, it won't hurt you.)

7. Add all the ingredients—except prunes and parsley—to a large saucepot.

continues

continued

8. Put in enough chicken broth or water to give it your desired consistency. Bring to a boil.

9. Carefully pour the whole thing into a large casserole dish, cover, and put it in the oven. Bake for 30 minutes.

10. Add the prunes, if desired, and bake an additional 15 minutes or until barley is tender and chicken is thoroughly cooked.

   Remove the bay leaf, sprinkle with the parsley, and serve.

Spicy Chili-Beer Gazpacho

Gazpacho looks like salsa and is more of a liquid salad than a soup. Serve it cold on steamy summer nights when it's too hot to cook. Chili beer is lager beer with a chili pepper floating in the bottle. It gives this cold soup a nice pepper burn and calls for a nice pale ale to wash it down. Serves six to eight. Here's what you'll need:

$2^1/_2$ cups V8 vegetable juice or tomato juice

12 oz. Crazy Ed's Cave Creek Chili Beer or other chili pepper beer

$^1/_2$ cup minced red onion

2 cups chopped cherry tomatoes or other sweet tomato

1 cup seeded, diced red bell pepper

1 cup peeled, diced cucumber

$^1/_2$ cup chopped green onions

$^1/_2$ cup chopped fresh parsley

$^1/_4$ cup chopped fresh basil

2 cloves minced garlic

$^1/_4$ cup freshly squeezed lime juice

2 tablespoons cider vinegar

1 tablespoon chopped fresh tarragon or $^1/_4$ teaspoon dried tarragon

salt and pepper to taste

1. Combine all ingredients in a bowl.

2. Pour half of the mixture into a blender or food processor and purée.

3. Return to bowl and stir well.

4. Cover and refrigerate for at least three hours.

Malty Meats

When cooking with meat, beer can be blended into a recipe, used as a sauce, or used as a marinade. You can even boil bratwurst in it. Beer can be substituted for broth or water to give any main dish an extra added attraction.

Low-Fat Brats, Brew, and Onions

This is a traditional dish using turkey or chicken bratwurst as a low-fat alternative. If you're on a high-fat diet, use regular pork or beef brats. Wash it down with a wheat, Dortmunder, alt, or Vienna-style beer. Serves four. Here's what you'll need:

2 tablespoons olive oil

3 cups thinly sliced yellow or white onions

1 minced jalapeño pepper (optional)

2 pounds turkey, chicken, or other bratwurst

24 oz. German or German-style dunkel (dark) lager

salt and pepper to taste

1. Add the olive oil to a skillet and sauté the onions over medium heat until clear.
2. Add the bratwurst and cook for about ten minutes.
3. Add beer and jalapeño pepper and simmer the mixture for about 20 minutes.
4. Remove the onions with a slotted spoon and arrange on plates.
5. Place the bratwurst on top of the onions.
6. Add salt and pepper to the beer mixture and pour over the bratwurst and onions.

Coc à la Rouge Bière

Coc à la Rouge Bière means chicken with red beer. This recipe uses a Belgian red ale. It makes beery the traditional French dish *coc au vin*, or chicken in wine. The premier Belgian red is Rodenbach. It costs a little more than your average beer, but you'll forget the cost once you taste this chicken dish. Serves four. Here's what you'll need:

1 whole cut-up broiler or roasting chicken (about 4 pounds)

4 tablespoons olive oil

$3/4$ cup chopped red onion

1 thinly sliced carrot

2 cloves minced garlic

2 tablespoons flour

2 tablespoons minced fresh parsley

1 tablespoon minced fresh marjoram or 1 teaspoon dried marjoram

1 bay leaf

$1/2$ teaspoon dried thyme

1 teaspoon salt

$1/2$ teaspoon black pepper

1 tablespoon brandy (optional)

12 oz. Rodenbach Belgian red ale or Rodenbach Grand Cru

$1/2$ pound sliced mushrooms

continues

continued

1. Wash the chicken thoroughly.

2. Pour the olive oil into a large soup pot and lightly brown the onion, carrot, and garlic.

3. Push the vegetables aside in the pot and brown the chicken.

4. Stir in the flour, parsley, marjoram, bay leaf, thyme, salt, and pepper.

5. Pour in the Rodenbach ale and the brandy.

6. Cover and simmer chicken over low heat until done, about one hour.

7. In the last five minutes of cooking, add the mushrooms.

   Serve the chicken on a hot platter with sauce and vegetables poured over it.

Flambéed Imperial Steak Au Poivre

Steak au poivre is steak with crushed black pepper. Half a bottle of imperial stout makes this a dish fit for a Czar and Czarina. Flambéing the meat in cognac at the end makes this meal as dramatic as Rasputin. Accompany the steak with barley wine in a brandy snifter. Here's what you'll need:

1-inch-thick strip sirloin or filet mignon steaks, about 1/2 pound of meat per person.

1 tablespoon whole peppercorns per steak

2 teaspoons salt

2 tablespoons butter

2 tablespoons olive oil

1 teaspoon Worcestershire sauce

2 tablespoons lemon juice

8 oz. Samuel Smith Imperial Stout or other imperial stout

2 oz. cognac or brandy (optional)

1. Trim fat from the steaks.

2. Crush whole peppercorns on a cutting board with a rolling pin. They should be coarse, not finely crushed.

3. Brush the steaks lightly with a small amount of the imperial stout.

4. Press the pepper into the steaks, and work it into both sides of the meat with the heel of your hand.

5. Over medium-high heat, sprinkle the bottom of a skillet with the salt.

6. When the salt begins to brown, add the steaks.

7. Reduce to medium heat and turn steaks, cooking to desired doneness.

8. In a separate pan, melt the butter and add the olive oil, Worcestershire sauce, lemon juice, and remaining beer.

9. Remove the steaks from the pan and discard pan drippings. Pour the butter/beer mixture over the steaks.

10. To flambé, make sure cognac or brandy is warmed to at least room temperature.

11. Return steak to skillet, turn heat on high, and quickly add the liquor. If it does not flame up, carefully touch the side of the pan with a match. In the unlikely event that the flames get out of hand, douse with baking soda. (Don't burn your house down!)

Foamy Fact

I've Heard of Steak and Ale, but this Is Ridiculous: A strong ale brewed in England uses beef or meat as a secret ingredient. Served at Levens Hall, Cumberland, the recipe was brought during the Crusades by Howard "From Beyond the Sea." It was buried during the 17th century and dug up later. The brew is called Morocco ale and is presumably not fat-free.

Krieky Pork Cutlets

This recipe calls for a sweetish cherry lambic to enhance the flavor of the boneless pork loin. It's low in fat, about five grams per serving. Eat this dish with a saison or strong Belgian ale on the side. Serves four. Here's what you'll need:

4 slices boneless pork loin (4 oz. each)	8 oz. kriek (cherry) lambic
1/4 teaspoon salt and pepper	1/2 cup chicken broth
1 teaspoon each butter and olive oil	1 teaspoon cornstarch
2 large shallots, finely chopped (about 1/3 cup)	1/3 cup half-and-half
	1 teaspoon Dijon mustard

1. With a meat mallet, pound each pork loin until it is 1/4-inch thick.

2. Sprinkle both sides with salt and pepper.

continues

continued

3. In a medium skillet, melt butter over medium heat and add olive oil.

4. Add the pork and brown for two minutes on each side.

5. Remove pork from pan and set aside. Add shallots to skillet and cook, stirring for one minute.

6. Add the kriek lambic and cook for two minutes. Add stock and cook for five minutes.

7. In a measuring cup, mix cornstarch into half-and-half and stir until it is dissolved.

8. Add the mixture to the skillet and simmer for two minutes. Stir in the mustard.

9. Return pork to skillet and simmer for three minutes.

   To serve, place pork on plate and pour sauce over it.

Foamy Fishy Dishes

Beer may be used liberally with meat and poultry dishes. Hops and malt, however, can overpower the subtle flavors of some seafood. With wise use, beer can make the most of crustaceans, chowders, and other fine finned flavors.

Crescent City Brown Ale Bouillabaisse

Bouillabaisse is basically a fisherman's stew that can be cooked up with whatever seafood is on hand. This recipe calls for shellfish and/or fish. Add a mild brown ale to sweeten up the pot and cut the heat of the Cajun spice and you'll be ready to let the good times roll. Wash this down with Dixie Blackened Voodoo Lager or other dark lager. Serves eight. Here's what you'll need:

3 tablespoons butter

4 pounds of any combination lobster tails, clams, shrimp, mussels, red snapper, salmon fillets, scallops, or halibut—all cleaned, boned, and removed from shell where necessary

1 teaspoon cayenne pepper

$1/_2$ teaspoon paprika

3 teaspoons salt

1 teaspoon black pepper

12 oz. brown ale

5 cloves minced garlic

4 medium tomatoes, diced

1 red onion, sliced

1 cup cubed potatoes

1–3 jalapeño peppers (to taste)

1 teaspoon saffron (optional)

3 tablespoons chopped parsley

4 cups fish stock or 1 cup clam juice mixed with 3 cups water

2 tablespoons lemon juice

1. Heat the butter in a large stock pot over medium heat.

2. Mix cayenne pepper, paprika, black pepper, and salt on a large plate.

3. Roll cleaned seafood in the seasoning or sprinkle seasoning on seafood.

4. Sauté seafood in butter for about three minutes. Add beer and simmer about eight minutes.

5. Add minced garlic, tomatoes, red onion, cubed potatoes, jalapeño peppers, saffron, and parsley. Cook for about one minute.

6. Pour in fish stock or clam juice and water. Simmer until potatoes are soft.

   Serve hot in large soup bowls with crusty French bread.

Wit Fish: Cod and Leeks in Orange-Wit-Tomato Sauce

Wit beer has a honey character and an orange finish. With a coriander overtone, it makes an excellent addition to this delish fish dish. I recommend using authentic Belgian wit beer with this recipe. A Trappist ale would make a great accompaniment to this meal. Serves four. Here's what you'll need:

1 teaspoon olive oil

3 large leeks, cut in half, cleaned and sliced

1 large sweet red pepper, diced

3 cloves garlic, slivered

3 medium potatoes, peeled and cubed

8 oz. wit beer

$1/3$ cup pitted green olives

1 medium tomato, chopped

$1/2$ cup orange juice

4 cod fillets (about 5 oz. each)

3 tablespoons fresh parsley or cilantro

1. Boil potatoes in a saucepan for 10 minutes.

2. Meanwhile, heat olive oil over a low heat in a large skillet.

3. Add leeks to skillet and cook for five minutes, stirring occasionally.

4. Add pepper and garlic and cook two more minutes.

5. Add beer, cooked potatoes, olives, tomato, and orange juice.

6. Lay the cod fillets on top of the vegetables and cook for 10 to 12 minutes, or until fish flakes with a fork.

7. Transfer fish to warm dinner plates.

8. Stir parsley into sauce, then spoon sauce over the fillets.

   Serve with green salad and crusty dark bread.

Doppel-licious Desserts

If you can't imagine beer-laced desserts, just think of rum cake or liqueur-filled chocolates and you'll get the idea. Dark doppelbocks, eisbocks, porters, and stouts can be poured directly over fruit and ice cream, or drizzled into coffee drinks. The only thing holding you back is your imagination.

Frozen Framboise: Raspberry Lambic Sorbet

This frozen treat gives a whole new meaning to the term ice beer. If you don't have an ice cream maker, follow the instructions for making it in the freezer compartment of your refrigerator. Serves four. Here's what you'll need:

$1/2$ pound fresh raspberries

$1/2$ cup sugar

$1 1/4$ cup water

2 teaspoons freshly grated ginger

1 cup chilled Belgian framboise (raspberry lambic)

1. Pour the water, sugar, and raspberries into a medium saucepan.

2. Bring to a boil, stirring occasionally.

3. Cook about five minutes until the raspberries are mushy. Allow to cool.

4. Pour the mixture into a food processor and purée until smooth.

5. Chill in the refrigerator, then pour in chilled framboise. Freeze in an ice cream freezer.

6. If you do not have an ice cream freezer, set the freezer compartment on your refrigerator at its coldest setting.

7. Pour the mixture into improvised molds (plastic cups or containers). Freeze covered for one to two hours, until nearly firm.

8. Remove icy mixture from containers, place in a large bowl, and beat with an electric mixer, or whirl in a food processor for two to three minutes.

9. Return to plastic containers and freeze two to three more hours until firm. For the smoothest texture, repeat this process again.

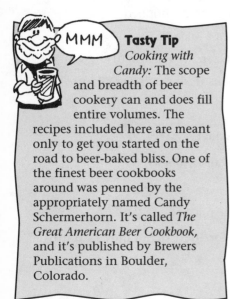

MMM

Tasty Tip
Cooking with Candy: The scope and breadth of beer cookery can and does fill entire volumes. The recipes included here are meant only to get you started on the road to beer-baked bliss. One of the finest beer cookbooks around was penned by the appropriately named Candy Schermerhorn. It's called *The Great American Beer Cookbook*, and it's published by Brewers Publications in Boulder, Colorado.

Quickie Ale Chocolate Cake

This is the easiest cake to bake, because the first step in making it is a trip to the grocery store where you'll buy whatever kind of instant chocolate cake mix you desire. Then pick a beer to use in place of the water called for in the recipe. Follow the rest of the instructions on the side of the box and see what happens. It should work great, but if it's a mess, don't blame me, just try it again. Kitchen science in action! Here's what you'll need:

➤ Store-bought instant chocolate cake mix that calls for water, oil, and eggs to be added to the mix. *Caution:* Do not use any mix that calls for milk.

➤ Any of the following beers: Kulmbacher Reichelbraü Eisbock, Irish stout, porter, doppelbock, old ale, imperial stout, or barley wine.

If the instructions call for 1 cup of water, use 1 cup of beer. If the instructions call for $1^1/_2$ cups of water, use that much beer. You get the idea. Follow the rest of the instructions on the box.

The Least You Need to Know

➤ Beer can be substituted for water or broth in many recipes.

➤ Beer makes an interesting ingredient for recipes from starters to desserts.

Part 4
Around the World in 80 Beers: A Beer-Lover's Travel Guide

A world traveler would be hard-pressed to find any city, town, village, or backwater outpost where there is no beer. Even in the Middle East, where the religion of Islam forbids the drinking of alcohol, beers are surreptitiously consumed—sometimes at great risk to the imbiber's life and limb. In some out-of-the-way locales where there is no commercially made product, beer is homebrewed from such local delicacies as corn, millet, and rice flour. And in brewing countries like Germany, one small village may have several breweries.

In Part 4 of this book, we're going to take a world tour and visit almost every country and region where beer is brewed, from Munich to Mali, in Africa. We're going to discuss a quick overview of each region's brewing history, beers brewed there, special events, and things not to miss if you visit. Jules Verne may have traveled around the world in 80 days, but we can sit back, relax, and travel 'round the world in 80 beers.

Note: I've tried to be very accurate about the addresses and phone numbers for each brewing site. However, area codes are changing with frightening regularity because of all the new fax lines, computer lines, and cell phones. In addition, Web site addresses change with great frequency. Please forgive any wrong area codes or Web site relocations you might encounter.

Chapter 15

Way Out West— Beer in the Western United States

In This Chapter

➤ An overview of the brewing scene in the United States west of the Mississippi River

➤ A region-by-region snapshot of brewpubs, microbreweries, breweries, beer festivals, and other beery sites

➤ Phone numbers, addresses, and Web sites related to western brewpubs, microbreweries, and breweries

---

The brewing scene in the United States is hot, hot, hot. The number of homebrewers is multiplying daily. Brewpubs and microbreweries are popping up almost everywhere. Microbrews are seen in TV sitcoms like *Friends* and discussed in national publications like *Time* and *Newsweek*. Even Wall Street has taken notice. Recent public stock offerings for Samuel Adams and Pete's Wicked Ale sold out in a matter of hours as the stock's prices climbed ever higher. (The stock's prices soon fell back to Earth. More on that in Chapter 22.) What's all this buzz about a simple drink like beer? I guess the answer is that Americans are an entrepreneurial lot and, to paraphrase the gold miners of 1849: "Thar's gold in them thar beers."

What's that mean for you and me? Options, entertainment, and plain old good times await eager brew trekkers across America. Cities like Portland, Oregon, seem to have a brewpub on every block. There's a beer *camp* in Kentucky (more on that later). And there's a slew of brew options for everybody, from the occasional imbiber to the true beer geek. So let's start where it all began, in California, and wind our way across the purple mountains' majesty and the amber waves of barley, from beer to eternity.

California Steamin'

California was claimed by the Spanish, English, and Russians in the centuries before the Gold Rush of '49—much to the chagrin of the Native Americans who had always lived there. Little is known about who was brewing what in the Golden State until 1837, when records tell us Adam Schuppert and a sailor named Billy the Brewer began making beer in San Francisco. When hoards of thirsty gold miners arrived a dozen years later, The Empire State Brewery was in full production in what is known today as the Mission District. By 1852, only three years later, San Francisco had grown from a few thousand folks to 36,000. There was one bar for every 100 men, women, and children living there.

When Fritz Maytag revived the Anchor Brewing Co. in 1965, another gold rush was born, this time for the more reliable gold in ale. After brewpubs were legalized in California in 1982, a veritable circus of copper pipe, old milking equipment, and new-fangled brewing systems was paraded before the ebullient public in bar after bar. More than a decade later, the California brew rush is still in happy progress.

California Hop Spots

MMM **Tasty Tip**
For complete information about all of California's delicious beer scene, pick up the *Celebrator Beer News* at P.O. Box 375, Hayward, CA, 94543; e-mail: CBeerNews@aol.com; Web site: http://www.celebrator.com. For a state-by-state listing of brewpubs and microbreweries on the Web, log on to the Institute for Brewing Studies brewery list at http://www.beertown.org/brews/brewlist.html.

If you were to begin at the Mexican border and head north through California, you would find at least 150 brewpubs and microbreweries, and at least that many beer festivals and celebrations. So let's hop in our brew-mobile, head on down toward San Diego, and work our way north through some of the most beautiful country on Earth.

In San Diego, the Karl Strauss brewpubs crank out an amazing variety of ales and lagers. Don't miss Karl Strauss' Brewery Gardens (9675 Scranton Road, Serrento Mesa in San Diego; 619-587-BREW), a 320-seat brewpub/restaurant, where you can wander five acres of manicured Oriental Gardens with a Koi pond, a crashing waterfall, babbling brooks, and quiet walking paths. You can also visit Karl's other brewpub: Karl Strauss' Old Columbia Brewery & Grill (1157 Columbia Street, San Diego; 619-234-BREW). Further up the coast, check out the dynamite porter at

La Jolla Brewing Company (7536 Fay Avenue, La Jolla; 619-456-BREW). La Jolla also offers a great happy hour, free pool tables, and free entertainment.

Brewpubs are the one thing the Los Angeles area does have a dearth of. A few notable exceptions are Belmont Brewing Co. (25 39th Place, Long Beach; 310-433-3891), and Manhattan Beach Brewing Co. (124 Manhattan Beach Boulevard., Manhattan Beach; 310-798-2744).

Santa Cruz is at the southernmost tip of Bay Area brewpub madness, which has a high density of suds makers. The Seabright Brewery Pub & Restaurant (519 Seabright Avenue, Suite 107, Santa Cruz; 408-426-2739) is three blocks from the ocean and features organic food. One of the first brewpubs in the U.S. since Prohibition ended is Buffalo Bills Brewery, (1082 "B" Street, Hayward; 510-886-9823). And don't forget Triple Rock Brewing in Berkeley (1920 Shattuck Avenue, Berkeley; 510-THE-BREW).

San Francisco flourishes with hot spots, including the elegant Gordon Biersch Brewery Restaurant (2 Harrison; 415-243-8246), the Twenty Tank Brewery (316 Eleventh Street; 415-255-9455), and Sankt Gallen Brewery (33 Bush Street; 415-296-8203). No trip would be complete without stopping by the Anchor Brewing Co., (1705 Mariposa Street; 415-863-8350), the company that started the craft brewing revolution in 1965. These tours are booked weeks in advance, so call ahead for reservations.

Foamy Fact

Too Brew to Be True: By 1860, the 40,000 inhabitants of San Francisco had 27 breweries operating within city limits—10 of them near North Beach. Twenty years later, there were 40 breweries, most of which made the "steam" beer style brewed today by Anchor Brewing Co. Steam beer, by the way, is now a registered trademark of Anchor Brewing.

Across the Golden Gate Bridge, you'll find the Marin Brewing Co. (1809 Larkspur Landing Circle, Larkspur; 415-461-4677), whose brewmaster and owner Brendan Moylan has won more than 15 medals at the Great American Beer Festival for his brews.

Northern California has a cornucopia of brewing landmarks. Napa Valley Brewing Co./Calistoga Inn (1250 Lincoln Avenue, Calistoga; 707-942-4104) offers mud baths, world-class dining, movie stars as guests—and of course—hand-crafted beer.

The Mendocino Brewing Co. (13351 Highway 101, Hopland; 707-744-1361) is the country's oldest post-Prohibition brewpub, opened in 1983; needless to say, it produces great brews to this day, with a new production facility coming online in the nearby town of Ukiah. Over in rural Boonville, Anderson Valley Brewing (14081 Highway 128, Boonville; 707-895-2337) used to make beer the old-fashioned way, in used milking equipment. Today a brand-new brewhouse is being built to keep up with demand for their high-quality product. Up in redwood country, Humboldt Brewing Co. (856 Tenth Street, Arcata; 707-826-2739) has world-class folk and blues entertainers singing over its suds. Go east to Chico and you'll find one of the country's original and largest micro-breweries at the Sierra Nevada Brewing Co. and Taproom (1075 East 20th, Chico; 916-893-3520). You'll holler "Eureka!" when you see the 19th-century–style tavern at the Lost Coast Brewery & Cafe (617 Fourth Street, Eureka; 707-445-4480).

The land of Bigfoot: Sierra Nevada Brewing in Chico, California. The Bigfoot Ale label is below.

Nevada Hop Spots

Nevada is known more for gambling than beer, but there are a few choice brewpubs in the land of buffet lunches and little old ladies with cups full of quarters. One of my favorite landmarks is the HOLY COW! Casino, Cafe & Brewery (2423 Las Vegas Boulevard South, Las Vegas; 702-732-2697), with 8,000 square feet of gambling, brewery, and eating. The black-and-white Holstein cow theme threatens to get out of hand here. Look out for the only 20-foot cow in red sunglasses on the Vegas Strip.

Over in the slightly quieter town of Sparks, you can drink an Ichthyosaur Pale Ale at the Great Basin Brewing Co. (846 Victorian Avenue, Sparks; 702-355-7711) in the renovated Victorian Square. The Union Brewery Co. (28 North C Street, Virginia City; 702-847-0328) has the racecar–driving owner's Indy 500 racecar parked in the middle of it, along with a beer museum.

Olympian Brews: The Pacific Northwest

The main contender for brewpub density is definitely the Pacific Northwest, where the damp, rainy climate has bred generations of ale drinkers similar to Scotland, Ireland, Wales, and England. In cities like Portland and Seattle, big, bad mega-brewers are losing market share as fast as the rain pours down Mount Rainier. And even tiny little towns in the rain forest can boast a brewery or two. From Mount Olympus to the Rogue River Wilderness in Oregon, the Cascade Mountains' creeks aren't the only things gushing profusely in the Pacific Northwest.

Oregon Hop Spots

Oregon is home to the ubiquitous McMenamin brothers, who operate 12 brewpubs and 33 taverns around the state that tend toward the counter-culture end of the brewing spectrum. The Hillsdale Brewery & Public House (1505 Southwest Sunset Boulevard, Portland; 503-246-3938) was the McMenamin's first and has a full menu with several vegetarian selections. The Thompson Brewery & Public House (3575 Liberty Road South, Salem; 503-363-7286) has psychedelic 1960s memorabilia with vegetarian and other food. The pièce de résistance is McMenamin's Edgefield Brewery (2126 Southwest Halsey, Troutdale; 503-667-4352), which is an upscale, elegant, 100-room hotel that started out as Multnomah County's poor farm in 1919. There's a winery, a brewery, gardens, two restaurants, a ballroom, a movie theater, European beer memorabilia, and an antique bar from the Portland Hotel.

Once a poor farm, the 100-room Edgefield Inn today boasts a brewery, a winery, a hotel, gardens, restaurants, a ballroom, and a theater.

Foamy Fact

Munich in the Rain: Oregon has more microbreweries and brewpubs, per capita, than any other state. It has a total of 54, giving those folks one craft brewery for every 50,000 Oregonians.

There's a new brewery where the old Rogue River Brewing used to be. It's called Siskyo Brewing Co. (31B Water Street, Ashland; 503-488-5061) and has been called the country's most beautiful brewery site, overlooking the wild Rogue River. And they've got some of the world's best beers and 21 kinds of pizza to boot.

Charming Eugene has its share of great brew, including the Eugene City Brewing Co./ West Bros. Bar-B-Q (844 Olive Street, Eugene; 541-345-8489). The Bay Front Brewery & Public House (748 Southwest Bay Boulevard, Newport; 541-472-1921) serves award-winning Rogue beer. The main Rogue brewery is housed in an old ship-building ware-house on the nearby water.

Foamy Fact

Saxer First Avenue: Oregon's first brewery was Liberty Brewery, built at First and Davis Streets in Portland in 1852 by a German immigrant named Henry Saxer. Saxer Brewing Co. in Lake Oswego is named after Herr Saxer.

Portland is crawling with highly recommended craft breweries, including B. Moloch Heathman Bakery & Pub/Widmer Bros. Brewing Co. (901 Southwest Salmon, Portland; 503-227-5700); Full Sail Riverplace Brewery (307 Southwest Montgomery, Portland; 503-222-5343); and BridgePort Brewing Co. (1313 Northwest Marshall, Portland; 503-241-7179). If you want to tour a large regional-style brewery, check out the Blitz-Weinhard Brewing Co. (1133 West Burnside Street, Portland; 503-222-4351). I've said it before and I'll say it again, any beer named Blitz is bound to be successful.

Oregon boasts some great beer festivals. In mid-July, the largest gathering of independent brewers in Oregon occurs at Waterfront Park in Portland for the Oregon Brewers' Festival (for more information, call 503-778-5917). Or check out the Brew & Brews Festival in mid-September in Corvallis (phone 503-754-6624).

Washington Hop Spots

Cross into the state named after the great beer lover who was also, incidentally, the father of our country. Washington is another state dense in brewery tradition. Cruising up I-5, drive up and see the blown top of Mount St. Helens outside of Woodland. When you're done, blow your mind with a tour of the gorgeous, glass-faced Pyramid Breweries building (110 West Marine Drive, Kalama; 360-673-2962) in Kalama. Their Espresso Stout is to die for, and this is where the first wheat beer since Prohibition was produced in America.

Visit the state capital in Olympia, and while you're there, visit Mary and Crayne Horton at their renowned Fishbowl Brewpub & Cafe (515 Jefferson Street Southeast, Olympia; 360-943-3650). Eat treats from their wood-fired oven and savor such delights as Trout Stout, Fish Tale Pale Ale, and Leviathan Barley Wine.

Seattle is beer geek paradise. In the University District, the Big Time Brewery (4133 University Way Northeast, Seattle; 206-545-4509) satisfies in a turn-of-the-century tavern, and sells growlers to go—so bring your own jug. The California & Alaska St. Brewery (4720 California Avenue Southwest, Seattle; 206-938-2476) is a cozy neighborhood brewpub with a wide selection of flavors. The Pacific Northwest Brewing Co. (322 Occidental Avenue South, Seattle; 206-621-7002), located in historic Pioneer Square, is as beautiful and elegant a brewpub as you'll ever find. Wood-clad conditioning tanks and a copper-topped bar are featured in this renovated warehouse. Down in Seattle's famous

Public Market you'll find the Pike Brewery (1432 Western Avenue, Seattle; 206-622-3373) run by beer *bon vivant* Charles Finkel. Charles also maintains the Museum of Brewing (Merchant du Vin, 140 Lakeside Avenue, Seattle 206-322-5022), which boasts a collection of brewing memorabilia.

Near the Kingdome is Pyramid Brewery and Hart Pub (1201 First Avenue South, Seattle; 206-68-BEERS; Web site at http://www.pyramidbrew.com) where Pyramid and Thomas Kemper beers are brewed and served. The pub has stately wood timbers and tables and serves a casual array of pub fare with fresh Pyramid and Thomas Kemper beers on tap. Tours are offered seven days a week. Another Seattle beer landmark is the Trolleyman Pub (3400 Phinney Avenue North, Seattle; 206-548-8000; Web site at http://www.halcyon.com/rh/rh.htlm), where Redhook Ales long brewed its ales before opening a new brewery in Woodinville. It's in an old trolley garage where the fireplace is the only thing allowed to smoke in the bar.

Tasty Tip
If you love your lager, the only brewpub in the Pacific Northwest dedicated to that drink is Thomas Kemper Brewing Co., located on the beautiful Olympic Peninsula. You can visit them for food, tours, and tastings at 22381 Foss Rd. Northeast, Poulsbo; 360-697-7899.

If you're heading into eastern Washington, the hop growing region of Yakima is where most of America's hops are produced. Visit some hop yards, then stop at Grant's Brewery Pub (32 North Front Street, Yakima; 509-575-2922) for some of the best brews in the world.

If you go way up north in Spokane, you don't have to be thirsty. Hale's Ales (East 5634 Commerce Avenue, Spokane; 509-534-7553) is the third oldest microbrewery in Washington. Fort Spokane Brewery (West 401 Spokane Falls Boulevard, Spokane; 509-838-3809) is built on the original sight of a long-vanished brewery that first opened its doors in 1889. The current brewpub is run by the great-great-grandnephew of those 19th-century brewers.

Washington's beer festival is held on gorgeous Bainbridge Island in mid-September; call 206-692-7293.

Alaska and Hawaii Hop Spots

I don't know how opposites like Alaska and Hawaii get lumped together, but if they do it in the weather reports, I can do it here.

Fiercely independent Alaska has been brewing in its own juices for quite sometime. The Alaskan Brewing & Bottling Co. (5429 Shaune Drive, Juneau; 907-780-5866) gets its beer water from the glacial runoff of the ice fields behind Juneau. Bird Creek Brewery (310 East 76th Street, Anchorage; 907-344-2473) is where folks in Anchorage get their beer.

> ### Foamy Fact
>
> *Wicki Wacki Beer:* In the decidedly warm climes of Hawaii, beer has had a tough history. Banned until 1900, today's Aloha brewers must deal with rent and labor costs that are about 60% higher than on the mainland. A six-pack seller can nail you for as much as $9 for a medium-quality beer. Old Hawaiian beer names like Primo, Pali, and Diamond Head are long gone. But the state finally legalized brewpubs in 1994.

California-based Gordon Biersch opened a traditional German-style brewpub in Aloha Tower Marketplace in Honolulu. Ali'i Brewing is experimenting with new Hawaiian hybrids such as Pineapple Pale Ale and Kona Coffee Stout. Kona Brewing Co. is rolling out the likes of Fire Rock Pale Ale on the Big Island of Hawaii. For more on the Hawaiian brewing scene, along with addresses and phone numbers of brewpubs there, contact *Brew Hawaii* at P.O. Box 852, Hauula, HI, 96717; 808-259-6884; e-mail: brew@lava.net.

Rocky Mountain High

Great beer takes great water, and some of the best H_2O in America tumbles from the snow-capped Rocky Mountains. That lovely landscape is also a major tourist destination, which makes it ripe for resort-area brewpubs. Throw in some thirsty skiers, movie stars, and cowboys, and you've got yourself a formula for beery success.

> ### Tasty Tip
> The folks who publish *Midwest Beer Notes* also publish the *Rocky Mountain Beer Notes*: 339 Sixth Ave., Clayton, WI; 715-948-2900. They've got the straight dope on the Rocky Mountain beer scene.

Idaho Hop Spots

When people think of Idaho think they of spuds instead of suds, which is too bad. Idaho has some of the most spectacular pristine wilderness in the lower 48 states. Up in Coeur d'Alene, T.W. Fisher's A Brew Pub (204 North Second Street, Coeur d'Alene; 208-664-2739) is the premier watering hole. Moscow boasts a university and two brewpubs: M.J. Barleyhoppers Brewery (507 South Main Street, Moscow; 208-883-4ALE) and Treaty Grounds Brewpub (West 2124 Pullman Road, Moscow; 208-882-3807). Down through the Snake River Wilderness into the Sun Valley area, you'll find the Sun Valley Brewing Co. (202 North Main Street, Hailey; 208-788-5777) in historic Hailey. They've won more gold and silver medals than I can list here, and they've got pub grub with a western twist. Up the road, check out Thunder Mountain Brewery (591 Fourth Street East, Ketchum; 208-726-1832) in Ernest Hemingway's beloved Ketchum.

If you're in Boise, you can chose between the Harrison Hollow Brewhouse (2455 Harrison Hollow, Boise; 208-343-6820) and the Table Rock Brewpub & Grill (705 West Fulton, Boise; 208-342-0944). North of Boise is the town of McCall, where the McCall Brewing Co. (807 North Third Street, McCall; 208-634-2333) offers astounding views of the mountains in the River of No Return Wilderness.

Montana Hop Spots

Folks up in Big Sky Montana have a slew of breweries all over their humongous state. From the Sawtooth Mountain grandeur of Missoula to the miles of prairie around Miles in the eastern part of the state, Montana's craft beer is a Butte.

In the western part of the state, the Iron Horse Brewpub (100 Railroad Street, Missoula; 406-721-8705) features beers brewed by Bavarian master brewer Jürgen Knöller. Slake your thirst in Bozeman at Spanish Peaks Brewing Co. & Cafe (120 North 19th Avenue, Bozeman; 406-585-2296). Billings is home to the Montana Brewing Co. (113 North Broadway, Billings; 406-252-9200) and the Yellowstone Valley Brewing Co. (2123-B, First Avenue North, Billings; 406-245-0918). Capital city Helena hosts the Brewhouse Brewpub & Grill (939 Getchell, Helena; 406-457-9390). While there you can tour the Kestler Brewing Co. (1439 Harris Street, Helena; 406-449-6214), a microbrewery. Miles from nowhere in the eastern Montana city of Miles City you can drink Cole Porter at the Golden Spur/Milestown Brewing Co. (1014 South Haynes Avenue, Miles City; 406-232-3544).

Utah Hop Spots

Utah has some of the most restrictive alcohol laws in the country, but brewpubs flourish in Salt Lake City, among the ski resorts of the Wasatch Mountains, and in red rock country. Brewpubs were first legalized in the state in 1986, but these folks have to keep the potency of their beer pretty low. When you're gazing at the spectacular sights, however, you might not notice.

Eddie McStiff's (57 South Main; Moab; 801-259-2337) dishes up the suds near Arches National Park. The Wasatch Brew Pub (250 Main, Park City; 801-645-9500) serves skiers on three floors. Squatters Pub Brewery (147 West Broadway, Salt Lake City; 801-363-2739) is located in a 100-year-old building.

Wyoming Hop Spots

Like the other sparsely populated states in the area, most of Wyoming's beer sights are in resort areas. Otto Brothers' Brewing Co. (1295 Northwest Street, Wilson; 307-733-9000) makes Moose Juice beer, gives tours, and has an Oktoberfest celebration near Jackson.

Jackson Hole Pub & Brewery (265 Milward, Jackson Hole; 307-739-BEER) is where to go after a tough day on the slopes.

Colorado Hop Spots

Colorado has the second-highest density of breweries per capita in the United States. A complete list of them here would be impossible, but here are a few highlights.

My favorite is the Flying Dog Brewpub (413 East Cooper, Aspen; 970-925-7464) in Aspen. This brewpub features such great beers as Rin Tin Tan, Doggie Style Beer, Hair of the Dog, and other canine brews. Flying Dog is right there in the middle of the wild and wacky promenade known as Aspen's Cooper Street Mall. While you're there you might have an opportunity to rub elbows with gonzo journalist Hunter S. Thompson in the Woody Creek Tavern (0002 Woody Creek Plaza, Aspen; 970-923-4585).

Gonzo artist Raolph Steadman designed this label for the Flying Dog Brewpub in Aspen, where all good road dogs meet.

Tasty Tip

MMM

Boulder is home to the Association of Brewers (303-447-0816), a non-profit organization devoted to collecting and disseminating information about beer and brewing for amateur and professional brewers. The association publishes dozens of books and several magazines about homebrewing, beer styles, brewing resources, and other topics. Every fall it puts on the Great American Beer Festival. The association can answer just about any question about beer and brewing.

Boulder boasts the Oasis Brewery & Restaurant (1095 Canyon Boulevard, Boulder; 303-449-0363), where the Egyptian motif will drive you Tuts. Up on Cripple Creek, the Wild Wild West Gambling Hall & Brewery (443 East Bennett Avenue, Cripple Creek; 719-689-3736) serves up Tex-Mex food with the loosest slot machines in town.

Other high-country brewpubs include: Carver Brewing Co. (1022 Main Avenue, Durango; 970-259-2545); Heavenly Daze Brewery and Grill (1860 Ski Times Square, Steamboat Springs; 970-879-8080); and Brewed & Baked in Telluride (127 South Fir, Telluride; 970-728-6324).

Down in Denver, the Wynkoop Brewing Co. (1634 18th Street, Denver; 303-297-2700) is Colorado's first—and formerly the world's largest—brewpub. (They were the world's largest until the 105,000-square-foot Red's opened in Edmonton, Canada. For more on that see Chapter 17.)

Colorado is also home of the Great American Beer Festival. For more on the GABF, see Chapter 10.

Happy Trails to Brew: Texas and the Southwest

It's dusty and dry in the Southwest. The cattle are lowing and the doggies are calling. What lonesome cowpoke hasn't dreamt of an ice-cold glass of beer while his spurs jingle-jangle-jingled across the parched sands? The new brewers of the purple sage have helped more than one cowgirl chase off the blues. So put down your saddle and lasso up a couple of the Southwest's best. Happy ales to you!

Texas Hop Spots

When Texas legalized brewpubs in 1994, a boom was on that made wildcat oil drilling look tame. Well, maybe not, but the brewed crude of Texas has fueled a spectacular comeback for craft-brewed ale in the Lone Star State. Texas—obviously a very big state—has more brewpubs than bluebonnets these days. And it's the only state in the Union where the passenger in a car is allowed to drink as long as the driver is sober.

MMM **Tasty Tip**
For a complete listing of Texas breweries and those of Arizona, New Mexico, Louisiana, Arkansas, Oklahoma, and Kansas, get a copy of the *Southwest Brewing News*, 1505 Lupine Lane, Austin, TX, 78741; 512-443-3607; e-mail: swbrewing@aol.com. An extra bonus: Yours truly is a regular contributor.

Austin is brew central with the Bitter End (311 Colorado Street, Austin; 512-487-2337) and the Copper Tank (504 Trinity Street, Austin; 512-478-8444). Tour the Belgian-style craft brewery of Celis Brewery (2431 Forbes Drive, Austin; 512-835-0884) and taste some lovely wits.

In Dallas, check out the Yegua (pronounced *yay wah*) Creek Brewing Co. (2920 North Henderson Avenue, Dallas; 214-824-2739). Houston has the Bank Draft Brewing Co. (2424 Dunstan Street 150; 713-522-6258). Down on the canals of San Antonio, visit the Boardwalk Bistro (4011 Broadway, San Antonio; 210-824-0100). For craft-brews in a bed and breakfast, visit the Fredericksburg Brewing Co. (245 East Main Street, Fredericksburg; 210-997-1646).

The Texas Brewers Festival in downtown Austin in early November is where the brews of Texas all come together for a roundup. For more information on that event, call 512-462-1855.

New Mexico Hop Spots

The Land of Enchantment is truly that. Towns like Santa Fe and Taos tug at a traveler's yearning to stay forever. For some enchanting brews, check out Santa Fe's first brewpub, opened in 1996. Wolf Canyon Brewing Co. (9885 Cerrillos Road, Santa Fe; 505-438-9840) offers breathtaking vistas of the Sangre de Christo Mountains and seats 130 inside and 280 outdoors. O'Ryans Tavern and Brewery (700 South Telshor Boulevard, Los Cruces; 505-522-8191) offers such delights as Atomic Dog Pale Ale and the ever-popular Dog Spit Stout. Speaking of atomic, blast by the Alamogordo Brewing Co. (817 Scenic Avenue, Alamogordo; 505-434-1540), where the first atomic bomb was detonated in 1945 and the beer might go nuclear at any minute. Albuquerque boasts the Rio Bravo Restaurant & Brewery (515 Central Avenue Northwest, Albuquerque; 505-242-6800) and Assets Grill & Brewery (6910 Montgomery Boulevard Northeast, Albuquerque; 505-889-6400).

Arizona Hop Spots

There's not quite enough beer in Arizona to fill the Grand Canyon, but there could be soon. Way up in the highlands of the state, Flagstaff boasts two brewpubs, Beaver Street Brewery and Whistle Stop Cafe (11 South Beaver Street, Flagstaff; 520-779-0079), and Flagstaff Brewing Co. (16 East Route 66, Flagstaff; 520-773-1442). Some like it hot, and if you like chili peppers floating in your beer, float into the Black Mountain Brewery (6245 East Cave Creek Road, Cave Creek; 602-254-8594). There are two Hops! on Camelback Rd. (7000 East Camelback and 2584 East Camelback), serving a lovely array of ales. In way-out Sedona, gaze at the beautiful red rocks and have a

Tasty Tip
A Scottsdale, Arizona company has invented writing paper made from beer. Before you think that's all wet, Bier Paper is made from barley, hops, and recycled beer labels. It looks like a "freshly poured lager" when held up to the light—golden brown and bubbly. Bier Paper—made by the world's oldest paper makers, Gmund in Germany—is 100% environmentally friendly. A 50-sheet box of $8^{1}/_{2}$-by-11-inch sheets sells for $12.95 and can be ordered through Le Desktop at 800-533-3758 in the U.S. and Canada, or 602-991-7270 elsewhere.

brew at Oak Creek Brewing Co. (2050 Yavapai Drive, Sedona; 520-204-1300). College-town Tempe boasts five brewpubs; the Bandersnatch (125 East Fifth Street, Tempe; 602-966-4438) is the oldest. Down in Tucson town, Gentle Ben's (865 East University Boulevard, Tucson; 520-624-4177) is where the college kids hang out.

Arkansas and Oklahoma Hop Spots

They have some weird beer laws in Oklahoma. Beer isn't allowed to be stronger than 3.2% alcohol by weight, 4.0% by volume, unless it's sold in an authorized liquor store. This really puts a crimp in the brewpub kettle. But if beer is outlawed, only outlaws will brew beer, so from the land of Pretty Boy Floyd, here's a quick tour of Oklahoma and Arkansas.

Take me back to Tulsa and order me a brew at Cherry St. Brewery (1516 South Quaker, Tulsa; 918-582-2739). O.K. City serves up Prairie Cuisine at the Bricktown Brewing Co. (1 North Oklahoma Avenue, Oklahoma City; 405-232-BREW). You won't know you're in Oklahoma when you go south of Norman and enter the Royal Bavaria (3401 South Sooner Road, Moore; 405-799-7666). The owner is from Bavaria and brews beer from a secret recipe he says was given to him by the Prince of Bavaria.

Arkansas is pretty dry except for Weidman's Old Fort Brew Pub (422 North Third Street, Fort Smith; 501-782-9898), Vino's (923 West Seventh Street, Little Rock; 501-375-8466), and Ozark Brewing Co. (430 West Dickson, Fayetteville; 501-521-2739).

Tasty Tip
For information about brew-pubs and breweries in the Midwest, pick up *Midwest Beer Notes*, 339 Sixth Avenue, Clayton, WI, 54004; Web address: http://realbeer.com/beernotes/.

Heartland Full of Beer: The Midwest

The Midwest spans the heart of America from Kansas to the Great Lakes. In most of these farm-belt states, brewing is generally restricted to college towns and bigger cities. Still, most of America's barley and a good portion of its meat, corn, wheat, and cheese comes from these areas and the food is fresh and abundant at the brewpubs. I've had some great beers in the middle West. Here's a quick tour from the Southwest to Northeast.

Kansas and Nebraska Hop Spots

Kansas is home of the Miracle Brewing Co. (331 South Emporia Street, Wichita; 316-265-7256), a microbrewery making such classics as Red Devil Ale and Purgatory Porter. The Free State Brewing Co. (636 Massachusetts Street, Lawrence; 913-843-4555) is located in a historic downtown district and caters to the college crowd.

In Nebraska, you'll find some of the finest food the heartland has to offer. Check out the Crane River Brewpub & Cafe (200 North 11th Street, Lincoln; 402-476-7766). The pub is run by Linda Vescio and Kristina Tiebel, who say they are reclaiming the brewers' art for women. In Omaha, of all places, you can find authentic Indian tandoori cooking and fresh-brewed beer at Jaipur Restaurant & Brew Pub (10922 Elm Street, Omaha; 402-392-7331).

Missouri Hop Spots

The Boulevard Brewing Co. (2501 Southwest Boulevard, Kansas City; 816-474-7095) serves up barbecue in the first brewery in Kansas City since 1903. In the shade of the Anheuser-Busch monster, you can visit the St. Louis Brewery (2100 Locust Street, St. Louis; 314-241-2337) and order some real beer. If you like great big Clydesdale horses and huge breweries, visit Anheuser-Busch (1 Busch Place, St. Louis; 314-577-2626) for a tour.

Iowa Hop Spots

The Front Street Brewery (208 East River Drive, Davenport; 319-322-1569) recovered from the Mississippi River flood of '93 and even named a beer Raging River Ale after the event. If you want to see a 1898 brewery on the banks of Big Muddy, check out the Dubuque Brewing & Bottling Co. (500 East Fourth Street, Dubuque; 319-583-2042). It's where Buffalo Bill's Pumpkin Ale is brewed, along with other great beers. In Cedar Rapids, you can visit the Cedar Brewing Co. (500 Blairs Ferry Road Northeast, Cedar Rapids; 319-378-9090).

South Dakota Hop Spots

They grow an awful lot of barley in SoDak, but if you want a fresh brew you have to go to Firehouse Brewing Co. (610 Main Street, Rapid City; 605-348-1915). It's a brewpub in (you guessed it) an old firehouse.

North Dakota Hop Spots

The warm and friendly folks in frigid North Dakota have only come to the craft-beer revolution recently. Fargo has two brewpubs. The Great Northern Restaurant and Brewery (425 Broadway, Fargo; 701-235-9707) serves great food and features wood-fired pizzas in a refurbished train depot. The Old Broadway Brewing Co. (16 Broadway, Suite 212, Fargo; 701-237-6161) is the college bar in a three-college town and a popular lunch hangout for the downtown crowd.

Minnesota Hop Spots

Downtown Minneapolis is home to a few good brewpubs, including The District Warehouse Brewing Co. (430 First Avenue North, Minneapolis; 612-333-2739) and Rockbottom Brewery #2 (825 Hennepin Avenue, Minneapolis; 612-332-7105). In St. Paul, Shannon Kelly's Brewpub (395 Wabasha Street North, St. Paul; 612-292-0905) makes a wicked stout. The Summit Brewing Co. (2264 University Avenue, St. Paul; 612-645-5029) offers thirst-quenching Saturday afternoon micro tours. Minnesota Brewing Co. (882 West Seventh Street, St. Paul; 612-228-9173) brews up such tasty treats as Pig's Eye Pilsner in a large plant built in 1902. The best beer in Minnesota is served up in the western suburb of Minnetonka at Sherlock's Home (11000 Red Circle Drive, Minnetonka; 612-931-0203).

So there you have it. From Minnesota to Monterey and from Washington to Wichita, there's a whole lot of brewing going on under the western skies. But you don't have to take my word for it. Get in a plane, train, or automobile and visit these wonder-brewers yourself. And if you do, tell 'em I sent ya, pardner.

The Least You Need to Know

➤ California, Oregon, and Washington are craft-brew heaven.

➤ You can find great brewpubs and microbreweries in every state west of the Mississippi River.

GO EAST YOUNG BEER...

Chapter 16

Yeast Is East—U.S. Beer East of the Mississippi River

In This Chapter

➤ An overview of the U.S. brewing scene in the East, mid-Atlantic states, and deep South

➤ A region-by-region snapshot of brewpubs, microbreweries, breweries, beer festivals, and other beery sites

➤ Phone numbers, addresses, and Web sites related to eastern U.S. brewpubs, microbreweries, and breweries

The microbrew revolution may have begun on the West Coast, but it wasn't long before the yeast worked its way east. In recent years, the Colonial ale tradition has been back in full swing from New England to the deep South. With plenty of refurbished warehouses in America's great old cities, brewers and restaurateurs have plenty of old bricks and tin ceilings to choose from.

Beer sales and brewing laws are a little tougher in the East, and a few states have had legalized pub brewing only in the past few years. But the East Coast is the home of great

Tasty Tip
For more information on New England and East Coast breweries, check out the *Yankee Brew News*, P.O. Box 520250, Winthrop, MA, 02152; 617-461-5693, or the *Ale Street News*, P.O. Box 1125, Maywood, NJ, 07607; 201-368-9101.

For a complete and up-to-date state-by-state listing of brewpubs and microbreweries on the World Wide Web, log on to the Institute for Brewing Studies brewery list. Their Web address is http://www.beertown.org/brews/brewlist.html.

brewers like George Washington, Thomas Jefferson, and Samuel Adams. So tour the breweries of America, hoist your glasses, and let freedom ring.

New England

The original colonies are where the U.S. brewing tradition started. Jean Vigne, one of the first white babies born in America, later grew up to establish a brewery in 1630, near Manhattan's Wall Street.

After the Revolutionary War ended, James Madison urged a high tariff on imported beer to stimulate America's fledgling brew industry. It worked. By 1810, there were 140 breweries in the original 13 colonies cranking out over 200,000 barrels a year.

Although mega-brewers dominated for half a century leading up to the 1980s, Jim Koch led the real beer charge with his Samuel Adams beers. Since then, ales from the East have regained their long-deserved respect and popularity.

Pennsylvania Hop Spots

The Keystone State was settled by German immigrants long ago. For some of that old-fashioned, high-quality lager, check out Stoudt's Brewing Co. (Route 272, Adamstown; 717-484-4387). The place is practically a beer theme park with a Black Angus restaurant, a brewery hall, an antiques mall, and a food court. Music plays on weekends all summer long. The Great Eastern Invitational Microbrewery Fest is held here in mid-June for two days and several other times during the year, and Stoudt's Beer Festival is held every Friday through Sunday from early July to September. If you can't have fun here, you better check yourself for a pulse.

In Pittsburgh, the Penn Brewery (800 Vinial Street at Troy Hill, Pittsburgh; 412-741-9400) has an authentic German-style beer hall. The Straub Brewery (303 Sorg Street, St. Mary's; 814-834-2875) opens an "eternal tap" (what you might call a bottomless beer mug) on tours seven days a week.

When the fellas who wrote the Constitution were finished, they retired to a Philadelphia pub to celebrate. There's still plenty of celebration going on at Dock Street Brewery & Restaurant (2 Logan Square, Philadelphia; 215-496-0413) with one of the largest selections of fresh-brewed beer anywhere. Dock Street holds the Six Months 'til Oktoberfest in late April. Samuel Adams contract brews most of its beers, but still cooks them up in its own small brewery at Samuel Adams Brewhouse (1516 Sansom Street, Second floor, Philadelphia; 215-563-2326).

Ascending into Space: *The inspirational mural behind the bar at Dock Street Brewery & Restaurant in Philadelphia.*

For real "roots" beer drinking, visit Penn's Tavern (Route 147, Fisher's Ferry; 717-286-4913). It was built in 1703 and still serves beer. Bube's Brewery (102 North Market Street, Mount Joy; 717-653-2056) is an intact 1800s brewery with three restaurants.

New York Hop Spots

The Empire State has quite a lot to offer. From Buffalo to Woodstock to Manhattan Island, dedicated folks are cookin' up some world-class ales and lagers. Over in the snowbelt, the Buffalo Brewpub (6861 Main Street, Williamsville; 716-632-0552) is housed in a former stagecoach stop and makes beer purer than the driven snow. In Troy, you can watch the

Bar Talk
The ante-diluvians were all very sober For they had no wine and brewed no October All wicked, bad livers, on mischief still thinking For there can't be good living Where there is not good drinking

—song by Philadelphian Ben Franklin, 1745

Hudson gurgle past from the deck at Troy Brewing Co. (417–419 River Street, Troy; 518-273-BEER). The Syracuse Suds Factory (210–216 West Water Street, Syracuse; 315-471-2253) sits in a historic building on the banks of the old Erie Canal. The Mountain Valley Brewpub (122 Orange Avenue, Suffern; 914-357-0101) has an extensive menu of slow-smoked food.

The Big Apple has a few brewpubs, including the Carnegie Hill Brewing Co. (212 West 79th Street, New York; 212-369-0808), Hansens Times Square Brewery (160 West 42nd Street, New York; 212-398-1234), and the Highlander Brewery (190 3rd Avenue, New York; 212-979-7268). Over on Pier 59, there's a microbrewery with a restaurant called the Chelsea Brewery (Pier 59/West 18th Street, New York; 212-336-6440). Over in Brooklyn, craft brews are served at Park Slope Brewing Co. (356 Sixth Avenue, Brooklyn; 718-788-1756).

Foamy Fact

First We Brew Manhattan: The first brewery in Manhattan was built in 1613 by Adrian Block on the southern tip of the island. The sheriff of New Amsterdam, Nicasius de Sille, wrote that "Beer is brewed here as good as in Holland, of barley and wheat. Good hops grow in the woods."

New Jersey Hop Spots

New Jersey is a latecomer to legalized brewpubs, but now you can enjoy fresh barley and hops in the Garden State. Check out Joe's Mill Hill Saloon and Brewcellar (300 South Broad Street, Trenton; 609-394-7222), Ship Inn (61 Bridge Street, Milford; 908-995-0188), and Triumph Brewing Co. (138 Nassau Street, Princeton; 609-924-7855).

Vermont Hop Spots

The rebels in Vermont do plenty of their own brewing. They're an independent lot and they've got the cold weather that keeps one indoors steaming up the mash tuns. Award-winning beers are brewed at Catamount Brewing Co. (58 South Main Street, White River Junction; 802-296-2248), a microbrewery that offers weekend tours with lots of tasting and a souvenir shop that's open all week. Otter Creek Brewing Co. (74 Exchange Street, Middlebury; 802-388-0727) makes a dynamite stout. McNeill's Brewery (90 Elliot Street, Brattleboro; 802-254-2553) serves up good food. The Vermont Pub & Brewery (144 College Street, Burlington; 802-865-0500) is the place to go in Burlington.

Maine Hop Spots

Ale can be a way of life this close to the Canadian border. If you want to rub elbows with George Bush, stop into the Kennebunkport Brewing Co. (Unit 6, 8 Western Avenue, Kennebunkport; 800-BREW-ALE). Bar Harbor is home to the Bar Harbor mini-microbrewery/bed and breakfast mentioned in Chapter 10. Bar Harbor also features the Lompoc Cafe & Brewpub (36 Rodrick Street, Bar Harbor; 207-824-4253). Great London porter is brewed in Portland at the D.L. Geary Brewing Co. (38 Evergreen Drive, Portland; 207-878-2337). While you're in Portland, check out Gritty McDuff's (369 Fore Street, Portland; 207-772-2739). The Maine Brewers' Festival is held in Portland in early November. For information, call 207-780-8229.

Massachusetts Hop Spots

The boys from Boston started the Revolution in 1776, and the men and women of today's Boston still carry on their beer traditions. Commonwealth Brewing Co. (85 Merrimac Street, Boston; 617-523-8383) is an Old English–style brewpub and Boston's original microbrewery. Jacob Wirth's (3337 Stuart Street, Boston; 617-338-8586) is Boston's second oldest restaurant (established 1868) and brews several German-style beers with singalongs on Friday nights. Boston Beer Co. (30 Germania Street, Boston; 617-368-5000) is the home of Samuel Adams (the beer, not the signer of the Constitution). And Boston Beer Works (61 Brookline Avenue, Boston; 617-536-2337) is across the street from Fenway Park. Boston hosts the WBUR Brewers Offering in late August. Call 617-353-3800 for details.

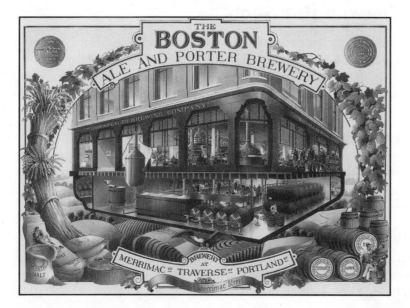

The Common-wealth Brewing Co. is New England's first brewpub and Massachusetts' oldest continuously operating brewery.

Away from the big city, John Harvard's Brewhouse (33 Dunster Street, Cambridge; 617-868-3585) serves brews to those who populate Hah-vahd Yahd. If you're lucky enough to be on Martha's Vineyard, check out The Brewery on Martha's Vineyard (43 Oak Bluffs Avenue, Oak Bluffs; 508-696-8400).

Foamy Fact

Here's One for Higher Learning: Harvard College began operating a brewhouse on campus in 1674. Harvard students were allowed to pay their tuition in wheat and malted barley. Students were given two pints a day, and Harvard brewed beer on campus until the end of the 1700s. Nathaniel Eaton, Harvard's first president, was ousted in part because he failed to provide enough beer rations.

Rhode Island Hop Spots

Rhode Island is a small state that took a little longer to change its brew laws to allow brewpubs, not having done so until the early 1990s. Today folks are catching up at Coddington Brewing Co. (210 Coddington Highway, Newport; 401-847-6690), Trinity Brewing Co. (186 Fountain Street, Providence; 401-453-2337), and Union Station Brewing Co. (36 Exchange Terrace, Providence; 401-274-2739).

Connecticut and Delaware Hop Spots

Connecticut, too, has come late to the brewpub game. Check out the Hartford Brewery (35 Pearl Street, Hartford; 203-246-BEER), the Main Street Cafe (877 Main Street, Willmantic; 860-423-6777), the New Haven Brewing Co. (458 Grand Avenue, New Haven; 203-722-2739), or the Post Road Brewing Co. (49 Boston Post Road, Waterford; 860-422-1200).

Delaware has a fairly new crop of brewpubs, including the Brandywine Brewing Co., (3801 Kenneth Pike, Greenville; 302-655-8000), Dogfish Head Brewings and Eats (320 Rehoboth Avenue, Rehoboth Beach; 302-226-2739), and Stewart's Brewing Company (Routes 40 and 72 Governors' Square, Bear; 302-836-2739).

The Mid-Atlantic States

From the nation's capital to the Blue Ridge Mountains, there's a whole lot of brewing in the East Coast's mid-section. For a complete rundown of mid-Atlantic brew happenings, pick up *BarleyCorn*, P.O. Box 2328, Falls Church, VA, 22042; 703-573-8970.

Maryland Hop Spots

Get down in Gaithersburg with fresh food, brew, and live music at Olde Towne Tavern & Brewing Co. (227 East Diamond Avenue, Olde Town, Gaithersburg; 301-948-4200). You can walk the streets of Baltimore or you can check out some ragin' Cajun cuisine and craft brew at Sisson's Restaurant & Brewery (36 East Cross Street, Baltimore 410-539-2093). Down on the docks, you can get hand-pulled, cask-conditioned beer at the Wharf Rat (206 West Pratt Street, Baltimore 410-244-8900). The Baltimore Brewing Co. (104 Albemarle Street, Baltimore 410-837-5000) is decorated with old Baltimore brewery stuff. And pick up some Cambridge-brewed Wild Goose beer at any beer store.

District of Columbia Hop Spots

Whether you're touring the Lincoln Memorial or lobbying your congressperson, the District has a few great beer monuments. Check out Capitol City Brewing (1100 New York Avenue Northwest, Washington, D.C.; 202-628-2222) or the other Capital City Brewing (2 Massachusetts Avenue Northeast; 202-842-2337). And you can toast your freedom at the Mid-Atlantic Beer Fest in mid-September. It's at H and 12th Streets, Washington D.C.; 703-527-1441.

Virginia Hop Spots

Yes, Virginia, there is a Santa Claus. And he's brought your state a few world-class places to have some beer. One of the world's most interestingly themed brewpubs is Bardo Rodeo (2000 Wilson Boulevard, Arlington; 703-527-9399). Owner Bill Stewart named his saloon Bardo, which, according to the *Tibetan Book of the Dead*, is the place where people go when they die. The brewery has a bright-blue Plymouth Fury crashing through the front window and a 240-foot wraparound mural inside showing scenes from Bardo. It's also huge, seating 900 inside and 300 outside, with 108 taps and at least 10 homebrews.

In Richmond you can visit the Cobblestone Brewery & Pub (110 North 18th Street, Richmond; 804-644-2739), or get some Big Nasty Porter at the Richbrau Brewery (1214 East Cary Street, Richmond; 804-644-3018).

West Virginia Hop Spots

West Virginy's oldest brewpub is West Virginia Brewing Co. (1291 University Avenue, Morgantown; 304-296-BREW).

Great Lakes Full of Beer

The Great Lakes region is surrounded by large cities full of thirsty folks, many of whose great-grandparents immigrated from the beer-loving countries of Europe. This is also where freighters full of North Dakota barley are shipped from Duluth, Minnesota to foreign destinations around the globe. The areas around the largest body of fresh water on the globe are full of surprisingly good brew.

Wisconsin Hop Spots

Wisconsin is known as the Dairy State, but with its German-American population, it should be known as the Beer State. In Appleton, the Appleton Brewing Co. (1004 South Olde Oneida Street, Appleton; 414-731-0507) won five gold medals at the GABF (Great American Beer Festival) in 1990. In Chippewa Falls, the Jacob Leinenkugel Brewing Co. (1–3 Jefferson Avenue, Chippewa Falls; 715-723-5558) is a regional brewery, now owned by Miller, that's been cranking out "Leinies" since 1867. Down near Madison, the Capital Brewery Co. (7734 Terrace Avenue, Middleton; 608-836-7100) boils up some award-winning lagers and offers a hop-draped Bier Garten where reading is encouraged. Another country brewery west of Madison, in the Bavarian-style town of New Glarus, is the New Glarus Brewing Co. (119 County West, New Glarus; 608-527-5850).

Tasty Tip
For up-to-date information on Great Lakes–area breweries, pick up a copy of *Great Lakes Brewing News* for free or order a copy from 214 Muegel Road, East Amherst, NY, 14051; 716-689-5841; fax 716-689-5789; e-mail: glbrewing@aol.com; or find them on the Web via the Real Beer Page, a site linking all things beer on the World Wide Web. Their Web address is http://realbeer.com.

In Milwaukee you can tour Miller Brewing Co. (3939 Highland Boulevard, Milwaukee; 414-931-BEER). Check out the real beer at the Water Street Brewery (1101 North Water Street, Milwaukee; 414-272-1195), or look up Randy at Sprecher Brewing Co. (701 West Glendale Avenue, Glendale; 414-964-BREW). When the big bad brewers in Milwaukee wouldn't let upstart Randy into their popular Milwaukee Summerfest, Randy started his own Sprecherfest, a great event every Labor Day weekend.

Other beer events in Wisconsin include the Wisconsin Microbrewer's Beer Festival in late May at Rowlands (25 North Madison Street, Chilton; 414-849-2534). The Great Taste of the Midwest in August can be found on the lakefront in Madison. And you can tour the Victorian Pabst Mansion, built in 1893 by Capt. Frederick Pabst, founder of the brewery.

Illinois Hop Spots

The Land of Lincoln has a good smattering of breweries. The Blue Cat Brew Pub (113 18th Street, Rock Island; 309-788-8247) is in the western part of the state with a glassed-in brewhouse and full menu. Down where Honest Abe was born you'll find Capitol City Brewing Co. (107 West Cook, Springfield; 217-753-5725).

> **Foamy Fact**
>
> *Da Bulls, Da Bears, and Mrs. O'Leary's Cow:* Today Chicago Brewing Co. (1830 North Besly Court, Chicago; 312-252-2739) brews a fine line of award-winning beers. But the original Chicago Brewing Co. was first established in 1847. The old Chicago Brewing was the city's first lager brewery, and the beer was stored in hand-dug, subterranean vaults that stretched two miles under the city. The gigantic brewhouses and malthouses burned when Mrs. O'Leary's cow kicked over a lantern and started the Great Chicago Fire in 1871. The brewery was never rebuilt.

Outside of Chicago, look for Mickey Finn's Brewery (412 North Milwaukee Avenue, Libertyville; 708-362-6688), a well-established watering hole for 17 years and a brew-pub for the last several. The Millrose Brewing Co. (45 South Barrington Road, South Barrington; 708-382-7673) is an elegant restaurant in a former cow barn. There are two Weinkeller Brewpubs (651 Westmont Drive, Westmont; 708-789-2236 and 6417 Roosevelt Road, Berwyn; 708-749-2276). Both feature fine dining and more than 500 beers, plus their own craft-brewed selections of beer.

The main buzz in Chicago is the world-famous Goose Island Brewing Co. (1800 North Clybourn, Chicago; 312-915-0071), where more than 30 styles of beer are brewed. Goose Island also hosts the Midwest Brewers' Oktoberfest in mid-September with more than 20 breweries featured. In excess of 100 imported beers are featured at the World Beer Festival in Maywood Park in late October. Call 312-880-1380 for information.

Indiana Hop Spots

The Hoosier State's selection of hop spots has grown in recent years. The Mishawaka Brewing Co. (3703 North Main, Mishawaka; 219-256-9994) near South Bend is worth the trip. In Indianapolis, check out the Broad Ripple Brewpub (842 East 65th, Indianapolis; 317-ALE-BREW). The Indianapolis Brewing Co. (3250 North Post Road, Indianapolis; 317-898-1235) is an established microbrewery. Another brewpub that's been around for a while is called the Oaken Barrel Brewing Co. (50 Airport Parkway, Greenwood, [just south of Indy]; 317-887-2287). Indianapolis also hosts the Alcatraz Brewing Co., "Best Beer Behind Bars," (Illinois Street at West Maryland; 317-488-1230), the Circle V Brewing Co. (8310 Craig Street; 317-59-59-ALE), and the Rock Bottom Brewery, (10 West Washington Street; 317-681-8180).

Michigan Hop Spots

Some of the best beer around is brewed at the Kalamazoo Brewing Co. (315 East Kalamazoo Avenue, Kalamazoo; 616-382-2338). Ann Arbor's college folks know that the best beer comes from Grizzly Peak Brewing Co. (120 West Washington, Ann Arbor; 313-741-7325). While in Detroit, drink up at Traffic Jam and Snug (4268 2nd Avenue, Detroit; 313-831-1265).

Ohio Hop Spots

The Buckeye State has a revitalized brewing industry, where hometown loyalty has helped make a few microbreweries successful players. The historic Brewery District of Columbus is a restored area where Columbus's German immigrants once brewed. The area has several brewpubs decked out in antique splendor. Check out Barley's Brewing (467 North High Street, Columbus; 614-228-2537), Hoster Brewing Co. (550 South High Street, Columbus; 616-228-6066), and Gambrinus Brewing Co. (1152 South Front Street, Columbus; 614-444-7769).

Cleveland used to be the Rodney ("I don't get no respect!") Dangerfield of cities. But with baseball's Indians making it to the World Series in 1995 and the opening of the Rock and Roll Hall of Fame, Cleveland is suddenly on tourists' must-see lists. A definite drop-in in Cleveland is the Great Lakes Brewing Co. (2516 Market Street, Cleveland; 216-771-4404), where Edmund Fitzgerald Porter, one of my favorite porters, is made. Great Lakes is a beautifully restored pub with a mahogany bar and a bullet hole in the wall left over from Cleveland's 1930s gangster days.

Way Down South in Dixie

Look away, look away. The South is all over the map when it comes to good beer. Brewpubs have been turning on their taps like crazy in boom states like Georgia, where craft brewing has recently been legalized. Meanwhile, there are still "dry" counties in Kentucky and Tennessee, and it's still illegal to brew at all in Mississippi. Through it all, however, there are plenty of dedicated folks bringing out the brews way down south in Dixie.

North Carolina Hop Spots

North Carolina has its share of brewpubs. The Spring Garden Brewing Co. (5804 Hunt Club Road, Greensboro; 910-299-3649) brews beer for several of its affiliated restaurants. Dilworth Brewing Co. (1301 East Boulevard, Charlotte; 704-377-2739) is the home of the Brew Pub Poets Society. And on the outer banks, the Weeping Radish Restaurant and Brewery (Highway 64 East, P.O. Box 1471, Manteo; 919-473-1880) adds the ambience of an authentic Bavarian pub, restaurant, and biergarten to historic Roanoke Island.

South Carolina Hop Spots

If you want white-sand scenery with your brew in South Carolina, visit the Hilton Head Brewing Company (7C Greenwood Drive, Hilton Head Island; 803-785-2739). For the best brew and smoked food in Charleston, visit Southend Brewery & Smokehouse (161 East Bay Street, Charleston; 803-853-HOPS).

Columbia boasts two brewpubs, Hunter Gatherer (900 Main Street, Columbia; 803-748-0540) and Columbia Brewing Company (931 Senate Street, Columbia; 803-254-2739).

Tennessee Hop Spots

Tennessee may be the home of Jack Daniel's whiskey, but it has its fair share of beer-making, too. The Big River Grille (222 Broad Street, Chattanooga; 423-267-2739) is a hit in Chattanooga. Take the last train to Clarksville and get a beer at the Black Horse Brewery (134 Franklin Street, Clarksville; 615-552-9499). Bosco's Pizza Kitchen & Brewery (7615 West Farmington Boulevard, Germantown; 901-756-7310) is the talk of Germantown.

Tasty Tip
For all the news there is about brews in the southland, pick up the *Southern Draft*, 120 Wood Gate Dr., Canton, GA, 30115; 770-345-1512. Or read all about it on the Web: http://realbeer.com/sodraft.

Nashville has both kinds of music—country and western. It also has great brews at Bosco's Nashville Brewing Co. (1802 21st Avenue South, Nashville; 615-385-0050), Big River Grille & Brewing Works (111 Broadway, Nashville; 615-251-4677), and Blackstone Restaurant & Brewery (1918 West End Avenue, Nashville; 615-327-9969).

Kentucky Hop Spots

Kentucky had long been a bootlegger's paradise, but today making your own home brew is legal. Just ask folks at the Kentucky Brewing Co. (122 West Maxwell Street, Lexington; 606-233-7821) or the Lexington City Brewery (1050 South Broadway, Lexington; 606-259-2739). Bring your banjos to the Bluegrass Brewing Co. (3929 Shelbyville Road, Louisville; 502-899-7070).

Up on the Ohio border is the Oldenberg Brewery (400 Buttermilk Pike, Fort Mitchell; 606-341-7223), which is a beer Disneyland. Five minutes from downtown Cincinnati, Oldenberg has a 12,000-square-foot beer hall so ornate it would make a Bavarian blush. It offers a biannual beer camp where counselors in khaki lead the beer-crazed through all aspects of beer worship. The Oldenberg has gift shops, entertainment and, oh yeah, it also brews beer. You should also check out the new Brewworks at the Party Source, which is a brewpub and eatery in a huge new complex in Covington (1115 Main Street, Covington; 606-581-2739).

Florida Hop Spots

There are several Irish-style pubs among the Florida palms. They include Irish Times Pub and Brewery (9920 Alt. AIA, #810, Palm Beach; 407-624-1504) and McGuire's Irish Pub and Brewery (600 East Gregory Street, Pensacola; 904-433-6789). Mill Bakery, Eatery, and Brewery (330 West Fairbanks, Winter Park; 407-644-1544, and 11491 South Cleveland Avenue, Fort Myers; 813-939-2739) are two brewpubs that focus on healthy eating and great bread. If you're lucky enough to be down in the Keys, check out Kelly's Caribbean Bar, Grill and Brewery (301 Whitehead Street, Key West; 305-293-8484). It's owned by actress Kelly McGillis.

Hops Grill and Bar is virtually everywhere in Florida. In no particular order, here are several of their locations: (4820 South Florida Avenue, Lakeland; 941-647-9117, 9826 San Jose Boulevard, Jacksonville; 904-645-9355, 327 North Dale Mabry Highway, Tampa; 813-871-3600, 14303 North Dale Mabry Highway, Tampa; 813-264-0522, 4502 14th Street West, Bradenton; 813-756-1069, 33086 U.S. Highway 19 North, Palm Harbor; 813-789-5678, and 18825 U.S. Highway 19 North, Clearwater; 813-531-5300).

Georgia Hop Spots

New laws make it easier to brew in Georgia and brewing they're doing. There's the Athens Brewing Co. (312 East Washington Street Athens; 770-549-0027), and two locations for the Texas Cattle Company, Border Grille & Brewery (2480 Riverside Drive, Macon; 912-741-1389 and 2067 Watson Blvd., Warner Robbins; 912-929-7070).

In hot Atlanta, several establishments are hanging out their brewing shingle. All the way from Massachusetts, there's John Harvard's Brew House (3047 Peachtree Road, Atlanta; 404-816-2739). And you can visit the Atlanta Beer Garten (3013 Peachtree Road, Atlanta; 404-261-9898), the Phoenix Brewing Co. (5600 Roswell Road, Atlanta; 404-843-2739), and the Buckhead Beer Exchange (3227 Roswell Road, Atlanta; 404-841-9754).

Alabama and Mississippi Hop Spots

Birmingham has The Magic City Brewery (420 21st Street South, Birmingham; 205-328-2739) and The Mill (1035 20th Street South, Birmingham; 205-939-3001). Or visit The Montgomery Brewpub (12 West Jefferson Street, Montgomery; 334-834-2739). If you're on the Gulf Coast, stop in at the Port City Brewery (225 Dauphin Street, Mobile; 334-438-2739).

If you want to drink craft-brewed ale in Mississippi, you'd better make your own or go to Alabama or Louisiana, because brewpubs aren't legal in Ole Miss.

Louisiana Hop Spots

Louisiana is the home of gumbo and Mardi Gras, where be-costumed people stumble about the streets for days on end. The best time to visit is during the New Orleans Jazz Festival in January. And if you're going to stumble, check out the Abita Brewing Co. (100 Leveson Street, Abita Springs; 504-892-5837), home of Turbo Dog beer. In the Crescent City you can visit the Acadian Brewing Co. (201 North Carrollton, New Orleans; 504-488-8274) or the Crescent City Brewhouse (527 Decatur, New Orleans 504-522-0571).

It's a big country, from New Orleans to Kennebunkport and from Key West to western Wisconsin. But now you know where to find the finest brews east of the Mississippi River. And new hop spots are opening every day. So pick up a brewspaper or log on to the Internet to get the latest brew news. Then drum up some cab fare, and get down with the best. Isn't that what life is really all about?

The Least You Need to Know

> ➤ You can find great craft-brewed beers almost everywhere in the eastern United States.

> ➤ There are brewpubs and microbreweries in every state east of the Mississippi River, except Mississippi.

Chapter 17

Canadian Brew-ha-ha

In This Chapter

➤ An overview of the brewing scene in Canada

➤ A region-by-region snapshot of brewpubs, microbreweries, breweries, beer festivals, and other beery sites

➤ Phone numbers, addresses, and Web sites related to Canadian brewpubs, microbreweries, and breweries

Americans know Canada as a friendly neighbor to the north with clean, safe cities and a magnificent sprawling wilderness. But what many Americans don't know (unfortunately) is that Canadian craft breweries brew world-class beers from some of the cleanest and clearest waters in the world.

O, Canada!

In the old days, Americans thought they were living it up when they were able to buy Molson, Labatt's, or (gasp) Moosehead beer. You know, something imported, something *exotic*. That was then. It's true that those companies actually did brew a few ale styles, about the only ones available in the U.S. But in the 1980s, after some of us got accustomed to craft-brewed ale, we realized that those Canadian giants pretty much brewed the same kind of highly filtered, low-hopped, corn-laden barley pop made by America's corporate brewers.

Canadians began strapping on their microbrewing boots a few years later than Americans did. And would-be Canadian brewers faced two huge problems. One was the complete stranglehold Molson and Labatt's have over beer sales in Ontario—Canada's most populous province. As hard as it is to believe, those two giant breweries *own* every single retail beer outlet, called Beer Stores, in the Ontario province.

Molson and Labatt's charge microbrewers a one-time fee of $22,900 (Canadian dollars) for each package size of each brand, plus a 60.6¢ per liter handling charge. That means a microbrewer wishing to sell four beer styles in Ontario must cough up almost $100,000 just to get their beer in the only retail outlet for their products. This, by the way, also profits their competition—the big breweries. In addition, Beer Stores sell beer by the six- or 12-pack only, and employees are prohibited from discussing anything about beer with customers. If you can imagine Budweiser owning every beer store in America, you'll get the idea.

Problem number two is Canada's strict regulatory environment and high taxes. Until recently, provincial liquor boards kept a stranglehold on brewpubs and microbreweries. There are Byzantine regulations, licenses, seating restrictions, and enough rules to drive a prospective brewpub owner to drink. And taxes on beer in Canada drive the price of an average six-pack over eight dollars (Canadian). A brewpub owner must fill out paperwork to pay three kinds of taxes to two branches of government. In the past few years, however, the regulations have loosened slightly (thanks to agitation by craftbrewers) and Canadian micros have come into their own.

The Canadian beer market was long protected from European and American imports. But under provisions of the North American Free Trade Agreement (NAFTA), the Canadian government decided to allow more American brews to be imported in 1995. They also scrapped the bizarre restrictions that limited the flow of beer between Canada's provinces.

Canada's high beer prices have spawned a major growth in all things homebrew. This includes homebrew clubs and homebrew supply stores. Brew-on-Premise (BOP) stores are a recent phenomenon; they are places where folks can go in and use professional-style kettles and other brewing equipment to make their own beer and cheat the government out of a few dollars worth of taxes. So Canada, like its southern neighbor, is returning to the beery ways of old, melding tradition with modern methods to savor some craft-brewed beer—no matter how they brew it.

Cherries Jubilee in the Atlantic Provinces

In the waters of the chilly Atlantic, Prince Edward Island and Newfoundland have no craft-brewing to speak of. Nova Scotia is another story. The Granite Brewery (1222 Barrington Street, Halifax; 902-422-4954; e-mail: granite@ns.sympatico.ca) brews a beautifully dry-hopped Extra Special Bitter and a hand-pumped, cask-conditioned dark ale called Peculiar. If you need a room with a brew, check out Heather Motel Lounge, named HomeBrewpub (130 Ford Street, Stellarton; 800-565-4500). There's plenty of fruit brewing going on at Paddy's Pub and Brewery (42 Aberdeen Street, Kentville; 902-678-3199; e-mail: paddys@fox.nstn.ca), where you can get Cherries Jubilee ale or Apple Cider. Homebrewers in Nova Scotia can join homebrew clubs Brewnosers in Halifax or the poetically named Fellowship Against Repulsive Tasting Suds (FARTS) in Waterville.

Tasty Tip
The Real Beer Page on the World Wide Web has a special page dedicated to Canadian beer. It is the most comprehensive guide I've seen for the Great White North. You can surf on Canadian beer by visiting http://realbeer.com/canada/.

The main claim to beer fame in New Brunswick is the Moosehead Brewery (89 Main Street, Saint John; 506-635-7000), which was built in 1867 in St. John. There's also a Taps brewpub (78 King Street, Saint John). Picaroons Brewing Co. (349 King Street, Fredericton; 506-455-2537) is a microbrewery that brews seven year-round beers and six seasonals.

Drinking "The End of the World" Ale in Quebec

The first brewery in Quebec was opened in 1649 when the French regime was trying to wean its none-too-sober soldiers off brandy and whisky. The brewery was opened under the direction of the governor of the colony. In 1786, John Molson began his company's long-running beer career when he opened his first brewery in Montreal.

Today's Quebec is probably the most enthusiastic province when it comes to craft brewing. And several of Quebec's brewers have taken to the Belgian beer tradition with a vengeance (southern Belgium is populated by French-speaking people as is Quebec). You can find triples, wits, and other Belgian styles lovingly brewed, wired, and corked just like on the Continent. Unfortunately, these beers are not widely available outside the beautiful province known as "La Belle Province."

Quebec has 12 brewpubs and 13 microbreweries, and that number is growing every year. While there aren't quite as many craft-breweries as in Ontario, Quebec's brewers are known for their enthusiasm and fresh approach. Some folks believe that Montreal is in close competition with Portland and Seattle when it comes to microbrew fever. Leading

Terms of Enbeerment
Brew-on-Premise (BOP) stores are a recent phenomenon. Folks who BOP are able to go into a storefront homebrewery where they can use professional-style kettles and other brewing equipment to make their own beer. BOPs offer dozens of different styles. When it's over, the homebrewer walks out with five cases of beer after spending one night brewing, then comes back three weeks later to bottle. The cost is around $100.

the charge is the Brasserie McAuslan (4850 Rue St. Ambroise, Bureau 100, Montreal; 514-939-3060; e-mail: http://www.mcauslan.com), a microbrewery whose products are snapped up on both sides of the border. Brewster Ellen McAuslan's St. Ambroise Oatmeal Stout is one of the best.

Microbrewery Unibroue (80 Des Carrières, Chambly; 514-658-7658) brews beer that might scare the faint of heart. They make an 8% Belgian strong ale called Maudite whose name translates roughly as "damned and burning in hell." It's based on the story of 17th-century *Voyaguer* fur trappers who sell their souls for a safe canoe *flight* home. Their l'Heroine beer has an alcohol content of 6.66%. La Fin Du Monde ("The End of the World") is a triple-fermented white beer. Most of their beers are bottle-conditioned and come in a corked bottle. Unibroue also brews a strong, spiced ale called Quelquechose, which is one of the only beers in the world that is supposed to be served hot.

Flying canoes, angels, devils, and the end of the world grace the labels of Unibroue's award-winning beers.

Brewpub hopping in La Belle Province has never been better. But in some cases, it can be down right beastly. La Cervoise (4457 Boulevard St-Laurent, Montreal; 514-843-6586) brews a beer called La 666, a mark-of-the-beastly offering among their other fine beers. La Cheval Blanc (809 Rue Ontario Est, Montreal; 514-522-0211) offers up such monstrous tasties as Loch Ness along with wit, cherry, raspberry, maple, and spice beers. Their strong Titanic ale goes down fast and doesn't come up again. Both Loch Ness and Titanic may be found in the United States.

Quebec City has L'Inox (37 Rue St-André, Quebec City; 418-692-2877), and up near Parc du Mont Tremblant there's La Diable (3005 Chemin Principal, Mont Tremblant; 819-681-4546).

Here's a complete list of Quebec's other brewpubs as of 1997:

➤ Gambrinus, Trois-Rivières

➤ La Microbrasserie St-Arnould, St-Jovite

➤ La Taverne du Sergent Recruteur, Montreal

➤ Le Bilboquet, St-Hyacinthe

➤ Le Vieux Copenhägen, St-Saveur-des-Monts

➤ Le Vieux Copenhägen II, Montreal

➤ Lion D'Or (Golden Lion Brewing Co.), Lennoxville

➤ Vessels and Barrels, Pointe-Claire

Here's a list of Quebec's other microbreweries:

➤ Beauce Broue Inc., St-Odilon

➤ Brasserie Aux 4 Temps, St-Hyacinthe

➤ Brasserie Brasal Brewery, Lasalle (Montreal)

➤ Brasseurs de l'Anse, l'Anse-St-Jean

➤ Du Bas-St-Laurent-Gaspésie, Cap-Chat

➤ La Brasserie Seigneuriale Inc., Boucherville

➤ Les Brasseurs de la Capitale Inc., Quebec

➤ Les Brasseurs du Nord, Blainville

➤ Les Brasseurs GMT, Montreal

Quebec Brewing Events

In the fall, folks in La Belle Province can enjoy the Festibière de Chamblya—a medieval beer festival with jugglers, medieval performers, and, of course, fabulous beer. It's held at Fort Chambly, 20 minutes south of Montreal on the shore of the Richelieu River. Great beer, food, and cheese are the order of the day, and a few breweries bring out their special products for tastings by the curious crowd.

Beers of the Great White North: A Siberian husky is the mascot of this husky beer.

The Canadian Amateur Brewers Association (CABA) holds the Great Canadian Homebrew Conference and Competition every March in Montreal. The event includes lunch, seminars, brewery tours, gourmet dinner, and competition awards. For more information, e-mail: brewerg@securenet.net.

C'est What? in Ontario

Ontario, the most populous province, has the most cruising for brews-ing. Not only are there 20 brewpubs and 28 microbreweries, but there are scores of homebrew supply shops and homebrewing clubs. The lovely city of Toronto has the bilingually named C'est What? (67 Front St. E., Toronto, 416-867-9499) and Al Frisco's (133 John Street, Toronto; 416-595-8201), along with a Granite Brewery (245 Eglington Avenue East, Toronto; 416-322-0723).

The Upper Canada Brewing Co. (2 Atlantic Avenue, Toronto; 416-534-9281) has transformed part of its brewery into an art gallery where local artists are given space to display paintings and photographs. The gallery is located near the brewery's retail store inside the plant and has regular gallery hours. Toronto's artists have dubbed it the Atlantic Avenue Brewery Gallery.

Up in the national capital of Ottawa you'll find Master's Brasserie and Brewpub (330 Queen Street, Ottawa; 613-594-3688). Addington's Brew Pub & Winery (575 Bank Street, Ottawa, 613-236-1641) and Major's Brew House (453 Sussex Dr., Ottawa; 613-789-7405) were both established in 1995 and both feature a wide range of styles.

Around Lake Superior, you can wet your whistle at Cellar Tap (320 Bay Street, Sault Ste. Marie; 705-946-2867) and Port Arthur Brasserie & Brewpub (901 Red River Road, Thunder Bay; 807-767-4415).

Here's a list of Ontario's other brewpubs:

➤ CC's Brewpub, Mississauga

➤ CEEPS Barney's Ltd., London

➤ Charley's Tavern, Windsor

➤ Denison's Brewing Co., Toronto

➤ Kingston Brewing Company, Kingston

➤ Lighthouse Brewpub, Bowmanville

➤ Lion Brewery (in the Huether Hotel), Waterloo

➤ Olde Heidelberg Brewery & Restaurant, Heidelberg

➤ Olde Stone Brewpub, Peterborough

➤ Pepperwood Bistro, Burlington

➤ Port Arthur Brasserie & Brewpub, Thunder Bay

➤ Tracks Brewpub, Brampton

Here's a list of Ontario's microbreweries:

➤ Amber Brewing Co., Mississauga

➤ Amsterdam Brewing Company, Toronto

➤ Conners Brewery, St. Catharines

➤ Copperhead Brewing Co., Nepean

➤ Creemore Springs Brewery, Creemore

➤ Durham Brewing Company, Pickering

➤ Elora Brewing Ltd./Taylor & Bate, Elora

➤ F & M Breweries, Guelph

➤ Glatt Brothers Brewing Co., London

➤ Gold Crown Brewery, Waterloo

➤ Great Lakes Brewing Company, Etobicoke

➤ Hart Brewing Company Ltd., Carleton Place

➤ Hogtown Brewing Co., Mississauga

➤ Kawartha Lakes Brewing Co., Peterborough

➤ Lakes of Muskoka Cottage Brewery, Bracebridge

➤ Magnotta Brewery Ltd., Scarborough

➤ Niagara Falls Brewing Company, Niagara Falls

➤ Old Credit Brewing Co., Port Credit

➤ Quinte Brewery, Belleville

➤ Robinson Brewing Co., Mississauga

➤ Trafalgar Brewing Company, Oakville

➤ Wellington County Brewery, Guelph

➤ Algonquin Brewing Company, Formosa

➤ Brick Brewing Company, Waterloo

➤ Lakeport Brewing, Hamilton

➤ Northern Breweries, Sault Ste. Marie

➤ Sleeman Brewing and Malting Company, Guelph

➤ Upper Canada Brewing Company, Toronto

Porter on the Prairies: Manitoba and Saskatchewan

Where the population thins out in chilly Manitoba, so do the brewpubs. In fact there are none, but there is one microbrewery doing the heavy lifting for the entire province. That would be Fort Garry Brewing Co. (Unit 13, 1249 Clarence Avenue, Winnipeg; 204-475-8995).

Saskatchewan is another story. Not exactly known for its wild and crazy fads, the province on the prairie has a bustling brewpub trade in Regina. The reason is due to a fluke in the law. When brewpubs began opening in early 1990, regulators decided to give them off-sale licenses to sell beers by *any brewery* for take away. This lucrative loophole causes more than one bar owner to throw in some brewing equipment to take advantage of the off-sale law. While a few brew beer as an afterthought, most brewpubs are living up to their demanding traditions.

Bushwakker Brewing Co. (2206 Dewdney Avenue, Regina; 306-359-7276) brews a line of organic beers, along with two dozen styles offered over the course of the year. Regina also has three Brewsters Brewing Co. & Restaurants (1832 Victoria Avenue East, Regina; 306-761-1500), (1686 Albert Street, Regina; 306-761-0784), and (480 McCarthy Boulevard North, Regina; 306-522-2739), which offer about a dozen craft-brewed beer styles. There's also a Brewsters over in Moose Jaw (8 Main Street North, Moose Jaw; 306-694-5580). I'm not sure where the name came from, and I don't want to know, but you can always visit the Hose and the Hydrant Brewing Co. (612 11th Street East, Saskatoon), one of Saskatoon's many brewpubs.

Here's a list of the other brewpubs in Saskatchewan:

➤ Barley Mill Brewing Co., Regina

➤ Bonzzini's Brewpub, Regina

➤ Checkers, Swift Current

➤ Chubby's, Yorkton

➤ Clarks Crossing, Saskatoon

➤ Fox and Hounds Brewpub, Saskatoon

➤ Last Straw, Regina

➤ Saskatoon Brewing Co. & Cheers, Saskatoon

Amazing Ales in Alberta

Alberta starts out on the high plains in the east and ends in the Canadian Rockies to the west—some of the most spectacular scenery in North America. This is big country. So as you would imagine, folks up here like to do things big. Besides possessing the world's biggest brewpub in the world's largest shopping mall, Alberta is also home to Big Rock Brewery (555 76th Street Southeast, Calgary; 800-242-3107). Big Rock recently opened an expansive four-acre, $16.5 million (Canadian) craft brewery, three times the size of its old facility. Big Rock's Cold Cock Winter Porter, Buzzard Breath Pale Ale, and Warthog Ale have garnered raves by folks on both sides of the 48th Parallel since the brewery's opening in 1985.

Wynkoop in Denver once claimed to be the biggest brewpub in the world. But that title has fallen to a new contender—Red's in Edmonton. Red's has an enormous 105,000-square-feet of space, room for 2,000 people, 28 bowling lanes, a 400-seat nightclub, a 300-seat restaurant, 24 pool tables, an 11-piece house band, an arcade with virtual reality games, two (count 'em, *two*) souvenir shops, and a partridge in a beer tree. Brewpub hardly seems a worthy term for this $12 million (Canadian) enterprise—brew-mall is more fitting. Red's is a project of the bowling-alley company Brunswick Indoor Recreation and is located in the world's largest shopping mall in Edmonton. If this project works, look for 10 more of these behemoths to be opened across the U.S. and Canada.

Alberta also boasts three Brewsters Brew Pub & Brasseries (834 11th Avenue SW, Calgary; 403-263-2739), (176–755 Lake Bonavista Drive, Southeast, Calgary; 403-225-2739), and (11620/104 Avenue, Edmonton; 403-482-4677). Folks in Calgary also stampede into Mission Bridge Brewing Co. (2417 Fourth Street Southwest, Calgary; 403-228-0100).

For all you need to know about real ale in Alberta, contact CAMRA at 204 Ranchview Place, Northwest, Calgary, Alberta, T3G 1R7; 403-239-3907; e-mail: penfoldj@cia.com. CAMRA sponsors Brewtopia—a festival of microbreweries from western Canada and the northwestern U.S. that aids the Alberta Theatre Projects group. And you homebrewers can join Marquis De Suds Homebrewers Club in Calgary.

Here's a listing of Alberta's other brewpubs:

➤ Grizzly Paw Pub & Brewing Company, Canmore

➤ West Trail Brewing Co./Taps, Edmonton

These are Alberta's microbreweries:

➤ Alley Kat Brewing Co., Edmonton

➤ Banff Brewing Co., Calgary

➤ Bow Valley Brewing Co., Canmore

➤ Brew Brothers Brewing Co., Calgary

➤ Flanagan & Sons Brewing Co., Edmonton

➤ Wild Rose Brewery Ltd., Calgary

Beautiful Brewpubs in British Columbia

British Columbia is home to spectacular scenery and Vancouver, one of the world's picturesque cities. And B.C. has its share of beautiful brews with eight brewpubs and twenty microbreweries. On charming Vancouver Island, Spinnakers Brewing Co. (308 Catherine Street, Victoria; 604-386-2739) was B.C.'s first brewpub and brews 23 different beer styles. Most are cask-conditioned and some are served from casks perched right on the bar. Victoria is also home to the Prairie Inn Cottage Brewery (7806 East Saanich Road, Victoria; 604-652-1575). Steamworks Brewing Co. (375 Water Street, Vancouver;

604-689-2739) brews a beer called Espresso and the formidable Ain't She Wheat, along with its other offerings. Victoria's other brewpub, Swan's Pub/Buckerfield Brewery (506 Pandora Street Victoria; 604-361-3310; e-mail: swans@islandnet.com), brews six year-round beers, including Pandora Pale Ale, along with 11 seasonals such as Dragon Lady Porter.

Cosmopolitan Vancouver is fertile brewing grounds. Granville Island Brewing Co. (1285 W. Broadway #214, Vancouver; 604-738-9463; e-mail: msimpson@cascadia.ca) is in the middle of the trendy shopping district. Viking lovers might want to visit Sailor Hägar's Brewpub (221 West First Street, North Vancouver; 604-984-3087). Another Vancouver watering hole is Yaletown Brewing Co. (1110 Hamilton Street, Vancouver; 604-688-0039; e-mail: brew@axionet.com) where you can drink up the likes of Old Hooligan Old Ale.

If you're "oot and aboot" in B.C., stop in at Black Mountain Brew Pub (2040 Old Joe Riche Road, Kelowna; 250-491-1020).

Here's a list of B.C.'s many microbreweries:

➤ Bastion City Brewing, Nanaimo

➤ Bear Brewing Company Ltd., Kamloops

➤ Bowen Island Brewing Co., Bowen Island

➤ Granville Island Brewing, Vancouver

➤ Hägar's Brewing Company, North Vancouver

➤ Horseshoe Bay Brewery, Horseshoe Bay

➤ Kimberly Brewing Company, Kimberly

➤ Mt. Begbie Brewing Company, Revelstoke

➤ Nelson Brewing Company, Nelson

➤ Okanagan Spring Brewery, Vernon

➤ Pacific Western Brewing Co., Prince George

➤ Russell Brewing, Surrey

➤ Shaftesbury Brewing Co., Delta

➤ Storm Brewing Ltd., Vancouver

➤ Tall Ship Ale Co., Squamish

➤ Tin Whistle Brewing Company, Penticton

➤ Tree Brewing Co., Kelowna

➤ Vancouver Island Brewing, Victoria

➤ Whistler Brewing Co., Whistler

➤ Windermere Brewing Company, Invermere

The Northwest Territories

The Arctic Brewing Co. in Yellowknife is the only territorial brewery in Canada and the northernmost brewery in North America. In the spectacular land of the midnight sun, dog team racing, fishing, hunting, hiking, and canoeing you can gaze at the northern lights while sipping on an Arctic Diamond dark beer.

Canada is a great big land with great big brews to match. From the Belgian-influenced beers in the east to the icy Arctic ales of the Northwest, Canada offers a rich and varied craft-brewed palette with which to paint your beery palate. Whether buying them imported in the U.S. or drinking them straight from the tap in the Great White North, you just can't lose with Canadian brews.

Stale Ale Alert

For years, a rumor persisted that Canadian beers like Labatt's and Molson were stronger than big-selling U.S. brews. People believed this because Canadians measured their alcohol content by volume, not weight. A 5% by volume Molson is really only 4% by weight—comparable to most American mass-brewed beers. With American micros measuring alcohol by volume, using the same method as Canada and the rest of the world, those rumors are beginning to fall by the wayside.

The Least You Need to Know

➤ Some of the world's greatest beers are made in Canada.

➤ Many of Quebec's breweries are following the Belgian beer style, while the rest of the provinces tend toward the English, Scottish, and Irish styles.

Chapter 18

Hands Across the Water: Great Beer in Great Britain and Ireland

In This Chapter

➤ An overview of the brewing scene in England, Scotland, and Ireland

➤ A region-by-region snapshot of brewpubs, breweries, beer festivals, and other beery sites

➤ Phone numbers, addresses, and Web sites related to brewpubs, microbreweries, and breweries in Great Britain and Ireland

Throughout the 18th and 19th centuries, brewers in Great Britain and Ireland developed the ale styles that most of us are familiar with today. Ironically, the reason most of us *are* familiar with those styles is that the American microbrewery revolution reintroduced the browns, porters, stouts, barley wines, and old ales of our great-great-grandparent's generation. When the rest of the world became enamored of lagers in the 1850s and switched to them exclusively, the British stubbornly stuck to their ales. Although about 40% of the beer sold in the United Kingdom these days is lager, the British Isle ale tradition lives on.

Ale is one thing, but British beer purists want only cask-conditioned ale. In fact, they're fanatics for what's known as *real ale*. These folks believe that the ale must be naturally carbonated in the barrel, and served from that barrel, or it's no good. Thanks to the

Campaign for Real Ale, there's no shortage of places to find real ale in Britain. All you need to do is join CAMRA, pick up one of their excellent pub (public house) guides, or hunt the information down on the Internet.

The Tun Always Whets on the British Empire: Beer in the United Kingdom

The British Isles have rich and colorful traditions steeped in history and ancient custom. Kings, queens, clans, and empires have risen and fallen like the icy waves of the North Sea. But the one tradition that has managed to withstand the ravages of time and emerge victorious is the practice of British ale.

MMM **Tasty Tip** For endless amounts of information about U.K. pubs on the World Wide Web, check out the Pubworld site (and its links) at http://www.pubworld.co.uk/.

MMM **Tasty Tip** There are more than 60,000 pubs in England. For a list of 1,400 "recommended" pubs, and 2,600 "Lucky Dips,"(whatever that means) pick up *The Good Pub Guide,* edited by Alisdair Aird. The book also lists specialties such as pubs with good gardens, pubs with great views, pubs near the motorway, and so on.

The British Isles have a history of brewing almost as old as the people themselves. Water-powered mills for grinding grain were first introduced in England in A.D. 500. This enabled folks to grind their own grain and render it useful in the brewing of beer. Homebrewed ale was common and folks drank it from horns and wooden cups. The Scots, because of the excessive cold climate and lack of fruit for wine, made a strong liquor from barley called *zithus,* which—according to historians—they drank to distraction.

The first set of laws regulating English ale sellers were decreed in 616 by Ethelbert, King of Kent. In the 900s, King Edgar ruled that there should be only one ale house per settlement. The church controlled most of the brewing at this point anyway, but the nobility was starting to realize that money and power could be associated with brewing. The issue was so important that a clause dealing with ale standards was included in the Magna Carta in 1215. By the 1300s, London had 1,700 taverns and breweries for its 35,000 residents. And the water was so polluted there that men, women, and children *had* to drink ale if they wanted to drink anything at all. Of course, much of this was a low alcohol affair known as small ale.

Today there are around 220 breweries in the U.K. and Ireland. They range from "rabbit hole" brewpubs to brewing giants like Bass and Guinness. To detail every incredible pub and brewery in the British Isles would take volumes. Anyone who has been to the U.K. knows that you can walk down almost any street—in any city, town, or village—

and find pleasing company and great ale. Still, there are a few monuments, shrines, and landmarks that any beer nut should visit if they are lucky enough to find themselves on the loose in the kingdom with a pocketful of pounds and a powerful thirst.

There are three kinds of British pubs—the tied house, the free house, and the brewpub. The tied house is a pub that's tied to a major brewery like Bass, Whitbread, or Watneys. Generally, a tied house will serve beer made only by the brewery it's connected to. You can tell a tied house by the signs in front advertising the ale of a major brewery.

Free houses are the most popular among beer nuts and guidebooks. These pubs are not owned or operated by any brewery, so are "free" to offer a wide choice of brews. Many free houses have real ale, a few lagers, and a couple of imports as well.

Brewpubs, as in North America, offer up the beer they brew on premise.

Tasty Tip
CAMRA's *The Good Beer Guide* lists pubs that serve "real ale." CAMRA also publishes a monthly brewspaper called *What's Brewing*, which it sends to its members. Both books are available at large bookstores or through CAMRA: 34 Alma Road, St. Albans, AL1, 3BW, Hertfordshire, England (0727-867201). Web address: http://camra.org.uk/.

British Firkin Brewpubs

Note: To dial these telephone numbers from anywhere but inside Great Britain, you must first dial 44, which is the country code for the U.K., or 353 for Ireland. The international operator is 011, so any number in England would be preceded by 011-44. Also remember it's five hours later in England than Eastern Standard Time. One other note: I've given prices for tours in British pounds, represented by this symbol: £. While exchange rates vary, a pound is worth approximately a little less than two U.S. dollars. In other words, £4 is worth about $8.

The most well-known of British brewpubs are the *"Firkin"* chain. All these pubs have the word *Firkin* in the name, such as The Fawn & Firkin, the Fedora & Firkin, the Falcon & Firkin, the Feline & Firkin, Philanderer & Firkin—you get the idea. These brewpubs are hard to miss, as there are 72 of them.

The Falcon & Firkin (360 Victoria Park Road, London; 0181 985-0693) has a full-featured children's play-room and sells kids' T-shirts that say "I'm a Firkin half-pint." The brewpub with the longest name I've ever heard of is near Carnaby Street: The Fanfare &

Terms of Enbeerment
A **firkin** is a small beer keg that holds nine Imperial gallons or 72 pints. Two firkins make up a kilderkin, two kilderkins make up a barrel, and one-and-a-half barrels equal a hogshead, or 54 Imperial gallons.

Firkin The Horn the Horn the Lusty Horn Is Not a Thing to Laugh to Scorn (38 Great Marlborough Street, London W1V; 0171 437-5559) sells T-shirts with such lovely messages as "Get Wind of a Firkin Good Hangover" and "Let off Some Wind at the Fanfare." Other Firkin brewpubs include the Feast & Firkin (229 Woodhouse Lane, Leeds; 0113 245-3669), Feline & Firkin (9 Princess Street, Wolverhampton)—try their Pussy Ale—the Felon & Firkin (26 George Street, Leeds), the Ferret & Firkin (114 Lots Road, London SW10; 0171 352-6645), and the Fiddler & Firkin (14, South End, Croydon, Surrey; 0181 680-9728). For a complete list of the six dozen Firkin brewpubs, write The Firkin Brewery, Tamebridge House, Aldridge Road, Perry Bar, Birmingham B42 2TZ, England, or visit the Firkin Info-List on the Internet at http://www.compulink.co.uk/~dalecu/firkin.htm.

Stale Ale Alert
Don't even *think* of having even a pint if you're driving in England. You'll need all your senses intact. They drive on the left there, mate, which is dangerous for North Americans who are trained to look left, then right before crossing a street on foot. In England you have to look right first, as the cars come from that direction—and quickly. Some crosswalks say "Look Right!" but most don't.

The most famous Firkin beer is the notorious Dogbolter, a 5.6% dark strong ale. Folks who do the "Firkin Crawl" visit 12 of London's 24 Firkin pubs in one day and receive a free T-shirt if they make it to the end.

All Firkin beers are unpasteurized and unfiltered. They're brewed from East Anglia malt, Kentish Fuggles, and Goldings hops. The water is "Burtonized" or treated with brewing salts to make it as hard as the water of Burton-on-Trent. Most pubs use wooden casks to store and serve the beer, but some brews have carbon dioxide or nitrogen added to them while serving. The chain is owned by brewing giant Carlsberg-Tetley, which plans to continue opening more brewpubs in the profitable chain.

Some purists reject the "Firkinization" of U.K. pubs and prefer folks who brew on a smaller scale. If you're one of those folks, there are plenty of other brewpubs around, though not as easy to locate. Consult your CAMRA guide.

For those looking for a bed and brewpub, check out Royal Clarence Hotel (The Esplanade, Burnham on Sea, Somerset; 01278-783138). In Dorset, you can visit the Poole Brewery (68 High Street, Poole, Dorset; 01202-685288).

For an extensive list of bed and breakfasts with real ale, visit the Web site of Real Ale and A Bed: http://indigo.stile.le.ac.uk/~gc16/beer/index.htm.

A Snapshot of CAMRA

The Campaign for Real Ale is the godfather of the North American craft-brewing movement. The organization's methods, practices, and especially their festivals promoting real ale have been widely imitated. Startled by the wave of small brewery closings in Britain, CAMRA began its crusade in 1971 and succeeded in educating millions to the value of real ale. CAMRA is an independent consumer organization staffed mainly by volunteers and supported by individual members. Corporate entities such as breweries or pubs are not allowed to join. CAMRA's mission is to act as champion of the consumer in relation to the U.K. and European beer industry. It promotes quality, choice, and value in all things related to beer. CAMRA supports pubs as a focus for community life and it campaigns for a greater appreciation of traditional beers and cider. CAMRA also lobbies for fairer tax laws for small brewers, defends pubs from eviction by landlords, fights takeovers and mergers, and encourages brewers to produce a wider range of beer styles.

CAMRA boasts that for 50 years—until its founding—there were no new ale breweries in the U.K. Now there are more than 200 new brewers producing real ale. CAMRA's membership has grown from 20,000 in 1989 to 48,000 today. There are 180 local branches of CAMRA that produce guidebooks and hold real ale festivals. Lobbying tactics include petitions, threatened boycotts, publicity stunts, funeral marches, laying wreaths outside closed breweries, and so forth.

CAMRA's rallying point is real ale, which is cask-conditioned beer—a living product that continues to undergo secondary fermentation in the cask and is served without artificial carbonation. Bottle-conditioned beers, which ferment in the bottle, are also real ale. CAMRA is keen on real ale because secondary fermentation allows character and flavor to develop, whereas pasteurization and filtration reduce flavor. Contrary to myth, rumor, and innuendo, real ale is not cloudy, flat, or warm. It is served at cellar temperature, about 55°F, and clears in the cask. It's not as carbonic as American mega-swill, but it's lively and bubbly in the mouth.

Real ale must be handled with care and treated properly or it will go bad. It cannot be transported overseas and has a limited shelf life. Very few breweries still use wooden casks for their beer. Three who do are Samuel Smith, Theakstons, and Wadsworths. The aluminum casks that real ale come in are expensive and preserve the beer for only two or three days after they are tapped. British beers that we drink in North America are kegged, not cask conditioned, and according to CAMRA "should *never* be described as real ale."

> **Tasty Tip**
> England and Wales have more than 100,000 miles of public footpaths that wind through field, farm, and forest. Hiking, or as the Brits say, rambling, is an extremely popular sport. Not only can you visit ancient ruins, castles, and the like, but you can ramble from pub to pub. You can walk miles carrying a pack or pay to go on a walking tour where your luggage is carted from town to town on a truck. Those tours include everything (except beer) and start at $200 a day.

Pub Grub: Bloaters, Haggis, and Dead Man's Leg

Some travelers to the U.K. think the words "English cuisine" are an oxymoron. Most Americans are not used to eating mutton, suet, or fried tomatoes (for breakfast). The Brits have a sense of humor about their food names as well as their beer names. (If you've ever had an Old Fart, a Pussy Ale, or a Fizzy Dick, you know what I mean.)

If you're going to be visiting pubs, you'll definitely encounter "pub grub"—some of the most affordable food you'll find. And judging English cuisine from pub grub would be like judging American cuisine from food offered in bars and saloons. Be that as it may, forewarned is forearmed. So here's a little list of traditional British foods, and what they are.

➤ Bubble and Squeak: Cabbage mixed with leftover potatoes and fried until brown with a nice crust.

➤ Clotted Cream: Fresh milk that is allowed to stand for 24 hours, then heated slowly and cooled. (Don't mix with stout.)

➤ Cock-a-leekie: A thick stew made from chicken, leeks, and prunes. (See Chapter 14 for a recipe.)

➤ Cornish Pasties: Pastry turnovers stuffed with beef and potato.

➤ Bloaters: Smoked fish grilled in butter—tastes better than it sounds.

➤ Bangers and Mash: Bangers are sausages; mash is mashed potatoes. When served for breakfast this might be accompanied by bread, tomatoes, and mushrooms—all fried in bacon grease.

➤ Dead Man's Leg: A sponge roll stuffed with strawberry jelly and served with hot custard. (Looks like a chopped-off leg, get it?)

➤ Fish and Chips: For those a little squeamish around bloaters, fish and chips will get you through many a meal. Greasy but good. By the way, chips are what we Yanks call French fries, and what we call potato chips are called "crisps."

➤ Haggis: A traditional Scottish dish. If you eat this you might not want to know what's in it, but here goes: A dish made with sheep heart, liver, offal, suet, and oatmeal.

➤ Pan Haggarty: Potatoes, onions, and grated cheese browned like a pancake in beef fat.

➤ Steak and Kidney Pie: Why someone would put kidney in with their steak is anyone's guess, but it tastes better than it sounds.

➤ Streaky Rashers: What Americans call bacon.

➤ Toad-in-the-Hole: English sausage baked in batter.

Surrey with a Fizz on Top: British Microbreweries

Great Britain is well-known for its big-name breweries—Bass, Courage, and Whitbread. But there are dozens of small, fiercely independent breweries scattered throughout the U.K. Some of these smaller breweries have been run by the same family for generations. Others are just a few years old. A few of them offer tours—some of them free. If you want to rub elbows with some dedicated, friendly folks and absorb some local color, these tours are just what the brewer ordered.

Surrey's Pilgrim Brewery (11c West Street, Reigate, Surrey RH2 9BL, England; 173 722 2651) was founded in 1982 and moved to its current site in 1985. Its first beer was Pilgrim's Progress, brewed from water that percolates down through the incredibly chalky hills called the North Downs. Owners David and Ruth Roberts (and Breeze the dog) welcome you to visit, but please call first. You can visit their Web site at http://www.breWorld.com/PILGRIM.

Jeff Lucas (a.k.a. Lou the Brew), and his wife Maggie started the Bridgwater Brewing Company (Lovedere Farm, Goathurst, Bridgwater, Somerset, TA5 2DD; 01278-663996) in 1993. The goal of the small brewery was to offer beers redolent of traditional West Country ales. They have succeeded with such exemplary brews as Copperknob and Bluto's Revenge—a 6% porter. The BBC, as it's called, is located on a rural site in Goathurst, a few miles outside of Bridgwater. Lou the Brew was a watchmaker by trade who found he had some time on his hands (sorry!) and decided to start brewing with Maggie. The Lucases are always happy to welcome small groups of visitors, although they recommend April through October as the best time to visit. Pint glasses of hospitality flow freely and walking may be a problem for some after a night of revelry. This is a highly recommended tour. You can book a visit by calling Maggie or Lou at the brewery.

Foamy Fact

Your Rent is Brew: In medieval times, English rent and taxes were often paid in homemade ale. Sometimes beer was the only form of currency available, and it was considered as good (or better) than gold. Feudal landholders often requested ale in lieu of coins.

The British ale tradition is wide and deep. But the Freedom Brewing Co. (Parsons Green, Fulham; 0171 731 7372) was established in 1995 with the aim of brewing the best lager in England. Living up to the standards of the Reinheitsgebot, Freedom's lagers are fully lagered for four to six weeks. Freedom's lagers have won rave reviews from critics and the public alike. Freedom Brewery is open for tours every Saturday from 10:30 A.M. to 2:30 P.M.

between May and September. Tours cost £5.00 per head and include beer and barbecue. No prior booking is necessary. Contact Ewan Eastham.

You can visit a microbrewery within the ancient city walls of York at the York Brewery (Toft Green, Micklegate, York; (01904) 621162; e-mail: sc@yorkbrew.demon.co.uk). Founded in 1996, it's the first brewery in the city to open in forty years. York Brewery was designed not only as a workplace but also as a tourist attraction, and there are specially designed viewing galleries from which the whole brewing process can be seen.

Tour times are 11 A.M., 12:30 P.M., 2:30 P.M., 4 P.M., and 6 P.M. Monday through Friday. There's a limited number of spots on each tour, so reserve your place by telephone or e-mail. It costs £3.00 per adult, £1.50 for 14- to 17-year-olds, and it's free for 13-year-olds and under. There's plenty of ale for the grown-ups. You can visit York Brewery's Web site at http://www.yorkbrew.demon.co.uk/visits.html.

The "Peculier" British Breweries

Breweries in Britain do not generally offer tours to folks who just turn up at their door. You can call or write weeks before your planned visit to arrange tours. Some of the most popular breweries, however, have a *two-year* waiting list for tours. A few breweries do have brewery museums or tourist spots where you can go to steep yourself in the misty beer lore of yore. Tours usually cost £4 to £7 but include food and plenty to drink. Some of these breweries are independent family brewers, some are giant conglomerates. What they all have in common is tradition, quality, and history.

Fuller ales are well-known on both sides of the pond. Fuller's Griffin Brewery (Chiswick Lane South, Chiswick, London W4 2QB; 181 994 3691) is nestled between the River Thames and Hogarth Roundabout, the busiest junction in the U.K. Fuller's beers have won more CAMRA Beer-of-the-Year Awards than any other brewery. A brewery has stood at this site in Central London since the days of Oliver Cromwell. The historic brewery is open for 90-minute tours four days a week. After the comprehensive tour, visitors can go to the Hock Cellar, where brewing artifacts and memorabilia are on display. They can also sample a full range of draft real ales. Tours take place every Monday, Wednesday, Thursday and Friday at 10 A.M., 11 A.M., 1 P.M., and 2 P.M. The prices are £4.00 per adult and £2.50 per child (14 and older).

Oxford is known for more than its famous university. It's also recognized for Morrells Brewery (St. Thomas Street, Oxford, OX1 1LA; 186 581 3000). It's the oldest surviving family-run business in Oxford. Parts of the brewery date to the 16th century, and the Morrell family has run the brewery for more than 250 years. Today a 100-year-old kettle bubbles away next to a state-of-the-art, stainless-steel mash tun.

The tour takes visitors through a thousand years of Oxford's brewing history. Tourists taste the malt, smell the hops, and drink the beers. Tours start at the Brewery Gate pub next to the brewery. Walk-in tours last one hour and are conducted daily at noon from June 1 to September 30 and are limited to Saturdays and Sundays from October 1 to May 31 (except Christmas/Boxing Day and New Year's Eve/Day). The Brewery Gate Shop sells an extensive range of brewing souvenirs, clothes, books and a wide variety of pub wares.

Foamy Fact

Rolling Rails of Ales: The invention of the railroad train in the 1820s led to a massive expansion of breweries in England. By 1840, railroad trains allowed brewers to ship beer all over the country; whereas a horse and wagon had been limited to within a 20-mile radius of the brewery. Bass Brewery in Burton went from 10,000 barrels-a-year production in 1837 to 60,000 barrels a year 10 years later thanks to the Midland railroad system. Bass increased to 900,000 barrels a year by 1876 thanks to the brewery's 11 rail engines.

The George Bateman & Son Brewery (Salem Bridge Bry, Mill Lane, Wainfleet, Skegness, Lincolnshire; 1754 880317) was founded in the Lincolnshire town of Skegness on the North Sea 1874. Today Bateman makes a wide range of ales including Dark Mild, XB, Valiant, Salem Porter, Victory Ale, and XXXB, CAMRA's "Beer of the Year" in 1986. This family-run brewery offers tours to anyone over the age of 16. For £10.00 per person you get a "Brewery Tour with Pie and Peas." This includes a one-hour tour of the brewery, samples of Bateman's Good Honest Ales in the Windmill Bar, and then a trek to a local pub for a supper of shepherd's pie, chips, and peas. For £30.00 per person, the tour includes a stay at a Wainfleet bed & breakfast.

Founded in 1758, the Samuel Smith Brewery (Tadcaster, Yorkshire, LS24 9DSB, England; 093 783 2225) is Yorkshire's oldest. Charles Dickens wrote about it in *A Tale of Two Cities*, and it's still a family-owned brewery. Samuel Smith beers, like the famous Taddy Porter and Imperial Stout, are fermented in giant, 12-foot-square, slate-stone fermenters that impart a unique flavor to the brew. Water from the beers is drawn from a 200-foot-deep well. I'd walk across England for a Sammy Smith beer fresh from the brewery. It's well worth the trip to charming Tadcaster.

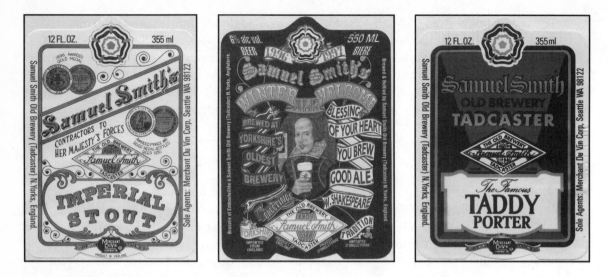

Charles Dickens wrote of the amazing beers brewed at Samuel Smith's in Tadcaster, England. The 1758 brewery is a must-see for any beer traveler.

The folks in Masham have been mashing the particularly named Old Peculier at the T&R Theakston Brewery (Wellgarth, Masham, Ripon, North Yorks, HG4, 4DX; 176 589 544) since 1827. Theakston is the last of the world's breweries to still employ its own cooper (barrel maker). If you visit the brewery you can see Clive Hollis build 150-pound, 36-gallon, Polish-oak barrels by hand. These barrels, which gently mellow the beer, can last up to 60 years. Little has changed at the Theakston brewery since the "new" brewhouse was built in 1875—except the gristmill is now powered by electricity instead of steam. The brewer says, "Our suppliers want our hop filter for their museum. We need it to make our beer." The Old Peculier folks extend a welcome to visitors, and more than 20,000 people a year take them up on it.

The Caledonian Brewery (42 Slateford Road, Edinburgh, EH11 1PH, Scotland; 131 337 1286) is Scotland's premier brewery that turns out award-winning Golden Promise organic ales and MacAndrews Scotch Ale (the latter of which is called Edinburgh Strong Ale in Scotland). Founded in 1869, the Caley brewery is a survivor of fires, shut-downs, and attempted takeovers. The company was rescued from extinction in 1986 by local politicians, the financial community, and brewery workers. Today, the direct-fired kettles, the last used anywhere, are producing ales enjoyed the world over.

For centuries, the kilt-clad, bagpipe-playing soldiers of Scotland were referred to as the Jocks. Old Jock has been brewed by the same family in Peeblesshire for seven generations.

Tours are conducted from 10 A.M. to noon and from 2 P.M. to 4 P.M. Monday, Tuesday, Wednesday, and Thursday; and on Friday between 10 A.M. and noon. The 90-minute tour includes tastings from Caledonian's extensive portfolio of 13 hand-crafted cask ales plus one of Anderson the Baker's famous pies. The cost is £5.00 per person. Trips are for clubs and organizations, but if you call you might get in on one. Call Willie Verdin or fax him at 131 337 1282 to arrange a spot.

Hopping Through Brit Brew History

After visiting dozens of ancient abbeys and castles, you might want see how the salt of the earth really lived. Well, the lives of the malt of the earth have been well preserved in dozens of brewing museums and historical attractions. A few of the best-known attractions are listed here.

Foamy Fact

Now That's *Old Ale:* Scottish and Newcastle Breweries in Edinburgh have brewed a beer using dried yeast sediment found in a clay jar in a 3,500-year-old Egyptian tomb known as the Sun Temple of Nefertiti. The brew was reconstructed using analysis of the Nile's waters and a recipe written in ancient hieroglyphics. It's primarily wheat with a little coriander and naback fruit thrown in for flavor. The beer is mostly for folks in the beer industry and the rest goes to the Egyptian Exploration Society. (By the way, folks who reconstruct ancient beer recipes are called palaeozymoligists. Try saying that three times fast—or even once slowly.)

Kent is known the world over for its Golding hops. If you want to see the graceful verdant vines in all their hoppy glory, you can pay a visit to The Whitbread Hop Farm (Beltring, Paddock Wood, Kent, TN12 6PY; 162 287 2068). This is a family park with the history of hop farming, horses, a zoo, hot air balloons, a restaurant, and other special events. And it's open all year round.

The Bass Brewery Museum (P.O. Box 220, Horninglow Street, Burton upon Trent, Staffs, DE14 1JZ; 01283 511000) in Burton upon Trent takes visitors through 200 years of British brewing history. The museum is free and has hands-on exhibits, a restaurant, and horses. Of course, there's a bar serving fresh Bass ale. Open every day except Christmas Day, Boxing Day and New Year's Day. From 10 A.M. weekdays, 10:30 A.M. weekends. Last admission 4 P.M.

The Traquair House Brewery (Innerleithen, Peeblesshire, The Borders, EH44 6PW, Scotland; 089 683 0323) is a 50-room mansion that boasts it is the oldest inhabited house in Scotland. Parts of the building date to the year 1107. Traquair House ale is first mentioned in an account of a visit by Mary Queen of Scots in 1566, and they still have the receipt from the purchase of their current brewkettle—paid for in 1738. While the 20th Laird of Traquair, Peter Maxwell Stuart, was exploring the four-story manor house in 1965, he came across the disused brewery. Soon he put the original equipment back to work. The four-barrel brewery is one of the world's smallest. The precious and expensive beer is exported to the United States and other countries and the Traquair house receives 50,000 visitors annually. Not to be missed.

Great British Beer Festivals

CAMRA sponsors something like 180 festivals every year. They tend to be around the same time of year in each locality. There are Winter Ale Fests, Valentine's Fests, and on and on. The main CAMRA event is The Great British Beer Festival. It's held every August, usually in London. There's live entertainment, food, family rooms, and more real ale than any one human could possibly drink. In fact, there are 500 brands, not including ciders and foreign bottle beers. Each year, 42,000 or so people gather in the Grand Hall at Olympia to chug more than 250,000 pints of beer. For more information contact CAMRA at Tel. +44 (0) 1727 867201, Fax. +44 (0) 1727 867670.

Brewing on the Emerald Isle

Folks in Ireland have raised barley for about 5,000 years, and history shows the Celts have been making beer since the Bronze Age. As in England, the church was in charge of brewing up until the 1600s. St. Patrick was said to employ his own personal brewer. Although beer wasn't quite as popular as whisky when Arthur Guinness started making beer at St. James's Gate in Dublin in 1759, a new era of Irish brewing was born. Guinness ale swept through the Emerald Isle and England as well. The brewery invented Guinness Extra Stout in 1820 and the rest, as they say, is history. By 1914, the Guinness brewery was the largest in the world. Although it has been dwarfed in modern times by megaliths such as Coors, Guinness is still the largest stout brewery in the world.

Foamy Fact

Of Irish Kings and Celts: In Ireland, a land of fantastic fables, there is also a story concerning ale—of course. Legend has it that Brian Boru, an 11th-century Celtic king, was riding his horse one day when a magical cloud descended upon him. Out of the cloud appeared a Celtic god with a beautiful young girl by his side. The bonny lass handed the king a glass of tasty, red Irish ale. The king passed it on to his people, and a tradition was born. This was centuries before Sir Arthur Guinness handed Guinness Extra Stout to king and commoner alike.

Ireland is famous for its ale, but there's not a lot of craft brewing going on. With Guinness (St. James's Gate, Dublin; 01 536700), Murphy's Lady's Well Brewery (Leitrim Street, Cork; 021 503371), Beamish & Crawford (South Main, Cork; 021 276841), and Smithwick & Sons (Saint Francis Abbey Brewery, Kilkenny; 056 21014) operating on such a small island, I guess only a few people have tried to compete. Guinness does offer daily tours, has a charming gift shop, and you can see several of their 500,000-pint brew-kettles. Now that's a lot of Guinness! You can visit the Guinness Web site at http://wombatix.physics.ucg.ie/misc/guinness.html.

Dublin presently has one microbrewery. Support The Porter House (Parliament Street, D2, Dublin) and maybe a few others will take the cue.

Dublin pub crawling can be astounding. The Temple Bar district offers street performers, traditional dancers, and great Irish music around every corner. A tour group offers the Literary Pub Crawl, complete with actors reading Joyce, Yeats, and Beckett, in the pubs where the poets got their beery inspiration. For more information call 01 540288.

I recommend forays into rural areas like County Cork, the Wicklow Mountains, and the west coast in general. Every town, large and small, has charming pubs with great Irish beer. There's a Web site (of course) dedicated to Irish brewing and pubs with all the latest updates. Check it out: Beer Hunting in Ireland at http://www.tiac.net/users/tjd/bier/ireland.html.

The Least You Need to Know

➤ Great pubs are to be found everywhere in the United Kingdom, including Scotland and Ireland.

➤ If you want the best, pick up the real ale guides from CAMRA or find information on the Internet.

➤ Most U.K. brewery tours cost money and need an advanced reservation.

Chapter 19

The Bubbly Golden Triangle: Continental Europe's Great Brewing Nations

In This Chapter

➤ An overview of the brewing scene in the Netherlands, Belgium, Germany, and the Czech Republic

➤ A region-by-region snapshot of brewpubs, breweries, beer festivals, and other beery sites

➤ Phone numbers, addresses, and Web sites related to continental Europe's brewpubs, microbreweries, and breweries

The European continent is home to the world's greatest beer culture. With traditions dating back at least a thousand years, the countries of Belgium, Germany, and the Czech Republic have breweries and historic beer sites in hundreds of cities, towns, and villages. Great pubs, of course, are on practically every block. The area between Belgium, Germany, and the Czech Republic can be called the bubbly golden triangle for all the unique and delicious beer styles that originated there. They include the lambics, wheats, and strong ales of Belgium; the bocks, dunkels, rauchbiers, and alts of Germany; and the Pilsners and dark lagers of the Czech Republic.

Because of the exchange rate, American tourists often suffer from "sticker shock." The high cost of almost everything in Europe, from hotel rooms to gasoline to food, puts a dent in many budgets. But incredible local beers are usually the most affordable commodity around—especially at beer stores. Beer prices in cafes are about the same on either side of the pond.

One note: most—but not all—small breweries that are not brewpubs do not give tours to the general public. The ones that do require that you write them well in advance and give them a choice of times when you expect to visit. If you're lucky, they'll find an English-speaking guide to give you the tour. If you don't speak the language, you might try learning a few words to ask questions and receive answers. A book published in Amsterdam, *Elsevier's Dictionary of Barley, Malting and Brewing,* has brewing terms in five languages (German, English, French, Italian, and Spanish) with an index in each language. But beer is an international language and nodding heads, giving thumbs up, and happy sighs of pleasure can replace dictionaries. So after visiting castles, museums, and other typical tourist sites, just remember that local color and history can be found, too, a stone's throw away in a pub or brewery.

Addressing the Addresses

Before I start I'd like to give a hint about the following addresses and telephone numbers. European addresses look different from those in North America. When looking at an address and phone number like this—Walplein 26, B-8000 Bruges; 050 345935—the first word, Walplein, is the street name. The number following is the address on the street (although sometimes the street address is in front of the street name). The letter/number B-8000 is the postal code, like the U.S. zip code, and the last word, Bruges, is the name of the city.

The telephone numbers should work if dialed as I've written them. I can't figure out why some have six numbers, some have eight, and some have nine. I don't know if *anyone* knows. These are the numbers as written in directories, so good luck. In some instances, telephone numbers were unavailable.

Each country has its own code if you call from another country. In this chapter, the country codes for dialing are: 31 for the Netherlands; 32 for Belgium; 49 for Germany; and 42 for the Czech Republic. Again, I recommend calling or writing well ahead of time to schedule any brewery tours.

The Never, Neverland of the Netherlands

The folks in the Netherlands have always been known for their sophisticated approach to enjoyment. The Dutch beer tradition is no exception. The tiny country has almost 30 breweries and Amsterdam has scores of "brown cafes," so named for their tobacco-smoke stained ceilings. The Netherlands is probably easiest on the pocketbook and has some of the best public transportation in Europe, including hundreds of miles of paved bicycle trails. Bikes are a great way to see the country because it's as flat as day-old beer.

Maximilaan Cafe (Kloveniersburgwal 6–8, NL-1012 CT Amsterdam; 020 6242778) is the city's first brewpub. Its specialty is a deep-copper, spicy, wheat-bock ale, but it also serves great food cooked in beer.

When Don Quixote tilled at windmills, he probably couldn't imagine one with a brewpub inside. But that's exactly what you get at 't IJ (Funnenkade 7, NL-1018 AL, Amsterdam; 010 228235). Another Amsterdam brewery cafe is De Drie Ringen Brouweerij (Kleine Spui 18, NL-3811 BE, Amsterdam; 033 620300). And no trip to Amsterdam would be complete without a visit to the Heineken Brewery (Stadhouderskade 78, NL1072 AE, Amsterdam; 020 5239239), which offers tours daily at 9:30 A.M. and 11 A.M.

Maastricht, in southeastern Netherlands, has quaint, cobbled, narrow streets and was founded by the Romans in 50 B.C. Today the locals like to boast that they have a church for every week of the year and a pub for every day of the year. They also have two world-renowned breweries—St. Christoffel (14 Brede Weg, 6042 GG Roermond; 04750 15740) and Brouwerij De Ridder (Oerverwal 3–9; Postbus 3072, NL-6202 NB Maastricht; 043 216057) which offer tours by appointment. If you want to visit the only Trappist brewery in the Netherlands, call in advance to Beirbrouwerij De Schaapskooi (Eindhovensweg 3, Postbus 394, NL-5000 AJ, Tillburg; 013 358147).

The national beer consumer's organization in the Netherlands is PINT (Postbus 3757, NL-1001 AN, Amsterdam; 010 212262). It is dedicated to support-ing the Netherlands' beer culture. It puts on beer festivals and publishes PINT Nieuws six times a year with events, calendars, reviews, and the like. The *Good Beer Guide to Belgium & Holland,* by Tim Webb, is available through CAMRA. See Appendix B for CAMRA's address and Web site.

Tasty Tip
No, Benelux is not a vacuum cleaner. Belgium, the Netherlands, and Luxembourg collectively are called the Benelux countries. There's probably more innovative brewing going on in these three small nations—especially in Belgium—than almost anywhere else in the world. On the World Wide Web, Peter Crombecq's Benelux Beer Guide (http://www.dma.be/p/bier/beer.htm) offers exhaustive and pithy Benelux beer news. Crombecq's site tells you about the 100 best Benelux beers, and lets you gaze at an archive containing 4,200 beers.

Holland-Daze Festive Occasions

The main beer festival in the Netherlands is the Noordelijk Bierfesival at Huize Mass, Vismarkt 52, NL-9701 BL, Groningen; 050 420267. It's two days in mid-April and features beer from 25 small breweries in the Netherlands, Belgium, and Germany.

Tilting at Windmills: Historic Netherlands Beer Sites

Folks interested in Dutch beer culture from centuries past can visit Biermuseum de Boom (Houttil 1, NL-1811 JL Alkmaar; 072 113801), which has displays on brewing, malting, and barrel-making along with a café. There's also the Bierreclamemuseum (Haagweg 375, NL-4813 XC, Breda; 076 220975), open Sundays 11 a.m. to 8 p.m. Or check out Brouwerijmuseum Raaf, Rijksweg 232, NL-6582 AB, Heumen; 080 581117) with old brewery equipment and a cafe, open daily.

Between the Duvel and the Deep Blue Sea: Belgian Breweries

If our solar system was divided by beer locales, Belgium would be the Milky Way—an endless array of stellar beauties. There are more breweries per capita in Belgium than in any other country in the world. Belgians brew more styles than the rest of the world combined. And until the American craft-brewing revolution, there were more brewing companies in Belgium than in the entire Western Hemisphere. But if you want to peer right into Belgian beer history, you don't need a telescope. Just find a print of *Peasant Wedding*, a painting by Pieter Bruegel the Elder, painted in 1568. In it you'll see ruddy-faced peasants whooping it up with giant clay pitchers full of tawny-brown, murky, foamy beer. In *Still Life with a Glass of Beer, Brazier, and Clay Pipe*, by Jan Jansz van de Velde (1620–62), you can see a perfect rendition of ale as seen by a Dutch master. By the time these paintings were made, the Belgian beer tradition was already half a millennium old.

Tasty Tip

MMM

If you expect a country with multifarious breweries to have a multitude of guidebooks, you'd be right. The bible of Belgian brewing is *The Great Beers of Belgium*, by Michael Jackson (the British beer writer, not the singer). Also, CAMRA publishes *A Selective Guide to Brussels Bars*.

Belgium is really two countries, the Flemish Dutch-speaking north and the Walloon French-speaking south. Brewing in the region that is today's Belgium began as home brewing on farms. In the 11th century, abbeys began brewing beer commercially. Six still do today. During the 16th and 17th centuries, Belgium and the Netherlands were in the center of world commerce. Brewing was a profitable and entrenched business. The grand 17th-century guild houses of Belgian brewers still stand in all their glory on the Grand-Place in Brussels. Belgium is a relatively moderately-priced, and often overlooked destination for tourists.

Before World War I decimated many parts of Belgium, there were 3,000 breweries there. Alas, today only 150 are left, and that number is shrinking due to consolidation and modern economics. Still, there are a few dozen Belgian breweries using techniques and recipes that are 500 years old. So it's not hard to find beery entertainment in Belgium. In fact, there are still 400 beer brands to choose from, and more than 60,000 taverns to drink them in.

The Trappist Tours

The Trappist monasteries of Belgium bring back impressions and emotions from times long past. The monks' serene demeanor and reverent devotion to their beliefs is rare and unusual as the 20th century draws to a close. The Abbaye de Notre-Dame d'Orval (6823 Villers-devant-Orval; 061 311060) is in the beautiful Ardennes Valley on the border of France. Although Orval has been brewed "only" since 1931, the abbey has been there since the 1100s. Visits may be arranged in advance. The monks also make delicious whole-grain bread and a mild cheddar-like cheese resembling port-salut.

Chimay ales have been brewed at Abbaye de Notre-Dame de Scourmont (6483 Forges; 060 210311) since 1863. The Trappist brothers use only organic ingredients and pure well water. The rustic Abbeye de Notre-Dame de Saint-Rémy (5430 Rochefort; 084 213181) brews Rochefort beers and is perhaps the most beautifully located and least famous of the abbey breweries. To the northeast of Antwerp you'll find the Abdij der Trappisten (2140 Malle; 033 1205353), where the decidedly amazing Westmalle beers are brewed.

The Bruegel Route: Belgium's Lambic Region

No trip to Belgium would be complete without a trip to the Lambic (or Lembeek) region in the Senne Valley south and west of Brussels. This region is known as Payottenland. Like the Trappists, lambic brewers are fiercely autonomous artisans from a bygone era. Lambic breweries look like old barns filled with dust, aging hops, aged brewing equipment, and gushing oak casks full of fermenting brew. (The casks, following tradition, are never cleaned on the outside but are well-scrubbed inside.) High in the rafters, large brass cooling vessels full of wheat and barley juice invite a mélange of lusty wild yeasts to breed with wanton abandon in the thick wort. The final product is not an ale, not a lager, but something untamed and spontaneous from the microflora of the Senne Valley. Virtuoso blenders mix old and young lambics to synthesize a perfect gueuze. Pounds and gallons of cherries (kriek) and raspberries (framboise) are aged in the lambic for months to create the planet's most ambrosial potion. Finally, the blend is bottled, corked, and wired shut. Some bottles are wrapped in gaily decorated tissue paper.

The road that runs through the region is called the Bruegel Route because these are the people and landscapes that inspired the great painter's work. Frank Boon (Fonteinstr 65, B-1502 Lembeek; 023 566644) runs the only lambic brewery left in the town of Lembeek. His artisanal blends are the center of lambic nirvana. His brews are 100% spontaneously fermented and he uses no syrups or extracts in his Kriek and Framboise.

The Lindemans Brewery (257 Lenniksebaan, 1712 Vlezenbeek; 025 960390) has produced astonishingly lovely lambics in aged oak since 1811.

The De Troch Brewery (20 Lange Straat, B-1741 Wambeek; 025 821027) is less than orthodox, adding exotics such as pineapple and banana to its lambics. But De Troch's Chapeau Gueuze Lambic is mouth-watering.

One of the oldest breweries in the region is Liefmans (200 Aalst Straat, 9700 Oudenaarde; 055 311392). This Oudenaarde brewery dates from 1679, although the nearby Abbey of St. Arnoldus was making beer here as early as 1084. St. Arnold also happens to be the patron saint of brewers. Liefmans was run in the 20th century by a ballet dancer named Madame Rose, whose picture used to grace every bottle. Liefmans brews its Frambozenbier with Flanders brown ale, not lambic, and it's a complex and piquant ale.

Liefmans in Oudenaarde has been brewing since 1679. In the nearby Abbey of St. Arnoldus, St. Arnold—the patron saint of brewers— was making beers in 1084.

Kwak, the Devil, and Sudden Death: Belgium's Ale Breweries

Maybe it's the holy righteousness of the Trappist monks. Maybe it's a result of being squashed between Germany and France. Whatever the cause, Belgium's secular brewers have some of the most fatalistic beer names around. There's Duvel (Devil)—and its not-really wicked imitation Lucifer. There's Mort Subite (Sudden Death) and Delirium Tremens (as in the D.T.'s, the drinker's disease). Of course, there's also Bos Keun (Easter Bunny), Kwak, La Chouffe (the gnome), and—my favorite—Saison de Silly. The latter, by the way, comes from the town of Silly, where the brewery's been operating for four generations.

Whatever the names, Belgium has scads of brewing monuments that don't just belong to the saints. Stop by the Brasserie Moortgat (Breendonkdorp 58, B-2870 Breendonk-Puurs; 038 867121), where Duvel is made, and see the sign that says "Shhh...Duvel is ripening here." A visit to Wallonia, in the French-speaking part of Belgium, would not be complete without stopping at Brasserie Dupont (5 Rue Basse, 7904 Tourpes-Leuze; 069 662201). The 1850 farmhouse brewery is the spot where Saison Dupont is brewed. The owner also sells eggs out of the "executive" office.

Rodenbach is one of the world's most unique beers, aged for two years in giant wooden oak tuns. If you stop by the Brouwerji Rodenbach (133–141 Spanje Straat, 8800 Roeselare; 051 223400) you can see the "Burgundy of Belgium" fermenting in some 300 of the vessels in the 1820 brewery.

At 8% Kwak is one strong beer with a taste that can take you back to the Renaissance. It's been made in Buggenhout for 200 years by Brouwerij Bosteels (Kerkstr 92, B-9225 Buggenhout; 052 332282).

Foamy Fact

Café Society: Belgium calls itself "Beer Lovers' Paradise" because of its multifarious breweries. There's one beer café for every 170 people in the country. That's down, however, from the turn of the century when there were 200,000 cafés—one for every 32 people.

Lovers of the cloudy and thirst-quenching Flemish wit beer can pass the days in a wheaty haze touring the wit breweries. The style's been brewed in Hoegaarden since at least 1380. The last of Hoegaarden's wit breweries closed in 1957. But the De Kluis Brouwerij van Hoegaarden (Stoopkenstraat 46, B-3320 Hoegaarten; 016 767676) was reestablished in 1965 by Pierre Celis, who now brews his famous wit beer in Austin, Texas.

Another must-see is the town Bruges, one of Europe's most well-preserved medieval cities. Belgian lace, pralines, and charming cafes make up the city scene. The Brouwerij De Gouden Boom (Golden Tree) (Langestraat 45, B-8000 Bruges; 050 330699) is near one of the city's main canals. Blanche de Bruges beer is made in this brewery, which is more like a working museum on industrial archeology. Tours are conducted daily. Also in Bruges is Huisbrouwerij Straffe Hendrik (Walplein 26, B-8000 Bruges; 050 345935), a small brewery that gives tours Monday through Saturday, March through September.

Belgian Historical Sites

A country so rich in history should have a lot of historic brewing sites. And Belgium does. Aside from the fact that many of the above breweries are historic in and of themselves, there are plenty of other Belgian hop spots. Tourists can see the history of Bruges brewing in the Bruges Brouwerij Mouterij Museum (10 Verbrand Nieuweland; B-8000 Bruges 050 330699) which is set in an old malt house. It's open Thursdays through Sunday, June to September.

The spectacular and palatial Confederation of Belgium Brewers Museum (10 Grand-Place, B-1000 Brussels; 025 114987) is in the Brewer's Guildhouse and laid out like an 18th-century brewery. It includes a small sample bar, and it's open Monday through Friday year round and on Saturday, from April to October. This is a must-see.

The Musee Bruxellois de la Gueuze (Rue Gheude 56, Brussels; 025 2028910) is an homage to the winy, tart gueuze beer. It's a living museum with the Cantillon Brewery. It's open Monday through Friday, with guided tours on Saturday—but make reservations.

The Nationaal Hopmuseum (71 Gasthuisstraat, Poperinge) is a museum of hops and hop cultivation and tours that include samples of local beer. It's open daily July to August and Sundays and holidays, May to September.

24 Hours of Belgian Beer Festivals

The big beer festival in Belgium is the 24 Hours of the Belgian Special Beers which translates in Belgian to the OBP Beer Festival in Antwerp in November. It's run by De Objective Bierproevers and lasts two days. The exact date of the festival changes from year to year, so call 00–32 3 2324538, e-mail: PCrombecq@AntwerpCity.be, or go the Web site: http://www.dma.be/p/bier/7_2_uk.htm.

The Leuven Bierfest is held in Louvain in mid-May and the Adriaan Brouwer Bierfesten is held in Oudenaarde in June. The Carnaval de Binche in Binche is held in February as it has been since the 14th century.

Many Hans Make Beer in Germany

No country loves beer more than Germany. Folks there drink astounding amounts of it daily and have been for more than 500 years. The first lagers were brewed in Germany, as well as dozens of other styles. And the country has 1,500 breweries dotting the landscape—that's 40% of the world's total. Those breweries make more than 5,000 brands. (If you drank two per day, it would take you 6.75 years to taste them all.) The exact number of brands is impossible to determine, because some are available only a few weeks a year during a specific religious feast or other festival. Most of Germany's breweries are in the western part of the country. The former East German brewing industry was badly mismanaged under Soviet rule. Public transportation is abundant in Germany, but accommodations can be very expensive. Food comes in heaping helpings.

With dozens of breweries in every region, there is no dominant brand of beer in Germany. The country's best selling brand, Warsteiner, only fills 5% of the market (as opposed to Anheuser-Busch's 45% of the U.S. market).

To put it mildly, Germany is heaven for lovers of fresh, locally brewed beer. If you fancy eccentric, back-road brands and unconventional brewing artisans, then Deutschland is the place for you. But you better move fast. Unfortunately, like other European countries, Germany is expecting a brew shake-up due to the changing tastes of young people who prefer lighter Pilsner over the "old-fashioned" dunkels and altbiers.

Bavarian Brew: Ja, Ja

Bavaria is the engine from which most of Germany's beer power flows. A third of the world's breweries—and 70% of Germany's—are located in this southeastern state. Nearly every village in Bavaria has a brewery.

Munich, Bavaria's capital, has 13 breweries and hosts the annual Oktoberfest, the world's most famous beer fest. The first place for a beer tourist to visit in Munich would have to be the famous Hofbräuhaus (Am Platzl 9, D-8000 Munich; 221672). The name means royal beer hall, and they aren't kidding. The Hofbräuhaus was built in 1589 by Duke Wilhelm V and seats 4,500 folks on three levels.

Munich is also home to brewers whose beers are readily available in the U.S. All have beer gardens open to the public. Three of them are Spaten-Franziskaner (Marsstr 46–48, D-80018, Munich; 08

Tasty Tip
The *Beer Drinkers Guide to Southern Germany* by James Robertson is an indispensable guide to Bavarian beer establishments. CAMRA publishes the *Good Beer Guide to Munich and Bavaria*. For really good Web links to the best of German beer, visit Germany Beer Links: http://www.tiac.net/users/tjd/bier/germany.html.

951220), Hacker-Pschorr (Hochstr 75, D-8000 Munich; 089 510 6800), and Löwenbräu (Nymphenburgerstr 4, D-8000 Munich; 08 952000).

Some of tastiest beer can be found away from the big city. One of the world's great organic beer brewers is Brauerei Pinkus Müller (Kreuz Straase 4–10, Münster, Nordrhein-Westfalen; 0251 45151–52). The brewery was founded in 1816 by Johannes Müller and the beer is currently brewed by Barbara Müller, the family's first brewster. Next door at the Pinkus Home Brew Haus you can buy an altbierbowle—a drink made by pouring Pinkus Altbier over a bowl of seasonal fruit.

Seventeen kilometers from Munich is Aying, the storybook village of 1,000 beer enthusiasts. The Brauerei Aying (1 Zornedinger Strasse, 8011 Aying; 080 958815) brews up such specialties as Fortunator Doppelbock (called Celebrator in the U.S.), Maibock, and Altbairisch Dunkel. The brewery was founded in 1848 and has been presided over by the Inselkammer family for six generations. Ayinger beers and the brewery itself continue to win awards year after year.

The oldest bock brewery in Germany is the Einbecker Bräu Haus (4–7 Paper Strasse, 3352 Einbeck, Lower Saxony; 055 617970), where the brewery's tower says *"Ohne Einbeck gäb's kein Bockbier"* or "If not for Einbeck there would be no bock beer."

The Georg Schneider & Sohn brewery (1–5 Emil Ott Strasse, 8420 Kelheim; 094 417050) in Kelheim is the world's oldest wheat beer brewery. It began production in the heart of Bavaria in 1607 and makes one of the most complex and delicious wheats the world has ever seen.

Foamy Fact

The Monk Drunk Lunch: There's a reason monks are such energetic brewers: religious fasts. The Bible tells them to abstain from solid food during times like Lent but does not mention beer, also known as liquid bread in Bavaria. Case in point: The Andechs Monastery has been brewing beer since 1455. A member of its board says: "Try an experiment. Go without eating anything for a few hours. Then drink a liter of Andechser Doppelbock (7% alcohol by volume). You won't feel like eating because you won't be hungry."

Kulmbach is a picturesque town in the rolling foothills of the Bavarian Alps. It is also home to three breweries. The Erste Kulmbacher Union (EKU) (EKU Strasse 1, D-95326 Kulmbach; 092 218 2281) has a modern, architecturally striking brewhouse that stands in stark contrast to the ancient castle that overlooks the city. EKU brews E.K.U. "28" and Kulminator doppelbock, two high-quality, high-gravity lagers. Real ice bock beer (eisbock) was invented in Kulmbach by the Reichelbräu Aktien-Gesellschaft (9 Lichtenfelser Strasse, Kulmbach; 092 217051). The chocolaty, roasty flavor of Eisbock gives this potent lager a smooth, powerful flavor.

If you're a lover of smoked beer, the city of Bamberg is on your to-do list. "It's like liquid ham!" the tourist board said about the rauchbier brewed in the nine breweries in and around the city. Once the seat of power of the Holy Roman Empire, Bamberg, population 70,000, sits nestled between seven hills. There are more than 100 breweries ringing the city. The most famous rauchbier brewery is the Brauerei Heller-Trum (Schlenkerla, 6 Dominikaner Strasse, 8600 Bamberg; 095 156060), which makes Aecht Schlenkerla Rauchbier Märzen (available in the U.S.). They've been making rauchbier since 1678. The other rauchbierhaus in Bamberg is a brewpub called Zum Spezial (Obere Koenig Strasse; D-8600 Bamberg; 24304). The Kaiserdom Privatbrauerei (Breitaecker Strasse 9, D-8600 Bamberg; 095 160450) was established in 1718 and is world-famous for its rauchbier. The most dramatic brewing process anywhere takes place at the Rauchenfels Brewery (Ketschenbacher Strasse 25, D-8632 Neustadt/Coburg). Rauchenfels makes steinbier, which is produced by plunging rocks heated to 2,200°F into the wort. The bubbling, crackling, steaming result is a thing to behold.

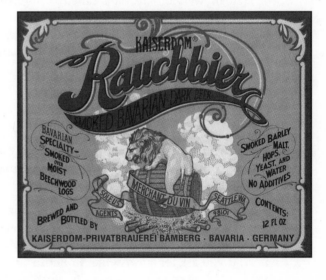

Smokin' brews of Bamberg: These rich and flavorful smoky beers are brewed with malt smoked over beechwood logs.

Foamy Fact

100% Proof: In case you need further proof that Germans love their beer, here are some fascinating figures. Germans drink 253 pints of beer a year for every man, woman, and child in the country. That's 20 pints ahead of the Czechs, their nearest contender. The Bavarians? They drink a whopping 400 pints a year per capita. They pick it up at birth.

More than one brewer has been called a prince by his appreciative audience. If you journey to Kaltenberg, 30 miles west of Munich, you can see the storybook castle of a real prince where a spicy, dark lager is the specialty of the in-house brewery. Prince Luitpold of Bavaria has been running the Schlossbrauerei Kaltenberg (8 Schloss Strasse, 8085 Geltendorf; 081 938071) since he was in his twenties. The castle's König Ludwig Dunkel is *kräusened,* dry hopped, and lagered for six weeks. The castle has a restaurant called the Bräustüberl and a tavern called Ritter Schwemme. Prince Luitpold also has a brewpub, Das Kleine Brauhaus, in Munich's Luitpold Park where wheat beer is brewed.

The state brewery of Bavaria is called Weihenstephan in the city of Freising. Weihenstephan claims to be the oldest brewery in the world, and records show monastic brewers produced beer there as early as 1040 and continue to this time. The building, however, is "newer"—built in the 1600s. There is also a world-famous, state-run brewing college there—the University Faculty of Brewing.

North to the Weisse of Berlin

Bavaria, in the south, is the most famous German brewing state with its countless breweries. But the northern part of the country has many brewing styles in its own right. Berlin, Dortmund, and Cologne also help make Germany the most brewery-laden country in the world.

For a wheat beer obtainable nowhere else, one must travel to Berlin to drink Berliner Weisse. It's been called the champagne of beers for its fruity tartness, pallid golden color, and frothy bubbles. Light in alcohol (about 3% by volume) this cloudy beer is up to 60% wheat. If you ask for a weissebier in Berlin, servers will ask "rot oder grün?" They're asking you "red or green?" That's because the beer is often served with a red raspberry syrup or green woodruff syrup to cut the acidic intensity of the brew. The red, green, and natural yellow beers together are sometimes compared to a set of traffic lights. Only two producers still brew Berliner Weisse. The smaller is the Berliner Kindl Brauerei (50 Werbellin Strasse, New Kölln, 1000 Berlin; 030 689920), whose original brewhouse was taken apart and physically removed by the Russians after World War II. It was never to be seen again. The only other brewer of authentic Berliner Weisse is the Schultheiss-Brauerei (28–48 Methfessel Strasse, Kreuzberg, 1000 Berlin; 030 780030), which was founded in 1840. Berlin also has seven brewpubs.

Dorts to You: Dortmunder

Dortmunder is the biggest brewing city in Germany, mainly because of the two giants, Dortmunder Actien Bräuerei (DAB) and its rival Dortmunder Union Brewery (DUB). Beer making has been going on in Dortmunder since 1293, and there are several brewpubs and small breweries there as well. The full-bodied lagers associated with the city are drier than Munich beer and less hoppy than traditional Pilsner.

Check out Dortmunder's brewpubs like Hoevel's (Hoher Wall, D-4600 Dortmunder). Wenker's (Marketplatz, D-4600 Dortmunder) is owned by Kronen Brauerei (Kronenburgallee 1, D-4600 Dortmund; 023 154130), Dortmunder's independent and oldest brewery.

Catch a Kölsch in Cologne

Cologne (Köln in German) has more than a dozen breweries in its city limits and several others nearby. Most of them specialize in the local style known as Kölsch. Cologne's Guild of Brewers dates back to 1396. The pale, golden top-fermenting drink is cleaner and less fruity than most ales. As it is an appellation like Burgundy, you won't find Kölsch brewed anywhere else. If you're in the city don't miss any of its fine brewpubs.

Privat Brauerei Gaffel-Becker (41 Eigelstein, 5000 Köln; 022 1160060) is in a spot known to have a brewery since 1302. The owner collects drinking glasses and advertising material and has established a museum in the brewpub. Brauhaus Heller (33 Roon Strasse, 5000, Köln; 022 1242545) is in a cavernous basement full of gargoyles and stained glass. The Malzmühle (6 Heumarkt, 5000 Köln; 022 1210118) is a brewpub whose name means "malt mill." P J Früh (12–14 Am Hof, 5000 Köln; 022 12367618) is a large and bustling late 19th-century brewpub.

Alt for a Malt in Düsseldorf

Düsseldorf is the home of altbier, that hoppy German ale in the old style. Düsseldorf is a beautiful city on the Rhine River with a touristy Old Town area containing three alt brewpubs. Zum Schlüssel (43–47 Bolker Strasse, Düsseldorf) name means "the key" in English. Im Füchschen (28 Ratinger Strasse and Schumacher, Ost Strasse, Düsseldorf) has a quaint brewery. Its name means the "little fox." The Zum Uerige (1 Berger Strasse, Düsseldorf; 021 184455) was originally built in 1830 and is decorated in photos of local writers and actors. Folks say it brews the best altbier in the world.

Alt German Historic Sites

The Brauerei Museum (Markischestr 85, D-4600, Dortmund) is a museum owned by Kronen Beer Works. It's open Tuesday to Sunday and entrance is free, but they don't give samples.

The Brauereimuseum (39–41 Heilgengeist Strasse, Lueneburg; 41021) was a working brewery for 500 years. The German Museum of Brewing (St. Jakobs Platz 1, D-8000 Munich; 23 32370) is in historic Munich.

Rock and Bocktoberfest

The superstar of brew festivals is held each year in Munich. In America it's spelled Octoberfest; in Germany, Oktoberfest. It doesn't matter how you spell it because it actually begins in September—the second-to-last Saturday in September to be exact. It ends on the first Sunday in October and lasts 16 days. More than six million people from all over the world descend on Munich for two weeks of smelling, drinking, and spilling beer. That's about 10 million liters in all. And don't forget the food. Revelers at an average Oktoberfest consume 830,000 sausages, 750,000 chickens, 65,000 pork knuckles, and 60 whole oxen. The whole shootin' match nets Munich around $1.2 billion.

Oktoberfest was first celebrated on September 17, 1810. Ostensibly the event was a horse race to commemorate the wedding of Bavarian crown Prince Ludwig von Bayern and Princess Theresa von Sachsen. King Maximilian—the prince's father—saw the event as an excuse to create a sense of Bavarian nationalism in his newly enlarged kingdom. Ludwig had a wandering eye, however, and was forced to abdicate his throne in 1848 when he had an affair with Irish-born dancer Lola Montez. But that's another story.

Oktoberfest has rollercoasters, ferris wheels, and more than 700 stalls and sideshows. But the main attraction is the beer, which cognoscenti feel is getting weaker and lighter every year. Oktoberfest used to be about Märzenbier (March beer, so called because it's brewed in the month of March for consumption in October). But lately the darker, reddish-brown brew has disappeared at Oktoberfest replaced by a pale, golden lager called helles (light) Märzen. Märzen is still served by Munich pubs during the fest but it's hard to find.

Oktoberfest takes place in nine canvas tents, each bigger than a football field, with each seating about 9,000. Off

Tasty Tip
If you're going to Oktoberfest, it's important that you make reservations up to five *months* in advance. You need reservations to get into the tents where full meals are served with (relative) Germanic precision. If you're not sitting down, it's very hard to get served. Standing around with no beer at Munich Oktoberfest is no fun, and lots of people end up that way. Check with your travel agent or check out the Oktoberfest Web site at http://www.munich-tourist.de.

the main avenue there are five more tents. In all, about 100,000 can sit and drink. As the night wears on, dancing ensues on the tables. Ever-smiling waitresses can carry six full-liter mugs of beer in each hand. Be sure to tip them well.

If you're still thirsty after Oktoberfest, you must be part Bavarian. Whatever the case, the Canstatter Volksfest begins in late September and runs to mid-October in Stuttgart. It was established in 1818 by the King of Wurtemberg as a harvest fest, but was really meant to compete with the Munich bacchanal. A lot less touristy, this one's for the locals and the beer is better to boot.

If you're not too enthralled with helles Märzenbier, check out the Starksbierfest in Munich in March. The name means "strong beer fest" and celebrates the annual release of the doppelbocks. If you can remain standing after several hours of drinking these 8% behemoths, your lederhosen need dry cleaning. Prost!

Foamy Fact

Limited to Local Lager: An ancient edict states that only breweries within Munich's city limits can participate in Oktoberfest. This means the annual billion dollar fest is a bonanza only to Munich's big six *brauereis*—Löwenbrauerei, Paulaner, Hacker-Pschorr, Spaten, Hofbräu, and Augustiner. Prince Luitpold, who runs his castle brewery in nearby Kaltenberg, cannot participate in Oktoberfest. Ironically, the prince is a great-great grandson of Ludwig III, who started the whole shebang in 1810. Luitpold tried to circumvent the rules by opening a small brewpub in Munich, but the city council changed the rules to say only breweries operating before 1970 could participate in Oktoberfest. This caused Luitpold to lose a bet with another brewer, so the Prince had to walk the 27 miles from Kaltenberg to Munich carrying a full mug of beer.

Czech Out This Pilsner

After the Germans, the Czechs drink more beer than anyone else. And with a beer culture that goes back more than 500 years, the Czech Republic can claim equal footing with Britain, Germany, and Belgium as a highly evolved brewing country. And that's in spite of fifty years of Soviet malevolence.

Many of the Czech Republic's eighty breweries are being snapped up by foreign interests. If you go, Czech is a very hard language for English-speakers to read and understand. But it has very cheap public transportation and accommodations. Food can be of poor quality and regrettable.

In the country that invented Pilsner, you can bet your barley that most of the Czech beer culture revolves around the soft, herbal-hoppy, sweet malt lager that made Bohemia famous. And a lot of Czech pub crawling has to do with who pours the best Pilsner. Beer is still a great bargain in the republic, with prices ranging from 25 cents a bottle in a grocer's store to $1.25 for a half-liter (about a pint) in a café. The latter price, by the way is considered outrageously expensive by old-timers.

As you are probably aware, the Czech Pilsner beer—called Pilsner Urquell and brewed at the Prazdroj Brewery—is the most imitated beer on earth. American mega-brewed beers are laughable simulations of the style, and Budweiser copied their name directly from Budvar beer. Pilsner beer originated in the Czech city of Plzen. Though Urquell is much-imitated, brewers in other European countries do not directly use the name. Instead, the Germans call it pils. Others call it pilsener. The beer's unique characteristics can be actualized only by using Saaz hops (grown near Plzen), Moravian and Bohemian barley, and the extremely soft water that the Prazdroj pumps from wells directly beneath its brewery.

Brewing in Plzen began in earnest in the 13th century when King Wenceslas granted brewing rights to burghers (landowners) in the region. In 1842, the Burghers Brewery—now Prazdroj—was established to take advantage of the latest brewing techniques that had been developed in Copenhagen (where Carlsberg had pioneered the lagering process), Munich, and Vienna. By 1870 the brewery was exporting Pilsner beer to London, Paris, Vienna, and Moscow. By 1874 it had arrived in America. By 1913 it was Europe's largest brewery.

Foamy Fact

I'll Havel a Pilsner Please: Czechoslovakia, now the Czech Republic, suffered under Soviet domination until 1989. That affected the brewing industry as well as people's lives. One person whose life was directly touched was dissident playwright Vaclav Havel, who became the Czech president after the fall of the Soviet Union. The Commies didn't like Havel's plays so they exiled him to Eastern Bohemia, where he was given a job moving beer kegs at a brewery. Soon he was transferred to the filtration department where his bosses bugged the cellars hoping to tape record "anti-socialist" pronouncements from the playwright. When the microphones were discovered, the disgraced brewmaster was forced to resign. Havel used the experience to pen the play *The Brewery*.

Prague is the largest city in the Czech Republic. It seems like everybody is moving there to enjoy the rich tapestry of beautiful and historic architecture, monuments, museums, theaters, music halls—and of course, beer halls. You can visit attractions that were frequented by the likes of Mozart, Kafka, and Einstein. If you want to visit the world's oldest brewpub (and third largest), go to the U Fleku (1 Kremencova, Prague; 02 296417) built in 1499. Famous for its one beer, a dark lager, the large clock on the outside of the brewpub is a Prague landmark. Although the club is around 500 years old, it's inexplicably in a part of the city called New Town. At night the club becomes a cabaret for which reservations must be made in advance. The largest brewer in the Czech Republic is the Staropramen Brewery (Nadrazni 84, CS-150 54, Prague; 02 538541). Staropramen's 12% lager is very popular in Germany. On weekends, busloads of Germans descend on the brewery's old-fashioned beer hall, called U Trojice (located next door to the brewery). At U Trojice, music, dancing, beef stew with dumplings, and all the beer you can drink are the order of the day. It may be crowded, but any beer that Germans travel hundreds of miles to imbibe must be worth the effort.

A visit to the superb restaurant run by the Urquell Brewery (U Prazdroje 7 CS-304 97 Plzen; 019 34031) in Plzen is the best way to enjoy the freshest Pilsner in the world. The brewery is open only to group tours, but the beer hall is open to everyone. About 100 miles south of Prague is the town of Ceské Budejovice, also known in German as Budweis. This is where the "Beer of Kings" is brewed. Although Anheuser-Busch has been trying to buy the Budweiser Budvar (Karoliny Svetle 2, CS-370 54 Ceske) for years, local pride will not allow it—so far. Some believe it's only a matter of time until the American giant takes over the Czech artisanal brewery.

Tasty Tip
The *Prague Pub Guide,* written by Sarah Shaw, and published by Pragolem Guides, gives you the lowdown on Bohemian brew-ha-ha. Ms. Shaw also publishes a weekly pub-crawl column in the *Prague Post,* a weekly newspaper printed in English. North American visitors to the Czech Republic might also want to stop by the American Hospitality Center (Male namesti 14, Prague), where friendly English-speaking hosts have plenty of tourist information. The center is open 10 A.M. to 6 P.M. or until 8 P.M. in summer. Czech it out.

This Bud's NOT For You

Ceske Budejovice was once home to forty-three breweries, including the Royal Court Brewery of Bohemia. The Pilsner-style Budejovicky Budvar or Budweis was first brewed there in 1843. German immigrant Adolphus Busch liked the beer so much that he, uh…borrowed its name and used it for a product he cranked out at his brewery in St. Louis. Busch even borrowed the slogan "Beer of Kings" and switched it around to "King of Beers." The Czech brewery sued and an agreement was reached: Anheuser-Busch could sell its Budweiser in the U.S. and Latin America. Budweis could sell its beer in Europe and the former Soviet Union. Under the 84-year-old agreement, the Americans are shut out of beer-selling in Germany and Austria. It's sold as Bud in other parts of Europe. Bud's been ruing the day it agreed to that division, and literally hundreds of court battles have ensued over the past century. So with the fall of Communism, Anheuser-Busch has been trying to win the Czechs over. They built a $1 million cultural center, sponsored a sports team, and they're even handing out scholarships and English lessons. But the Czechs still say no go. Other large breweries are also trying to buy the Budvar brewery, just to make the world's largest brewer squirm. Because of this little, er…problem, folks in North America will never get to taste a *real* Budweiser. Unless they go to Europe.

Czech Out These Festivals

Prague throws a beer party every single day at the Hotel International (Koulova 15, CS-160 45, Prague; 31 18201). The daily event lasts from May 15 to November 30 and features brass bands, storytelling, dance, folklore, a complete dinner, and all the Pilsner Urquell you can drink.

There's a brewing and malting trade show in the Czech Republic called PIVEX at the Brno Fairgrounds. It's in late May and lasts five days. It's open to the general public.

Pivo Historic Sites

If you're at the Urquell factory, you can visit the Pivovarske Museum (Veleslavinova Ul 6, CS-304 97 Plzen; 019 33989), which is a brewery museum in a Gothic-era malthouse. It is open Tuesday afternoons and Wednesday through Sunday.

The Least You Need to Know

➤ Belgium, Germany, and the Czech Republic make up the great brewing nations of continental Europe.

➤ Belgium has the most beer styles, followed by Germany.

➤ The German region of Bavaria is ground zero for hundreds of breweries in almost every city, town, and village.

Chapter 20

Old World Wort: Beer Across Europe

In This Chapter

➤ An overview of the brewing scene in the other European countries, including France, Italy, Switzerland, and the Scandinavian countries

➤ A region-by-region snapshot of brewpubs, breweries, beer festivals, and other beery sites

➤ Phone numbers, addresses, and Web sites related to brewpubs, micro-breweries, and breweries in other parts of Europe.

There's plenty of beer outside of Europe's Golden Triangle, but for one reason or another it doesn't get much press. The Scandinavian countries are beautiful, friendly, and well worth seeing. But they are astonishingly *expensive,* even by European standards. Regulations on beer are more in line with Prohibition days. Taxes are stratospheric. A six-pack of average brew in Norway can cost about $15. (And homebrewing is illegal.) A far cry from the Czech Republic's two-bit bottles. As for southern Europe—they drink wine. You wouldn't expect people in France's Bordeaux region to go nuts over an all-malt beer. While any connoisseur knows that a great beer can be as complex and interesting as a great wine, most experts concede that a 3,000-year old wine culture can't change overnight.

I've ranked the following countries in order of how many breweries they have and how much interest in beer they collectively hold. Countries with Germanic backgrounds obviously have more of a taste for beer. The Romantic countries can put a good beer on the table, but you might have to look a little harder to find it.

The addresses in this chapter are as complete as possible, based on the information that was available. The telephone codes for the various European countries are as follows: 43 for Austria; 45 for Denmark; 358 for Finland; 33 for France; 39 for Italy; 47 for Norway; 7 for Russia; 34 for Spain; 46 for Sweden; and 41 for Switzerland. For a thorough listing of most breweries in each country, go to the Institute for Brewing Studies' Brewery List Index. Reach the Web site at http://www.beertown.org/brews/brewlist.html.

Vienna Malts in Austria

Austria has beautiful mountains, great skiing, and a hefty number of breweries. Old-fashioned Vienna-style beer, first brewed there in 1842, has been the inspiration for many mass-produced lagers the world over. There are about 50 breweries in Austria and a new-found respect for unusual styles. Like Germany, no single brewery dominates the country, but rather several regional brands are popular. As in most other mountainous countries, travel, food, and lodging are relatively expensive. For more information, boot up the Austrian Beer Guide on the Web: http://www.lib.uchicago.edu/keith/austrian-beer.html.

Austria is heavily influenced by German brewing tradition. Brewing began there well over one thousand years ago and was a major industry by the 1600s. Beer was first mentioned in Austrian tax records in 990.

Brauhaus Nussdorf (1 Freihof Gasse, Nussdorf, Vienna; 1 372652) is near the Danube and brews what some feel are the best beers in Vienna. They are served on the premises in the Bier Heurige. Their Old Whisky Bier is made from whisky malt and has a smoky flavor. Nussdorf also brews a stout that's hard to find on the continent. Wieden Bräu (Universität Wien, IV Bezirk, Waaggasse 5. Phone: 1 58 60300) is a brewpub with a small brewery that produces a helles, a märzen, and a dunkel. The Brauerei Hirt (Rt. 83/E7, Friesach) has been a brewery since 1270 and has a beer garden and restaurant. Braeu (Town Center, A-6280 Zell am Ziller; 052 822313) is a historic hotel with a brewery and the Braeustuebl Restaurant.

MMM

Tasty Tip
Austrian food is similar to German food, and most of it is your basic meat-and-potatoes fare. Schnitzel seems to be the favorite food. Here are some typical Austrian schnitzel specialties:

Wiener schnitzel is the classic. It's a veal cutlet pounded thin, breaded, and sautéed, usually with sauce. Turkey and pork are alternatives to veal. *Zigeunerschnitzel* is "gypsy" style with a mildly spiced sauce of tomatoes and peppers. *Naturschnitzel* is an unbreaded schnitzel. *Jägerschnitzel* is hunter-style, with a mushroom sauce. Other non-schnitzel specialties include, Leberknödel Suppe, a soup with liver dumplings; and Gulasch, a Hungarian meat stew spiced with paprika.

Austrian Edelweiss is brewed light (Kristallklar), dark (Dunkel), and with yeast in the bottle (Hefetrüb).

Austria has several large breweries worth checking out. Brauerie Goesser (Goess, Leoben; 03842 22621) brews one of Austria's most popular export beers. It's made in a former monastery founded in 1020 and has a small beer museum. Brauerei Eggenberg (Eggenberg 1, Postfach 44, A-4655 Vorchdorf; 076 14345) brews the amazing blond Urbock 23.

If you're interested in an Austrian beer festival, the Gauderfest in Zell am Ziller is held the first weekend in May. It's a 400-year-old song-filled celebration. A special beer called Gauderbier is brewed for the occasion.

Of historic interest, the Beer Museum in Laa an der Thaya (025 225010) is open weekends May through September. The Griechenbeisl (Fleischmarkt 11, Vienna) is a 500-year-old tavern.

Viking Ale in Scandinavia

Judging by Scandinavian restrictions on alcohol and its consumption, it's hard to believe that these folks are the descendants of the ale-crazed Vikings. Or maybe that's why it's so restricted. Whatever the case, homebrewing is an ancient tradition in the northlands. Until recently, beers were brewed in Sweden and Denmark using herbs like bog myrtle, juniper, and angelica—ingredients that are throwbacks to the Viking era.

Foamy Fact

Bloody Good Ale: The act of christening ships was originally a Viking custom. Between the 8th and 10th centuries, the beer-crazed warriors sprinkled ale mixed with human blood on a ship's bow. Viking warriors also bled themselves into each other's ale as a brotherhood ceremony. But the ale was brewed by women only, and all brewing vessels were exclusive property of women—to be passed down to their daughters. When a Viking died, his or her property was sold off. One-third of the proceeds went to buy the funeral ale served at cremation.

Just the Faxe in Denmark

Most of the brewing in Denmark is done by the giants, Carlsberg and Tuborg. There are a few smaller breweries popping up here and there.

Tasty Tip

MMM

If you're ever lucky enough to be in Copenhagen, you can enjoy the arts thanks to Denmark's premier beer. The controlling interest in the Carlsberg Brewery is the Carlsberg Foundation, which gives money to scientific pursuits and is a patron of the arts. When founder Jacob Christian Jacobson died in 1887, his will revealed that he had left his entire brewery to the foundation. The foundation supports the Carlsberg Museum, which is visited by 150,000 people a year. The museum houses works by Gauguin, Degas, Monet, and Bonnard. The Foundation has also funded planetariums, Nobel Prize–winning scientists, telescopes in Chile, and countless other projects.

Lager may have been invented (or invented itself) in Bavaria, but it was the folks at Carlsberg Brewery (Elephant Gate, 140 Ny Carlsbergvej, Copenhagen; 33 271314) who first isolated and refined the yeast. Carlsberg gives guided tours Monday through Friday at 9 A.M., 11 A.M., and 2:30 P.M. They give free samples and have a brewery museum. If you want to see Copenhagen's other huge brewery (which is also owned by Carlsberg), visit the Tuborg Brewery (54 Strandvejen, Hellerup, Copenhagen; 33 272212), which gives tours with free samples Monday through Friday at 10 A.M., 12:30 P.M., and 2:30 P.M. The Faxe Bryggeri (DK-4640 Fakse, Copenhagen; 53 713700) gives tours Monday through Friday.

The Bryggeriet Apollo (Vesterbrogade 3, DK-1620, Copenhagen, 33 123313) is Copenhagen's premier brewpub and the first in Denmark.

I Did It Norway

Norway is known for its sparkling, clean waters—perfect for brewing. The country also has a beer-purity law, similar to the Reinheitsgebot. Drinking, however, is tightly restricted and expensive. A pint of beer in a Norwegian pub can cost more than $9. Like Sweden, Norway has a three-class brewing system. Class I beers have no alcohol. Class II beers are 3.5% alcohol by volume. Class III beers, over 5.6%, may only be bought in state-owned stores called *Vinmonopol*—and they are very heavily taxed—$3 for a .35l-milliliter (about 11 ounces) bottle of beer. For more information, visit the Web site Norway Beer and Brewpubs at http://pekkel.uthscsa.edu/beer/nor.html.

Norway's largest and most well-known brewery is Ringnes (Postboks 7152, Homansbyen, Oslo; 02 309500). The Aass Brewery (Postboks 1107, Drammen; 03 832580)—pronounced "orse," and meaning summit—has a mid-1800s brewery near Oslo, where the public is invited to cultural events. The Oslo Mikrobryggeri (Bogstadvn 6, Oslo; 02 569776) is one of Oslo's brewpubs. If you go way up north in Norway, visit the Macks Olbryggeri (Storgaten 5, Tromso; 08 384800), the northernmost brewery in the country where the beer is served with seagull's eggs on the side.

Soaking Up Suds in Sweden

Sweden has a brewing tradition dating to the 1200s. By the 1600s, King Magnus wrote down laws concerning beer production and Swedish brewers had their own trade guild. Modern Sweden has a strict three-class beer system like Norway's. This causes much Ingmar Bergman-type weeping and wailing among brewers and beer nuts alike.

Pripps Bryggerier (Bryggeriv 10, Bromma; 087 577000) is Sweden's biggest brewery and most popular export. The brewery was actually founded by a Scottish settler named Carnegie in the late 1700s. Carnegie Porter is still brewed by Pripps and is a welcome dark ale in a land of light lagers.

Bar Talk
Hont i haret.
(Literal translation: "Pain in the roots of my hair.")

—Swedish term for hangover

Sweden has several microbreweries. They are: Gamlestadens Bryġgeri in Are, Fors Nya Bryggeri in Gothenburg, Vivungs Bryggeri in Grangesberg, Hallsta Bryggeri in Halmstad, and Nordsjo Gardsbryggeri in Skruv.

Sweden holds the Midsommar Festival on the third weekend in June. There are celebrations, Maypoles, smorgasbords, beer, and aquavit (a strong liquor flavored with caraway seeds). The festivities are country-wide. Check with local tourist boards.

For more information about Swedish brewing, contact the Swedish Beer Consumers' Association, Svenska Olframjandet (Box 16244, S-103 25 Stockholm; 086 693630).

Finnish Your Beer in Finland

As you might imagine, folks who live as close to the North Pole as the Finns need something to keep them warm. There's a lot of brewing going on up there. There are even breweries making sahti, a traditional Finnish beer made of malted barley, malted rye, and spiced with juniper. The wort is sparged through a bed of juniper twigs which flavors the sahti. Some folks mash *sahti* in a hot sauna. The libation is also consumed in the sauna. Finns also brew a 100% rye malt beer called kotikalja. The Finns have adapted local berries of the northern climates—such as cloudberry, hawthorn berry, and Arctic bramble—to beer and liquors. Finns grow their own barley and have been growing hops since at least the 1400s.

Terms of Enbeerment
Sahti, a drink that dates back to the 9th century and is traditionally brewed by women in Finnish households, is uncarbonated and made from barley malt, 10% to 20% rye malt, and baker's yeast.

If you're planning a trip to Finland check out the list of Finnish breweries on the Internet: http://s-kanslia-3.hut.fi/Olutturisti/Finland/.

If you want to see sahti brewed, you can visit breweries where it's made. Finlandia Sahti (Suokulmantie 237, Matku ([30 km from Forssa]; 949 208024) is open to visitors from 2 P.M. to 12 P.M. everyday. Joutsan Sahti (Jousitie 76, Joutsa; 947 883403) has been brewing since 1985. Lammin sahti (Liesontie 554, Lammi; 917 6335 444) is available in Helsinki pubs.

Furrow Your Bräu in Switzerland

Switzerland has more than 30 breweries, but they sort of operate as a cartel. The Swiss don't seem too interested in beer culture, but there are a few outstanding Swiss brews available in North American markets. Everything in Switzerland is pricy. A ham and cheese sandwich in a Zurich sidewalk café costs $15 at current exchange rates. But Switzerland is one of the most beautiful countries on earth and you certainly can drink well while you're there.

MMM **Tasty Tip**
For all the ups and downs of Swiss beers, brewing, and history, pick up *Schweizer Bierbuch* by Karl Thoene, published by FSW, Gotthard Strasse 61, CH-8027 Zurich; 01 2012611.

The smallest brewery in Switzerland is Country Inn and Brewery Frohsinn (Romanshorne Strasse 15, CH-9320 Arbon; 071 461046). It's got an adjoining guest house and tavern.

Brauerei Hürlimann (Brandschenkestr 150, CH-8027 Zurich; 012 882626) brews Hexenbräu—according to the label only on full-moon nights. Spelled Huerlimann in English, the brewery also produces the 14.7% Samichlaus beer every December 6. The beer is lagered for one year and sold on the following December 6. The brewery has a museum with beer steins, a stable of Belgian horses, and free samples. Tours by appointment.

Hürlimann holidays: Hexenbräu is brewed only on full-moon nights, perfect for Halloween. Samichlaus is 14.7% alcohol and is referred to as "Santa Claus" beer for Christmas.

The Brauerei Feldschloesschen (CH-4310 Rhinfelden; 061 835011) is in an 1876 red and yellow brick building and brews some of Switzerland's better beers. There are tours, a museum, and a gift shop. The brewery also has its own Tudor-style train station.

The Brauerei Waedi-Brau-Huus (Florhof Strasse 13, CH-8820 Waedenswil; 017 801566) is a demonstration brewery that uses organic hops and barley. Along the same lines is the National Experimental Brewery (Engimatt Strasse 11, CH-8059 Zurich; 01 2014244) with public access by appointment. They've got a large collection of beer ads, coasters, cans, and steins.

Fermentation au France

When it comes to appreciating the finer things in life, we usually revert to words of French origin such as connoisseur and gourmet. But oddly enough, there's one word missing from the French vocabulary—"brew." There's a word for ferment, but beer must be brewed before it can ferment. Be that as it may, people in France are drinking more beer than ever. But most great beers served in Parisian cafés and bars are of Belgian origin. And it can be pricy. Reports of $9 bottles of Anchor Steam are true. But travel in France is fun. The food is excellent, prices are fair, and public transportation is good. If you're in France, you're forgiven for skipping the beer in favor of something red.

If you want to experience the great French beer tradition, forget Paris (no, not the Billy Crystal movie) and head up to the northeastern part of the country. That's where the world's greatest wine country proudly brews bière de garde. This area, known as the French lowlands, contains about 20 artisanal breweries in the Artois, Picardy, and French Flanders regions. Most are about 20 miles from Belgium's borders. Hops have been grown in the area since A.D. 822, and brewing was conducted at Abbey of Saint Bavas-les Esquerines in Lilles as early as 967.

France's finest farmhouse ales— bière de garde from antiquated artisan breweries in northern France.

Many of the charming farmhouse bière de garde breweries are very small and antiquated. The Brasserie Bailleux (Place du Fond des Rocs, 59570 Gussignies; 27 668861) is tucked away in the village of Gussignies, right on the border. It's a restaurant with a revivalist brewery and is open on weekends. A small brewery in the small town of Annoeullin has been making bière de garde since 1905. The Brasserie d'Annoeullin (4 Grand'Place, 59112 Annoeullin; 20 857857) has been a family operation for five generations. Yves Castelain is the proprietor and grandson of the founder of Brasserie Castelain (13 Rue Pasteur, Bénifontaine, 62410 Wingles; 21 403838). Monsier Castelain brews St. Amand, Castelain (called Ch'ti in France) and Jade. The latter is the only certified organic beer in France. Theillier (11 Rue de la Chaussée, Louvignies, 59570 Bavay; 27 631018) has buildings dating to 1670. The Brasserie de St. Sylvestre (St. Sylvestre-Cappel, 59114 Steenvoorde; 28 401549) is a classic farmhouse brewery in operation since the mid-19th century.

Tasty Tip
Paris is notorious for its rude waiters. If you want to avoid effrontery from a guy making seven bucks an hour, stand at the bar. While the barkeep might be just as rude, the same beer is cheaper at the bar. Beer is priced higher for customers sitting down in the restaurant, and even more pricey for those sitting down outdoors at a sidewalk table. If you hang at the bar then sit down, however, expect the waiter to demand a few francs' tip for the work of seating you.

The Alsace region of France around Strasbourg has been German territory at different times in history. The German influence is evident in the half-timbered buildings and the brewery density. Several large-scale breweries offer tours there. Francaise de Brasserie (4–10 Rue St. Charles, BP 43, F-67301 Schiltigheim; 88 629080) is a Heineken brewery that gives tours in French, English, and German Monday through Friday. The Brasseries Kronenbourg (68 Rte. d'Oberhausbergen, BP13 F-67200 Strasbourg; 88 274159) also gives daily tours. For a most unusual, peat-smoked beer, visit the Grande Brasserie d'Adelshoffen (87 Rte. de Bischwiller, F-67302 Schiltigheim; 88 839020). French brewing giant Fischer also operates near this site. Schiltigheim is also home to the Beer Festival early every August. For more information about the event, call 88 83900.

Visitors to Lyon might want to visit the some of the city's brewpubs. The Barrel House (Rue Sainte Catherine, 69001 Lyon) has free concerts from Wednesday to Saturday. Le Chantecler (Boulevard de la Croix Rousse, 69004 Lyon) has four different homemade beers.

For historic French brew vibes, the Chateau d'Etoges (4 Rue Richebourg, F51270 Etoges; 26 593080) is a pub with a rich history as a former coaching inn of French kings. There are also several museums dedicated to beer in France. They are Musee de la Biere (510 Ave. de la Republique, F-52100 St. Dizier), Musee Francais de la Brasserie (62 Rue Charles

Courtois, F-54210 St. Nicholas de-Port; 83 469552), and Musee European de la Bierre (Rue de la Citadelle, F-55700 Stenay; 29 806878).

Bock in the U.S.S.R.: Russian Bear Beer

Beer in Russia can go from the yucky to the downright dangerous. After 70 years of Communist rule, most of the old Russian brewery industry is in shambles. Bars can be some of the scariest places in wild Moscow. Some pour half a glass of beer and fill the rest with polluted tap water. Most good hotels serve European imports which are available for Western currency only. But in a place where you can see the Moscow circus for six cents, a person should be able to find a decent beer.

If you're an American, you are welcome at the Liberty Bar at the U.S. Embassy where you can drink Budvar, Pilsner Urquell, and even American Bud. The Embassy is guarded by U.S. Marines and their residence has a bar. The Marine House has a party every other Friday, where all are invited. This is a tradition around the world. Proceeds held fund the annual Marine Ball. Another tip: Look for Irish bars. A perfectly poured pint of Guinness has saved many a night.

A few adventurous Americans have opened brewpubs in Russia. Other brew-crazed Westerners have set up microbreweries. Pips (4–24 Krylatskye Kholmy; 414 1904) is a brewpub that looks like a one-story bunker. Don't be intimidated by video cameras, the big steel fence, and two security guards out front. They're for *your* protection. Inside you'll find a white-tablecloth restaurant. Wealthy Russians and foreign businessmen dine on homemade ice cream and sausages and crayfish. Pips was established in 1990. Russia has at least two microbreweries: Pivovarennij Zadov in Volgograd and Petrobier in St. Petersburg.

Foamy Fact

Gimme a Number 128: The former Soviet Union is actually the fifth-largest brewing nation in the world after the U.S., Germany, Britain, and Japan. Russia still produces its share of suds, but the transition to a free-market economy has caused chaos in the beer sector. Old Soviet breweries had names like State Brewery 128 (PBZ 128). Others date back to before the 1917 Revolution. The Aldris Brewery in Riga, Latvia was built in 1865.

Birra Good Beer in Italy

Folks in Italy produce and consume a surprising amount of beer, but their romance is with the grape. Per capita consumption of beer is rising in Italy, although at 30 liters per person, it's less than one-tenth of Bavarian consumption.

Peroni (Zona Industriale la Stada 56, I-35100 Padua; 049 773802), founded in 1846, has breweries all over Italy. Italy's other big brand, Moretti (Viale Venezia 9, I-12040 Sommariva Perno; 0432 203441), is owned by Canada's Labatt. Moretti makes a great doppelbock called La Rossa Doppio Malto.

Italy hosts the Fiera della Birra at Largo Fiera della Pesca (I-60100 Ancona; 071 58971). This beer and pub exposition is held in mid-July.

The Grain in Spain Is Made to Entertain

Like Italy, there's a lot of beer production in Spain, but most of it is light lager. Beer has been brewed in Spain since the 1500s, when emperor Charles V ruled. Chuck was born in Belgium. San Miguel (Carbonero y Sol 1–1A, E-28006 Madrid) is probably Spain's most well-known brewery. La Cruz del Campo (Avda de la Innovacion, Edif Arena 3, E-41007 Seville; 54 480800) has a visitor's center with samples.

Can You Say Brewery?

The word "brewery" is spelled and pronounced dozens of different ways across the European continent. I couldn't begin to tell you how to pronounce the word in each country, but I can tell you what to look for when you're traveling "over there." At least when you see a sign that says beirbrouwerij in Holland, your mouth can begin to appropriately water, if not say the word correctly.

Austria: brauerei

Belgium: brasserie (in French-speaking Wallonia), brouwerij or huisbrouwerij (house brewery) (in Flemish Belgium)

Czech Republic: pivoary or pivovar

Denmark: bryggerierne, bryggeriet, or bryggeri

France: brasserie

Germany: brauerei or privatbrauerei (private brewery)

Hungry: sorgyar

Luxembourg: brasserie

Netherlands: brouwerij, bierbrouwerij (beer brewery), or brouwhuis (brewhouse)

Norway: bryggeri

Poland: browar

Portugal: cervejas

Spain: fabricas de cerveza

Sweden: bryggerier or bryggeri

Switzerland: brauerei

And while we're at it, here's how to order a beer in almost any language around the globe:

African: Bier

Armenian: Quarec'ur

Chinese: Pijiu

Czech: Pivo

Danish: Øl

Dutch: Bier

French: Biere

Gaelic: Leann

German: Bier

Greek: Bere

Hawaiian: Pia

Hungarian: Sor

Icelandic: Bjor

Indonesian: Bir

Irish: Beoir

Italian: Birra

Japanese: Biiru

Lao: Bia

Latin: Cerevisia

Lithuanian: Alus

Norwegian: Øl

Old English: Beor

Old Norse: Bygg

Polish: Piwo

Portuguese: Cerveja

Romanian: Bere

Russian: Pivo

Spanish: Cervesa

Swahili: Pombe

Swedish: Ol

Thai: Beer

Turkish: Bira

Ukranian: Pivo

Vietnamese: Bia

Welsh: Cwrw

Yiddish: Beer

The Least You Need to Know

➤ Austria and Switzerland brew a wide range of great beer.

➤ The greatest brewing tradition in France is in the bières de garde region in the northeastern part of the country.

➤ The Scandinavian countries are dominated by a few higher-quality brewing giants, but craft breweries are springing up in many cities.

➤ Countries like Spain, Italy, and Russia have a centuries-old beer tradition, but brewers tend to brew only the light lagers.

Chapter 21

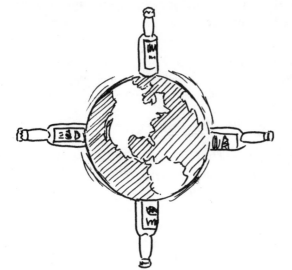

The Four Barleycorners of the Globe: Beer Culture Across the Planet

In This Chapter

➤ An overview of the brewing scene in places other than North America and Europe, including Mexico, Japan, Australia, Africa, and China

➤ A region-by-region snapshot of brewpubs, breweries, beer festivals, and other beery sites

➤ The history of brewing in each country and native beers brewed by indigenous societies

With a few exceptions, the world's beer culture is strongly influenced by Germany, the Czech Republic, and Great Britain. Beers from China to Argentina to Fiji are pretty much based on Vienna-style lager, Czech Pilsner, and English ales. In fact, most of the world's older breweries (including those in North America) were built by European colonists or immigrants. Many of the breweries in Third-World countries are still owned by large European brewing conglomerates.

This chapter blankets the world in beer, highlighting countries not mentioned in previous chapters. It's a wild journey from South America to Asia to the Middle East that proves how all-pervasive barley, hops, and yeast really are. It *is* possible to drink your way around the world in 80 beers—or 800. And you don't have to go anywhere. Beer drinkers are notorious armchair travelers. So pour a glass and dim the lights. It's going to be a bumpy ride.

> *Note: Addresses and phone numbers are not readily available for breweries and brewpubs in the Third World. If you visit, you should be able to find these places by making local inquiries.*

Wasting Away Again: Beer in Latin America

To further prove how ubiquitous fermented grain is in all cultures, consider this: Several different styles of beer are native to South and Central America—they were made there for thousands of years before the Europeans began to move in, circa 1492. Of course, if you believe Thor Heyerdahl's theory that the Aztec and Mayan pyramid builders once sailed from Egypt, then the beer thing makes more sense. Others theorize that a beer made from a starchy manioc tuber, called *masato*, was made in the Amazon region 10,000 years ago—even before Sumerian beer.

Foamy Fact

Here's Spit in Your Beer: More than 1,000 years ago, natives in Amazonia grew corn for a beer called chicha. Chicha is brewed to this day by women who sit in a circle, chew on corn, and spit the juice into a large bowl. The enzyme ptyalin from their saliva converts the starches in the corn to fermentable sugars. Chicha is fermented for 48 hours, then undergoes secondary fermentation in clay pots buried in the ground. There are several kinds of chicha. Chicha picante is served with hot pepper sauce and lemon. Chicha de jora is brewed to 38% alcohol by volume. And fruitilada is a rare kind of chicha made with strawberries, cinnamon, mace, and cilantro.

Besides chicha, the indigenous folks of the upper Amazon in Brazil once brewed a black beer from roasted grain, not unlike a stout. This beer style has been revived and is sold in North America under the name Xingu (shin-gu). In Central America, the Mayan people made beer from fermented cornstalks. The Aztec, Pueblo, and Tarahumar tribes brewed beer called *Tesguino* or *Tiswin* from sprouted maize.

Xingu Black Beer is a modern creation brewed from an ancient recipe that brewers claim evolved in the Amazon region more than a thousand years ago.

The Europeans brought brewing techniques from their homelands in the 16th century. The first European-style brewery in the Americas was opened on December 12, 1543 in Mexico. Records show this brewery paid the Spanish treasury 100 pesos a year in taxes.

By the mid-1800s, German and Swiss immigrants were flooding into the Americas. The first modern-style brewery was built in Mexico City in 1845 by a Swiss immigrant who used sun-dried barley and molasses.

Today, breweries in Latin America and the Caribbean tend toward light, watery lagers. Heavily malted beers aren't desired or deemed necessary when the humidity is pushing 100%. Consequently, the beers brewed in the equatorial regions of the Western Hemisphere are mostly run-of-the-mill Vienna- and Pilsner-style lagers. The economics of keeping lager very cold for long periods of time results in short lagering times for most equatorial beers. The porters, old ales, and bocks from days gone by are nearly extinct, although there are a few stouts still brewed.

Bermuda Quarts: Beer in the Caribbean

The azure islands of the Caribbean have been run on rum since the invasion of the Europeans. But Britannia ruled the West Indies seas during the 18th and 19th centuries and English ales formed the tastes of the region. By 1898 there were seven breweries operating in the Caribbean—four in Jamaica and one each in Barbados, Trinidad, and Cuba. After the Spanish–American War, a Brooklyn brewery came south and began brewing in Havana. The problem then, as now, was the shortage of fresh water on Caribbean islands. Today some breweries use desalinized water.

There are several craft breweries on the tourist-laden islands. Banks Barbados Breweries Ltd. operates in St. Michael, Barbados. Bermuda has two microbreweries, Bermuda Triangle Brewing and North Rock Brewing, both in Hamilton. The Carib Brewery in Trinidad and Tobago, is a large brewery founded in 1950. Carib brews an extra stout and a strong lager among its other beers.

In Nassau, Bahamas, the Commonwealth Brewery, Ltd. brews Kalik beer. The lager is named after the sound cowbells make when rhythmically shaken during the island's New Year's Junkanoo festival. In spite of water shortages and power outages, Kalik has become the island's best-seller. Desalinized water is "Burtonized" for brewing the 5% beer. Commonwealth Brewery is a joint venture between Heineken, Bacardi, and the Association of Bahamian Distillers.

The Cayman Islands have several breweries. The Banks DIH is a large brewery and the Buccaneer Brewery is a regional; both are located in George Town. In Grand Cayman, the Stingray Brewery handles the microbrewing chores and Santiago's is a brewpub. The La Villa De Torrimar in Guaynabo is Puerto Rico's microbrewery.

Jamaica is only one of the West Indies islands where folks believe stout is an aphrodisiac. And where there's stout, there's Guinness. The extra-stout company operates a brewery in the Spanish Town area of Kingston. Jamaica's most famous beer is Red Stripe, a soft, light lager that's brewed with 30% corn. Red Stripe was a dark ale until it was reformulated in 1934. Makers of Red Stripe, Desnoes, and Geddes also brew the wicked Dragon Stout, which is not a true stout, because it's bottom-fermented like a lager.

Heineken owns breweries in the Antilles and Trinidad.

Shaving Castro's Beer

Eduardo McCormack escaped Cuba in 1960 with the clothes on his back and $5 in his pocket. McCormack also carried in his head the secret recipe for Hatuey beer. Castro's Communist government had seized the Bacardi Brewery where Hatuey was brewed. Today, the dapper, silver-haired, 69-year-old McCormack is at it again. Bacardi-Martini

U.S.A. has introduced the flavorful, 5.5%-alcohol beer again, this time to Cuban–American enclaves in New Jersey and Florida. And the company hopes that the *Grande Cervesa de Cuba* will catch on elsewhere.

Hatuey was immortalized in Ernest Hemingway's *The Old Man and the Sea.* Hemingway lived just three miles from the brewery and would line his porch railing with full bottles of Hatuey. As he wrote, he would walk around the porch drinking from each bottle. Hatuey is named after an Indian chief who led the resistance against the Spanish in the 16th century and was ultimately burned at the stake. The beer bears a profile of its namesake on its blood-red label.

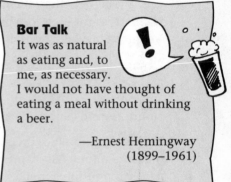

Bar Talk
It was as natural as eating and, to me, as necessary. I would not have thought of eating a meal without drinking a beer.

—Ernest Hemingway
(1899–1961)

My Corona: Mexico

Although Mexicans consume massive quantities of beer, it isn't a celebrated drink as it is in other parts of the world. Maybe it's the country's wine-loving Spanish roots. Or is it the close proximity to all that tequila?

Mexico's first large-scale brewery was established in Monterrey in 1890. One of the brewery's beers won Grand Prize at the Chicago International Beer Exposition in 1893.

Cuauhtémoc, the brewery that brews Carta Blanca, Tecate, and Bohemia, was also started in 1890. The brewer of the well-known Dos Equis is Cervecería Moctezuma. The company was established in 1894.

Modelo—the company that brews the perennial favorite Corona—was founded in Mexico City in 1925. Today Modelo is Mexico's biggest brewing company, dominating 72% of that country's beer exports. Modelo's production is greater than all but five American breweries and all of Canada's breweries.

By the 1970s, Mexico passed Canada as North America's second-largest brewing nation, mainly because of imports to the U.S. In 1986, Tecate sold 28% of its beer in the U.S. Today, Mexico's brewing scene is dominated by the big three, Cuauhtémoc, Moctezuma, and Modelo, but the country has slipped to third place in volume behind Brazil.

Tasty Tip
Baseball and Beer—Mexican Style: Yes, there is a Mexican Baseball Hall of Fame. It's at the gargantuan Cuauhtémoc Brewing Co. in Monterrey. Of course, there's a beer garden, and visitors can sample Carta Blanca and Tecate for free.

Central America

All the countries of Central America together produce only about six million barrels of beer a year—less than the monthly production of Anheuser-Busch. But the brewing tradition in the area goes back more than 1,000 years. As in Mexico, today's Central American breweries were founded by Swiss and German immigrants.

Of the three main breweries in Costa Rica, Cerveceria Costa Rica, is owned by Coca-Cola and Cerveceria Tropical is owned by Pepsi Cola. The Cerveceria Centroamericana is Guatemala's main brewery in Guatemala City. Cerveceria Hondurena is in San Pedro Sula, Honduras and exports Port Royal and Salva Vida brands to the United States.

Cerveceria Costa Rica brews Imperial Beer with pure spring waters from the Costa Rican rain forest. Imperial—a premium European-style lager—has one of the more stirring back labels ever printed on a beer bottle. It reads:

> *From the top of the mountains and volcanoes all through the rain forests and valleys, flow spring waters so rich and pure that they can only be compared with the integrity of freedom and democracy that fills the air in Costa Rica. Imperial will not only make you experience the richness of our nature, but also the essence of a whole nationality. Taste more than just a beer—taste the beer of Costa Rica.*

South America

The World Beer Survey on the World Wide Web is a place where people can go to vote for their favorite beers. A (very) unscientific poll elected these as the top 10 beers of South America:

1. Bavaria (Brazil)
2. Polar (Venezuela)
3. Xingu Black (Brazil)
4. Brahma Chopp (Brazil)
5. Xingu (Brazil)
6. Cordoba Negra (Argentina)
7. Cerveza Aguila (Colombia)
8. Antarctica Pilsen (Brazil)
9. Pilsen (Peru)
10. Serramalte (Brazil)

Only about 100 breweries remain in South America out of 1,000 at the beginning of the 19th century. Heavily populated Brazil is the second largest brewing nation in the Western Hemisphere after the United States and before Mexico. Other major brewing countries are Columbia and Peru. Chile, a major wine-producing country, has only one brewery.

Brahma beer, produced in Rio de Janeiro, Brazil, is the most popular beer in South America. But if you want to see how the native beer Xingu is made, visit the Xingu Brewery in Cacador. Cervejaria Astra in Papico is one of Brazil's microbreweries, brewing Astro Beer.

The Brazilian Oktoberfest is held in Blumenau.

In Bolivia, the Cerveceria Taquina in Cochabamaba operates a restaurant and gives tours. The Bavaria Brewery in Colombia is a slice of Germany in Bogota.

Foamy Fact

Wonder Women: Amazonian women maintained power and status through their skill as chicha brewsters, and do so to this very day. The Chaco tribes still drink a lot of chicha because they believe it helps them dream. When brewing chicha, brewsters take great care to keep the spirits of the dead from entering the beer. They drop lumps of charcoal into every pot. When the old women drink, they sprinkle a few drops on the ground for the goddess of Chicha. The old brewsters look over the beer-drunk men as if they were children. Morning hangovers are cured by chewing on bark and roots.

Sake to Me: Beer in Asia

The collective countries known as Asia cover a large portion of the globe and are home to almost half the world's population. *Sake,* a type of rice beer, is the indigenous drink of the Orient. As in other non-European countries, barley beer was introduced by travelers from the Western Hemisphere. Most Asian beer is lager and is brewed with up to 40% rice. In some areas, traditional, beer-type drinks are fermented from coconut sap, sweet potatoes, or other fermentable plants.

Terms of Enbeerment
Sake is Japanese rice wine. It's not really wine, however. Sake is brewed from rice grain, so it's technically beer. Sake has an alcohol content of 16% to 21% by volume.

Countries with strong fundamentalist Muslim factions have closed breweries and out-lawed drinking. Most countries still have at least one brewery in their capital city and, of course, Guinness and Heineken are likely to be found almost anywhere.

The Suntory Also Rises in Japan

Legend has it that the first beer made in Japan was brewed after the American Navy, led by Commodore Perry, sailed to Japan in 1853. A Japanese student visited the "smoky black ships" and was offered a beer. The student later found a Dutch textbook on brewing and made his own beer. In 1869, the Japanese government, looking to create industrial development, sent a researcher to Germany. Soon after, the government opened the Sapporo brewery on the islands of Hokkaido.

A brewery started by an American company called Wiegand and Copeland passed into Japanese hands in 1870 and became the Kirin brewery, currently the world's fourth largest. The other breweries making up Japan's "Big Four" are Asahi and Suntory.

Japanese beers are made to the highest technical standards and are very clean. Although the Japanese breweries make barrels of flavorless lagers such as Dry Beer, a few like Kirin and Asahi brew strong, dark, top-fermenting stouts. Sapporo, Asahi, and Kirin also brew a traditional German dark-lager style called black beer.

The Sapporo Beer Brewery in Funabashi has a beer garden and a beer hall, and conducts tours in English and German, weekdays with reservations. The Kirin Brewer in Yokohama is open to tours Tuesday through Sunday.

Foamy Fact

No Score for the Big Four: Sapporo, Kirin, Asahi, and Suntory, Japan's so-called Big Four breweries, tenaciously fought off the creation of craft breweries until 1994. The biggies even ran ads trying to persuade the beer-drinking public that only they knew how to make beer. But as they say, once you've gone bock, you never go back. The micro revolution has hit Japan. Brewpubs and microbreweries will no doubt soon be as ubiquitous there as in North America.

The Otaru Beer microbrewery is 30 minutes from Sapporo. It has a German-style restaurant and brewery. Other Japanese microbreweries include Kirishima Highland Brewery Ltd., in Kagoshima-Ken, Uehara Brauhaus in Nishikanbara-Gun, and Uehara Shuzo Co. Ltd./Echigo Brauhaus, a brewpub in Nishinkanbara-Gun. Most of Japan's microbreweries are concentrated in the Osaka area.

In Kobe, there's a sake museum in a historic brewery district. The Kikumasamune Shiryokan (1-9-1 Ozaki Nishimachin, Higashi-nada-ku; 078 854 1029) offers tours, videos, and sake tastings.

Here's a subjective list of the top 10 Asian beers:

1. Tsingtao (China)
2. Kirin (Japan)
3. Sapporo (Japan)
4. San Miguel (Philippines)
5. Ob (Korea)
6. Asahi (Japan)
7. Singha (Thailand)
8. Tiger Beer (Singapore)
9. Kirin Ichiban Shibori (Japan)
10. Asahi Super Dry (Japan)

Singha Sing Low in Southeast Asia

The first brewing company to operate in Southeast Asia was La Fabrica de Cerveze de San Miguel, founded in 1890 in the Philippines. The brewer of the popular San Miguel lager was founded eight years before the Spanish surrendered control to the United States in the Spanish–American War.

The main beer buzz in Korea is the Oriental Brewing Co. in Seoul, which makes the well-known OB Lager.

In Singapore, the popular Tiger Beer is brewed by the Asian Pacific Breweries (APB), founded in 1930. APB offers group tours of its Singapore brewery Monday through Friday. There's also a souvenir shop and the Tiger Tavern for tasting Anchor Pilsener, ABC Extra Stout, and of course, Tiger.

Foamy Fact

Put a Tiger Gin In Your Tank: The advertising slogan for Singapore's Tiger Beer is "Time for a Tiger." It was often printed on bar clocks. British author Anthony Burgess used the motto as the title of a book he published in 1946. In 1960, Tiger offered Burgess all the beer he cared to drink during a visit to Singapore. Burgess declined. He later wrote: "It was too late, I had become wholly a gin man."

275

While in Singapore, check out the Orang Utan Brewery and Pub (17 Jink Kim Street). It's a brewpub whose proceeds help support endangered wildlife.

The Boon Rawd Brewery in Thailand has produced the delicious, thirst-quenching lager Singha since 1934.

One of Germany's largest breweries, Paulaner, has recently opened a brewpub in Bangkok. The Paulaner Brauhaus is very popular and even holds an Oktoberfest. It's located in the President Park complex on Sukhumvit Soi 22. The prices are upscale, the food is standard German fare, and the beer is great.

South China Brewing Company runs a microbrewery in Aberdeen, Hong Kong.

China

China is the number one brewing nation in Asia, with yearly per capita consumption at around 56 pints. In the past several years, China's beer production has skyrocketed and it has surpassed Germany as the world's second largest beer-producing nation after the United States.

Stale Ale Alert
News item from the Chinese newspaper *People's Daily:* Last year more than 6,000 Chinese consumers were blinded or injured by exploding beer bottles. The glass was either poorly made or had been reused for more than 10 years. The pressure of the carbonated beer caused the bottles to explode. (Presumably these beers were never exported outside China.)

Mongolians and other ethnic groups have been brewing in China for thousands of years. Historians believe that sake was first brewed under the Emperor Ta-yu in 2207 B.C. Sake was deemed illegal almost as soon as it was invented. Many emperors tried to outlaw rice wine, and Confucius wrote of the dangers of the drink, but its consumption continued unabated.

As Western traders established a presence in China, Western lager quickly followed. When millions of Chinese became addicted to opium, Western brewers used the slogan "American Alcohol Cures Opium" to fight back against religious prohibitionists.

The Tsingtao (now Qingdao) Brewery—which looks like a Bavarian village—was built by Germans in 1897 to supply colonists and colonial military forces. The Qingdao brewery in Shandong gives tours.

Foamy Fact

The Drunk Poet's Society: Around the third century A.D., a group of Chinese poets known as the Seven Sages of Bamboo Grove made drunkenness a way of life. Their leading sage was Liu Ling, who later drowned while drunk on sake. Liu Ling was leaning out of a boat to embrace the moon's reflection in the water when he went down and didn't come up. In ancient societies, drunkenness was thought to allow the human spirit to achieve a higher state of consciousness. Go figure.

After the Communist revolution, the Chinese government nationalized all the breweries and increased the number of hop farms. Today's Chinese beers are made with all Chinese-grown ingredients. With free-market economics creeping into modern China, entrepreneurs are opening microbreweries in small towns to supply brew to some of the country's one billion people. Beer is sold everywhere and, at 20¢ to 35¢ for a 22-ounce bottle, is cheaper than bottled water. Tsingtao is the most recognized Chinese beer in the U.S., but it's hard to find in China because it is exported for hard currency. Anheuser-Busch recently bought a stake in the brewery.

In a joint venture with Chinese brewers Ginsber, Bass Brewers have begun brewing its famous Tennent's lager in China. Bass jumped into the venture because China is the fastest-growing beer market in the world, thanks in part to the government's attempts to wean people away from high-alcohol spirits like sake and steer them toward beer, the "drink of moderation."

Taj Malt Hall in India

Alcohol is not universally accepted in India, but a brewing industry thrives in some states. The leading breweries in India are Kalyani Breweries in Calcutta, Mohan Nagar Brewery in Uttar Pradesh, and Solan Brewery in Mimachal Pradesh. Mohan Nager brews the famous Taj Mahal.

One of the best stouts east of England is Lion Stout from the island nation of Sri Lanka.

Foamy Fact

Drunk with a Trunk: Illegal brewers in India have more to worry about than the law. Officials in 1996 reported that a herd of 45 thirsty elephants destroyed six illegal beer breweries in two days. The animals were looking for water but found beer instead. Mahendra Pande, the district forest officer said: "Elephants are notorious for their fondness toward beer and are great guzzlers."

Chunder Down Under in Australia

The Australians are often proud of their massive consumption of beer. Pubs in Australia once closed at 6 P.M. in a feeble attempt to control the beer-imbibing populous. This led to the "Six O'Clock Swill" where folks would drink as much as possible before closing time. Maybe that's why the country has more terms for vomit than any other (chunder, technicolor yawn, shout at your shoes, etc.)—sort of like the Eskimo's 48 words for snow.

Today, Australia is trying to downplay the beer-swilling image. Per capita consumption is down and microbreweries and brewpubs are introducing the concept of quality over quantity.

For a great rundown on beers down under, check out the Aussie Beer Page on the World Wide Web: http://www-personal.usyd.edu.au/~bcollins/OZBEER.HTML.

Australian beer was first brewed with malted corn and gooseberries by John Boston in 1796. But the country's hot climate was not conducive to ale brewing, and there was a shortage of barley and hops. It wasn't until the mid-1800s that Aussies could get a decent beer.

The original Castlemaine Perkins brewery was founded by a few Irishmen in 1850 and named after a castle in Ireland on the River Maine. Miners working the gold strike of 1853 enriched Castlemaine enough to open breweries in Melbourne, Sydney, Newcastle, Adelaide, Perth, and Brisbane. The currently ubiquitous Castlemaine XXXX Ale was first sold on Friday the 13th, September 1878. The beer has been something of a national standard for more than a century. In 1980 Castlemaine merged with another popular brand, Toohey's. Today Castlemaine XXXX is exported to more than 40 countries and is one of the most popular lagers in England. (In the U.S. Castlemaine XXXX is brewed by Coors.) Castlemaine XXXX is called "Fourex" and is the answer to the question "How does an Aussie spell beer?"

Coopers Brewery—Australia's only major ale producer—brews Coopers Sparkling Ale in Adelaide, South Australia. Adelaide sparkling ale is a style unto itself—cloudy, carbonic, fruity, and flavorful. Coopers was founded in 1862 by a Yorkshireman, Thomas Cooper, and is run today by the sixth generation of Coopers. In 1985, the company built its own malt works. This beer is highly recommended by brew enthusiasts.

The national treasure of Australia, Coopers brewery—founded in 1862—is hand-crafted, bottle-conditioned ambrosia.

Another recognizable Aussie beer is Swan, which originated in Perth, Western Australia, far from the populous metropolitan centers of the east. Frederick Sherwood founded the Swan Brewery in 1857.

Foamy Fact

Australian for Beer, Mate: Giant blue cans of Fosters Lager are famous the world over. The company's commercial spokesman in Australia, comedian Paul Hogan, later went on to become Crocodile Dundee of movie fame. Fosters is named—ironically—for a pair of American brothers who started Foster Brewing Co. in Melbourne in 1887. The Foster brothers stayed in the country barely 18 months before returning home, never to be heard from again. Fosters is brewed by the huge conglomerate Carlton & United, which owns over 100 breweries. By the way, the Fosters sold in America is brewed in Canada.

Sydney's brewpubs include the Lord Nelson Brewery Hotel and the Pumphouse Brewery at Darling Harbor. Tankstream Brewing Company is a Sydney microbrewery.

Other Australian microbreweries include A.P.K. Brewery in Canaberra City, Hahn Brewing Co. in Lane Cove, and the Geelong Brewing Company, Ltd. in Moolap.

The Sail & Anchor Pub Brewery is an English-style brewpub in Fremantle. The Good on Yer, also in Fremantle, has been a brewpub since 1952. Australia's brewpubs include The Redback Brewery and Hotel in North Melbourne, and the quaintly named Loaded Dog Pub, a brewpub and restaurant in Melbourne.

If you're ever in Tasmania, visit the Tasmanian Breweries in Hobart where you can get a historic brewery tour.

Every July the National Festival of Beers is held at the Story Bridge Hotel in Kangaroo Point. The fest features more than 50 Australian beers on tap.

Keelin' in New Zealand

Captain James Cook was New Zealand's first brewer in 1773, though the concoction he made would not be recognized by anyone today as beer.

Steinlager is probably the most well-known brew from New Zealand. It's brewed in Auckland by Lion Breweries, which dates to 1859. New Zealand's other major brewer is the New Zealand Breweries, with plants in Christchurch and Dunedin.

The Shakespeare Brewery in Auckland is New Zealand's first brewpub. Other boutique beer spots include the Metropolitan Breweries, Ltd. in Henderson, the Roaring 40's Brewery and the Timpany Brewery in Invercargill. Taranaki is the home of the Whitecliffs Brewing Co., and Pahiatua is where DB Breweries, Ltd. is located. Onekawa is home to Hawke's Bay Ind. Brewery Ltd., a brewpub.

Foamy Fact

Gimme a Pint of Stinking Water: When Captain James Cook landed in New Zealand in 1773, the first thing he did was (you guessed it) set up a brewery. He made a beer-like beverage from the local manuka and rimi tree branches. The good captain threw in a little molasses for good luck and called it beer. The natives, however, called it "stinking water." So much for *that* cultural exchange.

Micronesia

Proving once again that the micro revolution is everywhere, there's even a microbrewery on the far-flung Marshall Islands. Marshall's Best Micro Brewery (P.O. Box 477, Majuro, MH 96960-0477; 011 692 6255 325) brews it Pacifically, I mean specifically, for beer lovers.

The Hinano Brewery is where Tahitian dreams are brewed. The Carlton Brewery in Walu Bay, Suva, Fiji gives tours at 3 P.M. weekdays. South Pacific Lager is brewed in Port Moresby, Papua New Guinea in one of the world's more out-of-the-way breweries.

Ancient Traditions in Africa and the Middle East

Africa is the cradle of civilization—and of beer brewing. The brewer's art was practiced in Egypt and Sumeria eight millennia ago. From ancient Egyptian brewing dynasties to tiny huts, the first Europeans exploring Africa found an astounding number of beers brewed by tribes everywhere. Beer was brewed from native grains, grasses, and other fermentable materials, including palm sap, cassava flour, sorghum, millet, and later maize. Some of these ingredients are still used in commercially brewed African beers. At one time there were more than 100 native beer styles.

Many traditional beers are thin, sour, mild, milky, and porridge-like. Strong beers are used for ceremonial purposes. Tribes still drink beer through hollow reed straws stuck in a communal pot. Beer straws were first pictured in ancient Egyptian hieroglyphs more than 5,000 years ago.

Of course, European colonists in the 19th century brought their beer traditions with them as they built dozens of breweries across the continent. Most of the breweries were built in Nigeria, Kenya, South Africa, and Zaire. As the Euro-brews were made available, many of the ancient traditional beers all but disappeared.

Foamy Fact

Hard Time Brewing: There are almost 200 breweries in Africa today, but the hot climate prevents cultivation of hops and barley. Coupled with the impoverished economies of most African countries, the importation of raw materials for beer is difficult or impossible. Breweries with the backing of international companies like Heineken are most able to produce quality beers.

Jan van Riebeeck started brewing in the Cape of Good Hope in 1658. The first professional brewers arrived in Cape Town, South Africa about 40 years later. By 1860 there were more than 60 breweries in the area.

With its Dutch influence, brewing is big in prosperous South Africa. Now that apartheid is at an end, look for more beery investment in this diamond-producing country. Africa's leading brewery is South African Breweries, Ltd. (SAB) with its famous Lion and Castle Lager. The Claremont, Rosslyn, and Durban breweries all offer tours.

South African micros include Die Huisie Brewery in Bethlehem, Kew Bros. Brewery in Boksburg, Saint Georges Brewery in Johannesburg, Farmers Brewery in Kwa Lulu Natal, and Rawdons Hotel and Brewery in Nottingham Road. There's even a Firkin Brewpub, of English fame, in Sandton. Mitchell's Kynsna Brewery in Kynsna offers tours with tastings weekdays at 10:30 A.M.

In Nigeria, the Star Brand is brewed by Nigerian Brewery, Ltd. in a joint venture with Heineken. The brewery also makes beer in Chad, Ghana, and Sierra Leone. The Banjul Breweries, Ltd. in Gambia brew the award-winning JulBrew Lager. Kenya Breweries, Ltd. in Nairobi was founded by a gold prospector and two farmers, one of whom was later killed by an elephant. The company brews Tusker, White Cap, and Pilsner.

Here's a subjective list of the top 10 African beers:

1. Mamba Beer (Ivory Coast)

2. Tusker (Kenya)

3. Carling Black Label (South Africa)

4. Amstel (South Africa)

5. Flag Special (Morocco)

6. Raven Stout (South Africa)

7. Lion (South Africa)

8. Forester's Lager (South Africa)

9. Windhoek Urbock (Namibia)

10. Castle (South Africa)

The Drinks Africa event is the African International Wine, Spirits, and Beers Exhibition. It takes place in mid-November in South Africa.

Strange Brews in the African Tradition

Foods that are fermented constitute a substantial portion of the traditional African diet. Cereals, tubers, and beans are transformed by the biological process to foods higher in nutritional value, palatability, and flavor. In some cases the foods are detoxified and protected from pathogenic microbes. A good example is a drink called shakparo beer, which has a large social, economic, ritual, and nutritional role in the Savannah regions of the Republic of Benin. It's brewed from malted sorghum, also called guinea corn. The beer has a full body, long aftertaste, fruity pleasant sourness, and a complex aroma. It's very thirst-quenching, cloudy, and yeasty with a brownish-pink color. Shakparo is about 8% alcohol by volume and has a short shelf life of about 24 hours. The drink is brewed primarily by women, and as in other indigenous societies, brewing prowess ensures status for brewsters.

Other native African beers in the same family are bantu beer (called kaffir before the South African revolution), pombe (East Africa) dolo (Burkina Faso, Mali), burukutu (Nigeria), pito (Ghana and Nigeria), bouza (Egypt, Ethiopia), merisa (Sudan), hemeket or zythum or zythos, (Ancient Egypt), shukutu (Benin and Togo), Tchakpalo (Benin, Burkina Faso, Cote d'Ivoire), bil-bil (Cameroon).

Scheherazade in the Middle East

Beer was first brewed in what is now modern Iraq. But since the 1970s, there has been a resurgence of fundamentalist Islam—which strictly forbids the consumption of alcohol. Many breweries that once thrived in the region have closed. The main breweries still operating in the Middle East are Al Chark in Syria, the Jordan Brewery in Amman, and the Efes Brewery in Turkey. Iran's breweries have been shut down since 1980.

There once was a legendary Iraqi beer called Scheherazade. That was before George Bush, Saddam Hussein, and various geopolitical forces got in the way. In order to appease religious fundamentalists, Saddam shut down the Iraqi Brewery where the beer was brewed.

Israel and the Maccabeers

Tempo Beer Industries, Ltd., controls 90% of the brewing in Israel. Tempo's flagship brand is Maccabee, a premium lager. The country also brews Gold Star and Malt Star, as well as American Budweiser, under license.

> **Foamy Fact**
>
> *Take My Beer—Please!* The Jewish beer tradition is as old as the Hebron hills. The Book of Isaiah mentions shekar, the beer of the time and also the Hebrew word for intoxication. The ark-building Noah was "not of the grape, but of beer," and his oldest son, Shem, was a brewer who made beer from barley, dates, and honey. During the Jewish captivity in Babylon, they brewed a potent beer called sicera, thought to prevent leprosy. Some scholars believe that the manna from heaven that the wandering Hebrew tribes received was actually a bread-based beer called boosa.

You probably worked up a thirst on that heady trip around the world. Now you know that if you get tired of your locally made craft brew, you can go to a well-stocked bottle shop and taste brews from Guatamala to Guinea. They may not taste like brews you're used to but there's an exotic edge that can't be beat. Plus you can pair them with cuisine from the region where they are brewed. So next time American brew won't do, pick up a Tusker. Kenya?

The Least You Need to Know

➤ Most beer brewed outside Europe and North America tends toward the light Pilsner-style lager, although there are a few stouts here and there.

➤ Mexico, Brazil, and China are some the top brewing nations in terms of quantity.

➤ Japan and Australia are home to high-quality brewing giants, and more craft breweries are opening in those countries every year.

➤ South America and Africa have ancient beer traditions and still homebrew indigenous beers.

Part 5
Will Work for Ale: The Business of Beer

O.K. So you've sniffed beer, tasted beer, played games with beer, and even cooked dessert with the stuff. You're beer-flow bananas. But where's the cash flow? I mean, everybody likes a good brew, but it can be a real drain on your pocketbook. Great beers can be $10 a bottle. And going to their country of origin? Yikes. If you have to ask how much, you probably can't afford it. "There's got to be a way," you think, "to make all this beer love pay off." As one who makes his living off "the flat of the canned," I can say: "Yes Virginia there is a Beer-a-clause." But as Ringo Starr once said: "It don't come easy."

Part 5 of this book will delve into the not-so-secret finances of beer. We'll take a look at the buying and selling of beer cans and other paraphernalia. We'll explore the foaming up and falling flat of beer stocks on Wall Street and elsewhere. I'll even give a short course on beer writing (for what it's worth). And we'll lay out the economic realities of opening your very own craft brewery. We'll wrap up the book with every-thing you need to know to get started making your own beer. If you want to be the next Jim Koch, brewer of Samuel Adams, you'll need to learn how to brew your own.

Chapter 22

Buying into Beer

In This Chapter

➤ The buying, selling, and collecting of beer cans, trays, openers, and postcards

➤ The lowdown on buying stock in breweries

➤ Tips if you're going to invest

Some folks collect stamps. Some folks collect records. Some folks even collect spouses. But the truly beer-crazed collect beer cans, bottle openers, beer signs, and other beer baubles. And those who can afford it—or just don't want a mess of collectibles cluttering up the garage—collect shares of brewery stock.

Collecting beer paraphernalia is more than collecting cans. Old items bearing beer names and brewery logos include signs, posters, matches, mirrors, and T-shirts. Some folks even collect brewery equipment and antique beer trucks. And buying stock in up-and-coming breweries is more than ponying up on the Big Board. A lot more. Or sometimes less. This chapter starts with the basics—beer cans—and ends with the abstruse—brewery stocks.

Like anything related to brew geekdom, buying into beer is a hobby. (Unless you put your life savings into beer stock.) It's fun, it's entertaining, and it's cheaper than a bass boat. So if you've got a thing for a 1950s beer tray from Pittsburgh Brewing, go ahead and indulge yourself. Some day it might be worth more than your bass boat.

Dancing the Can-Can: Beer Cans and Other Valuables

Buying, selling, collecting, and exhibiting beer gewgaws is called *breweriana* (brewery-ana). These items, also called breweriana, may include beer cans, coasters, crates, lights, lighters, matchbooks, clothing, caps, openers, old signs, posters, tap handles, trays, glasses, and steins.

Terms of Enbeerment
Breweriana is the hobby of collecting beer paraphernalia and artifacts such as beer cans, coasters, bottle openers, tap handles, and beer trays. These geegaws are also referred to as breweriana.

MMM   **Tasty Tip**
For wide-ranging information on beer cans, contact The Beer Can Collectors of America, which was founded in 1971 and currently boasts 4,200 members. BCCA has a great Web site at http://www.bcca.com. The page has a show calendar and FAQs, and offers advice on buying and selling breweriana. They'll even hook you up with a BCCA member in your area for consultation. BCCA also has some of the best links available to other beer and brewery pages.

For years, brewerianans (brewerianiacs?) labored in obscurity, seeing each other at yearly conventions or making the rounds at flea markets and trade shows. Two things have changed—the resurgence of the brewing industry in the United States, and the explosion of interest in the Internet. Suddenly folks are talking about beer. And they're talking about breweriana. So if they need to know the net worth of a beer can from the Eisenhower era, they can look it up on the World Wide Web.

President Jimmy Carter changed the world when he legalized homebrewing in 1976. That law led—in a roundabout way—to today's microbrewery revolution. But Carter was also fraternally responsible for America's first wide-spread interest in breweriana. In the days of polyester suits and disco, the president's brother, Billy Carter, was nationally known for his beer-swilling, sleazoid ways. Whether cutting dubious deals with Third World dictators or urinating on runways while press cameras were rolling, Billy took full advantage of his 15 minutes of celebrity. And when Billy was broke, he lent his name to Billy Beer, produced by Falls City Brewing Co., in Louisville, Kentucky and a few other breweries nationwide. The beer didn't even last as long Carter's presidency, but a lot of folks thought they were going to get rich by scooping up all the Billy Beer they could load in their pickup trucks. As would be expected, the Billy boom fell as flat as the cheap swill in the can. Today, a Billy Beer can in perfect shape is worth about 50¢. One might be able to pass it off at a flea market for a dollar or two. Billy's antics aside, the can brought notice to folks who collect such things.

Billy Beer spawned a late-1970s rash of collector's cans. One was the J.R. Ewing beer can from the television show *Dallas*. The other was the *M*A*S*H* beer can. Both are worth the same as Billy's can.

There are, however, many noble, rare, and worthwhile beer tchotchkes to collect and some are worth quite a bit of cash. And most of them were free or very inexpensive when they were first manufactured. So forget the poseurs. If you desire to own talismans with a brewery's name on them, you're not alone. There are so many breweriana fanatics around that you'll find plenty of company.

Tasty Tip
For breweriana information, contact the mother of all beer can collectors, the American Breweriana Association, Inc., P.O. Box 11157, Pueblo, CO, 81001; 719-544-9267. The organization has more than 300 books on beer, breweriana, and brewing in its lending library. It also publishes a bimonthly magazine. You can be a member for little more than $25 a year.

Any Way You Can It

The first attempt to put beer in a can was in 1909 when a Montana brewer tested the idea with American Can Company. The beer's flavor was ruined when it reacted with the metal. Cans were soon canned due to World War I and the rationing of metal. Prohibition came along in 1918 putting beer can research on hold once again. When beer finally was put into cans, two styles were initially developed, the flat-top can and the cone-top can.

Here Comes Old Flat Top

After Prohibition ended in 1933, packaging companies were working hard to perfect a beer can without the "tinny" taste. American Can finally patented the "Keglined" process in 1934. American Can offered to install canning equipment at a New Jersey brewery and guarantee against losses if the container flopped.

The Gottfried Krueger Brewing Company of Newark finally test-marketed canned beer in October 1934. Some 2,000 units of Krueger's Special Beer were given out in the new container. The guinea pigs liked it. On January 24, 1935, Krueger's Finest Beer and Krueger's Cream Ale went on sale in Richmond, Virginia. The company figured that if the cans bombed, Richmond was far enough away not to ruin its reputation in Jersey. The can was readily accepted and by August, Krueger was selling 200,000 12-ounce cans of beer a day. Pabst Brewing saw Krueger's success and took the beer can nationwide. Those early cans had opening instructions on them and are worth about $300 to $400 in good condition.

Metal flat-top cans were produced from 1935 until the 1960s when pull-tab cans were introduced. The old cans had to be pierced by a sharp can opener or "church key."

Cone Top the Beer-barian

Continental Can Company developed the cone top in September 1935. This "metal bottle" was a called a Cap-Sealed Cone Top. The style appealed to smaller brewers who could use it on their existing bottling machinery. Crown Cork and Seal also entered the market with their "Crowntainer." The Gottlieb Heileman Brewing Co. in La Crosse, Wisconsin was the first to use the cap-sealed cone top. In August 1935, Joseph Schlitz Brewing Co. in Milwaukee took the cone top nationwide. The first quart cone top was introduced in 1937. The cone top lasted until 1960 when the Rice Lake Brewing Co., in Rice Lake, Wisconsin stopped using them.

Recycling with Aluminum

Aluminum cans first appeared in the unlikely location of Honolulu, Hawaii when Primo Brewing Co. first used them for their beer in 1958. Aluminum did not catch on for quite a while, but Rainier Brewing Company of Seattle recognized the benefits of lightweight recyclable cans in early 1970 and was the first brewery to go all aluminum. Pittsburgh Brewing Co. was the last to use steel cans, giving them up in 1985. Later cans were alloys of aluminum with steel or tin to ease opening.

> **MMM** **Tasty Tip**
> Breweriana is available from pubs, breweries, beer distributors, marketing specialists, gift and souvenir shops, individual collectors, and breweriana shows. Real can hounds search for their tin treasures in old abandoned buildings, especially old farmhouses, hunting cabins, barns, and even outhouses. Sometimes cans are found under floorboards and between walls of old buildings. Most rural residences had garbage dumps 50 yards behind the houses, where cans might be found.

Pop Goes the Beer Top

Pittsburgh Brewing Co. began selling cans that didn't require a can opener. "Pull-top" cans were first sold in 1962. Schlitz went nationwide with the "Pop-Top" beer can in March 1963. After a decade of cut fingers and sliced toes from pull tabs, "Sta-Tab" cans were introduced in 1975. The first company to use stay tabs was the Falls City Brewing Company of Louisville, Kentucky. Stay tabs have stayed with us to this very day.

Getting Your Can in Gear

One reason breweriana is so popular is that (unfortunately) so many breweries have gone beer-belly up—their numbers declined 83% from 1946 to 1975. In the case of breweriana, breweries are gone but not forgotten. Some collectors wax nostalgic over brews they swilled when they were feisty youngsters. Others use breweriana as an excuse to get together with a like-minded group of beer-lovers to meet, swap, organize, and jaw the night away. And, unlike porcelain dolls or antique autos, breweriana is inexpensive to get into and easy to understand.

You can start your collection next time you're in a bar. Items such as matches, coasters, and napkins are meant as giveaways. Brewers understand the advertising value inherent in having their logo stuck up on your wall—or on your forehead. Many brewpubs sell pint glasses, T-shirts, posters, and the like. So you can start for nearly nothing. And, if you put your totems away for about 40 years, they might be worth something when you're old and gray. (Unless you're already old and gray.)

Stale Ale Alert

Don't swipe anything that belongs to the bar. Some folks love to swipe ash trays, bar towels, and beer glasses when they drink at a bar. This stuff is not public property, and this is considered stealing. This also helps drive up the price of beer for the rest of us. Many brew-pubs give away coasters, matches, and other tchotchkes. Beer glasses and T-shirts may usually be purchased at a decent price. All you gotta do is ask.

Tips for Potential Brewerianiacs

Beer cans are just the most obvious collectibles in the world of breweriana. Companies like Coors, Anheuser-Busch (A-B), and Guinness sell a stunning array of items sporting their logo, including golf shoes, underwear, and furniture. In fact, the A-B catalog lists more than 5,000 items. As any collector knows, the more there are of something, the less they're worth. Modern Bud cans won't be worth anything until the 29th century. But microbreweries sell promotional items that may gain in value because of their small production number and their regional value.

Foamy Fact

Big Bucks for Battered Beer Cans: The record take for a beer can auction was a cool half million in 1992. The collection belonged to the late Kermit Dietrich, who ran the annual Bavarian festival in Barnesville, Pennsylvania. A sign for the Columbia Brewing Co. in Shenandoah, Pennsylvania brought in $6,500. A quart cone-top can from Old Reading Brewing Co. in Reading, Pennsylvania brought in $1,000.

A few tips for would-be collectors:

➤ The obvious: Rare and old items are worth the most.

➤ To get a head start, join a local breweriana club. You'll find beer, camaraderie, publications, and lots of free advice.

➤ Check prices in breweriana books and magazines or on the Internet before you buy anything expensive. Better yet, consult with an expert. Antique shows and flea markets tend to overprice things.

➤ Focus! True brewerianiacs focus on one or two kinds of items to collect—openers or bar towels, for instance. Others get all the items they find from one specific brewery.

➤ Flea markets, swap meets, second-hand stores, and garage sales sometimes have valuable breweriana at good prices. There are even breweriana auctions and mail auctions.

➤ Because neon signs are made in smaller numbers (and they're harder to get), they hold their value better than other beer items.

➤ If you're getting into this to get rich, find another hobby. You would have to quit your job and become a breweriana fanatic full-time to squeak by.

Foamy Fact

Six Grand for a Can: In 1980, an auction was held to sell the largest collection of flat-top beer cans in the world. A single Tiger beer can and a single Rosalie Pilsner can brought $6,000 each in an auction where people submitted bids by mail. A single cone-top can of Gibbon's Bock beer brought in $3,750.

Cans, Coasters, and Cups: Breweriana for What It's Worth

Every little item with a beer name or logo on it has its own set of obsessive aficionados. Some things are worth money, some are beautiful only in the eye of the beer-holder. If you don't know whether you're really a tap-handle person or a beer-poster person, here are the ins and outs of every little bit of breweriana:

➤ Bar towels are mainly made in Great Britain. They're about 8 by 18 inches and have the names of beer brands on them. Great for collecting or mopping up spills, they may be purchased at pubs in Great Britain and probably won't gain in value until the next century or so.

➤ Beer bottles (empty ones) are pretty much worthless, unless you're a homebrewer who likes to refill them with your own suds. They're heavy, they break, and they take up scads of space. The exceptions to the rule are very old bottles or those with raised, embossed lettering.

➤ Bottle caps aren't worth much unless they're very old. The advantage to collecting is that they're easy to display and don't take up a lot of room.

➤ Bottle labels are a good way to start a collection. If you just love the label on your favorite beer, chances are the brewery will send you some for a couple of bucks (if not for free). A self-addressed, stamped envelope is also a good thing to send with your request. It's good advertising for the brewers. Call and ask. Although relatively indestructible, labels need to be stored like old magazines. Heat, light, and moisture are killers over time. Many new breweries have funny beer names or beautifully designed labels suitable for framing. Old beer labels may be very valuable if in good condition.

Tasty Tip
If you want to save a non-twist-off cap without bending it, place a quarter over it before prying off with a bottle opener.

➤ Bottle openers are useful items that are easy to find. Fun to use, but not worth much money unless rare or old.

➤ Cans make up the mother lode of breweriana, but they're not as popular as they once were. Whole collections can be picked up at shows. Cans are harder to store. Old ones rust, they also dent, but they have plenty of value to some folks—sentimental or otherwise.

Foamy Fact

Cheap Aluminum Siding: When John Milkovisch got tired of mowing his lawn, he paved it over with concrete. When he got tired of painting his house, he started covering it with empty beer cans. He ended with a total of about 50,000. John's gone, but his wife Mary still lives in the house on 222 Malone Street in Houston, and she entertains tourists by the busload who come to see her "Beer Can House" (call 713-926-6368 for information on tours).

➤ Coasters that are old and rare have been sold for more than a few hundred dollars. Most of them aren't worth much, and if they're stained, forget it. Coasters are easy to display in a frame.

➤ Glassware with beer names and brewery logos can be worth quite a bit of money depending on where it's from. A 19th-century glass decorated with the logo of the long-defunct Anaconda Brewing Co. in Montana recently sold for better than $1,000. If you want your glassware to be worth something in the next century, don't drink beer from it—put it on display.

➤ Matchbooks don't last very long, so older ones are hard to find and may be worth a few bucks. Obviously, they should be kept in good condition and not used for lighting your cigar.

➤ Posters and postcards, like matchbooks, tend to fall apart. If they are older and in good condition posters keep their value. There are many reprints of old posters that may be found at gift shops.

➤ Signs are not something you would want to collect if you live in a small apartment. Neon is expensive and fragile. Older tin and wood signs keep their value. Modern signs are made from plastic and cardboard, so aren't worth much.

➤ T-Shirts with silk-screened designs on them are everywhere. Some craft breweries and brewspapers print up gorgeous, funny, or outrageously sloganed T-shirts. If you want your favorite T-shirt to be worth something in the future, put it in the closet and forget it. Drooled beer stains down the front detract from value. T-shirts are so popular that there's a T-shirt of the month club called Brew Tees (800-585-TEES).

➤ Tap handles are not usually available to the general public and the ones that are tend to be pricey. Like T-shirts, the craft-brewing industry has started a revival in unique and interesting tap handle designs. I've seen them shaped like fish, apple cores, wizards, grasshoppers, and several other strange forms.

➤ Trays represent a 1950s kind of image of a waitress bringing out a tray full of brimming golden brews. The old trays with intricate beer logos and pictures can be worth quite a few bucks. Dents, rust, and wear detract from the price.

The World's Largest Collection

Probably the largest collection of breweriana in one place was at the Oldenberg Brewery and Entertainment Complex in Fort Mitchell, Kentucky. In 1987, Oldenberg bought a million-piece collection of world-wide breweriana from Herb Haydock, who started collecting it in 1951. Oldenberg forked over 1 million dollars for the collection, which included everything from toothpicks to golf clubs. The collection was so huge that Oldenberg could display only half of it at once. The geegaws threatened to overcome brewing at the brewery. Oldenberg sold the thing lock, stock, and beer barrel to Miller Brewing in 1996, which is mum about plans for the collection, although a few pieces have been displayed at the Great American Beer Festival in Colorado. Now Oldenberg displays "a few" items—150,000 pieces it has collected from microbreweries.

Tasty Tip
Nashville, Tennessee, is home to country music, and it's also home to the Museum of Beverage Containers, which displays more than 300,000 beer and soda cans. The phone number is 615-859-5236.

Brewers today are prone to give their beers some goofy names such as Turbodog, Old Jock, and Freudian Sip Ale. Lest you think that weird beer names are anything new, check out the names of beer from defunct (and some still operating) breweries. These names were mostly unintentionally funny. Maybe that's why many of the breweries are gone but not forgotten.

➤ $1,000 Natural Process Beer—Gettleman Brewing, Milwaukee

➤ Autocrat Pilsner—Manhattan Brewing, Chicago

➤ Bean and Bacon Days Premium Beer—Walter's Brewing, Eau Claire, Wisconsin

➤ Bub's Beer—Walter's Brewing

➤ Clyde Ale—Enterprise Brewing, Fall River, Massachusetts

➤ Cremo Beer—Cremo Brewing, New Britain, Connecticut

➤ Dorf Bohemian Lager—Drewry's, Chicago

➤ Fehr's Liquid Gold Beer—Frank Fehr Brewing, Louisville, Kentucky

➤ Grossvater Beer—Renner Brewing, Akron, Ohio

➤ King Turkey Beer—August Schell Brewing, New Ulm, Minnesota (still operating regionally, making great beer)

➤ Kool Beer, Nu Deal Beer, Happy Hops Lager Beer—Grace Bros. Brewery, Los Angeles

➤ Mule Head Beer—Wehle Brewing, West Haven, Connecticut

➤ Sick's Select Beer—Sick's Seattle Brewing and Malting Company

➤ Sir Lady Frothingslosh Pale Stale Ale—Pittsburgh Brewing (still brewing Iron City, Samuel Adams, and other beers)

➤ Soul Mellow Yellow Beer—Maier Brewing, Los Angeles

➤ Sweet Life Premium Quality Beer—Cumberland Brewing, Cumberland, Maryland

➤ Tuxedo 51 Premium Beer—Tuxedo Brewing, Chicago

➤ Wacker Premium Beer—Wacker Brewing, Lancaster, Pennsylvania

➤ Wurstest 79 Dark Beer—Spoetzl Brewing, Shiner, Texas (still making Shiner Beer)

Drinking Your Shares: Buying and Selling Brewery Stock

In August 1995, Redhook Ale Brewery in Seattle went public and sold shares of stock in its brewery. Wall Street went nuts. The net worth of Redhook's stock jumped 60% *in one day!* In a feeding frenzy usually reserved for computer stocks, the brewery, little-known outside Washington, became one of the most talked-about stocks on Wall Street. When Boston Beer Company (brewers of Samuel Adams) and Pete's Brewing Co. (Pete's Wicked Ale) saw the Redhook success, they, too, went public. Boston's stock jumped 65% and Pete's 54% in the days that followed.

Of course, folks who bought those stocks at their highest level learned the number one lesson of Wall Street—what goes up must (usually) come down. They lost money. The stock's value decreased 30% in the following weeks.

With so many breweries trying to raise the large capital investments required by the beer business, we're likely to see more offerings like this in the near future. But things have changed. Wall Street is a love-'em-and-leave-'em kind of place. When Pyramid Breweries, also in Seattle, went public a few months later, their stock *fell* the first day. As Redhook CEO Paul Shipman said: "The investment bankers had already forgotten microbreweries and went on to bagels." Wall Street analysts said the craft-beer boom was a fad, soon to fade. They were wrong.

It's a long way between Wall Street and Main Street. The craft-brew industry has been growing at a rate of 46% a year since 1986. Industry analysts expect craft beer to fill up 8% of the total United States beer market by the year 2000, up from 2% in 1995. When you're looking at a $50-billion-a-year market, you're talking about Redhook, Pete's, and a thousand other breweries, vying for a $4 billion chunk of funds. That's *real* money—even on Wall Street.

What's that mean to the beer investor? It means that some of the smartest craft brewers are going to be seeing big, fat, bottom lines in the coming years. One or two of them might even get as big as Miller or Coors by the time a baby born today is done with college. Maybe. But like gambling in Vegas, the standard advice is: Don't bet more than you can stand to lose.

Foamy Fact

Stock's Up on Beer: The Wall Street roller coaster is a wild ride and not grounded in reality. Look at the stock price in 1996 of Boston Beer and Pete's for example. If you multiplied the number of shares sold by their going price, Boston and Pete's were both worth around $570 million on paper. Coors, the nation's third-largest brewer, is worth about $725 million. Those numbers show how absurd it all is. Coors shipped more than 20 million barrels of beer in 1995 with a total of $1.7 billion in sales. Boston Beer shipped 961,000 barrels. Pete's shipped only 348,000. How can those small brewers be worth almost as much as Coors? They're not. *An interesting note:* At one point, the owner of Boston Beer, Jim Koch, had holdings worth more than $100 million—more than August Busch III holds in Anheuser-Busch. Real ale equals real money. At least in the funny money terms of Wall Street.

There are more than 1,000 craft breweries out there today, with a new one coming on line almost every day. They're all trying to raise a dime, and the number of self-underwritten deals nationwide is growing as fast as yeast in a fermenter. What that means is a lot of folks are sitting around in rooms writing up business plans with grandiose projections showing how much money an investor can stand to gain over five or 10 years. The breweries are printing up stock and selling it to anyone who is interested, usually for a couple bucks a share, with a minimum buy of $1,000 or so. It's all perfectly legal, if certain laws are followed.

The good news is that there is a 23-to-1 opening to closing ratio for craft breweries. The bad news is that some of them are going to fail, and maybe the one you sunk a few grand into is one of them. The self-promoted stocks are more venture capital deals than stock offerings—breweries want to raise capital while selling off only 49% of the company, thus retaining control. Just because you love beer doesn't mean you're going to get rich from it. What these stocks do offer is investment in a solid business, if it succeeds. Portland Brewing Co., offers its stockholders a free pint of beer a day for life. Now *that's* what I call a dividend.

Breweries with a good track record are the safest investments. Redhook and Boston Beer had been around for more than 10 years before making their offerings. Other smaller brewers might offer stock to expand their bottling line or enlarge their facilities. These folks have past earnings that you can examine for comfort and hope.

Taking Stock in Your Investments

If you're going to invest in breweries, there's a lot of standard advice that applies to any investor. Make sure the company has a good product, savvy management, and is making money. The obvious question: Is the company supporting itself selling beer? If the business fails, stockholders are last in line to get money, behind suppliers, the government, banks, and other creditors.

Don't expect dividends. Any profits a young company generates will be plowed back into the business. That's as it should be. But the more you risk, the more you should expect to gain. Whatever you pay for the stock, you obviously want it to go up. Fast-growing companies are hard to value by traditional means. But if the product is there and the demand is there, the stock will be worth more over time. The final word: Although craft brewing is definitely not a fad, investing in it at astronomical prices is.

Foamy Fact

Stock's Up on Beer: The world's first digital initial public offering was the brainchild of Andrew D. Klein, a Harvard stock lawyer turned craft brewer. Spring Street Brewing Co. sold stock on the Internet and raised $1.6 million, virtually overnight. The craft brewers of Wit and Amber Wit beer didn't have to share any of the proceeds with Wall Street underwriters. Anyone with a computer and a modem could peruse the offer, download it, and e-mail a subscription directly to the company. The company, registered in 22 states, sold more than 800,000 shares of common stock for $1.85. Folks wishing to buy and sell the stock can do so using the company's bulletin board on its Web page, avoiding broker's fees and commissions.

If you're interested in following the bubbly beer stocks on the ticker tape or in the newspaper, you need to know their stock names. Boston Beer Company is SAM. Pete's Beer is WIKD. Pyramid Breweries is HOPS. And Redhook is HOOK. By the way, Pyramid used the money raised to build a brewery near San Francisco. Pete's, a contract brewer, is planning to build its own $30 million plant in California. And Redhook bought a brewery in New Hampshire and paid off some debt.

Beer Writing: Getting Your License to Swill

Some folks think I have the easiest job in the world. I work about 20 hours a week at home (in my sweatpants or less). I get lots of free beer. Occasionally I get free trips in this country and abroad. "How can I get a job like yours?" they ask. Well if I told you that, I might get too much competition, and soon I'd be out there slogging away in the real world like everyone else.

I can say this. If you've got a knack for the written word, a computer, and an e-mail address, brewspapers and beer magazines are always looking for *interesting* articles. They need stuff that is unique—that hasn't been written a hundred times before. If you wanted to review all the brewpubs in Nebraska, and take some pictures of them, you just might get published if you know how to put words together. But if you write about something that's been covered extensively, then you can wallpaper your office with rejection letters.

If you've never been published, you might want to try doing something with a local angle for a local brewspaper. Or you could even try a neighborhood paper. Write to the editors and ask for writer's guidelines. Usually the business or variety sections of newspapers have interest in beer stories. If you think you have a good idea, write it up in a paragraph or two and query the editor to see if there's any interest in your story. The *Editor and Publisher Yearbook* lists every daily in the U.S. as well as their phone numbers, addresses, e-mail addresses, and names of their section editors.

After you've been published many times, you can move up to the national magazines. If you're good and you can communicate well, you might start getting paid. But don't give up your day job. The money comes in fits and spurts, sometimes months go by without even a glimmer of cash. And brewspapers don't pay that much to start with.

Before my editors in the beer business have me killed, let me also add this: If you submit a work for publication, don't expect an answer for a few months. Even if they like it, it may be another few months before it's published and you get your money. Some publications offer only free magazines or less, no money changes hands. If you *do* want to get published eventually, don't start calling editors on the phone every other day and bugging them. These folks can get so inundated with submissions that it takes time to sift through them all. They'll let you know if they want your work. Or you can give them a call after four weeks or so. Now aren't you glad you asked?

> **Tasty Tip**
> *S.O.B.s (Scribes of Beer) Unite:* If you are truly interested in writing about beer, you can contact the North American Guild of Beer Writers, P.O. Box 20268, Alexandria, VA 22320-1268; 703-567-1962. E-mail: jdorsch@mnsinc.com. They have useful information of interest to Scribes of Beer.

The Least You Need to Know

➤ You can start a nice collection of breweriana for a small amount of money, but if you want to get serious, you can spend a fortune.

➤ Many breweries are offering shares of stock to the general public, and in some cases, the shares are gaining net worth quickly.

➤ Many stock offerings are overvalued and folks have lost money on them.

➤ If you have an unique take on a beer topic and you can write well, you may be able to get an article published in a local newspaper, brewspaper, or beer magazine.

Chapter 23

Are You Totally Nuts? Starting Your Own Brewery

In This Chapter

➤ The steps necessary to start a brewpub or microbrewery

➤ The cost, licenses, regulations, and realities of the venture

➤ Advantages of starting brewpubs

➤ Advantages of microbreweries

Starting a brewery is for the totally committed. Some folks who try it end up committed—to an asylum. But seriously, brewing beer and running a brewing operation is hard work with long hours, and pennies for profit on a huge investment. It is satisfying work, however, and if you're successful, it's possible to make a comfortable living brewing and selling beer. Money or not, 90% of the folks I know who brew beer are not in it to get rich. They do it for the love of the craft and to satisfy a certain outlaw mentality inherent in beer-making. Not that they would mind getting rich.

As you might imagine, starting a brewery is a tricky business in itself. There are strict city, state, and federal laws governing the production and sale of alcoholic beverages. There are employees to hire, buildings to lease or buy, forms to fill out, taxes to pay. Knowing how to make beer won't cut it. You need to have a working knowledge of how to run a business. Sure, you get to drink a lot of beer, but it's not quite as much fun when you're pouring 2,000 gallons of spoiled beer down the sewer at 2 o'clock in the morning. And your brewmaster just found a better job elsewhere. And the Bureau of Alcohol, Tobacco and Firearms is coming in for an audit at 8 A.M. the next morning.

There are, however, a lot of positive aspects to owning a brewery. These include:

➤ You can exercise your culinary creativity in your beer recipes.

➤ There is great personal satisfaction in brewing massive quantities of good beer.

➤ You can be your own boss.

➤ Brewers enjoy positive interaction with the general public—especially those in the brewpub business.

➤ The micro business is populated by many talented, creative, and colorful folks, some of whom will become your comrades in "barms."

➤ You never have to buy beer again, and what beer you do buy is tax deductible.

Every year, thousands of otherwise sane folks get the call. They mortgage their homes and kiss their families good-bye to go live in a brewery 18 hours a day. Could you be one of them?

Reality Bites: Opening a Brewery

Every spring thousands of starry-eyed, would-be brewers attend the National Craft-Brewers Conference and Trade Show sponsored by the Institute for Brewing Studies. They gaze at shiny copper brewing systems, shake hands with maltsters, check out bottling systems, and ponder cleaning agents. Hundreds of bottles of beer from every craft brewery in the country are offered as inspiration to the hopeful future microbrewers. Attendees sit in rapt attention as beer legends like Michael Jackson and Fritz Maytag give lectures. There are always a few folks who have made a million in the past year doling out sage advice. By the end of the four-day trade show, the novices are ready to go back to their home towns and open a brewery to the applause of their friends and family. There's only one small problem.

Opening a small craft brewery today costs a minimum of about one million dollars. If you want a decent restaurant to go with the brewery, you're talking another million. What do you get for that million? Lots of things obvious and not so obvious.

Let's talk about a microbrewery. Start with a copper, 20-barrel brewing system, with fermenters, hoses, bells, and whistles. That should come in at about $300,000 or so. A small bottling line will set you back about $75,000 or more. Remodeling and improving a leased building could run another $150,000. You've got to put in huge drains, angled floors (for proper drainage), vents, electrical hook-ups, and other nuts-and-bolts stuff. For a brewpub, a restaurant kitchen and seating for the public is an entirely different, and pricey, project. Of course, if you've never done this before, you're going to need a professional brewing consultant, a lawyer, an accountant, and other high-buck folks. Call it a hundred grand for professional costs. Little things like utility hook-ups, office supplies, deposits, kegs and bottles, a delivery van, promotional materials, and advertising could top out at another $100,000. To brew beer you need to pay a licensing fee to the state you live in and give them a surety bond, which is money against taxes you will have to pay when you start brewing. The feds require another bond in lieu of excise tax.

Have we hit a million yet? Oh yeah, labor costs. Start-up salary and benefits for three beer grunts and a head brewer should run you about $120,000. Then you need operating capital to carry your costs until you start selling beer. You can expect to turn a profit—say in about three years. Still want to start a brewery?

> **Tasty Tip**
> This book cannot go into the thousands of details necessary to bring a brewery to fruition. The library is a good place to find books about writing business plans. If you call your local Bureau of Alcohol, Tobacco and Firearms (BATF) agent, he or she can steer you toward information you will need for government compliance. The Association of Brewers sells dozens of books on brewery operations. It has books on financing and insurance, yeast fermentation, marketing and distribution, business plans, and brewery planners.

Who's Gonna Buy It? The Feasibility Study

David Heidrich, President of Oldenberg Brewery, compares brewery owners to spies. Some do it for the money. Others do it for the fun, excitement, and ideological reasons. The brewers who succeed are usually the latter. Heidrich also points out that the spy business is considerably less complicated and cheaper to get into. But if you still imagine your name on a brewery cranking out suds in the 22nd century, you have to do a *feasibility study* to decide if the area where you live can make you beer-mortal.

These are some of the things considered in a feasibility study:

> ➤ Site considerations determine if the area has proper access roads for the brewery to truck in

> **Terms of Enbeerment**
> A **feasibility study** is a project conducted by a group of people to determine whether a brewpub or micro-brewery will be financially successful in a particular area or region. You can conduct a feasibility study yourself, or pay a professional.

and out equipment and if people can find the place. Traffic counts are done, road maps are studied, sight distances are checked. City zoning laws must be consulted. Your operation should not be too close to a school, hospital, church, or library. There are horror stories of people who had invested thousands in a brewpub only to have the church across the street shoot down their dreams. On the other hand, a nearby sports arena, hotel convention center, or busy shopping mall can add desirability to the site.

➤ Building improvements can put you in the red in days. Breweries and restaurants are huge electricity, gas, and sewer consumers. Anyone less than brilliant should hire plumbers, electricians, and carpenters to check out the site. Tanks that hold 2,000 gallons of beer weigh better than 16,000 pounds *each*. Put four or five of those in an old building with no footers, and you're going to have a disaster. In large cities, getting gas lines hooked up can take months.

➤ Demographics are important, especially for brewpubs. Is your location near a retirement community full of sober old folks who go to bed at 9:30 P.M.? Is it near a college full of beer-swilling frat boys? The neighborhood where you build is as important as your product. Check out historical information about the area, population age trends, income trends, and population growth trends.

➤ Competition is good for consumers but not for manufacturers. Microbrewers have to contend with hundreds of new beers being rolled out every year. There's competition from giant brewers with unlimited budgets, as well as the hundreds of folks like themselves who are opening craft breweries. Shelf space in most beer stores is limited. Brewpubs have to compete with other brewpubs and even restaurants that don't brew their own beer. The flip side is that a brewpub operates in a much less hostile environment than a microbrewery—there can be as many brewpubs as restaurants. And if a town has 10 strong competitors, the consumer market is strong and may offer success.

Feasibility studies are best done by a third party. You are not going to be impartial if you *really* want to open a brewery in your town. Trouble is, outsiders will charge about $20,000 for the work—and might tell you to forget it. Another problem is that banks generally require an outsider's study before they'll lend you a dime.

Raising the Dough

Most people can't whip out their checkbook or Visa card and plunk down a cool million for a brewery. Where, oh where can a brew geek get that kind of money? Well, it's easier said than done.

The first thing anyone who opens a business needs is a business plan. A builder uses a blueprint to erect a building. A business plan acts as the blueprint for the hundreds of elements than need to be pulled together to build a better beer. The first thing folks with a million dollars to lend want to see is a *pro forma profit and loss statement.* That statement lists the cost of every piece of equipment from the office computer to the brew kettle. The cost of malt, hops, bottles, utilities, boxes, soap, and toilet paper must be estimated. Salaries and benefits have to be agreed upon. Below is a sample of a pro forma cash budget from a hypothetical company.

Pro Forma Cash Budget

Year	1	2	3	4	5
Cash Receipts					
Cash Sales	$771,430	1,542,886	2,314,290	3,085,772	3,582,215
Interest Income	$2,725	2,725	2,725	2,725	2,725
Total Cash Receipts	$774,155	1,545,611	2,317,015	3,088,497	3,584,940
Cash Disbursements					
Cost of Goods Sold	$309,038	538,076	807,114	1,075,883	1,344,854
General & Administrative	$417,885	474,725	563,132	630,139	674,249
Equipment			35,000	12,500	
Loan Installment	$0				
Total Cash Disbursements	$726,923	1,012,801	1,370,246	1,741,022	2,031,602
Annual Before-Tax Income	$47,232	532,810	946,769	1,344,750	1,553,338

Net cash flow 10-year total $16,354,446

Equity break-even point in 3rd year

Internal rate of return for 5-year period is 36.95%

Terms of Enbeerment
Pro forma is Latin for "according to form." In a business plan, the **pro forma profit and loss statement** lists the total amount made from selling a product minus the complete cost of producing it. The resulting number is the profit (or loss). In other words, if a brewery makes $350,000 a year and it costs $290,000 to produce all the beer, the profit is $60,000. Pro formas are usually projected for five years into the future.

Once you have a page or two with your projected costs, the fun begins. Get out your crystal ball and guesstimate how may pints of beer and hamburgers your brewpub is going to sell every year for the next five years. Figure out what you have to charge for each plate of French fries to make a profit. If you're opening a microbrewery, guess how many six-packs you're going to move from day one until day 2,000. Get out a computer spreadsheet program and record it. If you fudge the numbers, you're only hurting yourself. The biggest killer of small businesses is undercapitalization. Make sure you're going to have enough money to operate until the business is profitable. Below is a sample detail of sales projections from a hypothetical microbrewery. Don't try this at home.

Detail of Sales Projections for 1st Year's Operations

Total Production: 3,000 31-gallon barrels (bbls)

2,500 bbls sold as 134,775 6-packs @ $5.20 each	$716,430
500 bbls sold as 1,000 kegs @ $55 each	55,000
Interest on cash reserve	2,725
Total gross operating income	774,155

General & Administrative Estimated Expenses

Federal brewer's stamp—renewed annually	500
Building carrying costs	73,625
Gas and electric utilities	15,945
Water and sewer	4,200
Business insurance	2,000
Building insurance	3,775
Equipment maintenance	5,000
Labor salaries	76,800

Management compensation	170,000
Taxes and benefits for workers	56,040
Education, training, and travel	10,000
Total G & A expenses	417,885

Cost of Goods Sold Estimated Expenses

Federal excise tax @ $7 per bbl	21,000
Brewing ingredients	98,263
Bottles and packaging @ $1 per 6-pack	137,775
Advertising	52,000
Total C & S expenses	309,038

Total estimated operating expenses	**$726,923**

Summary

Gross operating income	774,155
Operating expenses	726,923
Net profits before tax	$47,232

After you've got the numbers, the rest of your business plan should define your market, detail your site, explain your distribution system, list the resumes of your board of directors, and explain your product and why it's different from all the other beers. Name your beers with clever names, give the background of the microbrewery revolution, explain the brewing process, and back it up with photocopied newspaper articles about successful breweries, and other warm and fuzzy information. If you can't write well, hire a professional author (me, for instance). A plan that reads well works well. It must dramatize the inherent beauty of your project, and convey your ability to make it happen.

Once you've got a business plan, pay someone who reads them every day to read yours. Ask for a critique. Chances are they can tell you half a dozen things you've forgotten to include.

Once you've got a dynamite business plan, it's time to go begging—I mean, shopping—for capital. Unless you've been running a brewery or restaurant for a few years, you can forget most banks. They won't generally lend to inexperienced folks who might actually *need* the money. If possible, take on a partner that *has* run a restaurant or brewery. You'll probably thank your stars you did anyway once the thing gets off the ground. Experienced people are important. Banks want collateral, and if you want to offer up your home, car, boat, stocks, or firstborn child for about 50% collateral on the loan, start praying and sign on the dotted line.

Hitting up rich relatives is always a good idea. After that, try to find several dozen private investors who will pool their money to back your brewery. Many folks will show interest, but only 1% will ever write a check. Print up lots of business plans. Ask old friends, family acquaintances, business clients, *everyone*. Expect lots of rejection, but keep your eye on the ball.

Many cities have venture capital clubs. These are groups of folks who meet once a month and pool their resources. They *want* to give money to possible winning projects. They also want a huge chunk of the business, say 90%. Venture capitalists will give you 20 minutes to make a presentation for them. Restaurants have a huge failure rate (much worse than brewpubs), so many of these folks are skeptical. Emphasize *brewpub*, not restaurant.

In the end, the best way to raise money is to need less of it. Some folks build their own brewing equipment out of old dairy machinery. Restaurant auctions offer equipment for a dime on the dollar. Some folks have started in a barn in their back yard. Some start *very* small and work their way up. Pete's Wicked Ale started in Pete's wicked garage.

Once you've put your million in the bank, the fun is just beginning. It's the last time you'll get any peace and quiet for about five years.

Foamy Fact

Overnight Success in 17 Years: Pete Slosberg recently went public with Pete's Brewing Co., and made it big overnight. But things didn't always go that well for the self-described Palo Alto "beer fanatic." Pete began homebrewing in his kitchen in 1979. After developing a great recipe for American Brown Ale in 1986, he begged and borrowed $50,000 to start Pete's Brewing Co. The beer won an award at the GABF, and Pete went home to pound the pavement and get established in the Bay Area. One night a sheriff called Pete and said the small, makeshift brewery doors would be locked in 96 hours due to unpaid bills. Pete called his friends together, and they bottled and warehoused the first cases of Pete's Wicked Ale. Pete sold the beer, began contract-brewing it, and the rest, as they say, is beer-story.

Brewing by the Rules

If you've decided on a site, and figured you could make your fortune there, you've got to ask Uncle Sam and Aunt Sammy if you can be licensed as a maker of alcoholic beverages. If you've ever been convicted of a felony, forget it. The Bureau of Alcohol, Tobacco and Firearms will not allow felons to open a brewery. They also bar folks who have been convicted of alcohol-related misdemeanors (like selling hooch out of their car trunk). Having DWIs does not look too good, but will not prevent you from getting a brewer's license. Anyone who owns more than 10% of the brewery must fit these requirements.

To get a license to brew beer, the BATF must get a pre-license inspection of the brewery. Each brand of beer must be registered. Exact copies of the beer labels must be registered and approved by the state and federal governments. Then the brewer must get a permit from the BATF and must supply the bureau with a floor plan, equipment description, and names of partners and directors. The process must begin when the brewer starts buying equipment, because it takes months for the BATF to get around to approving everything. The catch is they can approve your license only *after* the brewery is set up. So you better make sure you're going to get approved before you drop $300,000 on a shiny new brew system.

Breweries need to comply with regulations written by the U.S. Environmental Protection Agency, the Food and Drug Administration, state and city pollution control agencies, local department of health boards, local building departments, and waste control commissions.

Potential brewers are surprised to know that water and sewage requirements are very tough. But it takes more water to clean brewing equipment than is actually used to make beer. Caustic soaps are the main cleaner and they are polluting. If a brewer needs to dump a bad batch of beer, he or she must call the BATF so the brewery doesn't have to pay taxes on the juice. The brewer must also call the city sewer plant and warn them that the beer is on the way.

The laws are always changing and bureaucrats hate surprises. The gov'mint folks can make your life a living hell, so you better pretend they're Santa Claus, not the devil. The wheels of administration move slowly, so give them plenty of time.

Burgers, Beer, and Bottles: Brewpubs vs. Microbreweries

Do you want to run a restaurant brewery or a beer factory? There are plenty of advantages and disadvantages to both. Here are a few succinct points to illustrate the difference:

➤ Brewpubs are *two* operations, the making of food and the brewing of beer. If you don't know how to run a restaurant, this is not the business for you.

➤ Brewpubs need more employees than micros. Dedicated workers can make a business—disgruntled workers can kill it.

➤ Brewpubs must be in the daily business of pleasing their customers on myriad levels from hot soup to clean rest rooms. Microbrewers need only to brew, bottle, ship beer, and give an occasional tour.

➤ Brewpubs require good food and good beer in a good atmosphere. The food and brew brings people in. The atmosphere attracts them the second time.

➤ As in real estate, the three most important aspects to a brewpub are location, location, location. Microbreweries can be tucked away on some inexpensive piece of industrial land.

➤ With a brewpub, your food and beer need to appeal to a large cross-section of the general public. With a micro you can specialize in one or two styles if you brew them really well, and can aim them at your desired market.

➤ Brewers at brewpubs can use their creativity to offer a wide range of styles brewed in small batches. Some brewpubs offer up to 10 styles. Microbreweries have to concentrate on making three or four styles perfectly and consistently.

➤ Microbreweries usually bottle their product, which is a time-consuming headache. Micros must also recall their beers—or sell it at a loss— if the beer has been on store shelves too long—another expensive killer.

➤ The markup on beer is better at a brewpub because there are no bottling, shipping, or distribution costs. And brewpubs sell it at retail prices. If a micro can achieve good sales and distribution, however, the sky is the limit as far as possible earning potential.

School Days, Brew Daze

If you still think you want to open a brewery, you need to get yourself an education. Formulating beer recipes, handling yeast, and dealing with government compliance are no joke. If you've made a few batches of homebrew and think you're ready to be the next Auggie Busch, you're in for a rude awakening. Fortunately, there are people out there who are ready to help.

Here is a list of some brewing schools:

➤ There are two major beer schools in the U.S. One is at the University of California in Davis, the other is the Siebel Institute of Technology in Chicago (4055 West Peterson Avenue, Chicago, Illinois, 60646-6001; 773-279-0966; fax: 773-463-7688.

Web site: http://www.siebel-institute.com/welcome; e-mail: siebelinstitute@worldnet.att.net.). In addition, the American Brewer's Guild (1107 Kennedy Place, Suite 3, Davis, California, 95616; 800-636-1331. Web site: http://www.mother.com/abg; e-mail:abgbrew@mother.com.) offers two-day courses in cities from coast to coast.

➤ In England, contact the Institute of Brewing, 33 Clarges Street, London, W1Y 8EE, England; (011-44) 171 499 8144.

➤ The world's most respected brewing school is the German Technische Universitat Weihenstephan, Technische Universitat Munchen, Verwaltungsstelle, Weihenstephan, Freising 8050, Germany.

Tasty Tip
Wanted: Vat Vassals and Suds Serfs: There are several ways to learn brewing on a large scale. One is to apprentice yourself to a craft brewery. Beer slaves usually don't get paid much, but they get free beer, and there's no better way to learn than through hands-on experience. Many micros use part-time interns. In other cases of reverse slavery, the beer slave pays the brewer for the privilege of working in the brewery. If beer slavery doesn't appeal to you, consider attending beer school.

Most of the courses offered by brewing schools last from two days to ten weeks. A ten-week diploma course in brewing science and technology at Siebel can cost about $8,000. One-month courses cost about half that much. Weekend courses can run from $300 to $1,000. The four-week course at the American Brewer's Guild in Davis is about $7,000. Room and board must also be paid for by the student. Living in a hotel and eating in restaurants for a few months can also add up. Students *are* offered discounts by local hotels.

Some of the things students learn at beer school are such weighty topics as the theory and practice of the brewing process, product formulation, quality assurance, government regulations, and practical business management. Other exciting topics are brewing microbiology and microscopy, sensory evaluation of beer, beverage packaging, off-flavors and the brewing process, brewhouse calculations, and the ever-popular pipe matrices and valving systems.

One thing is for certain. If you are reasonably intelligent and you complete one of these 4- to 10-week courses, you will be ready for an exciting life as a craft brewer. Consider it a $9,000 investment in your future. Even if you don't open your own brewery, there are plenty of jobs out there for someone who can practice the art and science of brewing.

Hello Mudda, Hello Fadda: Beer Camp

If you still shudder when your recall summer camp with its plastic lanyards and slimy, frog-filled swimming hole, you might need a weekend at Oldenberg Beer Camp. That's right, beer camp. The Oldenberg Brewery and Entertainment Complex in Fort Mitchell, Kentucky was established in 1986. Five minutes from downtown Cincinnati, the place has a 12,000-square-foot beer hall, a breweriana museum, a beer garden, and live entertainment every weekend. Twice a year, they offer a three-day beer camp to 255 lucky beer nuts. For a mere $400 (plus transportation to and from Cincinnati) a beer camper can immerse himself or herself in an unending supply of beer and beery loquaciousness. Oldenberg Beer Camp offers lessons on brewing beer, tasting beer, cuisine, beer lectures from industry leaders, entertainment from a theater troupe, and a "brewffet" of 360 brews.

Not the camp you remember: The Oldenberg Brewery and Entertainment Complex, home of the world's only beer camp.

The weekend begins when folks from all over the country check into the Drawbridge Inn near the brewery. Campers are assigned to groups named after beer styles. (Hey, I'm in the Porter Group!) Counselors attired in teal polo shirts keep track of the hoppy campers. Campers receive name tags, manuals, books, and camp T-shirts. (To fit over campers' beer "muscles," T-shirts come in XL and XXL only.)

Campers get a tour of the 25,000 barrel-a-year Oldenberg brewhouse. They meet the brewmaster and sample beer in various stages of development from sweet wort to bottled product. Then it's on to the American Museum of Brewing History and Arts, where the 150,000-piece breweriana collection is kept. Dinner the first night consists of six-foot-long hero sandwiches and lots of beer.

Opening ceremonies on Friday night begin with the singing of the Beer Camp Theme Song, which begins with "Beer, beer, we love to drink beer!" and ends several verses later with "And pour me another beer!" An hour-long beer tasting with 10 beers gets things moving, then it's time to wobble over to the 360-beer brewffet. There, every kind of beer imaginable is offered, from Keystone Light to Belgian ambrosia. Guides advise drinking the expensive stuff first. By midnight, hoppy campers crawl back to their hotel rooms.

On day two, an artery-clogging breakfast is followed by the ceremonial tapping of a keg of Oldenberg beer. The Beer Camp Theme Song is sung once again. A lecture detailing the history of brewing is followed by another tour of the beer museum. Then an extended tasting of beers precedes the midday meal. Saturday afternoon is spent bar hopping in Cincinnati's Over-the-Rhine neighborhood, which contains bookstores, art galleries, taverns, and a brewpub. Before dinner, campers do arts and crafts, mainly building obscene statues from old beer cans, duct tape, toilet paper, and caulk. Saturday dinner is a five-course feast of beer and food match-ups. Another round of the camp song, then it's back to the brewffet.

Sunday is officially dry (thank goodness), and hangovers are soothed by short, 19th-century temperance plays from a local theater troupe. The troupe also enacts "Foamio and Brewliet." Awards are handed out, certificates are signed, photos are taken, and at noon, camp is over. Time to go back to reality, five pounds heavier, a million brain cells lighter, and fuzzy memories of beery love stamped forever into the mind.

The Bottling Bottom Line

The first people who went out there to start craft breweries were flying by the seats of their pants. An amazing amount of them succeeded beyond their dreams. That was then. Today, most consumers have at least a passing knowledge of the craft-beer boom. And there's plenty of competition for those who want to jump into the brewing biz with both feet.

If you're one of those hard-working fanatics who wants to pop the top of your own beer, you should think about getting an education on the subject. And a degree in business doesn't hurt either. A weekend at beer camp or a brewer's convention will show you the inner workings of the beer crafter's trade. Regardless of the nay-sayers, the foamy beer boom has yet to be capped. So if you think a career in brewing is for you, do it. Follow your dreams. Even if you're seeing them through the bottom of a glass.

The Least You Need to Know

➤ It takes at least one million dollars to open a craft brewery in the United States.

➤ You need restaurant and brewing experience to successfully run a brewpub.

➤ Almost everything you need to know to run a brewery is taught at various brewing schools.

Chapter 24

Brew It Yourself: Homebrewing Beer

In This Chapter

➤ Everything you need to know to brew beer at home

➤ The equipment you need and what it costs

➤ Step-by-step instructions for brewing a five-gallon batch of beer

If you have a deep and abiding interest in homebrewing, you're not alone. Today there are more than 1.5 million Americans who regularly turn their kitchens into small beer breweries. They are supplied by over 1,500 homebrew supply shops and backed up by 600 homebrew clubs. These folks are joined by amateur brewers all over the planet who invest their time and energy into producing premium, hand-crafted beer in their homes.

As with any other hobby, there are fanatics, and those who brew once or twice a year. This chapter covers the basic equipment, recipes, and skills a beginner needs to learn homebrewing. It may look complicated at first, but don't worry. Homebrewing is fun. If you can cook, you can make beer. And even if you can't cook but can follow instructions, you can still make beer.

Getting Your Kit Together

If you invest about $100 in equipment, you could be drinking top-quality beer for less than 40 cents a bottle. Of course, you can buy cheap swill for that price. But a great porter, like one you can make, costs more than twice that much. And the satisfaction of drinking and sharing homebrewed beer with friends and family is a priceless joy. Most homebrewers do it for the satisfaction, camaraderie, and excitement of concocting one-of-a-kind brews. Saving a few bucks on beer is incidental. Homebrewing is a labor of love.

Just like building a large brewery, homebrewing requires an up-front investment to get the wort rolling. Most homebrew supply shops offer complete kits with everything you need to start for about $100. Then there's another $20 to invest in malt, hops, and yeast, which will give you ingredients for five gallons of beer—53 12-ounce bottles, or two cases plus five bottles.

Bar Talk
Relax...don't worry...have a homebrew!

—Charlie Papazian, author of the homebrewer's "Bible," *The Complete Joy of Homebrewing*

Tasty Tip
Let Your Fingers Do the Brewing:
If you're going to brew, look in the Yellow Pages under "Beer Homebrewing Equipment and Supplies" for a homebrew supply shop near you. If you live in a rural area, these places do lots of mail-order business, so you can get your home brewery via UPS. If you don't have listings in your Yellow Pages, look at the advertisements in the magazines listed in Appendix B.

I seriously recommend following Monsieur Papazian's advice to relax and not worry. Homebrewing ain't rocket science. It's easy if you carefully follow instructions and employ patience. You might make a few funny tasting beers, but unless you seriously mess up, they'll still be drinkable. Learn from experience and by your third or fourth batch, you'll be brewing like a pro. After a while, you might be ready to take the plunge and become an advanced homebrewer, which actually is a little like rocket science.

The law allows each adult in a household to brew 100 gallons of beer per year, with a maximum of 200 gallons per household. This boils up to 40 five-gallon batches. If you have anything else to do in life, like work at a job, you're probably not going to make that much beer. It *is* illegal to sell homebrew under any circumstances, so you must give it away if you want others to enjoy it.

Besides selling everything you need to make beer, homebrew stores usually offer inexpensive classes in homebrewing. Sometimes the classes are free. If there's more than one store in your town, you might want to shop around. Homebrewing is a growing trend, however, and it's hard to get deals on homebrew equipment unless you find someone who is giving it up and selling second-hand equipment.

When you assemble all your homebrewing equipment, it looks vaguely like tenth-grade science class. Here's a list of things a beginner needs to make five-gallon batches of homebrew:

➤ *20-quart stainless steel or enamel brew kettle.* Maybe your mother or grandmother used to can fruit and vegetables in a giant blue enamel pot. Maybe it's sitting in her basement. You can use it if it's not chipped, scratched, or dented. If you can't borrow one, you must purchase a brew pot for $30 to $40. This is your largest homebrewing investment. Beginners can get by with a cheaper 16-quart model, but I recommend the 24-quart size in case you want to move up to advanced homebrewing. The larger pot costs only about $10 more. Make sure it's stainless steel or enamel. Aluminum or cheap metal imparts a weird flavor to the beer.

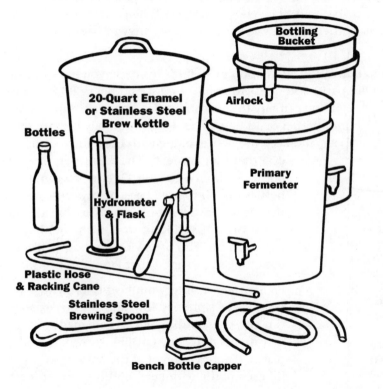

With the equipment pictured here, you can brew your own beer.

➤ *Airlock.* Airlocks fit over a hole in the primary fermenter to let CO_2 gasses escape. They also prevent outside air from entering—and possibly contaminating—the fermenting beer. There are several types of airlocks, which cost about $1. Ask your supplier how to use them properly—it's easy.

➤ *Bottle caps.* Bottle caps or *crowns* fit over the top of your freshly filled beer bottles. Some have cute expressions printed on them like "Real Beer" or "Relax. Don't worry. Have a homebrew." These caps cost about $4 for 60. I recommend oxygen-absorbing bottle caps. These caps have a liner that absorbs oxygen in the neck of the beer bottle. This oxygen can produce off-flavors in the beer.

➤ *Bottle capper.* A bottle capper fastens caps to your filled beer bottles. Cappers come in all manner of shapes and styles. The expensive ones are easier to use, but if you're on a budget, an inexpensive bottle capper will cost about $10. Bench cappers cost about $30.

➤ *Bottle washer.* A bottle washer is a copper device that screws onto your kitchen faucet and shoots pressurized water into beer bottles. This is the best way to wash bottles, and a bottle washer costs about $11. A bottle brush ($3) helps get the goo off the bottom of dirty beer bottles (which you shouldn't have anyway—see "Tasty Tip" below).

➤ *Bottles.* You need to put your beer in bottles when it's ready, so you have to plan ahead. (This is the fun part.) You need either 53 12-ounce bottles or 30 22-ounce bottles to hold your beer. You can buy fresh clean bottles from your supply store for about $10 for 24 12-ounce bottles or 12 22-ounces. Or you can buy beer in returnable bottles, drink the beer, and keep the bottles along with the handy, cardboard case that they come in. The deposit on those bottles is about $2 a case. Or else you can use bottles from imported beer, or any brown bottles that *do not* have twist-off caps. The threaded neck of the twist-offs will not work with your bottle caps. You can also use swing-top bottles like those used for Grolsch and other European beers.

Tasty Tip
Brown bottles are best for homebrewing, as they keep out light. Bottles that use non-twist off caps are mandatory. If you want to save up a collection of bottles from beer you drink, rinse your bottles thoroughly as soon as you're done drinking the beer. If you let the bottles sit dirty for days, blue-green gunk will grow in the leftover beer at the bottom of the bottle. That stuff is difficult to remove, and will spoil any beer it comes in contact with. Don't bother trying to remove the labels, it's more trouble than it's worth.

➤ *Bottling bucket.* After your beer is fermented, it needs to be siphoned into another bucket so you can bottle it. Bottling buckets are made of high-density polyethylene (HDPE), known as food-grade plastic. There's a spigot at the bottom so you can fill each bottle with beer. Bottling buckets cost $10.

➤ *Brewing spoon.* I recommend buying a spoon that is used only for homebrewing. Wooden kitchen spoons hide plenty of beer-killing bacteria. A slotted, metal brewing spoon with an 18-inch handle costs about $5.

➤ *Flexible plastic hose and racking cane.* Three to four feet of clear, plastic hose is necessary to siphon beer from one bucket to the next. It must be kept clean at all times as bacteria can grow in it and ruin your beer. A racking can is a hard, clear, plastic tube that goes into your primary fermenter when you need to siphon beer from it. Make sure your plastic hose fits over the racking cane. The cost is about $5 for hose and cane.

➤ *Floating thermometer.* A brewer's thermometer floats in the wort and allows you to measure its temperature so that you know when it's cool enough to add yeast. A very important instrument for advanced brewing, a good thermometer should cost about $6.

➤ *One-quart measuring cup.* Buy a brand-new, one-quart, glass measuring cup. Old ones that have been on kitchen duty for years have scratches and bacteria that will come back to haunt you. Make sure the measuring cup is glass and don't use it for anything other than brewing beer. Measuring cups cost about $4 at any discount store.

➤ *Primary fermenter.* This is a white, seven-gallon bucket with an air-tight lid that you pour your wort into after it's done boiling. The wort ferments into beer in the primary fermenter. Fermenters cost about $10. Some folks use narrow-necked, five-gallon glass bottles (called carboys), like those that come with bottled water. Carboys are much harder to clean than the plastic buckets (and they break).

➤ *Rubber stopper.* The rubber stopper is a cork with a hole in the middle, also called a drilled stopper. It stops up the hole in the lid of the primary fermenter, then holds the stem of the airlock. They come in various sizes. You need one that fits in your primary fermenter. They cost about $1 or less.

➤ *Cleaners and sanitizers.* Homebrewers quickly learn that they spend more time cleaning than anything else. All equipment that comes in contact with beer must be *extremely* clean, if not sterile. Regular household soap will not do the job. Some folks use chlorine bleach to sterilize their equipment, but I feel that bleach essence is hard to remove from plastic buckets and hoses. It's also very polluting when it goes down the drain. Homebrew stores sell B-Bright, a powder that cleans perfectly, costs $2, and is non-polluting. If you really need something sterilized quickly, keep a bottle of cheap 100-proof vodka on hand. (This also comes in handy after your wort boils accidentally over onto the stove. Drink the voddy!)

➤ *Triple-scale hydrometer (optional).* Hydrometers determine the original gravity of your beer and allow you to figure its alcoholic content. They come with instructions. You also need a long flask to hold the wort in order to measure it with the hydrometer. Both cost about $10. This is an optional piece of equipment for a beginner.

Hop to It: Get Your Ingredients Together

The simplest way to get everything you need to brew your first batch of beer is to buy a recipe kit from your supply store. These kits include malt, hops, yeast, and step-by-step instructions to brew whatever style of beer you chose. Kits come in all styles from pale ale to German alt to oatmeal stout. They're priced from $20 to $30 depending on the flavor. Using them is quick and easy, and you'll learn enough to start formulating your own recipes later on.

If you're adventurous and want to brew beer without a pre-assembled kit, you need a recipe. Fortunately, recipes are everywhere, from the Internet to homebrew books. Whether you use a kit or not, here's a basic list of ingredients you'll be working with as you delve into the joys of homebrewing.

Get Loose with Barley Juice: Malt Extract or Malt Powder

Beer is made from malted barley that has been mashed, lautered, and sparged. This is a very complicated procedure for a novice. Not to worry. Beginner homebrewing is only as complicated as opening a can of malt extract and pouring it in a kettle of boiling water. Malt extract is a thick syrup resembling dark honey in color and consistency. It is basically wort with most of the water removed, and it's the essence of malt sugar. Yeast will readily turn it into beer. Supply shops also sell bags of malt powder which is malt syrup with *all* the water removed.

Some extracts are *hopped,* which means the hops are already in the syrup and you don't need to buy any. Can this be any easier?

Many types of malt syrup come from Great Britain and Australia. Some come in cans weighing 3.3 pounds, which is 1.5 kilos. It takes six to seven pounds of dried or syrup malt to make a five-gallon batch of beer. Many suppliers sell three-pound bags of locally-produced malt syrup considerably cheaper than the English imports. It works just as well. Malt syrup comes in light, amber, dark, and wheat styles that correlate with beer styles. Bulk syrup costs about $2 a pound, imports can cost twice as much.

Hop Shopping

Homebrew supply shops sell several types of hops in different forms. Hop oils are the easiest to use—just pour them in the wort. They lack the full flavor of hop pellets or loose-leaf hops, however. Your recipe will call for different kinds of hops. Pellets are the easiest, because they don't need to be filtered out. Hop pellets cost about $1.25 an ounce. A five-gallon recipe can use up from two to four ounces of hops of varying varieties. The following instructions call for hopped malt syrup, so you don't need to worry about hops right now.

A New Yeast on Life

Many beer kits call for dried yeast, and it's acceptable and easy to use—just mix it up and pour it into the cooled wort. Today, however, there are many varieties of liquid yeast available that are far superior in flavor to dried yeast. They're a little more complicated to use because they must be mixed with malt powder to get them "started" at least one day before use. But the liquid yeasts come with complete instructions, and your homebrew supply dealer will show you how they work. Dried yeast costs $1 to $2 per batch. Liquid yeast comes in all styles, from Dusseldorf ale to California lager to Belgian Trappist Ale. It's well worth the investment at $4 per package, but must be kept refrigerated until use.

Primo Sugar for Priming

After you've fermented your beer, and you're ready to bottle it, the beer needs to re-ferment in the bottle so it has a foamy head when you pour it later on. To achieve this, dextrose, or corn sugar, is added just prior to bottling. This is called priming, and is somewhat akin to the bottle-conditioning done by commercial breweries. Three-fourths of a cup of priming sugar goes into a five-gallon batch of beer. Homebrew shops sell dextrose for less than $1 a pound.

> **Stale Ale Alert**
> If you're a novice homebrewer, plan on making ale-style beers. Don't even *think* of brewing lagers. Unless you have a place to keep a five-gallon bucket of beer at a steady 33°F for at least four weeks, the true lager flavors won't come through. Fanatics have old refrigerators in their basements just for lagering.

Miscellaneous Malt

Your homebrew shop will have an entire supply of real malted barley in addition to the concentrated malt syrups and powders. Many of these malts are described in detail in Chapter 3. This malt needs to be milled and mashed, which is the domain of the intermediate and advanced brewer.

Bubble, Bubble, Boil, and Brew Beer

All right then. You have your kit together, and you've assembled all the gear necessary to brew up some suds. Ready to brew? *Not so fast!* I hate to sound like your parent, but you've got to clean the kitchen before you start. You're going to be handling large pots full of boiling liquid and you'll be glad the counters have been cleaned and cleared. The warm, sticky wort is a magnet for all sorts of bacteria. Not only that, but the dust and cobwebs in the cracks where the walls meet the kitchen ceiling are home to beer-spoiling microscopic monsters.

Stale Ale Alert
Nothing that grows in beer is as dangerous as the bacteria that grows in meat and eggs such as *e coli* or salmonella. Beer killers won't kill you. But you might get sick while pouring 50 bottles of beer down the drain, so keep it clean.

I can't over-emphasize how much of brewing is cleaning. It's all in good fun, but you don't want to eagerly open the product of your labors in a few weeks and have it floating with mold. Cleaning the entire kitchen isn't mandatory, but I can tell you from long years of experience, it's better to start with a clean, clear work space than to trip over some clutter and spill boiling wort all over the place. (The stuff is a bear to clean up.)

One more note: Again, I hate to be a stick-in-the-mud, but if you're going to be brewing beer, you're probably going to be *drinking* beer. That's fine, but the entire brewing process takes more than two hours. I don't recommend getting roaring drunk while your trying to throw around five gallons of sterile wort. *Especially the first time.* When it comes to bottling, drunkenness can cause disaster. Pace yourself. To paraphrase Kenny Rogers: "There'll be time enough for drinking, when the brewing's done."

So, before you begin:

1. Clean, dry, and put away all the dirty dishes in the kitchen sink.

2. Clear all the counters and wipe them down with a clean, soapy rag, rinse, and dry. Do the same with the kitchen stove.

3. Look up. Are the cabinet doors above the stove dusty and grimy? Give them a quick wipe.

4. Take out the festering trash, sweep the floor, and get any junk that might trip you up, out of the way. If you have kids and pets, put the pets in the yard and send the kids to a movie.

5. Take a deep breath, think of cracking the top of a fresh homebrew in a few weeks, and begin.

Wort's Brewing?

These are the steps you're going to take to make great homebrew. I'm going to spell them out quickly at first, then explain them in more detail as a step-by-step process. You're going to:

1. Put 1¹/₂ gallons (six quarts) of water in your brewpot and put it on the stove over a medium heat.

2. Dissolve your malt extract in the water and bring it to a boil.

3. Heat the liquid *uncovered* at a rolling boil for one hour.

4. While the wort is boiling, you will sanitize your fermenter, cork, airlock, thermometer, and (optional) hydrometer with a sanitizing solution. Then you will thoroughly rinse the equipment with fresh water.

5. After one hour, turn off the brewpot then add three gallons of cold water to your clean fermenter.

6. Add the malt in the brewpot to the cold water in the fermenter.

7. Measure the temperature of the liquid in the fermenter. It should be about 78°F.

8. Pitch the yeast into the liquid.

9. Add the rubber stopper and airlock, then put the bucket of brew away for 8 to 14 days.

10. Sterilize beer bottles and siphon beer into them. Cap the bottles.

11. Age for 10 to 14 days.

12. Have a party and drink the beer!

Tasty Tip
Brewing beer takes about four hours from cleaning the kitchen to the final cleaning of the brewpot. Bottling takes another two hours or more. You need to plan ahead, so you have a free day to brew, then a free day seven days later to bottle. Beer can sit longer than seven days in the fermenter, but it's not a good idea to leave it more than 14 days. That's why homebrewers tend to their hobby on weekends.

Now, in loving detail, the above steps with everything you need to know to brew beer but were afraid to ask.

Note: all instructions are for brewing five gallons (20 quarts, 40 pints, 80 cups, 640 ounces, 18.9 liters) of beer. All temperatures are in degrees Fahrenheit.

1. Put 1¹/₂ gallons (six quarts) of water in your brewpot and put it on the stove over a medium heat.

   a) For best results, use bottled water or filtered water. Tap water in most cities is not the greatest, but will work fine. The better the water the higher-quality the final product.

   b) You want to go to step 2 while the water is still lukewarm, not boiling.

2. Dissolve your malt extract in the brewpot water and bring it to a boil.

   a) Most beer kits have about six pounds of extract. This is what you need for five gallons of medium-strength beer.

   b) Some older beer kits come with instructions to add table sugar. *Don't do this.* This is an old-fashioned way of boosting alcoholic content that will make your beer taste terrible. If the instructions call for three pounds of sugar, use three pounds of dried malt extract or syrup.

   c) Malt syrup is *very* thick and sticky. Immerse the can of syrup in a sink full of very hot tap water for 30 minutes to thin it enough for easy pouring. Wipe the rim clean before opening. Pour the syrup into the brewpot. Use a spatula to get all of the syrup out of the can, and add some warm water to dissolve the final goo stuck to the bottom. You don't have to worry about sterility at this point, because the wort will boil for an hour.

   d) After the syrup is in the brewpot, stir it thoroughly with your clean brew spoon until it is dissolved in the water.

3. Heat the liquid *uncovered* at a rolling boil for one hour.

   a) Check the clock and note the time (write it down) so you know when an hour has passed.

   b) Keep the brewpot on a medium-high flame at a slow rolling boil. *Do not cover or it will boil over!*

   c) Don't turn the heat on the pot and walk away. Keep an eye on it. If the sticky wort boils over, it is hellish to clean off the stove.

   d) If the pot looks like it's about to boil over, turn off the flame and throw a handful of ice cubes into the pot.

   e) Stir every 10 minutes, paying particular attention to the bottom of the brewpot, where the syrup has a tendency to scorch.

4. While the wort is boiling, sanitize your fermenter, cork, airlock, thermometer, and optional hydrometer with a sanitizing solution.

   a) You must kill the ambient bacteria that lives everywhere in our world or your beer might be spoiled. These critters love to hide in scratches on the side of your bucket, so don't use any abrasive sponges or cleansers on the plastic.

   b) The next step is best done in a deep laundry tub or deep sink. If you don't have one, clean your bathtub thoroughly and do it there. But remember, the bathtub is crawling with germs and bacteria.

c) Pour two ounces of *unscented* household bleach in your fermenter. If you're using B-Brite or some other environmentally friendly cleanser, follow instructions on the label. B-Brite uses one tablespoon of the cleaner for each gallon of water.

d) Add five gallons of lukewarm water to the fermenter, dissolving the cleaner.

e) Put your airlock, rubber stopper, thermometer, (optional) hydrometer, flask and a clean measuring cup into the fermenter. Then gently force the plastic fermenter lid into the cleaning solution (you have to bend it a little).

f) After 30 minutes, turn the fermenter lid upside-down on a counter and place the smaller items on it. Empty the cleaning solution from the fermenter. Save cleaning solution in the measuring cup for cleaning the spoon later on. Then thoroughly rinse all of the equipment (except measuring cup) along with the fermenter bucket in hot water, making sure to remove all cleaner residue.

Stale Ale Alert
Caution! Do not mix bleach with any other cleaner, especially ammonia. Toxic gases will result.

5. After one hour, turn off the brewpot and then add three gallons of cold water to your clean fermenter.

   a) Turn off the boiling wort and cover.

   b) Measure three gallons of cold, clean water into the plastic fermenter.

6. Add the wort in the brewpot to the cold water in the fermenter.

   a) Put the plastic fermenter full of cold water it into a sink or tub.

   b) Remove the brewpot lid. *Carefully* pick up the brewpot with pot holders, and pour the wort into the plastic fermenter bucket.

   c) Add enough water to bring the total amount of liquid within four inches of the top of your fermenter (if it isn't already there).

   d) Clean your brewing spoon with cleaning solution in the measuring cup. Rinse. Use the spoon to thoroughly mix wort with water in fermenter.

7. Measure the temperature of the liquid in the fermenter. It should be about 78°F.

   a) Use your thermometer to measure the temperature of the wort. If the wort is too hot, it will kill the yeast you are about to add, and you won't have beer.

   b) If the wort temperature is higher than 80°F, cover the fermenter with its lid and run cold water into the sink it's sitting in. The cold water on the outside of the bucket will cool the wort within.

8. Pitch the yeast into the liquid.

a) If you want to take a hydrometer reading, make sure the hydrometer's sterile. Place it in the wort, and follow the instructions that came with it. This is optional for a beginner, but will tell you the alcoholic content of your brew.

b) Rinse the cleaning solution out of your measuring cup. Pour eight ounces of 90° to 100°F tap water into the cup. Take the water's temperature with your thermometer to make sure it is right. If the water is too hot it will kill the yeast.

c) Open the dried yeast package and pour it in the measuring cup. Shake it around to dissolve the yeast. If you're using dried yeast, you can use two packages to make sure you get good fermentation.

d) Cover the yeast in the measuring cup with a piece of fresh plastic wrap, and let it stand for about 10 minutes.

e) Pour the dissolved yeast into the wort, and stir vigorously with your *clean* spoon. Yeast needs oxygen to begin fermentation. Stirring rapidly oxygenates the water.

Tasty Tip

Even if you brew all the time, it's hard to remember your exact procedures from one batch to the next. That's why it helps if you keep good records of each brew. Write down brewing times, temperatures, ingredients, and other not-so-exciting details. This will help you re-create a beer you love, or help you troubleshoot if a beer comes out bad. Other things to keep track of include names and types of malt used, type of yeast used, fermentation times, days in bottle, and so on. There are books and computer programs that are as complicated as can be, but the old spiral binder works great, too.

9. Add the airlock and put the bucket of brew away for 8 to 14 days.

a) After you've pitched the yeast, press the fermenter lid on tightly.

b) Put the rubber stopper in the hole in the lid, and place the airlock into the rubber stopper. Make sure everything is tightly sealed.

c) Fill the airlock halfway with clean water or vodka.

d) Put the bucket of wort in a cool, dark place where the temperature (ideally) is a steady 60° to 65°. If you can't find a dark place to leave your beer, pull a black plastic garbage bag over it, but first punch a hole in the bag to allow the airlock to stick out.

e) Write down the date and time that you pitched the yeast.

f) You will hear the beer beginning to burble within 24 hours. After a few days, it will be burping away like crazy. *Do not open the fermenter or look inside or you risk contaminating the beer.* After three days the beer will be gurgling steadily.

g) Leave the beer alone for seven to 10 days from its original brewing date. This is the hard part for beginners: *You must wait.*

h) After seven days, go to your beer with a wristwatch. Listen to the time between bubbles burping from the airlock. When the bubbles are coming only every minute or so, prepare to bottle the beer the next day.

Bottle Your Work of Art

At this point your beer is perfectly drinkable—but flat. Most of the carbonation has been blown off through the airlock—that's the fascinating bubbling sound you've been hearing for a week. Advanced homebrewers may keg their beer at this point and use a tank of carbon dioxide to charge the beer when served. Since you're new at this, you're going to bottle your beer with priming sugar, so that it will have head in about two weeks. Pouring beer *you made* from a beer bottle is more fun than serving from a keg anyway. So here we go, it's time to coddle your bottles.

You will need to assemble this equipment in order to bottle your beer:

➤ 2 small saucepans

➤ $^3/_4$ cup dextrose (priming sugar)

➤ Bottle capper

➤ Bottle caps

➤ Bottle washer

➤ Bottles

➤ Bottling bucket

➤ Plastic hose and racking cane

➤ Sanitizer

1. Sterilize you beer bottles and equipment.

   a) Your beer bottles should either be brand new or, if used, thoroughly rinsed after you drank the beer out of them. But they still need to be sterilized before you fill them with beer.

   b) This is best done in a clean laundry sink, but can be done in a kitchen. Attach your bottle washer to the faucet in your sink. Press each beer bottle onto the bottle washer to give it a blast of clean water. Set aside. Do this to enough beer bottles to contain 640 ounces of beer.

Stale Ale Alert
Caution: Do not submerge entire beer bottles in buckets of cleaning solution to sterilize. The glue and paper labels on used beer bottles turn to mush and will seriously contaminate your beer.

c) Fill your bottling bucket with two to three ounces of *unscented* bleach, or five tablespoons of B-Brite or other cleaner. Add five gallons of lukewarm water.

d) Put your plastic hose and racking cane into the cleaning solution.

e) Fill each beer bottle to the very top with the cleaning solution, making sure to get the bottle rim. Set bottles aside.

f) After beer bottles are all full, leave them to soak in the cleaning solution and move to the next step.

2. Dissolve the priming sugar and sterilize the bottle caps.

    a) The priming sugar needs to be dissolved in water and brought to a boil in order to sterilize it. The bottle caps also need to be sterilized.

    b) Stir ³/₄ cup dextrose into 16 ounces of water in a small, clean saucepan. Bring to a boil, then cover and shut off the heat.

    c) Place as many bottle caps as you will need in a small saucepan. Then throw in *at least* six extra (you'll need them, I promise). Cover the caps with water, and bring them to a boil. Then shut off the flame and cover the pan.

    d) If you use oxygen-absorbing bottle caps, you can't boil them in water. They need to be soaked in vodka. (Don't worry—you can drink it afterward.) Follow the instructions that come with the caps.

3. Go back to the bottles, and rinse them once again with the bottle washer. Rinse your bottling bucket and other equipment.

    a) Empty the cleaning solution out of the bottles.

    b) Rinse each bottle with the bottle washer. Inspect the bottles to make sure they don't have gunk in them. Line up the bottles so that they are easily within reach when you need to fill them. Place them back in their original cardboard cartons if possible.

    c) Thoroughly rinse the cleaner from your bottling bucket, hose, and racking cane.

4. Prepare to siphon fermented beer into the bottling bucket. Add the priming sugar.

    a) Place your bucket full of fermented beer onto a table.

    b) Place the empty bottling bucket on the floor below the fermenter.

c) Carefully remove the airlock and rubber stopper from the fermenter. Put them down anywhere—you won't need them until the next time you brew beer.

d) Place the clean and sterile racking cane into the hole in the fermenter lid. Push it all the way down in the beer.

e) Pour the priming sugar liquid from the saucepan into the bottling bucket.

f) Attach the plastic hose to the racking cane.

g) Thoroughly wash your hands with a good soap and rinse well.

5. Siphon the beer into the bottling bucket.

a) Place your extremely clean hand around the end of the plastic tube.

b) Make sure the opening of the plastic hose is lower than the bucket of beer. In other words, get down on your hands and knees below the bucket of beer.

c) Slowly suck on your hand that is wrapped around hose to bring beer into the hose. Try not to put your mouth on the siphon hose.

d) Lower the hose into the bottling bucket. The beer should now flow freely from the fermenter to the bottling bucket. Don't drink the first liquid out of the bucket, as it will be yeasty gunk. It won't hurt you, but it's pretty chewy goo.

e) Try not to splash the beer or shake it up at this point. This adds oxygen to the beer, which you *do not want* at this point. Avoid splashing at all costs.

f) If you need practice siphoning beer, use water. Some folks cringe at the idea of your hand or lips on the siphoning hose, but your beer should be about 4% alcohol by now, enough to kill germs. Another method of siphoning is to fill the plastic hose with water. When you place the hose end lower than the fermenter, the pressure will pull the beer out and begin the siphon.

g) It will take a while for the beer to siphon into the bottling bucket. Don't worry about the last dregs in the fermenter, they're full of gunk.

6. Fill and cap the bottles.

a) After the beer is drained into the bottling bucket, carefully lift it up onto a table, without shaking it.

b) Attach your plastic hose to the spigot on the bottling bucket.

c) Fill each bottle with beer by pushing the hose down into the bottom of the bottle. Again, you do not want to shake, splash, or add oxygen in any way to the beer in the bottles.

d) Fill each bottle within about an inch of the top rim. When you remove the hose from the bottle, the level will go down. You should develop a rhythm to keep from overfilling the bottles.

e) Keep the beer bottles in their cardboard containers or somewhere that they won't spill. You don't want your precious brew going down the sink at his point.

f) After all the bottles are full, cap them with the bottle capper. I like to leave one bottle out to try after I'm done. It may be flat, but it sure tastes good!

g) If you drop a cap on the floor, it isn't sterile anymore. Use a clean one. If you run out, sterilize the last few caps you need with vodka.

h) If a bottle cap does not seat right, remove it and put on a fresh one.

i) Write down the date you bottled the beer on a few pieces of paper and tape them to the full cases.

> **Stale Ale Alert**
> Yeast and sugar make carbon dioxide. If that CO_2 has nowhere to escape—like in a sealed beer bottle—it will explode. If you use more than $3/4$ cup priming sugar, or bottle your beer before seven days, you might have real bottle rockets in your basement. If you hear beer bottles exploding, you can't drink the beer. If you try to open it, the beer will shoot out of the bottle and be pure foam. Use extreme caution when removing the unexploded beer bottles. Protective layers of clothing, gloves, and eye goggles are mandatory. But don't worry. Just don't over-prime your beer or bottle it too soon and you won't have a problem.

7. Hard part number two: Put the beer bottles away for 14 days.

   a) The priming sugar you just added needs to condition the beer and make the beer carbonated.

   b) Put the beer in a cool, dark place. If you don't have a dark place, throw a thick towel or blanket over the beer bottles. Do not refrigerate the beer or it won't become carbonated.

8. Thoroughly clean and rinse all the equipment you used, so it is sparkly fresh for your next batch. If you leave it dirty, even for a day, it will quickly become contaminated and ruin your next batch of beer. *Protect your investment.* Store your clean equipment in fresh garbage bags or boxes where it won't be in touch with dust and dirt.

9. Make sure the beer is good. Crank up the stereo and have a beer!

   a) It's about time! Take one of your beers out and check to see that it looks clear in the bottle.

   b) Chill it down to about 50°F, and pour it slowly into a glass, leaving the last quarter-inch of yeast gunk in the bottle.

c) Drink it! Enjoy it! Pat yourself on the back! Begin planning your next batch of brew.

See, that wasn't so hard. (Or was it?) You probably enjoyed your first batch of homebrew, even if it wasn't perfect. Part of the fun is that your skills sharpen each time you brew. If the beer was pretty good the first time, think of how good it will be in a year or three. Once you have a storeroom full of homebrew in various stages of fermentation and consumption, you'll be one satisfied homebrewer. Here's wishing great brew to you. Cheers!

The Least You Need to Know

➤ If you can cook, you can make beer.

➤ Homebrew supply shops have everything you need to get started and even offer cheap or free brewing lessons.

➤ There are many steps involved in homebrewing, but if you follow directions and keep everything clean, you should be able to make your own beer.

The 50 Best Beers in the World

People have often asked me to name the best beers in the world. It was a question I heard so much, that I decided to write a book called *The 50 Greatest Beers in the World* (Citadel Press, 1996).

Obviously, if you really like a certain beer and think it's the best, then it is for you. But I tasted over 2,000 beers and came up with a list of the world's best-brewed, hand-crafted worts of art. It was extremely difficult picking the top 50—a tough job, but it had to be done. If you're a beer lover, you should make sure you try these world-class brews.

1. Delirium Tremens—The humorously named Belgian lager, it's a strong, sweet, delicious offering from Ghent, Belgium.

You probably won't be seeing pink elephants after drinking Delerium Tremens, a strong Belgian beer.

2. Reichelbrau Eisbock—The world's first *real* ice beer that so many mega-breweries have laughingly tried to imitate. The beer is frozen, and the ice is removed, leaving behind a rich, powerful bock that is to die for.

3. Shakespeare Stout—A black, roasty ale named after the author who mentioned ale so many times in his plays. Any beer writer worth his malt would love a beer named after the Bard.

4. Duvel—Belgian for "devil," this is a devilishly deceptive beer, light in color, foamy as all get-out, and powerful as sin.

5. Caledonian Golden Pale Organic—A hoppy organic Scotch ale from Edinburgh. Great with haggis.

6. Chapeau Gueuze Lambic—Lambics are tart Belgian beers that are made with wild yeast and aged for several years. Chapeau is one of the best.

7. Samuel Smith's Taddy Porter—Lighter than stout, tastier than all get-out, Taddy Porter defines the style of beer originally brewed for carters, porters, and haulers in London's Victoria Station.

8. Aventinus Wheat Doppelbock—It's wheat beer, it's bock, and it's brewed in a 400-year-old German brewery that's the oldest wheat brewery in the world. What's not to love?

9. Lindemans Kriek Lambic—A Belgian Lambic brimming over with real cherries. Rosy-pink, bubbly, and sweet. Won the award for "Best Wine" at California's Summer Spectacular! A beer-hater's beer.

10. Murphy's Irish Stout—Ireland's pride and joy, it's not just for breakfast any more. A little bit of Celtic magic from the Emerald Isle.

11. Chimay Trappist Ale—Pronounced "she-may"—a strange twist from an ale made by celibate Trappist monks in Belgium. Smells of hidden cloisters, ancient tomes, and apple blossoms.

12. Grant's Scottish Ale—A big beer from the Pacific Northwest. Washington's answer to Scotland's favorite son.

13. Corsendonk Monk's Pale Ale—A creamy Belgian "Triple" style ale. Lowers blood pressure instantly.

14. Erdinger Weizenbock—The largest-selling wheat beer in Germany, and they drink a lot of weizen. Erdinger brews nothing but wheat beers.

15. Guinness Draught—Guinness invented the stout style and today exports it to 130 countries. Charged with nitrogen instead of carbon dioxide, this Guinness stout is black Irish gold.

16. Orval—Orval is the quintessential Trappist ale. And the Benedictine Brothers who brew it inhabit the oldest beer-brewing monastery in the world, established in the 12th century.

17. Samuel Smith Imperial Stout—This style was originally brewed for Catherine the Great and the Imperial Russian Court. It's chocolate cake in a bottle and worth a coup d'état or two.

18. Saison Dupont—A citrusy, Belgian farmhouse ale that's closer to champagne than beer. It's lovingly handcrafted in tiny batches by an eclectic family of Walloon brewers who also sells farm-fresh eggs out of the brewery office.

19. Pinkus Ur Pils—An organic German Pilsner that's as golden as sunshine and drinkable as artesian waters.

20. Grant's Imperial Stout—A Russian stout from Yakima, Washington—make sure you're sitting down when you drink this one.

21. Old Peculier—Spelled with an "-er" not an "-ar," this particular ale is still aged in hand-made casks cut from Polish maple. Brewed deep in the heart of Yorkshire, England, Old Peculier tastes like an expensive sherry.

22. Liefmans Frambozen—A gorgeous Flanders brown ale brewed with several pounds of raspberries per gallon, the bottle is wrapped in tissue paper festooned with angels dancing with raspberries. Peerless.

23. Samuel Smith Oatmeal Stout—The best way to consume oatmeal ever invented—brewed in giant fermenters called Yorkshire Squares that are cut from huge slabs of slate.

24. Royal Oak Pale Ale—Inviting as a crackling fireplace on a rainy autumn afternoon in Dorchester. Royal Oak is named for the exploits of King Charles II in his battles with Oliver Cromwell in 1651.

25. Pyramid Espresso Stout—A Seattle favorite that's so black you'll swear you're drinking coffee. A restorative.

26. Pilsner Urquell—The original Pilsner beer, often imitated never equaled. Called "a national treasure of the Czech Republic" by Vaclav Havel.

27. Holy Cleopatra!—Straight from Tutankhamen's favorite brewer, folks in Colorado go tuts over this one. One of the best Extra Special Bitters made in the U.S.A.

28. Aecht Schlenkerla Rauchbier Maürzen—Smoked ham in a bottle. This Bavarian lager is made from malt smoked over a beechwood fire. Singularly unique.

29. Old Crustacean—A barley wine from Rogue Ales in Newport, Oregon, it has a deep bass, or *basso profundo,* note of a fine port wine.

30. Rodenbach—Called the "Burgundy of Belgium" this beer is aged in ancient oak vats where it mingles with a unique yeast that makes it as tart as all get-out. It's transcendentally sour. Yahoo!

31. McAuslan's Griffon Brown Ale—A brilliant brown ale from a Montreal Brewery. Graced with the mythical griffin on the label, this beer flies like an eagle and growls like a lion.

32. Bigfoot Barley Wine Style Ale—It takes big shoes to make Bigfoot Barley Wine. Named after the large-pawed monster who lives right over the mountain from the Chico, California brewery, this beer stomps butt, dude.

33. Scrimshaw Pilsner Beer—The best Pilsner this side of the Atlantic—and this side of the continent—Scrimshaw comes from northern California where the beer is as big as the redwoods and smells just as sweet.

34. Geary's London Porter—Maine's answer to London's original style, Geary's is one of the tastiest porters in America.

35. Third Coast Old Ale—From world-famous Kalamazoo, Michigan, the U.S.A.'s Third Coast on the Great Lakes, this ale is so complex it's almost human.

36. Lindemans Gueuze Lambic—Another incredible lambic that's so sour it would make the Mona Lisa pucker.

37. Oasis Zosar Oatmeal Stout—Boulder, Colorado's Oasis Brewery brews with as much integrity as you can find without bringing in Trappist monks. Named after Zosar, who, besides drinking a lot of Egyptian beer, commissioned the first pyramids.

38. Flag Porter—This English porter is brewed from a traditional 19th century recipe and fermented with original 1825 yeast salvaged from a sunken ship in the English Channel. Need I say more?

39. Blackjack Porter—English porter is traditionally drunk with oysters—should Rocky Mountain porter be drunk with Rocky Mountain oysters? I don't know, but this stuff from the Left Hand Brewing Co., in Longmont, Colorado, is good. Period.

40. Redhook DoubleBlack Stout—Some brilliant Seattle-ite finally got the idea to pitch espresso coffee right into the beer, combining the city's two most famous products. Brewed with Starbucks coffee. Need I say more? Absolutely fabulous!

41. Samuel Smith Pale Ale—Most ales pale beside Samuel Smith. They've been in business since 1758, and they've never made a bad beer.

42. Barney Flats Oatmeal Stout—A northern California oatmeal offering from Anderson Valley Brewing Co. It's slippery, creamy, dark, and sweet as a Pacific May morning.

43. Pumpkin Ale—Brewer Buffalo Bill Owens went off the deep end and threw a 40-pound pumpkin in his brew kettle. Turns out George Washington did the same thing. Pumpkin pie in a bottle.

44. Samuel Adam's Triple Bock—Made by the country's biggest microbrewery—an oxymoron if there ever was one. At 17% alcohol, this beer enters the Guinness Book of Records as the strongest beer made. Tastes exactly like sherry. At $5 for a 7 oz. bottle, you won't have to worry about drinking too many.

45. Dock Street Bohemian Pilsner—A Bohemian Pilsner from the City of Brotherly Love. Ben Franklin would have been proud.

46. Thomas Hardy 1994—Fourteen percent alcohol by volume and named after a drunken British literary master. Thomas Hardy may be cellared for up to 20 years. An original vintage bottle from 1968 recently sold for $10,000.

47. Samichlaus Bier—Brewed by Hürlimann Brewery only on December 6 of each year, this Swiss lager is aged for 12 months before it's released prior to Christmas. Named after St. Nicholas. Now we know why his nose is so red.

48. Celebrator Doppelbock—A Bavarian double bock with dancing goats on the label. It's inky black with a profoundly dark taste—a rich elixir.

49. MacAndrews Scotch Ale—A Scottish ale with a Scottie dog on the label. Tastes of heather and honey.

50. Kwak—Not a duck, but a sweet strong beer from Buggenhout, Belgium, that was too good to leave off the list. Reminds one of the Saturday morning flea market in Bruges—pretzels, pastries, smoked ham, and oysters.

There are hundreds of great beers out there and more so-so ones. I hope I mentioned some of your favorites in the above list. Here are some beers that are terrific but did not make the top 50.

Abita Turbodog—Great name, great beer from the shores of Lake Pontchartrain down Loo-zee-anna way.

Anchor Steam/Porter—Fine beers from America's first microbrewery.

Bateman XXXB Ale—A wonderful triple-X English bitter.

Beavertail Dark Ale—A heather-scented Canadian ale that is closer to an India Pale Ale than a dark ale.

Big Shoulders Porter—One of the world's better porters. Brewed in Al Capone's sweet home Chicago.

Blue Moon Nut Brown Ale—A new offering by Coors trying to cash in on the micro market, brewed by F.X. Matt. A good nut brown.

Boon Faro Pertotale—A sweetened lambic from Belgium.

Frank Boon brews some of the few authentic lambics in the world.

Boon Gueuze—Probably the most sour beer on the planet—yum!

Boon Kriek—An extremely sour authentic Belgian fruit lambic.

Fraoch Heather Ale—It's brewed with heather flowers and Scottish malt—incredible.

Granville Island Bock—A Canadian bock.

Grimbergen Double Ale—A Belgian offering.

Hoegaarden—A lovely Belgian white beer.

Kostritzer Schwarzbier—Literally "black beer" from Kostritzer, a formerly East German brewery.

Mackeson XXX Stout—One of the best sweet stouts around.

Our Special Ale—A great holiday offering from Anchor Brewing Co. in San Francisco.

Pike Place Stout—A stout for everyday drinking, made by the brewery that's owned by Merchant du Vin, one of the country's premier importers.

Pyramid Wheaten—The first wheat beer to be brewed in America since Prohibition ended. Pyramid revived the style that hundreds of microbreweries have since copied.

Rogue Smoke Ale—Like the rest of the Rogues, a great ale.

Samuel Smith's Lager—The best English lager.

St. Georgen Braü Keller Bier—A Gold Medal–winning beer from Germany.

Schierlinger Roggen—A fantastic German rye beer.

Thomas Hardy's Country Bitter—A bitter ale from the folks who bring you the rare and expensive Thomas Hardy's Old Ale.

Thomas Kemper Hefeweizen—An American microbrewed product from Pyramid Breweries. Kemper Hefeweizen is a stunning example of a cool, refreshing beer in the style of Berliner Weisse—straight from the West Coast.

Watney's Cream Stout—About the only imported cream stout to be found in America. Although lacking lactose, still a top beer.

Weihenstephan—Beautiful beer from one of the world's oldest German breweries.

Yuengling Porter—A dark beer from America's oldest brewery.

Beer Books, Magazines, and Web Pages

Mirroring the growth of microbreweries and brewpubs, there's been a veritable cornucopia of beer publications offered in the past few years. You can buy them or find them—complete with beer-soaked pages—at your local library.

The Association of Brewers, Inc., is a Colorado non-profit corporation dedicated to brewers of beer and all those interested in beer and the art of brewing. They publish several excellent magazines. They also publish dozens of books on subjects ranging from cooking with beer to beer dictionaries to brewing science to yeast technology. Many of the books listed below can be found through the institute. They also sell T-shirts, breweriana, and homebrew equipment. They'll send you a free catalog.

Write to them: Association of Brewers, P.O. Box 1679, Boulder, CO 80306-1679, or check out their Web site at http://www.aob.org/aob.

Books

The 50 Greatest Beers in the World by Stuart Kallen. A plug for my last beer book, which ranks the world's best beers and explains ingredients, the brewing process, brewery histories, addresses, and phone numbers. A thirst-building book. May be found at your local book stores or ordered directly by calling Citadel Press at 800-447-BOOK.

Beer by Gregg Smith. A history of civilization and suds. Avon Books, 1995.

Beer Here by Stuart A. Kallen. A plug for my first beer book, which is a complete guide to almost 600 American microbreweries and brewpubs. Citadel Press, 1995.

Beer Companion by Michael Jackson. Authoritative information on brews and breweries. Illustrated with over 200 photographs. Running Press, 1993.

The Beer Directory compiled by Heather Wood. This book is a directory of breweries, brewpubs, microbreweries, well-stocked pubs and restaurants, beer festivals and celebrations, and beer-related retail stores, museums, organizations, and publications. And it's world wide from Alaska to Asia to Africa to Belgium and back. Storey Publications, 1995.

The Beer Enthusiast's Guide by Gregg Smith. This book tells you how to taste and judge beers from around the world. Everything you wanted to know about beer but were afraid to ask. Storey Communications, Inc., 1994.

Great American Beer Cookbook by Candy Schermerhorn. Cooking with Candy is easy. From the elegant to the downright sinful, Candy cooks 217 recipes with beer. It could change your life. Brewers Publications, 1993.

New World Guide to Beer by Michael Jackson. Beers of the world, over 100 photos. Running Press, 1988, reprinted 1990.

The Historical Companion to House-Brewing by Clive La Pensée. A fascinating look at the history of beer. Recipes from the 15th to the 19th centuries. Montag Publications, 1990.

The New Complete Joy of Homebrewing by Charlie Papazian. The bible of home-brewing. Many of today's brewsters and brewmasters started brewing with Charlie's book, which is loaded with helpful knowledge and encouragement. Charlie coined the phrase, "Relax, Don't Worry, Have a Homebrew." Avon Books, 1991.

The Secret Life of Beer by Alan Eames. This self-named "Beer King" is a cultural anthropologist as well as a great writer and funny guy. Full of amazing facts. Storey Publications, 1995.

Magazines and Brewspapers

Believe me, 'cause I know, keeping up with all the new beers introduced in the last few years is a full-time job. But there's help! Plenty of otherwise perfectly sane folks keep track of all this stuff for you so you can worry about other things—like how to pay for said beers. Most of these folks have been around for a while, and they're getting better all the time. What follows is an annotated list.

Ale Street News. A brewspaper about New York and surrounding areas, available for free in many brewpubs and bars. Subscriptions are available through Tony Forder, P.O. Box 1125, Maywood, NJ 07607; 201-368-9100.

All About Beer. A nationally published magazine all about beer, with new products, brewery openings and closings, reviews, etc. Published six times a year. Chautauqua, Inc., 1627 Marion Avenue, #41, Durham, NC 27705.

American Brewer. A magazine geared toward those whose business is beer, but still plenty of amusing articles and info about brewing for the layperson. Published by Buffalo Bill Owens, whose twisted take on life gives it that extra edge. American Brewer, Box 510, Hayward, CA 94543-0510; 800-731-BEER. Web site: http://www.ambrew.com/.

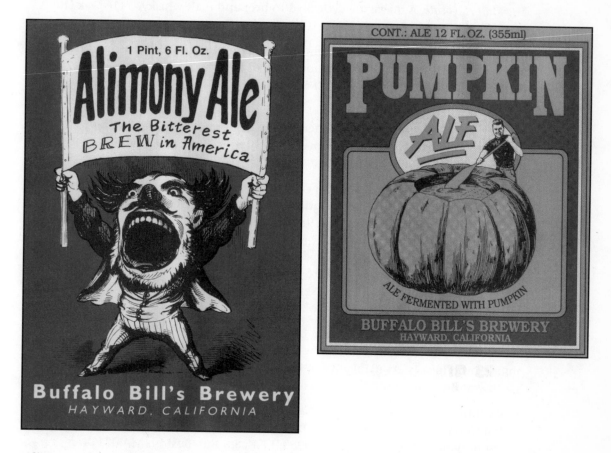

Alimony Ale and Pumpkin Ale are two brews made by Bill Owens, publisher of American Brewer.

American Breweriana Journal. A publication dedicated to brewing memorabilia and paraphernalia with microbrewery updates thrown in for good measure. American Breweriana Association, Box 11157, Pueblo, CO 81001.

BarleyCorn. A brewspaper for the mid-Atlantic region. George Rivers, BarleyCorn, Box 2328, Falls Church, VA 22042.

Brew Hawaii. Say "Aloha" to beer in the pineapple state. P.O. Box 852, Hauula, HI 96717; 808-259-6884. E-mail: brew@lava.net.

Celebrator Beer News. This one is free in most bars and liquor stores. Celebrator, Box 375, Hayward, CA 94543.Web site: http://celebrator.com.

The Malt Advocate. A magazine dedicated to beer and malt whisky. 3416 Oak Hill Road, Emmaus, PA 18049; 610-967-1083.

Midwest Beer Notes. A brewspaper concentrating on beer news from around the Midwest. Free at many bars and liquor stores or by subscription. Midwest Beer Notes, 339 6th Avenue, Clayton, WI 54004. Web site: http://realbeer.com/beernotes/.

The New Brewer. A magazine published by the Institute of Brewing Studies for the technical and business-oriented brewer. New Brewer, Box 1679, Boulder, CO 80306-1679.

Northwest Beer Journal. A brewspaper of the Pacific Northwest available free in many bars and liquor stores or by subscription. Northwest Publishing Company, 2677 Fircrest Drive SE, Port Orchard, WA 98366-5771.

Pint Post. 12345 Lake City Way NE, #159, Seattle, WA 98125; 206-527-7331.

Southern Draft. A brewspaper for the South. Free at many bars and liquor stores or by subscription. Southern Draft Brew News, 120 Wood Gate Drive, Canton, GA 30115; 770-345-1512. E-mail: brewnews@aol.com.

Southwest Brewing News. An amusing brewspaper published in Austin all about brewpubs and brewing in Texas, New Mexico, Arizona, and Southern California, among other places. Available free at many bars and liquor stores or by subscription. Southwest Brewing News, 11405 Evening Star Drive, Austin, TX 78739.

Yankee Brew News. A brewspaper of New England. Lots of history and fun facts along with reviews and information about breweries. Available free in bars and liquor stores or by subscription. YBN, Box 8053, J.F.K. Station, Boston, MA 02114.

Zymurgy. A magazine about homebrewing published by the American Homebrewers Association. Zymurgy, besides being the last word in the dictionary means "the art and science of brewing." AHA, Box 1679, Boulder, CO 80306-1679.

Beer-Related Web Pages

A thorough listing of beer-related Web pages can be found under the Yahoo banner: http://akebono.stanford.edu/yahoo/Entertainment/Drinks/Alcoholic Drinks/Beer.

The most comprehensive page dedicated to beer is the Real Beer Page: http://realbeer.com. You'll find links to all the breweries online and tons of info on beer all over the world.

American Brewer's Guild is a brewing school in Davis, California: http://www.mother.com/abg.

Anderson Valley Brewing: http://www.avbc.com/avbc/home.html.

Association of Brewers runs the Institute of Brewing Studies, the American Homebrewers Association, the Great American Beer Festival and Brewers Publications. They know everything there is to know about American brewing: http://www.aob.org.aob.

Aussie Beer Page is a guide to the land down under: http://www-personal.usyd.edu.au/~bcollins/OZBEER.HTML.

Austrian Beer Guide: http://www.lib.uchicago.edu/keith/austrian-beer.html.

Beer Can Collectors of America has a great web site: http://www.bcca.com.

Benelux Beer Guide: http://www.dma.be/p/bier/beer.htm.

Brasserie McAuslan in Quebec: http://www.mcauslan.com.

Buffalo Bill's Brewing: http://and.com/bb/bb.html.

Campaign for Real Ale (CAMRA): 34 Alma Road, St. Albans, AL1, 3BW, Hertfordshire, England (0727-867201). Web address: http://camra.org.uk/. E-mail: siebelinstitute@worldnet.att.net.

Students at Siebel Institute kick back after a hard day at beer college.

Finnish breweries and brewpubs: http://s-kanslia-3.hut.fi/Olutturisti/Finland/.

Firkin chain of brewpubs in Great Britain: http://www.compulink.co.uk/~dalecu/firkin.htm.

Germany Beer Links: http://www.tiac.net/users/tjd/bier/germany.html.

Guinness Extra Stout: http://wombatix.physics.ucg.ie/misc/guinness.html.

Pyramid Breweries Inc.: http://www.PyramidBrew.com.

Ireland Beer Hunting: http://www.tiac.net/users/tjd/bier/ireland.html.

Marin Brewing Co.: http://and.com/mbc/mbc.html.

Norway Beer & Brewpubs: http://pekkel.uthscsa.edu/beer/nor.html.

Oktoberfest in Munich, Germany: http://www.munich-tourist.de.

Pubworld site: http://www.pubworld.co.uk/.

Real Ale & A Bed is a British guide to bed & breakfasts that also serve "real" ale: http://indigo.stile.le.ac.uk/~gc16/beer/index.htm.

Redhook Ale Brewery: http://www.halcyon.com/rh/rh.html.

Siebel Institute of Technology has information on attending their brewing school: http://www.siebel-institute.com/welcome.

The Virtual Pub & Beer Emporium: http://lager.geo.brown.edu:8080/virtual-pub/.

Virtual Brewery Adventure: http://portola.com/TR/VBA/index.html.

Virtual Brewpub-Beer: the magazine: http://www.ambrew.com/.

York Brewery in England: http://www.yorkbrew.demon.co.uk/visits.html.

Terms of Enbeerment

Ale   The style of beer made with ale yeast, which ferments at the top of the wort. Ales are generally not aged as long as their cousins, lager beers. Ales are expressive, fruity, and complex in flavor.

Altbier   Literally "old beer" in German, altbier is the style that preceded lager. Altbier is a copper-colored German ale, usually associated with the city of Düsseldorf.

Barley   The main ingredient in beer, sprouted barley is kilned at high temperatures to turn it into malt.

Barley Wine   A very strong ale, 8% to 10% alcohol by volume.

Barrel   A term used to measure brewery output; one barrel equals 31 U.S. gallons of beer.

Beer   A fermented drink made mainly from malted grain and usually seasoned with hops. In German, *bier*.

Belgian Lace   The lovely pattern that a great beer head leaves on the side of the glass as the beer is drunk. Belgian beers are famous for their creamy, rich foam, as Belgium is famous for its lace.

Bitter   A British-style ale with a high hop content, making it, well...bitter.

Bock   A strong, usually dark, German lager, usually served in spring.

Bottle Conditioned   A beer that has yeast added to it right before bottling. The yeast causes the beer to referment and carbonation to develop naturally in the bottle. This is also known as *methode champenoise*—the method used in making champagne.

Bottom Fermented   A beer made with lager yeast, which ferments at the bottom of the beer tun. This lessens the chance of contamination and leaves a clearer beer.

Brewery   A place where beer is made.

Breweriana   Brewing memorabilia such as old beer cans, trays, and advertisements.

Brewpub   A tavern or restaurant that also makes its own beer, usually, but not always, for sale only on the premises.

Brown Ale   A mild, brown beer associated with Great Britain, where it is served in varying degrees of sweetness.

Cream Ale   An American-style beer that is mild, sweet, and golden in color. The style was originally brewed with ale *and* lager yeast, with the ale yeast fermenting at the top and the lager yeast fermenting at the bottom, hence the term cream.

Dark Beer   A general term for—you guessed it—dark-colored brown beer.

Doppelbock   Literally "double bock" in German. An extra-strong version of bock. In Germany, the names of most doppelbocks end with the suffix "ator," as in Kulminator (brewed by E.K.U.) and Animator (brewed by Hacker-Pschorr). Not for the faint of palate.

Dunkel   Literally "dark" in German. Dunkels are (what else?) dark beers.

Export   In Germany, export is a drier and less hoppy lager than most Pilsners. Every-where else, the term means "premium," which usually means nothing.

Framboise   A Belgian-style lambic beer with lots of raspberries added.

Fruit Beer   Any style beer that has…fruit added to it.

Gravity   The weight of a liquid when compared to an equal amount of pure water. This type of measurement is used to determine how much malt is in a beer, and hence, its alcoholic strength. If a beer has a specific gravity of 1.040, it is 1.04 times heavier than water.

Helles   Literally "pale" in German.

Hops   The cone-shaped flower of the female hop plant, used to flavor and bitter beer. Originally used as a preservative.

Imperial Stout   A very strong stout, 7% to 10% alcohol, originally brewed in Britain between 1780 and 1918 as an export to St. Petersburg in Czarist Russia.

India Pale Ale   A strong, bitter beer originally brewed in Britain for export to soldiers in India. Made strong to survive the long boat trip.

Kölsch   A light, delicate, golden ale associated with Cologne, Germany.

Kraeusen   Means "crown" in German. The process of kraeusening beer involves adding unfermented wort to the finished beer so that it develops natural carbonation (head). This process may take place in a fermentation tank or in the beer bottle, in which case it's called bottle-conditioning, which is easier to pronounce.

Kriek   A Belgian lambic beer with cherries added—elegant and delectable. Liefmans Kriek is made with Flanders brown ale, not lambic.

Lager   A beer made with lager yeast—that is, bottom fermented. Lagers are supposed to be stored for long periods at cold temperatures which gives the beer a soft, clean taste.

Lambic   A Belgian ale that is low in carbonation and fermented with wild yeasts that float into the brewery on the air in the fall season. The taste can almost resemble a fine sherry or cider.

Light beer   That American curse to good taste, light beer is usually a lightly-hopped, watered-down, low-cal imitation of Pilsner.

Maibock   Literally "May bock" in German, Maibocks, pale and tasty, are brewed in fall and brought out in spring to celebrate that season of love and awakening.

Malt   Grain, usually barley, that has been kilned to develop maltose sugars, those delicious molecules that yeast need to make alcohol and CO_2.

Malt Liquor   Not malty or a liquor, malt liquor is an Americanism for cheap, sweet beer that is high in alcoholic content. Some import beers are labeled as malt liquor because of their higher alcohol content. These malt liquors are generally much higher quality than American or Canadian malt liquors.

Märzenbier   A medium-strong, malty beer usually associated with Oktoberfests and fall celebrations. Märzen literally means "March" in German, which is the month the beer is *made,* for consumption the following fall.

Mash Tun   A copper or stainless steel cook-pot used for making beer. Tun means tub in German.

Microbrewery   A brewery that makes under 15,000 barrels of beer a year for sale off the premises. So-called microbreweries that produce more than 15,000 barrels, but still use high-quality ingredients, are now being called "craft breweries."

Mild   An English beer that is dark, lightly-hopped, and mild in alcoholic content.

Munich/Münchener   Munich, Germany, produces dark, spicy lagers with an almost coffee-like palate. These beers are called Münchener Dunkel. Light-colored beers from Munich are called Münchener Helles.

Oktoberfest   Legend has it that in the old days of Germany, before refrigeration, March was the last month that beer could be made, because the warmer temperatures that followed would bring out the wild yeasts and spoil any beer made later in the season. By October, the *Märzenbier,* or "March beer," was ready to be drunk, and millions of thirsty Germans were ready to celebrate the fall harvest with some freshly decanted brew. Today's version of Germany's Oktoberfest was started in 1810 to celebrate the marriage of the Crown Prince of Bavaria. The festival begins in late September and lasts 16 days, ending on the first Sunday in October. Millions of people attend the annual festival in

351

Germany, where some beer halls hold several thousand people. Mini-Oktoberfests are celebrated in many parts of the world. Many of the brewpubs in this book celebrate Oktoberfest.

Old Ale   Not ale that has been left in the back of your fridge too long, but a British term for a medium-strong, dark ale usually consumed in winter. Old ales can be aged for *several years*.

Pale Ale   A fruity, milder version of the English-style India Pale Ale.

Pilsener/Pilsner/Pils   The most imitated beer style in the world, Pilsner was the first commercially made lager beer. First perfected by Czech brewmaster Frantisek Poupe in the town of Pilsen, Czechoslovakia (then Bohemia), Pilsner Urquell beer was produced in 1842 to the accolades of all. "Pils" is pale in color, has a beautiful hop bouquet, and is almost as bubbly as champagne. Almost all beer produced by the U.S. brewing giants is an Americanized Pilsner that is less hoppy and not aged as long.

Porter   An English style that was first brewed in London in 1730, porter can be very bitter and very dark—almost black. It was originally brewed for hard workers like porters and carters who needed a bracing, nourishing brew.

Rauchbier   A smoky-flavored lager made around Bamburg and Franconia, Germany, produced with malt that has been wood-smoked. Another more dramatic way to make rauchbier is to heat rocks over a wood fire until they are red hot, then plunge them into the boiling wort. A Scottish-style smoked beer is made with malt that is kilned over burning peat. Some American microbrews sell peat-malted beer.

Reinheitsgebot   The German beer purity law that states that beer shall be made with only barley, hops, yeast, and water—with the exception of wheat beer, which has malted wheat added to it.

Saison   A mildly sour summer ale produced in Belgium and flavored with spices or herbs.

Scottish Ale   Scottish ales are a variation of the basic pale-ale style popular in England. Scottish ales are sweeter and less hoppy than pale ales. They may include darker malts and come in several alcoholic strengths.

Steam Beer   Steam beer is a uniquely American product first produced in California during the Gold Rush. It is produced using bottom-fermenting lager yeast at top-fermenting temperatures. Fermentation is carried out in long, shallow pans called clarifiers. At one time, 27 breweries made steam beer in the San Francisco area. Today, it is made exclusively by Anchor Brewing Company, which has registered the name, Anchor Steam, as a trademark.

Stout   Stouts are very dark, very heavy ales that are sometimes sweetened with sugar. In Ireland, Guinness—who invented the style—makes the most famous stout in the world. There are dry stouts and sweet stouts. Stouts are highly hopped and dry.

Top Fermented   Beer made with ale yeast, which works at the top of the liquid and falls to the bottom when done.

Trappist Ale   Strong, fruity ales made by Trappist monks in Belgium. It is bottled like champagne and is considered to be some of the finest beer in the world.

Ur/Urquell   Literally, "original source of" in German; hence, Pilsner Urquell is the original Pilsner.

Weisse/Weissbier/Weizenbier   *Weisse* means "wheat" in German, and the term is used for wheat beers that are anywhere from 20% to 60% wheat. Weizenbier is a refreshing summer drink with a clove-like bouquet. It is often garnished with a slice of lemon in the glass.

Wheat Beer   See Weisse.

Wort   The sweet liquid that is produced by cooking, or "mashing" malted barley during the beer-making process. Beer is called wort before the yeast is added to it.

Yeast   A single-celled fungus (sounds good doesn't it?) that turns sugar into alcohol and carbon dioxide. Beer is made with either top-fermenting ale yeast *(Saccharomyces cerevisiae)* or bottom-fermenting lager yeast *(Saccharomyces uvarum,* formerly *Saccharomyces carlsbergensis).*

Index

359